P9-CRG-529

THE COMPLETE YES MINISTER

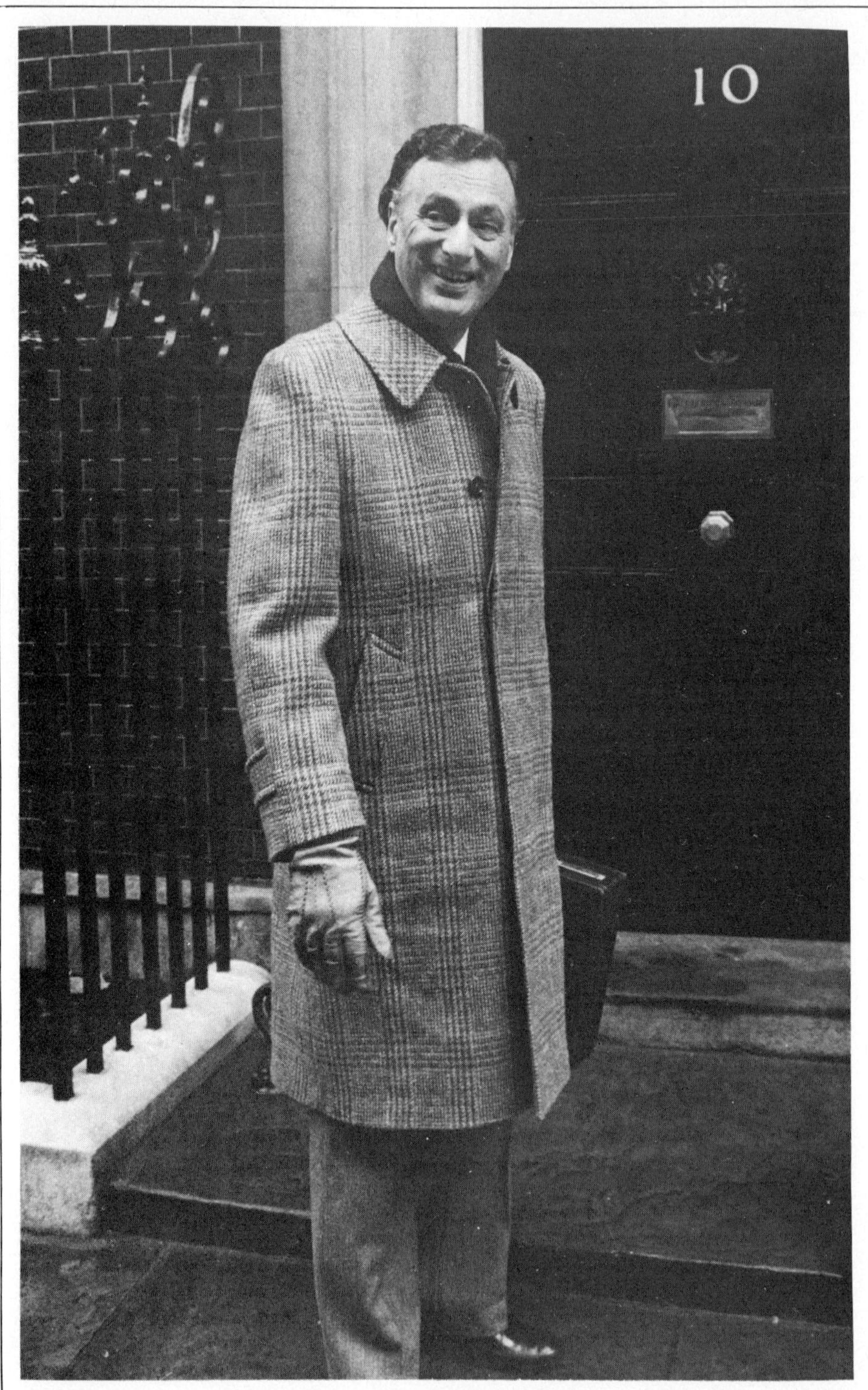
10

THE COMPLETE YES MINISTER

The Diaries of a Cabinet Minister
by
the Right Hon. James Hacker MP

Edited by Jonathan Lynn and Antony Jay

Salem House Publishers
Topsfield, Massachusetts

The BBC TV series *Yes Minister* were written by Jonathan Lynn and Antony Jay and produced by Sydney Lotterby and Peter Whitmore. The part of *James Hacker* was played by Paul Eddington, *Sir Humphrey Appleby* by Nigel Hawthorne and *Bernard Woolley* by Derek Fowlds.

First published by the
British Broadcasting Corporation

First published in the United States by
Salem House Publishers, 1987
462 Boston Street, Topsfield, MA 01983

ISBN 0 88162 272 9

Printed in England

Contents

Editors' Note

Some note of explanation is needed on the methods and guidelines that we have used in reducing these collected diaries of many millions of words to one relatively short volume.

James Hacker kept his diaries from the day on which he first entered the Cabinet. He dictated them into his cassette recorder, sometimes on a daily basis, more often at weekends when he was at his constituency home. His original plan had been simply to make notes for his memory, but he soon realised that there would be intrinsic interest in a diary which gave a daily picture of the struggles of a Cabinet Minister.

Before going into politics full time, Hacker had been first a polytechnic lecturer and, later, Editor of *Reform*. When the diaries were first transcribed they were hardly readable, having been dictated very much *ad lib*, rather like his polytechnic lectures. Furthermore, there were a number of discrepancies in his account of events, both within the book itself and when objectively compared with outside events. Being a journalist, Hacker had no particular talent for reporting facts.

Apart from the discrepancies, there was also a certain amount of boring repetition, inevitable in the diaries of a politician. Years of political training and experience had taught Hacker to use twenty words where one would do, to dictate millions of words where mere thousands would suffice, and to use language to blur and fudge issues and events so that they became incomprehensible to others. Incomprehensibility can be a haven for some politicians, for therein lies temporary safety.

But his natural gift for the misuse of language, though invaluable to an active politician, was not an asset to a would-be author. He had apparently intended to rewrite the diaries with a view to improving the clarity, accuracy and relevance of his publication. Towards the end of his life, however, he abandoned that plan because – according to his widow, Lady Hacker (as she now is) – he saw no reason why he should be the only politician publishing memoirs which adhered to those criteria.

The editors have therefore had to undertake that task, and in doing so found one further obstacle to clear understanding of the Hacker tapes. The early chapters of this volume had been transcribed from the cassette recordings during the great statesman's own lifetime, and he had glanced at them himself and made a few preliminary suggestions of his own as to selection and arrangement. But later chapters had yet to be transcribed when the bell rang for the Last Division and – curiously – it seemed that Hacker's speech became more and more indistinct, slurred and emotional as each recording session progressed. This may have been due to a fault in the recording machine, but it did not make our task any easier.

Nevertheless, these diaries constitute a unique contribution to our understanding of the way that Britain was governed in the 1980s and because Hacker wrote them in the hope that the public would understand more rather than less of the political process, we have edited the diaries ruthlessly. We encountered three principal problem areas in the editing process: chronological, technical, and interpretation.

First, chronology. Broadly, we tried to preserve the narrative element of the original diary, and thus we have tended to pursue particular stories and trains of events to their conclusion. At all times we have striven to maintain a chronological day-by-day account, even though the original tapes are much more confused. There is a slight risk of historical inaccuracy in this approach, because Hacker himself was deeply confused for most of his time in office and it could be argued that the diaries ought to reflect this confusion. But if we had allowed the diaries to reflect his confusion in full, the events that they relate would have become as incomprehensible to the reader as they were to him.

Technically, we have completed and punctuated sentences, unmixed the metaphors and corrected the grammar, unless by leaving the original we were able to give an insight into Hacker's state of mind.

Finally, interpretation. Where the book is ambiguous we have assumed that this is a deliberate exercise of his political skills. Although it is true that he was often unclear about the meaning of events, it is also the case that sometimes he was deliberately vague.

We believe that these diaries accurately reflect the mind of one of our outstanding national leaders; if the reflection seems clouded it may not be the fault of the mirror. Hacker himself processed events in a variety of ways, and the readers will have to make their own judgement as to whether any given statement represents

(a) what happened
(b) what he believed happened
(c) what he would like to have happened
(d) what he wanted others to believe happened
(e) what he wanted others to believe that he believed happened.

As a general rule, politicians' memories are less reliable about failures than successes, and about distant events than recent ones. Since Hacker's career, like all politicians', inevitably consisted mostly of failures, these diaries ran the risk of having only small historical value. But the fact that the great man had no time to make any alterations or excisions in the light of subsequent events has enabled us to select from the morass a document of unique value to students of that period of British history.

This book covers Hacker's entire career as the Minister for Administrative Affairs. This was his first experience in government. The Ministry had been created some years earlier as an umbrella ministry, along the lines of George Brown's Department of Economic Affairs in the Wilson government of the 1960s, to co-ordinate government administration. Theoretically it gave Hacker a roving brief, to investigate and control administrative inefficiency and overspending throughout the system, wherever it was to be found. Unfortunately the Department of Administrative Affairs was not only created to control the Civil Service, it also had to be staffed by the Civil Service. Readers will therefore be well aware of the inevitable result of Hacker's labours.

Nonetheless, it remains a slight puzzle to the editors of this volume that Hacker, who was such a master of blurring and obfuscation in his own political dealings, should have found such difficulty in dealing with a group of civil servants whose techniques were essentially similar. Hacker's innocence, as revealed in these diaries, is quite touching.

Later volumes under the title *Yes Prime Minister* will deal with Hacker's career as he failed upwards to Number Ten Downing Street, and thence to his final demise on his elevation to the House of Lords (as it then was).

We have, of course, had the benefit of other sources. Hacker was, inevitably, in ignorance of certain conversations and events which, had he known of them, would doubtless have altered his perceptions and his views. We are fortunate that under the Thirty-Year Rule all of Sir Humphrey Appleby's memos and minutes have become available to us. We are also fortunate that because Appleby was a first-class civil servant he had a total belief in the value of committing everything to paper. Thus we have also had the benefit of Sir Humphrey's own private diaries, and we would like to record our debt of gratitude to the Public Record Office and the Trustees of the voluminous Appleby Papers.

A final word of thanks. We were most grateful to have had a few conversations with Sir Humphrey himself before the advancing years, without in any way impairing his verbal fluency, disengaged the operation of his mind from the content of his speech. And we should like to express our thanks to the staff of St Dympna's Hospital for the Elderly Deranged, where he resided for his last days.

Above all, we are grateful to Sir Bernard Woolley, GCB, former Head of the Civil Service, who was Hacker's private secretary for the period covered by this volume. He has given generously of his time and checked our selection against his own memory and records. Nevertheless, any responsibility for errors and omissions is, of course, entirely our own.

Jonathan Lynn
Antony Jay

Hacker College, Oxford
September 2019 AD

1

Open Government

October 22nd

Well, perhaps it's the early hours of Friday, the 23rd now. I am most excited. I have just been returned to Parliament by Birmingham East. And after years in opposition, the party has finally won a general election and we're back in office.

After the result was announced I went to the celebration do at Alderman Spotteswoode's[1] and saw Robert McKenzie on the telly say: 'And so Jim Hacker's back, with an increased majority in his marginal constituency. After many years as a Shadow Minister he seems almost certain to get a Cabinet post in the new government.'

Robin Day seemed doubtful, though. I do hope Bob McKenzie's right.

October 23rd

I'm still hoping but I wonder if Robin Day knows something that I don't.

I've been sitting by the telephone ever since breakfast. No potential Cabinet Minister ever moves more than twenty feet from the telephone in the twenty-four hours following the appointment of a new Prime Minister. If you haven't heard within twenty-four hours, you're not going to be in the Cabinet.

Annie kept me supplied with constant cups of coffee all morning, and when I returned to the armchair next to the phone after lunch she asked me to help do the Brussels sprouts for dinner if I didn't have anything else to do. I explained to her that I couldn't because I was waiting for the call.

'Who from?' Sometimes Annie really is a bit dense.

The phone rang. I grabbed it. It was Frank Weisel, my special

[1] Hacker's constituency party Chairman.

political adviser, saying that he was on his way over. I told Annie, who wasn't pleased.

'Why doesn't he just move in?' she asked bitterly.

Sometimes I just don't understand her. I patiently explained to her that, as my political adviser, I depend on Frank more than anyone. 'Then why don't you marry *him*?' she asked. 'I now pronounce you man and political adviser. Whom politics has joined let no wife put asunder.'

It is awfully difficult for Annie, I know. Being an MP's wife is a pretty thankless task. But now that I may be a Minister, she'll at last reap the rewards!

The phone rang all day. Alderman Spotteswoode, the Gas Board, Frank, all sorts of useless people ringing up to congratulate me. 'On what?' I said to Annie: 'Don't they realise I'm waiting for the call?'

She said, 'You sound as if you're about to enter the ministry.'

'Yes,' I said, 'but which ministry, that's the whole point.'

Suddenly Annie screamed. I couldn't believe my ears. 'It was a *joke*!' she shouted, and started to pull her hair out. I decided that she must be a bit tense.

'Are you a bit tense?' I asked. She screamed again, and threw herself onto the floor. I thought of calling an ambulance, but was worried about the adverse publicity affecting my career at this crucial juncture – NEW MINISTER'S WIFE TAKEN AWAY IN STRAIT-JACKET.

'Are you a bit tense?' I asked again. Carefully.

'No,' she shouted – 'No, no, no, I'm not tense. I'm just a politician's wife. I'm not allowed to have feelings. I'm just a happy carefree politician's wife.'

So I asked her why she was lying face downwards on the floor. 'I'm looking for a cigarette. I can't find any.'

'Try the cigarette box,' I advised, trying to keep calm.

'It's empty.'

'Take a Valium.'

'I can't find the Valium, that's why I'm looking for a cigarette. Jim, pop out and get me some.'

I explained to Annie that I simply didn't dare leave the phone. Annie betrayed her usual total lack of understanding. 'Look, if the PM wants you to be in the bloody Cabinet, the PM will phone back if you're out. Or you can phone back.'

Annie will never understand the finer points of politics.

[*Hacker was very insecure about his cabinet prospects because he had previously run Martin Walker's campaign against the new PM for the leadership of the party. The question was whether the PM would be strong enough to ignore Jim Hacker or whether, in the interests of party unity, the PM would be obliged to give him a good job – Ed.*]

By the end of today I've heard on the grapevine that Bill's got Europe. Poor old Europe. Bill can't speak French or German. He hardly even speaks English, as a matter of fact. Martin's got the Foreign Office, as expected, Jack's got Health and Fred's got Energy.

I told Annie of these appointments, and she asked me if anyone had got Brains. I suppose she means Education.

October 24th

At last I'm a Cabinet Minister.

And today I had my first encounter with the Civil Service, and I must say I am very impressed.

I got the call from Number Ten at about 9 a.m., after a sleepless night, and immediately Frank Weisel and I caught the London train. I got a taxi to Number Ten, where I was asked by the PM to take over the Department of Administrative Affairs.

This is an important post. In the Cabinet ranking, about eighth or ninth I should think. On the other hand, Martin reminded me (when he phoned to congratulate me) that the DAA is a political graveyard, a bit like the Home Office, and the PM may have over-promoted me – a vengeful move. I am determined to get a grip on the DAA and prove to the PM that I'm not so easily taken care of.

I was expecting to be Minister of Agriculture, as I've shadowed Agriculture for seven years, and have many good ideas about it, but for some inexplicable reason the PM decided against this.

[*We found a memo from Sir Andrew Donnelly, Permanent Secretary of Agriculture, to Sir Arnold Robinson, Secretary to the Cabinet, imploring Sir Arnold to make sure that Hacker did not get Agriculture as he was too 'genned up' on it. Cabinet Papers show that Sir Arnold managed to convey to the PM that it would be better for Hacker not to go to Agriculture because 'he's been thinking about it rather too long and is perhaps in a bit of a rut' – Ed.*]

An official car met me as I came out of Number Ten, and I was driven straight to the DAA. I was met on the front steps by Bernard Woolley, who is to be my Private Secretary, and his assistant. He seems a likeable enough chap.

To my surprise he instantly knew who Frank Weisel was, as we got out of the car, though he pronounced his name 'Weasel', which always infuriates Frank.

We walked down miles of corridors. When we got to my office Frank had disappeared with the Assistant Private Secretary. Bernard assured me that Frank was being taken care of. They really are awfully nice and helpful.

My office is large, with a big desk, a conference table with lots of chairs around it, and a few armchairs arranged around a coffee table to form a conversation area. Otherwise, rather characterless. Bernard immediately went to the drinks cupboard.

'A drink, Minister?'

I nodded. 'Jim,' I said, as I want us to be on first-name terms.

'Gin?' he said, mishearing me.

'No,' I said, 'Jim. Call me Jim.'

Bernard said: 'If it's all the same to you, I'd rather call you Minister, Minister.'

'Minister, Minister?' It reminded me of Major Major in *Catch-22*. Then I realised what he meant. I asked him, 'Does that mean I have to call you Private Secretary, Private Secretary?'

Bernard said I was to call him Bernard. I'm sure that in the course of time I'll persuade him to call me Jim.

A moment later Sir Humphrey Appleby arrived. He is the Permanent Secretary of the DAA, the Civil Service Head of the Department. He is in his early fifties I should think, but – somehow – ageless. He is charming and intelligent, a typical mandarin. He welcomed me to the Department.

'I believe you've met before,' Bernard remarked. I was struck for the second time how well-informed this young man is.

Sir Humphrey said, 'Yes, we did cross swords when the Minister gave me a grilling over the Estimates in the Public Accounts Committee last year. He asked me all the questions I hoped nobody would ask.'

This is splendid. Sir Humphrey clearly admires me. I tried to brush it off. 'Well,' I said, 'Opposition's about asking awkward questions.'

'Yes,' said Sir Humphrey, 'and government is about not answering them.'

I was surprised. 'But you answered all my questions, didn't you,' I commented.

'I'm glad you thought so, Minister,' said Sir Humphrey. I didn't quite know what he meant by that. I decided to ask him who else was in the Department.

'Briefly, sir, I am the Permanent Under-Secretary of State, known as the Permanent Secretary. Woolley here is your Principal Private

Secretary. I, too, have a Principal Private Secretary, and he is the Principal Private Secretary to the Permanent Secretary. Directly responsible to me are ten Deputy Secretaries, eighty-seven Under-Secretaries and two hundred and nineteen Assistant Secretaries. Directly responsible to the Principal Private Secretaries are plain Private Secretaries. The Prime Minister will be appointing two Parliamentary Under-Secretaries and you will be appointing your own Parliamentary Private Secretary.'

'Can they all type?' I joked.

'None of us can type, Minister,' replied Sir Humphrey smoothly. 'Mrs McKay types – she is your secretary.'

I couldn't tell whether or not he was joking. 'What a pity,' I said. 'We could have opened an agency.'

Sir Humphrey and Bernard laughed. 'Very droll, sir,' said Sir Humphrey. 'Most amusing, sir,' said Bernard. Were they genuinely amused at my wit, or just being rather patronising? 'I suppose they all say that, do they?' I ventured.

Sir Humphrey reassured me on that. 'Certainly not, Minister,' he replied. 'Not quite all.'

I decided to take charge at once. I sat behind my desk and to my dismay I found it had a swivel chair. I don't like swivel chairs. But Bernard immediately assured me that everything in the office can be changed at my command – furniture, décor, paintings, office routine. I am unquestionably the boss!

Bernard then told me that they have two types of chair in stock, to go with two kinds of Minister – 'One sort folds up instantly and the other sort goes round and round in circles.' On second thoughts, perhaps that was another of Bernard's little jokes.

I decided that the time had come to be blunt and to tell them what's what. 'Frankly,' I said, 'this Department has got to cut a great swathe through the whole of the stuffy Whitehall bureaucracy. We need a new broom. We are going to throw open the windows and let in a bit of fresh air. We are going to cut through the red tape and streamline this creaking old bureaucratic machine. We are going to have a clean sweep. There are far too many useless people just sitting behind desks.'

I became aware that *I* was actually sitting behind a desk, but I'm sure that they realised that I was not referring to myself.

I explained that we had to start by getting rid of people who just make work for each other. Sir Humphrey was very helpful, and suggested that I mean redeploy them – which, I suppose, is what I *do* mean. I certainly want to reduce overmanning, but I don't actually want to be responsible for putting people out of work.

But, by the clean sweep and the new broom, I mean that we must have more Open Government. We made election pledges about this, and I intend to keep them. We must take the nation into our confidence. I said all this to Humphrey and Bernard who, to my surprise, were wholeheartedly in favour of these ideas.

Humphrey referred to my speeches on this subject in the House last year. And he referred to my *Observer* article, *Daily Mail* interview, and the manifesto.

I am most impressed that he knows so much about me.

Humphrey then produced draft proposals, to implement my policy in a White Paper. I was flabbergasted. The efficiency of the Civil Service is quite astounding. They even plan, Sir Humphrey tells me, to call the White Paper 'Open Government'.

All of these draft proposals are available to me within thirty-six hours of the new government being elected and within minutes of my arrival at my office. And on a weekend! Remarkable chaps. I asked Humphrey who had done all this.

'The creaking old bureaucratic machine,' he replied with a smile. 'No seriously, Minister, we are fully seized of the need for reform and we have taken it on board.'

I told him I was slightly surprised.

'I thought I'd have to fight you all the way,' I said.

Sir Humphrey remarked that people have funny ideas about the Civil Service.

'We are just here to help you formulate and implement your policies,' he explained.

He seems most sincere.

The draft proposals, which I have brought home tonight to my London flat in a red box, include 'Proposals for Shortening Approval Procedures in Planning Appeals'. Excellent. Sir Humphrey was able to quote from Hansard the rather amusing question which I'd asked earlier this year in the House:

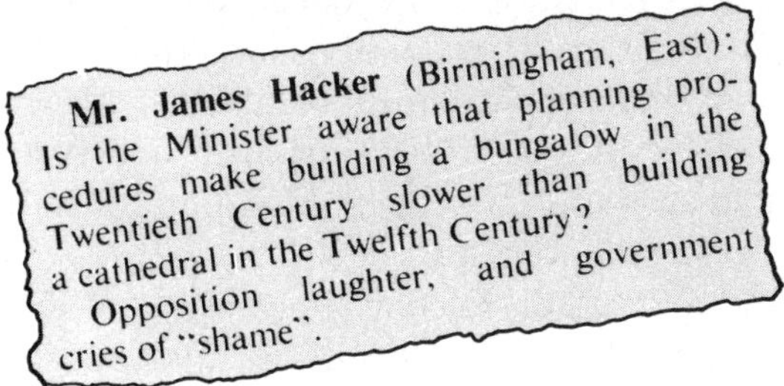
Mr. James Hacker (Birmingham, East): Is the Minister aware that planning procedures make building a bungalow in the Twentieth Century slower than building a cathedral in the Twelfth Century?
Opposition laughter, and government cries of "shame".

[*Actually they cried 'Bollocks' – Ed.*]

As it's Saturday, we have arranged to start things properly on Monday morning. But they've given me six red boxes for the weekend, four to be completed by tonight and two more tomorrow. Bernard tells me that the previous Minister got a bit slack about the paperwork, especially during the election campaign.

I'm certainly not going to be slack! I shall be a good Minister. I shall read everything they give me to read.

October 26th

I read all my boxes over the weekend. It took about nine hours. I caught the 7.15 a.m. train to Euston, the official car met me, and I was in the office by 9.20.

All the draft proposals for Open Government are superficially pretty impressive, but I happen to know that the Civil Service is pretty good at delaying tactics. I mentioned this to Humphrey at a meeting today. I think he's getting to know who's boss around here.

But first things first. The day started with the diary. I found to my surprise that there were numerous appointments in it already. I asked how this was possible, since they didn't even know who would win the election.

Bernard said: 'We knew there'd be a Minister, Minister.' I told him not to start *that* again.

Sir Humphrey explained, 'Her Majesty likes the business of government to continue, even when there are no politicians around.'

'Isn't that very difficult?' I asked.

'Yes . . . and no,' said Humphrey. I must say, I can't see how it's possible to govern without the politicians. I'm afraid that Humphrey might have delusions of grandeur . . .

My diary was pretty frightening. Cabinet at 10 on Thursday. Nine Cabinet committees this week. A speech to the Law Institute tomorrow night, a deputation from the British Computer Association at 10.30 tomorrow morning, University Vice-Chancellors lunch on Wednesday (another speech), opening the National Conference of Public Employers on Thursday morning (another speech), and so on.

I noticed that everything in the diary is in pencil, so presumably much of it can be and will be changed. I pointed out to Bernard that I have various other commitments.

Bernard looked puzzled. 'Such as?' he asked.

'Well . . . I'm on four policy committees of the party, for a start.'

'I'm sure you won't be wanting to put party before country,' said Sir Humphrey. I had never looked at it in that light. Of course, he's absolutely right.

They were going to give me three more red boxes for tonight, by the way. When I jibbed at this a bit, Sir Humphrey explained that there are a lot of decisions to take and announcements to approve. He then tried something on, by saying: 'But we could, in fact, minimise the work so that you need only take the major policy decisions.'

I saw through that ploy at once. I insisted that *I* would take *all* the decisions and read *all* the relevant documents.

They've given me five boxes for tonight.

October 27th

Today I found that we have a problem with Frank Weisel. It's Tuesday today, and I realised that I hadn't seen him since I arrived at the DAA last Saturday morning.

To be quite truthful, I didn't actually realise it till he barged into my office, shouting and carrying on, demanding to be let in.

It appears that he's been in the waiting room since Saturday. (I presume he went home on Sunday.) Bernard tried to tell him that he, Humphrey and I were in private conference, but I quickly sorted that out. I demanded that Frank, as my adviser, be given an office in the Department.

Sir Humphrey attempted to fudge the issue, saying that I had a whole Department to advise me now. Nonetheless I insisted.

'Well,' said Sir Humphrey, 'I believe we have some spare office space in Walthamstow, don't we Bernard?'

Frank was appalled. 'Walthamstow?'

'Yes, it's surprising isn't it?' said Sir Humphrey agreeably. 'The government owns property all over London.'

'But I don't want to be in Walthamstow,' explained Frank at the top of his voice.

'It's in a very nice part of Walthamstow,' put in Bernard.

'And Walthamstow's a very nice place. So I gather,' added Sir Humphrey.

Frank and I looked at each other. If they were not so charming and, well, gentlemanly, you might have thought they were trying to squeeze Frank right out.

'I need an office *here*, in this building,' said Frank, firmly and extremely loudly.

I added my agreement. Sir Humphrey capitulated at once, and told Bernard to find a suitable office right away. I then said, to make assurance doubly sure, that I expected Frank to have copies of all the papers that are given to me.

Bernard seemed surprised. 'All?'

'All,' I said.

Sir Humphrey agreed immediately. 'It shall be done – all the appropriate papers.'

In my opinion, these civil servants are not nearly so hard to deal with as people say. They are mostly very co-operative, and, even if not initially, always jump to it when spoken to firmly. I think I'm getting somewhere at last.

October 28th

After the last hectic four days, I have a little time to reflect – for posterity – on my first days in office.

First, I am impressed by the thorough grasp the officials at the DAA have of every situation. Second, how they are willing to co-operate fully, albeit under pressure, with Frank Weisel.

Thirdly, I am most struck by my dependence on these civil servants. I, like virtually all our new administration, knew nothing of the workings of Whitehall except what I'd learned second-hand. Because we have been so long in opposition, only three members of the government, including the PM, have ever held office before. I had never seen the inside of a red box, never met a Permanent Secretary, and had no idea how things were really done. [*This situation is similar to the one in which the Labour Government of 1964 found itself – Harold Wilson, the PM, was the only member of Cabinet who had previously been a Cabinet Minister – Ed.*] This makes us more dependent on our officials than most new governments. Thank goodness they are behaving honourably.

[*The following Monday, Sir Humphrey Appleby met Sir Arnold Robinson, Secretary to the Cabinet, at The Reform Club in Pall Mall. Sir Humphrey made a note about the meeting in his private diary.*]

November 2 MONDAY

Arnold and I compared notes about the new government. His new Cabinet is scarcely distinguishable from the last one. My new boy is learning the rules very quickly.

I sounded Arnold out about the American Ambassador – rumour has it he has been spending a lot of time with the PM.

[*It is interesting to observe that senior civil servants, perhaps because they have spent thirty years writing notes in the margin of a memo or minute, only write in the margin even if there is nothing else on the page – Ed.*]

Arnold and I compared notes [on 2 November] about the new government. His new Cabinet is scarcely distinguishable from the last one. My new boy is learning the rules very quickly.

I sounded Arnold out about the American Ambassador – rumour has it he has been spending a lot of time with the PM.

Arnold confirmed this. But was unwilling to say whether it was about defence or trade. He is anxious about a leak – therefore it is imperative that the Cabinet doesn't hear about it yet.

I concluded, correctly, that it is defence *and* trade, i.e. the new aerospace systems contract.

The aerospace contract would be a considerable coup for the PM, less than two weeks after the election. Of course, it's been in the pipeline for months, but the new PM will obviously take the credit.

It will mean four and a half billion dollars, and many new jobs in the Midlands and North-West. All in marginal seats, too – what a coincidence!

This is valuable information. I gathered from Arnold that it would, therefore, be a grave embarrassment to the PM if a hypothetical Minister were to rock the Anglo-American boat. Man overboard. The end of a promising new Ministerial career, in fact.

Therefore, I have ensured that the Weasel[1] receives a copy of the invoice

[1] Frank Weisel.

for the new American addressing machines. Naturally he has not received it, because it is sensitive. But I think that this is the right moment.

I instructed my secretary to ensure that the Weasel find the invoice near the bottom of a pile. Let the man feel he has achieved something.

[*Bernard Woolley joined Sir Humphrey and Sir Arnold at the club, for an after-dinner coffee while they drank their after-dinner brandy – Ed.*]

I asked young Bernard what he makes of our new Minister. Bernard is happy. So am I. Hacker swallowed the whole diary in one gulp and apparently did his boxes like a lamb last Saturday and Sunday. He'll be house-trained in no time.

All we have to do is head him off this Open Government nonsense, I remarked to Bernard. Bernard said that he thought that we were in favour of Open Government. I hope I have not over-promoted young Bernard. He still has an awful lot to learn.

I explained that we are calling the White Paper *Open Government* because you always dispose of the difficult bit in the title. It does less harm there than on the statute books.

It is the law of Inverse Relevance: the less you intend to do about something, the more you have to keep talking about it.

Bernard asked us, 'What's wrong with Open Government?' I could hardly believe my ears. Arnold thought he was joking. Sometimes I wonder if Bernard really is a flyer, or whether we shouldn't just send him off to a career at the War Graves Commission.

Arnold pointed out, with great clarity, that Open Government is a contradiction in terms. You can be open – or you can have government.

Bernard claims that the citizens of a democracy have a right to know. We explained that, in fact, they have a right to be ignorant. Knowledge only means complicity and guilt. Ignorance has a certain dignity.

Bernard then said: 'The Minister wants Open Government.' Years of training seem to have had no effect on Bernard sometimes.

I remarked that one does not just give people what they want, if it's not good for them. One does not, for instance, give whisky to an alcoholic.

Arnold rightly added that if people do not know what you're doing, they don't know what you're doing *wrong*.

This is not just a defence mechanism for officials, of course. Bernard must understand that he would not be serving his Minister by helping him to make a fool of himself. Every Minister we have would have been a laughing-stock within his first three weeks in office if it had not been for the most rigid and impenetrable secrecy about what he was up to.

Bernard is a Private Secretary. I am a Permanent Under-Secretary of State. The very word Secretary means one who can keep a secret.

Bernard asked me what I proposed to do. Naturally I did not inform him of my plans for the Weasel to make a great discovery. This would be putting too great a strain on Bernard's loyalty to Hacker.

I asked Bernard if he could keep a secret. He said he could. I replied that *I* could, too. [*Appleby Papers 14/QLI/9a*]

[*Hacker was, of course, in complete ignorance of the meeting described above – Ed.*]

November 5th

Guy Fawkes Day. Fireworks inside the office too. A fitting day on which to enforce the supremacy of parliament and HMG.

Frank Weisel came bursting into my office, waving a document, 'Have you seen this?' he enquired at four thousand decibels.

I was delighted that the civil servants were giving him all the papers now. I said so.

'They're not,' he said derisively. 'Not the *real* papers.'

'Which real papers aren't you getting?' I wanted to know.

'How do I know, if I'm not getting them?'

This is, of course, absolutely true. And I don't know what he can do about it. [*This, of course, is an example of what management consultants call the Light-in-the-Refrigerator Syndrome, i.e. is the light on when the door is shut? The only way to find out is to open the door – in which case the door is not shut any more – Ed.*]

But Frank did not want to discuss his problems in getting necessary information out of the officials.

'They think they're sending me the rubbish. But look what I've found – oho, we've got them, we've got them by the short and curlies.'

I still didn't know what he was talking about. Frank explained further.

'We've got Sir Humphrey-Bloody-Appleby and Mr Toffee-Nose-Private-Secretary-Snooty-Woolley just where we want them.'

He brandished a sheaf of papers under my nose. I *still* didn't know what he was talking about, but I do think he has a wonderful line in invective – perhaps I should let him write the draft of my conference speech next year.

I made Frank sit down, and explain calmly. He has found some ordinary office invoices that have tremendous political significance. The DAA has apparently bought one thousand computer video display terminals, at ten thousand pounds each. Ten million pounds of the taxpayers' money. And they are made in Pittsburgh!

This is shocking. Humphrey's been keeping very quiet about this. And I'm not surprised. We make computer peripherals in my constituency, Birmingham East. And we have rising unemployment. It is a scandal that the Civil Service is not buying British.

I sent for Humphrey. He was in meetings all day, but Frank and I will confront him with this tomorrow. I am deeply grateful to Frank. Sir Humphrey is going to be very surprised indeed that we have found out about this so fast.

November 6th

The meeting with Humphrey was a total success.

I showed him the invoices for the computer display terminals. He admitted that the DAA has purchased this brand for the whole of Whitehall.

'But they're not British,' I pointed out.

'That is unfortunately true,' he agreed, somewhat shamefaced.

'We make these machines in Birmingham East.'

'Not of the same quality,' he said.

This is very probably true, but naturally I can't admit it even if it is.

'They are better quality,' I said firmly. 'They come from my constituency.' I told Humphrey to cancel the contract.

He responded that it was beyond his power to do so, and that it could only be cancelled by the Treasury. He said it would be a major change of policy for the Civil Service to cancel contracts freely entered into. Especially with overseas suppliers.

He suggested (a trifle impertinently, I thought) that I should take it up in Cabinet. 'Perhaps they would postpone the discussion on the Middle East, or nuclear disarmament, to talk about office equipment.'

I could see that this was out of the question. I was faced with a dilemma. If it couldn't be cancelled, how was I to face my constituency party?

'Why need they know?' asked Sir Humphrey. 'Why need *anybody* know? We can see that it never gets out.'

I was staggered. Couldn't Humphrey see that to keep it quiet was directly contrary to our new policy of Open Government, to which he was as firmly committed as I?

Frank spelled out the only alternative. 'If the order can't be cancelled, it must be published.'

Humphrey asked why. For a moment I couldn't quite think of the answer. But Frank saw it at once. 'Two reasons,' he explained. 'First, it's a manifesto commitment. Second, it'll make the last Minister look like a traitor.'

Two unanswerable reasons. I really am very grateful to Frank. And he is running rings around Sir Humphrey. Perhaps Sir Humphrey is not as clever as I first thought.

Humphrey seemed very anxious about the idea of publication. 'But surely,' he said to Frank, 'you're not suggesting that the Minister should make a positive reference to this confidential transaction in a speech?'

'A speech!' said Frank. 'Of course! That's the answer.'

This is a superb idea of Frank's. My speech to the Union of Office Employees will deal with this scandalous contract. And we will release it to the press in advance.

I said as much to Humphrey. Frank said, 'There. Who's running the country now?' I felt his glee was a little juvenile, but quite understandable.

Sir Humphrey seemed even more worried. I asked him for his advice, which was totally predictable. 'I think it might be regrettable if we upset the Americans.'

Predictable, and laughable. I pointed out to Humphrey, in no uncertain terms, that it is high time that someone jolted the Americans out of their commercial complacency. We should be thinking about the British poor, not the American rich!

Humphrey said, 'Minister, if that is your express wish the Department will back you. Up to the hilt.' This was very loyal. One must give credit where it's due.

I said that indeed it was my express wish. Bernard then said he would circulate the speech, as soon as it was written, for clearance.

This is new to me. I've never heard of 'clearance'. More bureaucracy and pointless paperwork. This matter has nothing to do with any other department. And if another department disagrees, they can say so publicly. That's what Open Government is all about.

Humphrey pleaded with me to circulate the speech, if only for information. At first I opposed this, but he argued – quite convincingly, I thought – that Open Government demands that we should inform our colleagues in government as well as our friends in Fleet Street.

My final word to Humphrey, as the meeting concluded, was to see that the speech went straight to the press.

'Minister,' he said, 'we shall obviously serve your best interests.'

A notable victory by Frank and me, in the cause of Open Government.

[*A typescript of Hacker's speech has been found in the files of the DAA. It is annotated with suggestions by Frank Weisel and Bernard Woolley, with comments from Hacker – Ed.*]

DEPARTMENT OF ADMINISTRATIVE AFFAIRS

SPEECH TO THE UNION OF OFFICE EMPLOYEES

As you know, we have made a pledge to the people about Open Government. So let's begin as we mean to go on. The people have a right to know what I know. And I have discovered that only last month the previous government signed a contract to import ten million pounds worth of office equipment from America for use by the Service.

Civil Service bureaucracy. Frank

YES. GOOD! J.H

And yet an identical product - a better product - is made in Britain. By British workers. In British factories. So we are being fobbed off with second-rate American junk by high-pressure smart-alec salesmen from Pittsburgh while British factories stand idle and British workers queue up for the dole.

Unemployment benefit? B.W.

DOLE! J.H

Well, if the Americans are going to take us for a ride, at least the British people have a right to know about it. And we will fight them on the beaches, we will fight them

/over

November 9th

Today was disastrous. There have been some quite astounding turns of events.

My speech was completed. I was sitting in the office reading the press release when Bernard burst in with a minute from the PM's private office.

I have learned, by the way, that *minutes, memos* and *submissions* are all the same thing. Except that ministers send *minutes* to civil servants and to each other, whereas civil servants send *memos* and *minutes* to each other but *submissions* to ministers.

[*This is because a minute takes or orders action whereas a memo presents the background arguments, the pros and cons. Therefore, civil servants may send either to each other, as may politicians – but as a civil servant may not tell a Minister what to do he sends a submission, the very word designed to express an attitude of humility and respect. Minutes may, of course, also be notes about official meetings, and this meaning gives rise to the well-known Civil Service axiom that meetings are where civil servants take minutes but politicians take hours – Ed.*]

Anyway, the minute made it clear that we were all to be very nice to the Yanks for the next few weeks. I realised that my speech, which had gone out to the press, could not have been timed worse.

I was appalled. Not only by my bad luck. But I find it incredible that I, as a member of the Cabinet, should have no knowledge of forthcoming defence agreements with the Americans. Whatever has happened to the doctrine of collective responsibility that I learned about at the LSE?

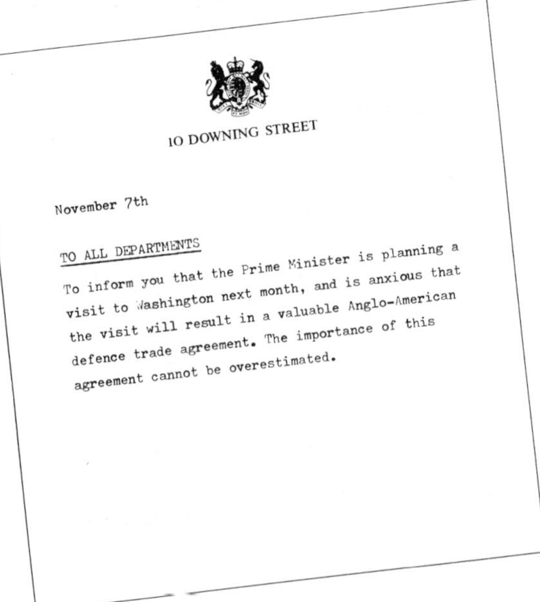

10 DOWNING STREET

November 7th

TO ALL DEPARTMENTS

To inform you that the Prime Minister is planning a visit to Washington next month, and is anxious that the visit will result in a valuable Anglo-American defence trade agreement. The importance of this agreement cannot be overestimated.

Sir Humphrey then hurried in to my office, looking slightly panicky.

'Sorry to burst in, Minister, but all hell's broken loose at Number Ten – apparently they've just seen your speech. They are asking why we didn't obtain clearance.'

'What did you say?' I asked.

'I said that we believe in Open Government. But it seemed to make things worse. The PM wants to see you in the House, right away.'

I realised that this could be the end for me. I asked Humphrey what was likely to happen. Sir Humphrey shrugged.

'The Prime Minister giveth – and the Prime Minister taketh away.'

I left the room feeling sick. As I started down the corridor I thought I heard Sir Humphrey add: 'Blessed be the name of the Prime Minister.' But I think I must have imagined that.

Humphrey, Frank and I hurried down Whitehall past the Cenotaph (how very appropriate that seemed!). There was an icy wind blowing. We went straight to the House. I was to meet the PM behind the Speaker's chair.

[*This does not mean, literally, behind the chair. It is the area of the House where the PM and the Leader of the Opposition, the two Chief Whips, the Leader of the House and others, meet on neutral ground to arrange the business of the House. The PM's office is to be found there too – Ed.*]

We were kept waiting for some minutes outside the PM's room. Then Vic Gould, our Chief Whip, emerged. He came straight over to me.

'You're a real pain in the arse, aren't you?' Vic really does pride himself on his dreadful manners. 'The PM's going up the wall. Hitting the roof. You can't go around making speeches like that.'

'It's Open Government,' said Frank.

'Shut up, Weasel, who asked you?' retorted Vic. Rude bugger. Typical Chief Whip.

'Weisel,' said Frank with dignity.

I sprang to Frank's defence. 'He's right, Vic. It's Open Government. It's in our manifesto. One of our main planks. The PM believes in Open Government too.'

'Open, yes,' said Vic. 'But not gaping.' Very witty, I don't think! 'In politics,' Vic went on relentlessly, 'you've got to learn to say things with tact and finesse – you berk!'

I suppose he's got a point. I felt very sheepish, but partly because I didn't exactly enjoy being ignominiously ticked off in front of Humphrey and Frank.

'How long have you been a Minister?' Vic asked me. Bloody silly question. He knows perfectly well. He was just asking for effect.

'A week and a half,' I told him.

'Then I think you may have earned yourself a place in the *Guinness Book of Records*,' he replied. 'I can see the headlines already – CABINET SPLIT ON U.S. TRADE. HACKER LEADS REVOLT AGAINST PRIME MINISTER! That's what you wanted, is it?'

And he walked away.

Then Sir Arnold Robinson, the Cabinet Secretary, came out of the PM's office. Sir Humphrey asked him what news there was.

Sir Arnold said the same things, only in Whitehall language. 'That speech is causing the Prime Minister some distress. Has it definitely been released to the press?'

I explained that I gave express instructions for it to go out at twelve noon. Sir Arnold seemed angry with Sir Humphrey. 'I'm appalled at you,' he said. I've never heard one civil servant express himself so strongly to another. 'How could you allow your Minister to put himself in this position without going through the proper channels?'

Humphrey turned to me for help. 'The Minister and I,' he began, 'believe in Open Government. We want to throw open the windows and let in a bit of fresh air. Isn't that right, Minister?'

I nodded, but couldn't speak. For the first time, Sir Arnold addressed me directly.

'Well, Minister, it's good party stuff but it places the PM in a very difficult position, personally.' That, in Sir Arnold's language, is about the most threatening thing that has ever been said to me.

'But . . . what about our commitment to Open Government?' I finally managed to ask.

'This,' replied Sir Arnold drily, 'seems to be the closed season for Open Government.'

Then Sir Humphrey voiced my worst fears by murmuring quietly: 'Do you want to give thought to a draft letter of resignation? Just in case, of course.'

I know that Humphrey was just trying to be helpful, but he really doesn't give much moral support in a crisis.

I could see that there was only one possibility left. 'Can't we hush it up?' I said suddenly.

Humphrey, to his credit, was completely baffled by this suggestion. He didn't even seem to understand what I meant. These civil servants really are rather naïve.

'Hush it up?' he asked.

'Yes,' I said. 'Hush it up.'

'You mean,' Humphrey was apparently getting the idea at last, 'suppress it?'

I didn't exactly care for the word 'suppress', but I had to agree that that was exactly what I did mean.

Humphrey then said something like: 'I see. What you're suggesting is that, within the framework of the guidelines about Open Government which you have laid down, we should adopt a more flexible posture.' Civil servants have an extraordinary genius for wrapping up a simple idea to make it sound extremely complicated.

On second thoughts, this is a real talent which I should learn to cultivate. His phrasing might help me look as though I am not changing my posture at all.

However, we were saved by the bell as the US Cavalry galloped over the horizon in the shape of Bernard Woolley hurrying into the ante-room.

'About the press release,' he began breathlessly. 'There appears to have been a development which could precipitate a reappraisal of our position.'

At first I didn't quite grasp what that meant. But he then went on to say that the Department had failed to rescind the interdepartmental clearance procedure, which meant that the supplementary stop-order came into effect, which meant that it was all *all right*!

In other words, my speech didn't go out to the press after all. By an amazing stroke of good luck, it had *only* been sent to the Prime Minister's Private Office. The Duty Office at the DDA had never received instructions to send it out *before* it was cleared with the PM and the FCO. Because of the American reference.

This wonderfully fortunate oversight seems to have saved my bacon. Of course, I didn't let Humphrey see my great sense of relief. In fact, he apologised.

'The fault is entirely mine, Minister,' he said. 'This procedure for holding up press releases dates back to before the era of Open Government. I unaccountably omitted to rescind it. I do hope you will forgive this lapse.'

In the circumstances, I felt that the less said the better. I decided to be magnanimous. 'That's quite all right Humphrey,' I said, 'after all, we all make mistakes.'

'Yes Minister,' said Sir Humphrey.

2
The Official Visit

November 10th

I am finding that it is impossible to get through all the work. The diary is always full, speeches constantly have to be written and delivered, and red boxes full of papers, documents, memos, minutes, submissions and letters have to be read carefully every night. And this is only *part* of my work.

Here I am, attempting to function as a sort of managing director of a very large and important business and I have no previous experience either of the Department's work or, in fact, of management of any kind. A career in politics is no preparation for government.

And, as if becoming managing director of a huge corporation were not enough, I am also attempting to do it part-time. I constantly have to leave the DAA to attend debates in the House, to vote, to go to Cabinet and Cabinet committees and party executive meetings and I now see that it is not possible to do this job properly or even adequately. I am rather depressed.

Can anyone seriously imagine the chairman of a company leaping like a dervish out of a meeting in his office every time a bell rings, no matter when, at any time of the afternoon or evening, racing like Steve Ovett to a building eight minutes down the street, rushing through a lobby, and running back to his office to continue the meeting. This is what I have to do every time the Division Bell rings. Sometimes six or seven times in one night. And do I have any idea at all what I'm voting for? Of course I don't. How could I?

Today I arrived in the office and was immediately cast down by the sight of my in-tray. Full to overflowing. The out-tray was completely empty.

Bernard was patiently waiting for me to read some piece of impenetrable prose that he had dug up, in answer to the question I had asked him yesterday: what are my actual powers in various far-flung parts of the UK, such as Scotland and Northern Ireland?

He proudly offered me a document. It said: 'Notwithstanding the provisions of subsection 3 of Section A of Clause 214 of the Administrative Procedures (Scotland) Act 1978, it has been agreed that, insofar as the implementation of the statutory provisions is concerned, the resolution of anomalies and uncertainties between responsible departments shall fall within the purview of the Minister for Administrative Affairs.'

I gazed blankly at it for what seemed an eternity. My mind just seemed to cloud over, as it used to at school when faced with Caesar's Gallic Wars or calculus. I longed to sleep. And it was only 9.15 a.m. I asked Bernard what it meant. He seemed puzzled by the question. He glanced at his own copy of the document.

'Well, Minister,' he began, 'it means that notwithstanding the provisions of subsection 3 of Section A of Clause 214 of . . .'

I interrupted him. 'Don't read it to me,' I said. 'I've just read it to you. What does it *mean*?'

Bernard gazed blankly at me. 'What it says, Minister.'

He wasn't trying to be unhelpful. I realised that Whitehall papers, though totally incomprehensible to people who speak ordinary English, are written in the everyday language of Whitehall Man.

Bernard hurried out into the Private Office and brought me the diary.

[*The Private Office is the office immediately adjoining the Minister's office. In it are the desks of the Private Secretary and the three or four assistant private secretaries, including the Diary Secretary – a full-time job. Adjoining the inner Private Office is the outer private office, containing about twelve people, all secretarial and clerking staff, processing replies to parliamentary questions, letters, etc.*

Access to the Minister's office is through the Private Office. Throughout the day everyone, whether outsiders or members of the Department, continually come and go through the Private Office.

The Private Office is, therefore, somewhat public – Ed.]

'May I remind you, Minister, that you are seeing a deputation from the TUC in fifteen minutes, and from the CBI half an hour after that, and the NEB at 12 noon.'

My feeling of despair increased. 'What do they all want – roughly?' I asked.

'They are all worried about the machinery for inflation, deflation and reflation,' Bernard informed me. What do they think I am? A

DEPARTMENT OF ADMINISTRATIVE AFFAIRS

INTERDEPARTMENTAL COMMITTE ON

ADMINISTRATIVE PROCEDURES

In the Chair	Sir Humphrey Appleby KCB
Present	Mr S J Unwin CBE
	Mr H B Christie CVO
	Mrs G E Williamson OBE
	Mr P F Warburton
	Miss L W McFarlane
Secretary	Miss G Fairbairn

1. The Minutes of the previous meeting were read and agreed.

2. Matters arising:

   (i) Notwithstanding the provisions of subsection 3 of Section A of Clause 214 of the Administrative Procedures (Scotland) Act 1978, it has been agreed that, insofar as the implementation of the statutory provisions is concerned, the resolution of anomalies and uncertainties between responsible departments shall fall within the purview of the Minister for Administrative Affairs.

What does this mean? J.H

/over

Minutes of a Meeting held at the Department of Administrative Affairs on November 2nd

Minister of the Crown or a bicycle pump?

I indicated the in-tray. 'When am I going to get through all this correspondence?' I asked Bernard wearily.

Bernard said: 'You *do* realise, Minister, that you don't actually *have* to?'

I had realised no such thing. This sounded good.

Bernard continued: 'If you want, we can simply draft an official reply to any letter.'

'What's an official reply?' I wanted to know.

'It just says,' Bernard explained, '"the Minister has asked me to thank you for your letter." Then *we* reply. Something like: "The matter is under consideration." Or even, if we feel so inclined, "under active consideration!"'

'What's the difference between "under consideration" and "under active consideration"?' I asked.

'"Under consideration" means we've lost the file. "Under active consideration" means we're trying to find it!'

I think this might have been one of Bernard's little jokes. But I'm not absolutely certain.

Bernard was eager to tell me what I had to do in order to lighten the load of my correspondence. 'You just transfer every letter from your in-tray to your out-tray. You put a brief note in the margin if you want to see the reply. If you don't, you need never see or hear of it again.'

I was stunned. My secretary was sitting there, seriously telling me that if I move a pile of unanswered letters from one side of my desk to the other, that is all I have to do? [*Crossman had a similar proposition offered, in his first weeks in office – Ed.*]

So I asked Bernard: 'Then what is the Minister for?'

'To make policy decisions,' he replied fluently. 'When you have decided the policy, we can carry it out.'

It seems to me that if I do not read the letters I will be somewhat ill-informed, and that therefore the number of so-called policy decisions will be reduced to a minimum.

Worse: I would not *know* which were the decisions that I needed to take. I would be dependent on my officials to tell me. I suspect that there would not be very many decisions left.

So I asked Bernard: 'How often are policy decisions needed?'

Bernard hesitated. 'Well . . . from time to time, Minister,' he replied in a kindly way.

It is never too soon to get tough. I decided to start in the Department the way I meant to continue. 'Bernard,' I said firmly, '*this* government governs. It does not just preside like our predecessors did. When a nation's been going downhill you need someone to get into the driving seat, and put his foot on the accelerator.'

'I think perhaps you mean the brake, Minister,' said Bernard.

I simply do not know whether this earnest young man is being helpful, or is putting me down.

November 11th

Today I saw Sir Humphrey Appleby again. Haven't seen him for a couple of days now.

There was a meeting in my office about the official visit to the UK of the President of Buranda. I had never even heard of Buranda.

Bernard gave me the brief last night. I found it in the third red box. But I'd had very little time to study it. I asked Humphrey to tell me about Buranda – like, where is it?

'It's fairly new, Minister. It used to be called British Equatorial Africa. It's the red bit a few inches below the Mediterranean.'

I can't see what Buranda has got to do with us. Surely this is an FCO job. [*Foreign and Commonwealth Office – Ed.*] But it was explained to me that there was an administrative problem because Her Majesty is due to be up at Balmoral when the President arrives. Therefore she will have to come to London.

This surprised me. I'd always thought that State Visits were arranged years in advance. I said so.

'This is not a State Visit,' said Sir Humphrey. 'It is a Head of Government visit.'

I asked if the President of Buranda isn't the Head of State? Sir Humphrey said that indeed he was, but also the Head of Government.

I said that, if he's merely coming as Head of Government, I didn't see why the Queen had to greet him. Humphrey said that it was because *she* is the Head of State. I couldn't see the logic. Humphrey says that the Head of State must greet a Head of State, even if the visiting Head of State is not *here* as a Head of State but only as a Head of Government.

Then Bernard decided to explain. 'It's all a matter of hats,' he said.

'Hats?' I was becoming even more confused.

'Yes,' said Bernard, 'he's coming here wearing his Head of Government hat. He is the Head of State, too, but it's not a State Visit because he's not wearing his Head of State hat, but protocol demands that even though he is wearing his Head of Government hat, he must still be met by . . .' I could see his desperate attempt to avoid either mixing metaphors or abandoning his elaborately constructed simile. '. . . the Crown,' he finished in triumph, having thought of the ultimate hat.

I said that I'd never heard of Buranda anyway, and I didn't know why we were bothering with an official visit from this tin-pot little African country. Sir Humphrey Appleby and Bernard Woolley went visibly pale. I looked at their faces, frozen in horror.

'Minister,' said Humphrey, 'I beg you not to refer to it as a tin-pot African country. It is an LDC.'

LDC is a new one on me. It seems that Buranda is what used to be called an Underdeveloped Country. However, this term has apparently become offensive, so then they were called Developing Countries. This term apparently was patronising. Then they became Less Developed Countries – or LDC, for short.

Sir Humphrey tells me that I *must* be clear on my African terminology, or else I could do irreparable damage.

It seems, in a nutshell, that the term Less Developed Countries is not yet causing offence to anyone. When it does, we are immediately ready to replace the term LDC with HRRC. This is short for Human Resource-Rich Countries. In other words, they are grossly overpopulated and begging for money. However, Buranda is *not* an HRRC. Nor is it one of the 'Haves' or 'Have-not' nations – apparently we no longer use those terms either, we talk about the North/South dialogue instead. In fact it seems that Buranda is a 'will have' nation, if there were such a term, and if it were not to cause offence to our Afro-Asian, or Third-World, or Non-Aligned-Nation brothers.

'Buranda *will have* a huge amount of oil in a couple of years from now,' confided Sir Humphrey.

'Oh I see,' I said. 'So it's not a TPLAC at all.'

Sir Humphrey was baffled. It gave me pleasure to baffle him for once. 'TPLAC?' he enquired carefully.

'Tin-Pot Little African Country,' I explained.

Sir Humphrey and Bernard jumped. They looked profoundly shocked. They glanced nervously around to check that I'd not been overheard. They were certainly not amused. How silly – anyone would think my office was bugged! [*Perhaps it was – Ed.*]

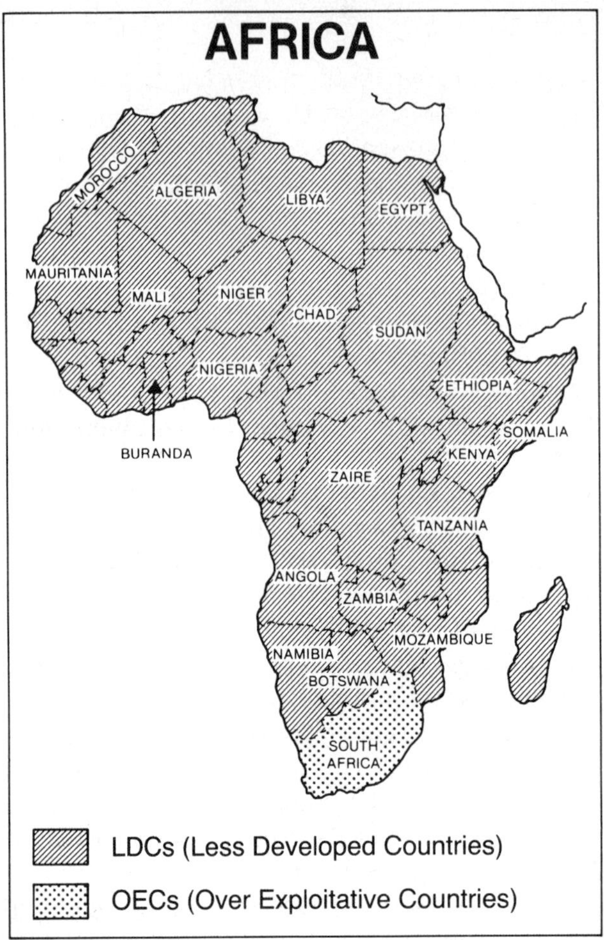

November 12th

On my way to work this morning I had an inspiration.

At my meeting with Humphrey yesterday it had been left for him to make arrangements to get the Queen down from Balmoral to meet the Burandan President. But this morning I remembered that we have three by-elections pending in three marginal Scottish constituencies, as a result of the death of one member who was so surprised that his constituents re-elected him in spite of his corruption and dishonesty that he had a heart attack and died, and as a result of the elevation of two other members to the Lords on the formation of the new government. [*The Peerage and/or the heart attack are, of course, the two most usual rewards for a career of corruption and dishonesty – Ed.*]

I called Humphrey to my office. 'The Queen,' I announced, 'does not have to come down from Balmoral at all.'

There was a slight pause.

'Are you proposing,' said Sir Humphrey in a pained manner, 'that Her Majesty and the President should exchange official greetings by telephone?'

'No.'

'Then,' said Sir Humphrey, even more pained, 'perhaps you just want them to shout very loudly.'

'Not that either,' I said cheerfully. 'We will hold the official visit in Scotland. Holyrood Palace.'

Sir Humphrey replied instantly. 'Out of the question,' he said.

'Humphrey,' I said. 'Are you sure you've given this idea due consideration?'

'It's not our decision,' he replied. 'It's an FCO matter.'

I was ready for this. I spent last night studying that wretched document which had caused me so much trouble yesterday. 'I don't think so,' I said, and produced the file with a fine flourish. 'Notwithstanding the provisions of subsection 3 blah blah blah . . . administrative procedures blah blah blah . . . shall fall within the purview of the Minister for Administrative Affairs.' I sat back and watched.

Sir Humphrey was stumped. 'Yes, but . . . why do you want to do this?' he asked.

'It saves Her Majesty a pointless journey. And there are three marginal Scottish by-elections coming up. We'll hold them as soon as the visit is over.'

He suddenly went rather cool. 'Minister, we do not hold Head of Government visits for party political reasons, but for reasons of State.'

He had a point there. I'd slipped up a bit, but I managed to justify it okay. 'But my plan really shows that Scotland is an equal partner in the United Kingdom. She *is* Queen of Scotland too. And Scotland is full of marginal constit . . .' I stopped myself just in time, I think, '. . . depressed areas.'

But Sir Humphrey was clearly hostile to the whole brilliant notion. 'I hardly think, Minister,' he sneered, clambering onto his highest horse and looking down his patrician nose at me, 'I hardly think we can exploit our Sovereign by involving her in, if you will forgive the phrase, a squalid vote-grubbing exercise.'

I don't think there's anything squalid about grubbing for votes. I'm a democrat and proud of it and that's what democracy is all about! But I could see that I had to think up a better reason (for Civil Service consumption, at least) or else this excellent plan would be blocked somehow. So I asked Humphrey why the President of Buranda was coming to Britain.

'For an exchange of views on matters of mutual interest,' was the reply. Why does this man insist on speaking in the language of official communiqués? Or can't he help it?

'Now tell me why he's coming,' I asked with exaggerated patience. I was prepared to keep asking until I got the real answer.

'He's here to place a huge order with the British Government for offshore drilling equipment.'

Perfect! I went in for the kill. 'And where can he see all our offshore equipment? Aberdeen, Clydeside.'

Sir Humphrey tried to argue. 'Yes, but . . .'

'How many oil rigs have you got in Haslemere, Humphrey?' He wasn't pleased by this question.

'But the administrative problems . . .' he began.

I interrupted grandly: 'Administrative problems are what this whole Department was created to solve. I'm sure you can do it, Humphrey.'

'But Scotland's so remote.' He was whining and complaining now. I knew I'd got him on the run. 'Not all that remote,' I said, and pointed to the map of the UK hanging on the wall. 'It's that pink bit, about two feet above Potters Bar.'

Humphrey was not amused – 'Very droll, Minister,' he said. But *even that* did not crush me.

'It is going to be Scotland,' I said with finality. 'That is my *policy* decision. That's what I'm here for, right Bernard?'

Bernard didn't want to take sides against Humphrey, or against me. He was stuck. 'Um . . .' he said.

I dismissed Humphrey, and told him to get on with making the arrangements. He stalked out of my office. Bernard's eyes remained glued to the floor.

Bernard is *my* Private Secretary and, as such, is apparently supposed to be on my side. On the other hand, his future lies with the Department which means that he has to be on Humphrey's side. I don't see how he can possibly be on both sides. Yet, apparently, only if he succeeds in this task that is, by definition, impossible, will he continue his rapid rise to the top. It's all very puzzling. I must try and find out if I can trust him.

November 13th

Had a little chat with Bernard on our way back from Cardiff, where I addressed a conference of Municipal Treasurers and Chief Executives.

Bernard warned me that Humphrey's next move, over this Scottish business, would be to set up an interdepartmental committee to investigate and report.

I regard the interdepartmental committee as the last refuge of a desperate bureaucrat. When you can't find any argument against something you don't want, you set up an interdepartmental committee to strangle it. Slowly. I said so to Bernard. He agreed.

'It's for the same reason that politicians set up Royal Commissions,' said Bernard. I began to see why he's a high-flyer.

I decided to ask Bernard what Humphrey *really* had against the idea.

'The point is,' Bernard explained, 'once they're all in Scotland the whole visit will fall within the purview of the Secretary of State for Scotland.'

I remarked that Humphrey should be pleased by this. Less work.

Bernard put me right on that immediately. Apparently the problem is that Sir Humphrey likes to go to the Palace, all dressed up in his white tie and tails and medals. But in Scotland the whole thing will be on a much smaller scale. Not so many receptions and dinners. Not so many for Sir Humphrey, anyway, only for the Perm. Sec. at the Scottish Office. Sir Humphrey might not even be invited to the return dinner, as the Burandan Consulate in Edinburgh is probably exceedingly small.

I had never given the ceremonial aspect of all this any thought at all. But according to Bernard all the glitter is frightfully important to Permanent Secretaries. I asked Bernard if Humphrey had lots of medals to wear.

'Quite a few,' Bernard told me. 'Of course he got his K a long time ago. He's a KCB. But there are rumours that he might get his G in the next Honours list.'[1]

'How did you hear that?' I asked. I thought Honours were always a big secret.

'I heard it on the grapevine,' said Bernard.

I suppose, if Humphrey doesn't get his G, we'll hear about it on the sour-grapevine.

[*Shortly after this conversation a note was sent by Sir Humphrey to Bernard Woolley. As usual Sir Humphrey wrote in the margin – Ed.*]

[1] K means Knighthood. KCB is Knight Commander of the Bath. G means Grand Cross. GCB is Knight Grand Cross of the Bath.

Bernard:

Have spoken to the Perm. Sec. at the F.C.O. about official visit to Scotland.

Unfortunately, our Minister had already spoken to the Foreign Secretary. I gather they are chums.

It appears that the Cabinet is utterly united on this matter. They have blatantly issued writs for three by-elections on the day of the visit.

It seems that the Burandan Consulate is rather a hutch. V. little space at the return dinner, and I shall not be going. Rather relieved, really.

However, Perm. Sec. at F.C.O. hinted that there are rumblings in the interior. Our man in Mungoville is expecting trouble. Possibly a coup d'état.

It may be that a friendly African country with Commonwealth connections is about to become a hostile L.D.C. with a Cuban connection.

In which case, all will be well.

H.A. 13/xi

DEPARTMENT OF ADMINISTRATIVE AFFAIRS

SCHEDULE FOR THE OFFICIAL VISIT OF THE PRESIDENT OF BURANDA

First Draft

14.00 The President disembarks, and is met by Her Majesty the Queen.

14.07 National Anthems:
God Save The Queen - 0.45 secs
Burandan Hymn - 3 minutes 25 secs approx.

14.11 Her Majesty the Queen and the President inspect Guard of Honour.

14.15 Speech of welcome by Her Majesty.

14.18 Brief reply by the President.

14.30 Proceed to cars, thence to Holyrood Palace.

15.00 Arrive Holyrood Palace.

[*Presumably by 'all will be well' Sir Humphrey was referring to the cancellation of the official visit, rather than another Central African country going communist – Ed.*]

November 18th

Long lapse since I made any entries in the diary. Partly due to the weekend, which was taken up with boring constituency business. And partly due to pressure of work – boring Ministerial business.

I feel that work is being kept from me. Not that I'm short of work. My boxes are full of irrelevant and unimportant rubbish.

Yesterday I really had nothing to do at all in the afternoon. No engagements of any sort. Bernard was forced to advise me to go to the House of Commons and listen to the debate there. I've never heard such a ridiculous suggestion.

Late this afternoon I was in the office, going over the plans for the Burandan visit, and I switched on the TV news. To my horror they reported a *coup d'état* in Buranda. Marxist, they think. They reported widespread international interest and concern because of Buranda's oil reserves. It seems that the Commander-in-Chief of the Armed Forces, who rejoices in the name of Colonel Selim Mohammed, has been declared President. Or has declared himself President, more likely. And no one knows what has happened to the former President.

I was appalled. Bernard was with me, and I told him to get me the Foreign Secretary at once.

'Shall we scramble?' he said.

'Where to?' I said, then felt rather foolish as I realised what he was talking about. Then I realised it was another of Bernard's daft suggestions: what's the point of scrambling a phone conversation about something that's just been on the television news?

I got through to Martin at the Foreign Office.

Incredibly, he knew nothing about the coup in Buranda.

'How do you know?' he asked when I told him.

'It's on TV. Didn't you know? You're the Foreign Secretary, for God's sake.'

'Yes,' said Martin, 'but my TV set's broken.'

I could hardly believe my ears. 'Your TV set? Don't you get the Foreign Office telegrams?'

Martin said: 'Yes, but they don't come in till much later. A couple of days, maybe. I always get the Foreign News from the telly.'

I thought he was joking. It seems he was not. I said that we must make sure that the official visit was still on, come what may. There are three by-elections hanging on it. He agreed.

I rang off, but not before telling Martin to let me know if he heard any more details.

'No, you let *me* know,' Martin said. 'You're the one with the TV set.'

November 19th

Meeting with Sir Humphrey first thing this morning. He was very jovial, beaming almost from ear to ear.

'You've heard the sad news, Minister?' he began, smiling broadly.

I nodded.

'It's just a slight inconvenience,' he went on, and made a rotary gesture with both hands. 'The wheels are in motion, it's really quite simple to cancel the arrangements for the visit.'

'You'll do no such thing,' I told him.

'But Minister, we have no choice.'

'We have,' I countered. 'I've spoken to the Foreign Secretary already.' His face seemed to twitch a bit. 'We are reissuing the invitation to the new President.'

'New President?' Humphrey was aghast. 'But we haven't even recognised his government.'

I made the same rotary gesture with my hands. 'The wheels are in motion,' I smiled. I was enjoying myself at last.

Humphrey said: 'We don't know who he is.'

'Somebody Mohammed,' I explained.

'But . . . we don't know anything about him. What's he like?'

I pointed out, rather wittily I thought, that we were not considering him for membership of the Athenaeum Club. I said that I didn't give a stuff what he was like.

Sir Humphrey tried to get tough. 'Minister,' he began, 'there is total confusion in Buranda. We don't know who is behind him. We don't know if he's Soviet-backed, or just an ordinary Burandan who's gone berserk. We cannot take diplomatic risks.'

'The government has no choice,' I said.

Sir Humphrey tried a new tack. 'We have not done the paperwork.' I ignored this rubbish. Paperwork is the religion of the Civil Service. I can just imagine Sir Humphrey Appleby on his deathbed, surrounded by wills and insurance claim forms, looking up and saying, 'I cannot go yet, God, I haven't done the paperwork.'

Sir Humphrey pressed on. 'The Palace insists that Her Majesty be properly briefed. This is not possible without the paperwork.'

I stood up. 'Her Majesty will cope. She always does.' Now I had put him in the position of having to criticise Her Majesty.

He handled it well. He stood up too. 'Out of the question,' he replied. 'Who *is* he? He might not be properly brought up. He might be rude to her. He might . . . take liberties!' The mind boggles. 'And he is bound to be photographed with Her Majesty – what if he then turns out to be another Idi Amin? The repercussions are too hideous to contemplate.'

I must say the last point does slightly worry me. But not as much as throwing away three marginals. I spelt out the contrary arguments to Humphrey. 'There are reasons of State,' I said, 'which make this visit essential. Buranda is potentially enormously rich. It needs oil rigs. We have idle shipyards on the Clyde. Moreover, Buranda is strategically vital to the government's African policy.'

'The government hasn't got an African policy,' observed Sir Humphrey.

'It has now,' I snapped. 'And if the new President is Marxist-backed, who better to win him over to our side than Her Majesty? Furthermore, the people of Scotland have been promised an important State occasion and we cannot go back on our word.'

'Not to mention,' added Sir Humphrey drily, 'three by-elections in marginal constituencies.'

'That has nothing to do with it,' I said, and glowered at him. He said, 'Of course not, Minister,' but I'm not quite sure that he believed me.

Then the phone rang. Bernard took the call. It was from Martin at the FCO.

Bernard listened, then told us that the new President of Buranda had announced his intention to visit Britain next week, in line with his predecessor's arrangements.

I was impressed. The Foreign Office was getting the news at last. I asked Bernard if the cables had come through from Mungoville. 'Not exactly,' he said. 'The Foreign Secretary's driver heard a news flash on his car radio.'

The upshot is that it would now be up to the PM to cancel the visit on my recommendation or Martin's. And I have decided it is on. Another policy decision. Quite a lot of them after all. Good.

November 26th

Today was the first day of the long-awaited official visit. President Mohammed's arrival was shown on TV. Bernard and I were watching in the office – I must admit I was slightly on tenterhooks in case he did turn out to be a bit uncouth.

A jumbo jet touched down, with BURANDAN AIRWAYS written on the side. I was hugely impressed. British Airways are having to pawn their Concordes, and here is this tiny African state with its own airline, jumbo jets and all.

I asked Bernard how many planes Burandan Airways had. 'None,' he said.

I told him not to be silly and use his eyes. 'No Minister, it belongs to Freddie Laker,' he said. 'They chartered it last week and repainted it specially.' Apparently most of the Have-Nots (I mean, LDCs) do this – at the opening of the UN General Assembly the runways of Kennedy Airport are jam-packed with phoney flag-carriers. 'In fact,' added Bernard with a sly grin, 'there was one 747 that belonged to nine different African airlines in one month. They called it the mumbo-jumbo.'

While we watched nothing much happened on the TV except the mumbo-jumbo taxiing around Prestwick and the Queen looking a bit chilly. Bernard gave me the day's schedule and explained that I was booked on the night sleeper from King's Cross to Edinburgh because I had to vote in a three-line whip at the House tonight and would have to miss the last plane. Then the commentator, in that special hushed BBC voice used for any occasion with which Royalty is connected, announced reverentially that we were about to catch our first glimpse of President Selim.

And out of the plane stepped Charlie. My old friend Charlie Umtali. We were at LSE together. Not Selim Mohammed at all, but Charlie.

Bernard asked me if I were sure. Silly question. How could you forget a name like Charlie Umtali?

I sent Bernard for Sir Humphrey, who was delighted to hear that we now know something about our official visitor.

Bernard's official brief said nothing. Amazing! Amazing how little the FCO has been able to find out. Perhaps they were hoping it would all be on the car radio. All the brief says is that Colonel Selim Mohammed was converted to Islam some years ago, they didn't know his original name, and therefore knew little of his background.

I was able to tell Humphrey and Bernard *all* about his background. Charlie was a red-hot political economist, I informed them. Got the top first. Wiped the floor with everyone.

Bernard seemed relieved. 'Well that's all right then.'

'Why?' I enquired.

'I think Bernard means,' said Sir Humphrey helpfully, 'that he'll know how to behave if he was at an English University. Even if it was the LSE.' I never know whether or not Humphrey is insulting me intentionally.

Humphrey was concerned about Charlie's political colour. 'When you said he was red-hot, were you speaking politically?'

In a way I was. 'The thing about Charlie is that you never quite know where you are with him. He's the sort of chap who follows you into a revolving door and comes out in front.'

'No deeply held convictions?' asked Sir Humphrey.

'No. The only thing Charlie was deeply committed to was Charlie.'

'Ah, I see. A politician, Minister.'

This was definitely one of Humphrey's little jokes. He'd never be so rude otherwise. Though sometimes I suspect that Humphrey says things he really means and excuses himself by saying 'only joking'. Nonetheless, I was able to put him down by patronising him with his own inimitable phrase. 'Very droll, Humphrey,' I said cuttingly. And I pointed out that as Charlie was only here for a couple of days he couldn't do much harm anyway.

Sir Humphrey still seemed concerned. 'Just remember, Minister,' he said, 'you wanted him here, not me.'

'If you'll excuse me, Humphrey, I must get on with my letters,' I said, trying to hide my irritation.

'Just before you do,' said Sir Humphrey, 'I'd be most grateful if you would glance at this brief on African politics.' He handed me a very bulky file. More paper. I declined to read it.

'No thanks,' I said. 'I think I'm all right on all that.'

'Oh good,' he said cheerfully, 'because one wouldn't want to upset the delicate power balance between FROLINAT and FRETELIN, would one?'

I think he could see that he'd got me there. So he pressed home his advantage. 'I mean, if the new President is more sympathetic to ZIPRA than ZANLA, not to mention ZAPU and ZANU, then CARECOM and COREPER might want to bring in GRAPO, and of course that would mean going back over all that old business with ECOSOC and UNIDO and then the whole IBRD–OECD row could blow up again . . . and what would HMG do if that happened?'[1]

[1] FROLINAT was the National Liberation Front of Chad, a French acronym. FRETELIN was the Trust For the Liberation of Timor, a small Portuguese colony seized by Indonesia: a Portuguese acronym. ZIPRA was the Zimbabwe People's Revolutionary Army, ZANLA the Zimbabwe African Liberation Army, (cont.)

The only initials I understood in that whole thing were HMG [*Her Majesty's Government – Ed.*]. As he had predicted, I said – as casually as I could – that I might as well glance through it.

'I'll see you on the train,' he said, and departed smoothly. I'm afraid he won a small moral victory there.

Bernard then tried to hurry me along to the House. But the huge pile of correspondence in my in-tray was now multiplying horrifyingly and apparently reproducing itself. 'What about all this,' I said helplessly. 'What can I do?'

'Well, Minister . . .' began Bernard, and his eyes flickered almost imperceptibly across to the out-tray a couple of times. I realised that I had very little choice. I picked up the whole pile of letters and moved them solemnly from the in-tray to the out-tray.

It was a funny feeling. I felt both guilty and relieved.

Bernard seemed to think I'd done the right thing. The inevitable thing, perhaps. 'That's right, Minister,' he said in a kindly tone, 'better out than in.'

November 27th

Last night was a horrendous experience, one that I do not intend to repeat in a hurry.

And today a massive crisis has yet to be solved. And it's all my fault. And I don't know if I can carry it off. Oh God!

I am sitting up in bed in a first-class sleeper, writing this diary, and dreading what the day has in store for me.

To begin at the beginning. Roy drove me from the House to King's Cross. I was there in plenty of time. I found my sleeper, ordered my morning tea and biscuits, the train was just pulling out of the station and my trousers were half off when there was a panic-stricken knocking on the door.

'Who is it?' I called.

(cont.) ZAPU the Zimbabwe African People's Union, ZANU the Zimbabwe African National Union. CARECOM is the acronym for the Caribbean Common Market and COREPER the Committee of Permanent Representatives to the European Community – a French acronym, pronounced co-ray-pair. ECOSOC was the Economic and Social Council of the UN, UNIDO the United Nations Industrial Development Organisation, IBRD the International Bank for Reconstruction and Development and OECD was the Organisation for Economic Co-operation and Development. GRAPO could not conceivably have been relevant to the conversation, as it is the Spanish acronym for the First of October Anti-Fascist Revolutionary Group.

It is not impossible that Sir Humphrey may have been trying to confuse his Minister.

'Bernard,' said Bernard's voice. It was Bernard. I let him in. He was breathless and sweating. I'd never seen him in such a state. Come to think of it, I've never seen any civil servant in such a state. They all seem so frightfully calm and controlled most of the time, in a funny way it's rather reassuring to see that they sometimes panic just like the rest of the human race, and that when they do they just run around like headless chickens.

Bernard was clutching a pile of large brown manila envelopes.

'Come in, Bernard,' I said soothingly. 'Whatever's the matter?'

'Read this, Minister,' he said dramatically, and thrust one of the brown envelopes at my chest.

I was thoroughly irritated. Bernard is endlessly pushing paper at me. I already had four red boxes on my bunk.

I thrust the envelope back at him. 'No I won't,' I said.

'You must,' he said, and back it came as though we were playing pass the parcel. 'This is top priority.'

'You always say that about everything,' I pointed out, and carried on removing my trousers.

Bernard informed me that he was offering me an advance copy of President Selim's speech for tomorrow (today now – oh my God!) which had been sent around by the Burandan Embassy.

I wasn't interested. These speeches are always the same: happy to be here, thanks for the gracious welcome, ties between our two countries, bonds of shared experience, happy and fruitful co-operation in the future, and all the usual drivel.

Bernard agreed that all of that rubbish was in the speech, but insisted that I read the important bits at once – bits he'd underlined in red ink. He then said he was distributing copies around the train. Round the train? I thought he'd gone completely crackers – but he explained that Sir Humphrey and the Foreign Secretary and the Perm. Sec. to the Foreign Sec. and our press officer and assorted other dignitaries were on the train. I hadn't realised.

I opened the envelope and saw the most appalling sight. A speech that we *cannot* allow to be delivered.

Burandans feel a special affinity with the Celtic peoples in their struggle for freedom. We, too, had to fight to break free from the chains of British colonialism. We bid you to recall your former greatness, to remember William Wallace, Robert the Bruce, Bannockburn and Culloden. The people of Buranda urge the Scots and the Irish to rise up against English oppression, cast off the Imperialist yoke and join the fellowship of free nations.

Minister: Your views urgently B.W.

Then Sir Humphrey came in, wearing, incidentally, a rather startling gold silk dressing gown with a red Chinese dragon all over it. I would never have thought of Humphrey in such a garment. Perhaps I wasn't all that impressive, in my shirt-tails and socks.

'Well Minister,' Sir Humphrey began, 'we appear to have been caught with our trousers down.' He went on to say that he didn't like to say that he'd told me so, but he'd told me so.

'We're going to have egg all over our faces,' I said.

'Not egg, Minister,' he replied suavely, 'just imperialist yoke.'

I asked him if he was trying to be funny. Because I certainly can't see anything funny about this situation. I think he said, 'No, just my little yoke,' but because of the noise of the train I'm not absolutely sure.

I reiterated that something had to be done. Three Scottish by-elections hang in the balance, not counting the effects on Ulster! 'This is a catastrophe,' I whispered.

Sir Humphrey did not exactly seem to be at pains to minimise the situation. 'It is indeed,' he agreed solemnly, piling on the agony. 'A catastrophe. A tragedy. A cataclysmic, apocalyptic, monumental calamity.' He paused for breath, and then added bluntly: 'And you did it.'

This was not exactly helping. 'Humphrey,' I reproached him. 'You're paid to advise me. Advise me!'

'All in all,' replied Sir Humphrey, 'this is not unlike trying to advise the Captain of the *Titanic* after he has struck the iceberg.'

'Come on,' I said, 'there must be *something* we can do.'

'We could sing *Abide with Me*.'

There was more knocking on the door and Bernard popped in. 'Minister, the Foreign Secretary would like a word.'

Martin came in.

'Ah, Foreign Secretary.' Sir Humphrey was being obsequious now.

'Yes,' said Martin. He knew who he was. 'You've read the speech?'

Before I could reply, Sir Humphrey interrupted: 'Yes, my Minister is concerned that the government will have egg all over its face. Scotch egg, presumably.'

I'm getting a bit tired of Humphrey's stupid puns. I asked Martin why Selim Mohammed would want to make such a speech here. Martin reckons it's for home consumption, to show the other African readers that he is a pukka anti-colonialist.

Bernard popped his head round the door, and suggested that we draft a statement in response to the speech. I thought that was a good idea. Whereupon he announced that he had brought along Bill Pritchard from the press office.

We had me and Humphrey and Martin and Bernard already in my sleeper. Bill Pritchard turned out to have the build of a rugger front-row forward. 'Room for a little 'un?' he enquired jovially, and knocked Humphrey forward onto the bunk, face first.

I asked Humphrey if a statement was a good idea.

'Well Minister,' he replied carefully as he stood up, still the mandarin in spite of his silly Chinese dressing gown. 'In practical terms we have, in fact, the usual six options. One, do nothing. Two, issue a statement deploring the speech. Three, lodge an official protest. Four, cut off aid. Five, break off diplomatic relations. Six, declare war.'

This sounded like rather a lot of options. I was pleased. I asked him which we should do.

'One: if we do nothing we implicitly agree with the speech. Two: if we issue a statement we just look foolish. Three: if we lodge a protest it will be ignored. Four: we can't cut off aid because we don't give them any. Five: if we break off diplomatic relations we cannot negotiate the oil rig contracts. Six: if we declare war it just *might* look as if we were over-reacting.' He paused. 'Of course, in the old days we'd have sent in a gunboat.'

I was desperate by this time. I said, 'I suppose that is absolutely out of the question?'

They all gazed at me in horror. Clearly it is out of the question.

Bernard had absented himself during Humphrey's résumé of the possibilities. Now he squeezed back into the compartment.

'The Permanent Under-Secretary to the Foreign and Commonwealth Office is coming down the corridor,' he announced.

'Oh terrific,' muttered Bill Pritchard. 'It'll be like the Black Hole of

Calcutta in here.'

Then I saw what he meant. Sir Frederick Stewart, Perm. Sec. of the FCO, known as 'Jumbo' to his friends, burst open the door. It smashed Bernard up against the wall. Martin went flying up against the washbasin, and Humphrey fell flat on his face on the bunk. The mighty mountain of lard spoke:

'May I come in, Minister?' He had a surprisingly small high voice.

'You can try,' I said.

'This is all we needed,' groaned Bill Pritchard as the quivering mass of flesh forced its way into the tiny room, pressing Bill up against the mirror and me against the window. We were all standing extremely close together.

'Welcome to the Standing Committee,' said Humphrey as he propped himself precariously upright.

'What do we do about this hideous thing? This hideous *speech*, I mean,' I added nervously, in case Jumbo took offence. His bald head shone, reflecting the overhead lamp.

'Well now,' began Jumbo, 'I think we know what's behind this, don't we Humpy?'

Humpy? Is this his nickname? I looked at him with new eyes. He clearly thought I was awaiting a response.

'I think that Sir Frederick is suggesting that the offending paragraph of the speech may be, shall we say, a bargaining counter.'

'A move in the game,' said Jumbo.

'The first shot in a battle,' said Humphrey.

'An opening gambit,' said Bernard.

These civil servants are truly masters of the cliché. They can go on all night. They do, unless stopped. I stopped them.

'You mean, he wants something,' I said incisively. It's lucky someone was on the ball.

'If he doesn't,' enquired Jumbo Stewart, 'why give us a copy in advance?' This seems unarguable. 'But unfortunately the usual channels are blocked because the Embassy staff are all new and we've only just seen the speech. And no one knows anything about this new President.'

I could see Humphrey giving me meaningful looks.

'I do,' I volunteered, slightly reluctantly.

Martin looked amazed. So did Jumbo.

'They were at University together.' Humphrey turned to me. 'The old-boy network?' It seemed to be a question.

I wasn't awfully keen on this turn of events. After all, it's twenty-five years since I saw Charlie, he might not remember me, I don't know what I can achieve. 'I think you ought to see him, Sir Frederick,' I replied.

'Minister, I think you carry more weight,' said Jumbo. He seemed unaware of the irony.

There was a pause, during which Bill Pritchard tried unsuccessfully to disguise a snigger by turning it into a cough.

'So we're all agreed,' enquired Sir Humphrey, 'that the mountain should go to Mohammed?'

'No, *Jim's* going,' said Martin, and got a very nasty look from his overweight Perm. Sec. and more sounds of a press officer asphyxiating himself.

I realised that I had no choice. 'All right,' I agreed, and turned to Sir Humphrey, 'but you're coming with me.'

'Of course, said Sir Humphrey, 'I'd hardly let you do it on your own.'

Is this *another* insult, or is it just my paranoia?

Later today:

Charlie Umtali – perhaps I'd better call him President Selim from now on – welcomed us to his suite at the Caledonian Hotel at 10 a.m.

'Ah Jim.' He rose to greet us courteously. I had forgotten what beautiful English he spoke. 'Come in, how nice to see you.'

I was actually rather, well, gratified by this warm reception.

'Charlie,' I said. We shook hands. 'Long time no see.'

'You don't have to speak pidgin English to me,' he said, turned to his aide, and asked for coffee for us all.

I introduced Humphrey, and we all sat down.

'I've always thought that Permanent Under-Secretary is such a demeaning title,' he said. Humphrey's eyebrows shot up.

'I beg your pardon?'

'It sounds like an assistant typist or something,' said Charlie pleasantly, and Humphrey's eyebrows disappeared into his hairline. 'Whereas,' he continued in the same tone, 'you're really in charge of everything, aren't you?' Charlie hasn't changed a bit.

Humphrey regained his composure and preened. 'Not quite everything.'

I then congratulated Charlie on becoming Head of State. 'Thank you,' he said, 'though it wasn't difficult. I didn't have to do any of the boring things like fighting elections.' He paused, and then added casually, 'Or by-elections,' and smiled amiably at us.

Was this a hint? I decided to say nothing. So after a moment he went on. 'Jim, of course I'm delighted to see you, but is this purely a social visit or is there anything you particularly wanted to talk about? Because I do have to put the finishing touches to my speech.'

Another hint?

I told him we'd seen the advance copy. He asked if we liked it. I asked him if, as we were old friends, I could speak frankly. He nodded.

I tried to make him realise that the bit about colonialist oppression was slightly – well, really, *profoundly* embarrassing. I asked him if he couldn't just snip out the whole chunk about the Scots and the Irish.

Charlie responded by saying, 'This is something that I feel very deeply to be true. Surely the British don't believe in suppressing the truth?'

A neat move.

Sir Humphrey then tried to help. 'I wonder if there is anything that might persuade the President to consider recasting the sentence in question so as to transfer the emphasis from the specific instance to the abstract concept, without impairing the conceptual integrity of the theme?'

Some help.

I sipped my coffee with a thoughtful expression on my face.

Even Charlie hadn't got it, I don't think, because he said, after quite a pause: 'While you're here, Jim, may I sound you out on a proposal I was going to make to the Prime Minister at our talks?'

I nodded.

He then told us that his little change of government in Buranda had alarmed some of the investors in their oil industry. Quite unnecessarily, in his view. So he wants some investment from Britain to tide him over.

At last we were talking turkey.

I asked how much. He said fifty million pounds.

Sir Humphrey looked concerned. He wrote me a little note. 'Ask him on what terms.' So I asked.

'Repayment of the capital not to start before ten years. And interest free.'

It sounded okay to me, but Humphrey choked into his coffee. So I pointed out that fifty million was a lot of money.

'Oh well, in that case . . .' began Charlie, and I could see that he was about to end the meeting.

'But let's talk about it,' I calmed him down. I got another note from Humphrey, which pointed out that, if interest ran at ten per cent on average, and if the loan was interest free for ten years, he was in effect asking for a free gift of fifty million pounds.

Cautiously, I put this point to Charlie. He very reasonably (I thought) explained that it was all to our advantage, because they would use the loan to buy oil rigs built on the Clyde.

I could see the truth of this, but I got another frantic and, by now, almost illegible note from Humphrey, saying that Charlie wants us to give him fifty million pounds so that he can buy our oil rigs with our money. (His underlinings, I may say.)

We couldn't go on passing notes to each other like naughty schoolboys, so we progressed to muttering. 'It sounds pretty reasonable to me,' I whispered.

'You can't be serious,' Humphrey hissed.

'Lots of jobs,' I countered, and I asked Charlie, if we did such a deal, would he make appropriate cuts in his speech? This was now cards on the table.

Charlie feigned surprise at my making this connection, but agreed that he would make cuts. However, he'd have to know right away.

'Blackmail,' Sir Humphrey had progressed to a stage whisper that could be heard right across Princes Street.

'Are you referring to me or to my proposal?' asked Charlie.

'Your proposal, naturally,' I said hastily and then realised this was a trick question. 'No, not even your proposal.'

I turned to Humphrey, and said that I thought we could agree to this. After all, there are precedents for this type of deal.[1]

Sir Humphrey demanded a private word with me, so we went and stood in the corridor.

I couldn't see why Humphrey was so steamed up. Charlie had offered us a way out.

Humphrey said we'd never get the money back, and therefore he could not recommend it to the Treasury and the Treasury would

[1] Hacker might perhaps have been thinking of the Polish shipbuilding deal during the Callaghan government, by which the UK lent money interest free to the Poles, so that they could buy oil tankers from us with our money, tankers which were then going to compete against our own shipping industry. These tankers were to be built on Tyneside, a Labour-held marginal with high unemployment. It could have been said that the Labour government was using public money to buy Labour votes, but no one did – perhaps because, like germ warfare, no one wants to risk using an uncontrollable weapon that may in due course be used against oneself.

never recommend it to Cabinet. 'You are proposing,' he declared pompously, 'to buy your way out of a political entanglement with fifty million pounds of public money.'

I explained that this is diplomacy. He said it was corruption. I said 'GCB,' only just audibly.

There was a long pause.

'What did you say, Minister?'

'Nothing,' I said.

Humphrey suddenly looked extremely thoughtful. 'On the other hand . . .' he said, '. . . we don't want the Soviets to invest in Buranda, do we?' I shook my head. 'Yes, I see what you mean,' he murmured.

'And they will if we don't,' I said, helping him along a bit.

Humphrey started to marshal all the arguments on my side. 'I suppose we could argue that we, as a part of the North/South dialogue, have a responsibility to the . . .'

'TPLACs?' I said.

Humphrey ignored the crack. 'Quite,' he said. 'And if we were to insist on one per cent of the equity in the oil revenues ten years from now . . . yes, on balance, I think we can draft a persuasive case in terms of our third-world obligations, to bring in the FCO . . . and depressed area employment, that should carry with us both the Department of Employment and the Scottish Office . . . then the oil rig construction should mobilise the Department of Trade and Industry, and if we can reassure the Treasury that the balance of payments wouldn't suffer . . . Yes, I think we might be able to mobilise a consensus on this.'

I thought he'd come to that conclusion. We trooped back into Charlie's room.

'Mr President,' said Sir Humphrey, 'I think we can come to terms with each other after all.'

'You know my price,' said Charlie.

'And you know mine,' I said. I smiled at Sir Humphrey. 'Everyone has his price, haven't they?'

Sir Humphrey looked inscrutable again. Perhaps this is why they are called mandarins.

'Yes Minister,' he replied.

3
The Economy Drive

December 7th
On the train going up to town after a most unrestful weekend in the constituency, I opened up the *Daily Mail.* There was a huge article making a personal attack on me.

I looked around the train. Normally the first-class compartment is full of people reading *The Times*, the *Telegraph*, or the *Financial Times*. Today they all seemed to be reading the *Daily Mail.*

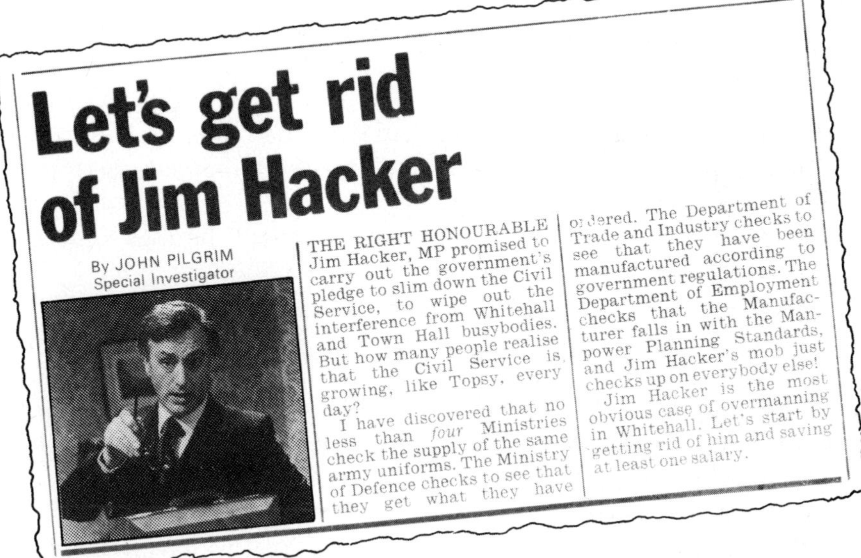

Let's get rid of Jim Hacker

By JOHN PILGRIM
Special Investigator

THE RIGHT HONOURABLE Jim Hacker, MP promised to carry out the government's pledge to slim down the Civil Service, to wipe out the interference from Whitehall and Town Hall busybodies. But how many people realise that the Civil Service is growing, like Topsy, every day?

I have discovered that no less than *four* Ministries check the supply of the same army uniforms. The Ministry of Defence checks to see that they get what they have ordered. The Department of Trade and Industry checks to see that they have been manufactured according to government regulations. The Department of Employment checks that the Manufacturer falls in with the Manpower Planning Standards, and Jim Hacker's mob just checks up on everybody else!

Jim Hacker is the most obvious case of overmanning in Whitehall. Let's start by getting rid of him and saving at least one salary.

When I got to the office Bernard offered me the paper and asked me if I'd read it. I told him I'd read it. Bernard told me that Frank had read it, and wanted to see me. Then Frank came in and asked me if I'd read it. I told him I'd read it.

Frank then read it to me. I don't know why he read it to me. I told him I'd read it. It seemed to make him feel better to read it aloud. It made me feel worse.

I wondered how many copies they sell every day. 'Two million, three million?' I asked Bernard.

'Oh *no*, Minister,' he answered as if my suggested figures were an utterly outrageous overestimate.

I pressed him for an answer. 'Well, how many?'

'Um . . . four million,' he said with some reluctance. 'So only . . . twelve million people have read it. Twelve or fifteen. And lots of their readers can't read, you know.'

Frank was meanwhile being thoroughly irritating. He kept saying, 'Have you read this?' and reading another appalling bit out of it. For instance: 'Do *you* realise that more people serve in the Inland Revenue than the Royal Navy?' This came as news to me, but Bernard nodded to confirm the truth of it when I looked at him.

'"Perhaps,"' said Frank, *still* reading aloud from that bloody paper, '"Perhaps the government thinks that a tax is the best form of defence."'

Bernard sniggered, till he saw that I was not amused. He tried to change his snigger into a cough.

Frank then informed me, as if I didn't already know, that this article is politically very damaging, and that I had to make slimming down the Civil Service a priority. There's no doubt that he's right, but it's just not that easy.

I pointed this out to Frank. 'You know what?' he said angrily. 'You're house-trained already.'

I didn't deign to reply. Besides, I couldn't think of an answer.

[*The Civil Service phrase for making a new Minister see things their way is 'house-training'. When a Minister is so house-trained that he automatically sees everything from the Civil Service point of view, this is known in Westminster as the Minister having 'gone native' – Ed.*]

Sir Humphrey came in, brandishing a copy of the *Daily Mail*. 'Have you read this?' he began.

This was too much. I exploded. 'Yes. Yes! Yes!!! I have read that sodding newspaper. *I* have read it, *you* have read it, *we have all bloody read it*. DO I MAKE MYSELF CLEAR?'

'Abundantly, Minister,' said Sir Humphrey coldly, after a brief pained silence.

I recovered my temper, and invited them all to sit down. 'Humphrey,' I said, 'we simply *have* to slim down the Civil Service. How many people are there in this Department?'

'This Department?' He seemed evasive. 'Oh well, we're very small.'

'How small?' I asked, and receiving no reply, I decided to hazard a guess. 'Two thousand? . . . three thousand?' I suggested, fearing the worst.

'About twenty-three thousand I think, Minister?'

I was staggered. Twenty-three thousand people? In the Department of Administrative Affairs? Twenty-three thousand administrators, all to administer other administrators?

'We'll have to do an O & M,' I said. [*Organisation and Method Study – Ed.*] 'See how many we can do without.'

'We did one of those last year,' said Sir Humphrey blandly. 'And we discovered we needed another five hundred people. However, Minister, we could always close your Bureaucratic Watchdog Department.'[1]

I'd been expecting this. I know Humphrey doesn't like it. How could he? But we are not cutting it. Firstly, it's a very popular measure with the voters. And secondly, it's the only thing I've achieved since I've been here.

'It is a chance for the ordinary citizen to help us find ways to stop wasting government money,' I reiterated.

'The public,' said Sir Humphrey, 'do not know anything about wasting public money. We are the experts.'

I grinned. 'Can I have that in writing?'

Humphrey got very tetchy. 'You know that's not what I meant,' he snapped. 'The Watchdog Office is merely a troublemaker's letter box.'

'It stays,' I replied.

We gazed at each other, icily. Finally Sir Humphrey said: 'Well, offhand, I don't know what other economies to suggest.'

This was ludicrous. 'Are you seriously trying to tell me,' I asked, 'that there's nothing we can cut down on?'

He shrugged. 'Well . . . I suppose we could lose one or two of the tea ladies.'

I exploded again. I told him not to be ridiculous. I told him I wanted facts, answers. I listed them:

[1] The Bureaucratic Watchdog was an innovation of Hacker's, to which members of the public were invited to report any instances of excessive government bureaucracy which they encountered personally. It was disbanded after four months.

1 How many people work here?
2 What do they all do?
3 How many buildings do we have?
4 Who and what is in these buildings?

I spelt it out. I demanded a complete study. First of all we'll put our own house in order. Then we'll deal with the rest of Whitehall. With a complete study, we'll be able to see where to cut costs, cut staff, and cut procedures.

Sir Humphrey listened with some impatience. 'The Civil Service, Minister,' he responded when I paused for breath, 'merely exists to implement legislation that is enacted by Parliament. So long as Parliament continues to legislate for more and more control over people's lives, the Civil Service must grow.'

'Ha!' Frank made a derisive noise.

Sir Humphrey turned towards him with a glassy stare. 'Am I to infer that Mr Weisel disagrees with me?'

'Ha!' repeated Frank.

Frank was getting on *my* nerves too. 'Frank, either laugh thoroughly, or not at all,' I instructed.

'Minister.' Humphrey stood up. 'I am fully seized of your requirements, so if you'll excuse me I think I'd better set the wheels in motion.'

After Sir H. left Frank told me that there was a cover-up going on. Apparently a North-West Regional controller has achieved cuts of £32 million in his region alone. And the Civil Service has suppressed news of it. I asked why. 'They don't want cuts,' said Frank impatiently. 'Asking Sir Humphrey to slim down the Civil Service is like asking an alcoholic to blow up a distillery.'

I asked Bernard if this story were true. Bernard said that he didn't know, but, if so, he would be aghast. I asked them both to check up on it. Bernard said he'd find out through the grapevine, and I arranged with Frank to do some more ferreting.

[*Sometime in the next few days Bernard Woolley had an interview with Sir Humphrey Appleby. Sir Humphrey wrote a memo following the meeting, which we found in the DAA Personnel Files at Walthamstow – Ed.*]

Woolley came at 5.15 p.m. to discuss the £32 million saved by the NW controller. I remarked that I was aghast.

Woolley said he also was aghast, and that it was incredible that we knew nothing of this.

He sometimes reveals himself as worryingly naïf. I, of course, know all about it. I am merely aghast that it has got out. It might result in our getting less money from the Treasury in next year's PESC review. [*PESC is the Public Expenditure Scrutiny Committee – Ed.*]

I felt I would learn more about Bernard Woolley if I made the conversation informal. [*To do so, Sir Humphrey would have moved from behind his desk to the conversation area, remarking that it was after 5.30 p.m. and offering Woolley a sherry – Ed.*] Then I asked him why he was looking worried. He revealed that he genuinely wanted the DAA to save money.

This was shocking. Clearly he has not yet grasped the fundamentals of our work.

There has to be some way to measure success in the Service. British Leyland can measure success by the size of its profits. [*British Leyland was the name of the car manufacturer into which billions of pounds of taxpayers' money was paid in the 1980s in an attempt to produce full employment in the West Midlands. To be more accurate, BL measured its failure by the size of its losses – Ed.*] However, the Civil Service does not make profits or losses. *Ergo*, we measure success by the size of our staff and our budget. By definition a big department is more successful than a small one. It seems extraordinary that Woolley could have passed through the Civil Service College without having understood that this simple proposition is the basis of our whole system.

Nobody had asked the NW controller to save £32 million. Suppose everybody did it? Suppose everybody started saving money irresponsibly all over the place?

Woolley then revealed another curious blind-spot when he advanced the argument that the Minister wanted cuts. I was obliged to explain the facts of life:

1 Ministers come, and Ministers go. The average Minister lasts less than eleven months in any Department.
[*In his ten years as Chairman of British Steel, Sir Monty Finniston dealt with no less than nineteen Ministers at the Department of Industry – Ed.*]
2 It is our duty to assist the Minister to fight for the Department's money despite his own panic reactions.
3 However, the Minister must be allowed to panic. Politicians like to panic. They need activity – it is their substitute for achievement.
4 The argument that we must do everything a Minister demands because he has been 'democratically chosen' does not stand up to close inspection. MPs are not chosen by 'the people' – they are chosen by their local constituency party, *i.e.* thirty-five men in grubby raincoats or thirty-five women in silly hats. The further 'selection' process is equally a nonsense: there are only 630 MPs and a party with just over 300 MPs forms a government – and of these 300, 100 are too old and too silly to be ministers, and 100 too young and too callow. Therefore there are

about 100 MPs to fill 100 government posts. Effectively no choice at all.

5 It follows that as Ministers have had no proper selection or training, it is our patriotic duty to arrange for them to make the right decision as often as possible.

I concluded by teaching Woolley how to explain the saving of £32 million to the Minister. I offered the following possibilities. Say that:

(a) they have changed their accounting system in the North-West.
or (b) redrawn the boundaries, so that this year's figures are not comparable.
or (c) the money was compensation for special extra expenditure of £16 million a year over the last two years, which has now stopped.
or (d) it is only a paper saving, so it will all have to be spent next year.
or (e) a major expenditure is late in completion, and therefore the region will be correspondingly over budget next year. [*Known technically as phasing – Ed.*]
or (f) there has been an unforeseen but important shift of personnel and industries to other regions whose expenditure rose accordingly.
or (g) some large projects were cancelled for reasons of economy early in the accounting period with the result that the expenditure was not incurred but the budget had already been allocated.

Woolley seemed to understand. I am concerned that he has not had adequate training so far. I intend to keep a close watch on him because, in spite of all this, I still think he shows promise.

He volunteered information that Frank Weisel was ferreting. Naturally, I arranged a government car to assist him. [*It was standard Civil Service practice to provide government cars for troublesome outsiders. The driver would, at the very least, be relied on to report where he had been, if only to account for the mileage.*

Drivers are one of the most useful sources of information in Whitehall. Their passengers are frequently indiscreet, forgetting that everything they say in the back seat can be overheard in the front. Furthermore, Ministers tend to forget confidential documents, and leave them behind in the car.

Information is Whitehall's most valuable currency. Drivers barter information – Ed.]

[*The following series of memos between Sir Humphrey Appleby and Sir Frederick Stewart were found in a Ministry file – Ed.*]

A note from Sir Frederick Stewart, Permanent Secretary to the FCO:

Foreign and Commonwealth Office
From the Permanent Under-Secretary of State

Dear Humphy,   10/xii

Am concerned that your minister is still trying to economise pointlessly.

Jumbo

A reply from Sir Humphrey to Sir Frederick Stewart:

DEPARTMENT OF ADMINISTRATIVE AFFAIRS

From the Permanent Under-Secretary of State

Dear Jumbo —

Am hoping it will be like all the other government economy drives — three days of press releases, three weeks of ministerial memos, then a crisis in the Middle East, and back to normal again.

H.

10. xii

A reply from Sir Frederick:

Foreign and Commonwealth Office
From the Permanent Under-Secretary of State

11/xii

Dear Humpy,

Hope you're right, but why take chances? I suggest another 'Operation Hairshirt'

"Economy begins at home. Set a personal example. Can't expect others to do what we don't do ourselves." etc.

Jumbo.

A reply from Sir Humphrey:

DEPARTMENT OF ADMINISTRATIVE AFFAIRS

From the Permanent Under-Secretary of State

Jumbo —

Good idea. Will try it. Thanks.

Self-denial is probably the answer, as always.

H.

P.S. See you at the Lord Mayor's dinner.

11 xii

[*Hacker's diary continues – Ed.*]
December 15th
Today we had the big meeting on expenditure cuts. Frank has been ferreting for a couple of weeks. The meeting didn't actually end the way I thought it would, but we do now have a real programme of action, though not the one I expected.

At the meeting were Sir Humphrey, Bernard, and Frank who had come up with what seemed to be some astounding revelations about wastage in our midst. I told Sir Humphrey that he would be pretty surprised by it all, and that the new facts seemed to be a frightening indictment of bureaucratic sloppiness and self-indulgence.

Sir Humphrey seemed very concerned and intrigued, and was eager to learn where there might be scope for dramatic economies.

Frank had prepared two files, one on Manpower and one on Buildings. I decided to look at Buildings first.

'Chadwick House,' I began. 'West Audley Street.'

'A huge building,' said Frank, 'with only a handful of people working there.'

Sir Humphrey said he happened to know about Chadwick House. 'It is certainly underused at the moment, but it is the designated office for the new Commission on the Environment. We're actually wondering if it'll be big enough when all the staff move in.'

This seemed fair enough. So I went on to Ladysmith Buildings, Walthamstow. It is totally empty.

'Of course,' said Sir Humphrey.

I asked him what he meant.

'Security, Minister, I can say no more.'

'Do you mean MI6?' I asked.

Sir Humphrey shook his head, and said nothing. So I asked him what he *did* mean.

'We do not admit that MI6 exists,' he replied.

I've never heard anything so daft. I pointed out that absolutely everyone knows that it exists.

'Nevertheless, we do not admit it. Not everyone around this table has been vetted.'

Vetted is such a silly expression. I remarked that it sounds like something you do to cats.

'Yes, but not ferrets, Minister,' said Sir Humphrey sharply, eyeing Frank. 'Ladysmith Buildings is top secret.'

'How,' I asked sarcastically, 'can a seven-storey building in Walthamstow be a secret?'

'Where there's a will there's a way,' replied Humphrey, with (I think) a twinkle in his eye. It was all quite amicable, but I could see that he had no intention of discussing anything that was remotely to do with security while Frank was present. I had no intention of asking Frank to leave, so, reluctantly, I was forced to move on to the next two white elephants.

'Wellington House, Hyde Park Road. Estimated value, seven and a half million pounds. Westminster Old Hall, Sackville Square, estimated value, eleven million pounds. Both buildings with a tiny staff, and entirely full of filing cabinets.'

'May I ask the source of these valuations?' Sir Humphrey enquired.

'Going rate for office property in the area,' said Frank.

'Ah. *Unfortunately*,' said Sir Humphrey in his most helpful tone, 'neither building would actually fetch the going rate.'

I asked why not.

'Wellington House has no fire escape or fire doors and the fabric of the building would not stand the alteration, so it can't be sold as offices.'

'Then how can *we* use it?' enquired Frank aggressively.

'Government buildings do not need fire safety clearance.'

'Why?' demanded Frank.

'Perhaps,' Humphrey offered, 'because Her Majesty's Civil Servants are not easily inflamed.' This time he chuckled. Another of his little jokes. He seemed to be increasingly pleased with himself. I don't care for this.

[*In fact, government buildings have to comply with most statutory fire requirements, but not with regard to means of escape! – Ed.*]

We were not getting very far with our economies, so I asked why Westminster Old Hall couldn't be sold as offices.

'It's a Class One listed building. Can't change current user designation. The Environment, you know.'

We were getting nowhere fast. Frank moved on, and suggested we sold 3 to 17 Beaconsfield Street.

'That,' said Sir Humphrey, 'has a three-level reinforced-concrete basement.'

'So?' I said.

'It is there in case,' said Sir Humphrey. I waited for him to complete his sentence, but after a while it became apparent that he thought he had already done so.

'In case?' I asked eventually.

'You know, Minister,' he said, his voice pregnant with hidden meaning. 'Emergency Government Headquarters, if and when.'

I was baffled. 'If and when what?'

Humphrey was now at his most enigmatic. 'If and when . . . you know what,' he replied so quietly that I could hardly hear him.

'What?' I wasn't sure I'd heard correctly.

'If and when you know what?'

'I *don't* know what,' I said confused. 'What?'

'What?' Now Sir Humphrey seemed confused.

'What do you mean, if and when you know what? If and when, I know what – *what*?'

At last Humphrey decided to make his meaning clear. 'When the chips are down, Minister, and the balloon goes up and the lights go out . . . there has to be somewhere to carry on government, even if everything else stops.'

I considered this carefully for a few moments. 'Why?' I asked.

Humphrey appeared to be absolutely staggered by this question. He explained to me, as if I were a backward five-year-old, 'Government doesn't stop merely because the country's been destroyed. Annihilation is bad enough, without anarchy to make it even worse.'

Obviously Humphrey was concerned about the danger of a lot of rebellious cinders.

However, this is clearly an MoD matter [*Ministry of Defence matter – Ed.*] and I can see it is beyond *my* power to do anything about 3 to 17 Beaconsfield Street.

There was one more virtually unused building on Frank's list. It was my last shot. 'What about the Central Registry?' I enquired, without any real hope.

'No planning permission,' said Sir Humphrey, with a bland smile of a man who knows he's won five rounds and is way ahead on points.

Frank suddenly intervened. 'How does he know all this?' he enquired belligerently, and turned accusingly to Sir Humphrey. 'You *knew* where I'd been.'

This hadn't occurred to me, but Frank was obviously right. I was about to lay into Humphrey on that score, when Humphrey said to me, most disarmingly: 'Of course we knew where he'd been. Why, was he supposed to be spying?'

I wasn't ready for that particular googly. I realised at once that I was on a very sticky wicket.

Humphrey pressed home his advantage. 'I mean, we *do* believe in open enquiries, don't we?'

There was no answer to this, so, in my most businesslike fashion, I closed the Buildings file. [*In any case, it would have been impossible to sell all these government buildings simultaneously. If you put government property in London on the market all at once, you would destroy the market – like diamonds – Ed.*]

I turned to Manpower. Here, I felt I was on rock-solid ground.

'Apparently,' I began, 'there are ninety civil servants in Sunderland exactly duplicating the work of ninety others here in Whitehall.'

Humphrey nodded. 'That stems from a cabinet decision. Job Creation in the North-East.'

At last we were in agreement about something. 'Let's get rid of them,' I proposed.

Frank chimed in eagerly, 'Yes, that would get rid of ninety civil servants at a stroke.' Somehow, the way Frank spits out the words 'civil servants' makes them sound more contemptible than petty thieves. If I were a civil servant I think Frank's style would offend me, though Sir Humphrey doesn't seem too bothered, I must say.

But he picked up Frank's phrase 'at a stroke'. [*Actually, Edward Heath's phrase, originally applied to price reductions which, needless to say, never occurred – Ed.*] 'Or indeed,' said Sir Humphrey, 'at a strike.'

'What?' I said.

'Personally, Minister, I should be wholeheartedly in favour of such a move. A considerable economy. But . . . I should remind you that it is a depressed area. Hence the original job creation scheme. It would show great political courage for the government to sack staff in a depressed marginal constituency.'

We sat for a while in silence. I must say, I think it was rather sporting of Humphrey to remind me that a marginal constituency was at stake. Normally civil servants take no interest in those vital political calculations.

Clearly, I couldn't possibly risk a strike up there. But I was feeling really hopeless about these economies by now. I decided to put the ball back into Humphrey's court.

'Look, Humphrey,' I said, 'this is all very well . . . but . . . well, I just don't believe that there are no savings to be made in the Civil Service. I see waste everywhere.'

'I agree with you, Minister,' came the reply, much to my surprise. 'There is indeed scope for economy . . .'

'Then . . .' I interrupted, '. . . *where*, for God's sake?'

And to my surprise, Sir Humphrey suddenly became very positive. 'I sometimes feel that the whole way we do things is on too lavish a scale. You know, cars, furnishings, private office staff, entertainment, duplicating machines. . . .'

This was marvellous. I couldn't agree more. I nodded enthusiastically.

'There is a difficulty, however,' he added. My heart sank again, but I waited to hear what it was. 'It does cause profound resentment if those at the top continue to enjoy the convenience and comforts they have withdrawn from those below them, not to mention the deeply damaging publicity. . . .'

He broke off, and waited to see how I reacted. I wasn't awfully keen, I must admit. It became clear that Humphrey's scheme was that he and I should set a personal example. Economy begins at home, and we can't expect others to do what we don't do ourselves, and so forth.

I challenged Humphrey. 'Would it really save that much?'

'Directly, no,' he said. 'But as an example to the whole public service . . . incalculable!'

Then Frank came up with the decisive argument in favour of Humphrey's plan. He pointed out that there would be lots of great publicity in it. He suggested the sort of newspaper headlines we'd be getting: THE MINISTER SHOWS THE WAY, or SLIMLINE GOVERNMENT, HACKER SETS EXAMPLE. We might even get a first-name headline: SAVE IT, SAYS JIM.

I gave Humphrey the okay to put the scheme into practice as soon as possible. I shall be interested to see how it works. At this moment, I have high hopes.

December 20th

Sunday morning. I'm writing this at home, in the constituency.

Haven't had time to make any entries in the diary for some days because this economy drive is creating a lot of extra work for me. However, I'm sure it's all going to be worth it.

It was a dreadful journey home on Friday night. I got home in the middle of the night. Annie had gone to bed. Apparently she'd made supper for us, and it had spoiled.

I'd tried to get a taxi to get me from Whitehall to Euston, but there was a thunderstorm and no taxis were available. So I'd gone by tube, carrying three red boxes which are immensely heavy when filled, and I'd missed the train at Euston. So I got home very tired and wet.

I apologised for waking Annie, and told her about my troublesome journey.

'What happened to the chauffeur-driven car?' she asked anxiously.

'I've got rid of it,' I explained proudly. 'I've also got rid of the chauffeur, all the grand office furniture, and the drinks cabinet, and half my private office staff.'

'You've been sacked!' she said. Annie often jumps to the most ridiculous alarmist conclusions. I explained that it was an economy drive and that I was setting an example of no frills, no luxuries and no privileges.

Annie couldn't seem to understand. 'You're bloody mad!' she exploded. 'For twenty years as a backbencher you have complained that you had no facilities and no help. Now you've been given them, and you're throwing them away.'

I tried to explain it, but she wouldn't let me get a word in edgeways. 'For twenty years you've wanted to be a success – why did you want it if it brings no greater comfort than failure?'

I explained that this move would give me much greater power in the end.

Annie was unimpressed. 'And how will you travel when you're Prime Minister? Hitch-hike?'

Why can't she understand?

December 21st

Great progress today with the economy drive.

The office work is getting a bit behind, with twelve fewer people in my Private Office. Bernard is working overtime, and so am I, but clearly we didn't need all those people out there, reading my letters and writing my letters, and making appointments and answering phones, and drafting replies to questions and – basically – protecting me from the outside world. I don't need all those people to shield me. I am the people's representative, I should be available to one and all, shouldn't I?

However, we have to avoid screw-ups like this morning, when I arrived an hour and a half late to open a conference. What made it even more unfortunate was that it was the Business Efficiency Conference!

And, because we've abolished the night shift for cleaners (a really useful economy, in my view), I had a cleaning lady in my office vacuuming. Bernard and I had to shout at the tops of our voices as we discussed the week's diary. But I'm sure these little wrinkles can be ironed out.

Tomorrow I have a vital meeting with Mr Brough, Director of Manpower Planning for the North-East Region, on the subject of staff reductions. I've never met him, but Bernard tells me he's eager to make cuts.

The biggest progress is in the media coverage I'm getting. A front-page story in the *Express*. Couldn't be better.

No luxury lunches in Hacker's new austerity regime

"ECONOMY begins at home", said Jim Hacker today, as he ate a sandwich off a paper plate to set an example to Britain's pampered army of bowler-hatted bureaucrats.

SIR BERNARD WOOLLEY RECALLS:[1]
I remember Jim Hacker's first economy drive only too well. I suspected, green though I still was, that Sir Humphrey Appleby had created a potentially disastrous situation.

It was impossible for me to run the Private Office single-handed, with just a couple of typists to help. Errors were bound to occur, and sooner or later there would be a calamity.

The calamity occurred sooner than even I expected. On 21 December, the day after Hacker had received some favourable publicity, Ron Watson arrived at the Department without an appointment. Watson was the General Secretary of the Civil Service Transport and Associated Government Workers.

He demanded to see the Minister at once, because of what he described as 'disturbing' rumours about cut-backs and redundancies affecting his members. The rumours were clearly generated by the numerous press stories of which Jim Hacker was so ludicrously proud.

I told Watson that nobody could see the Minister without an appointment,

[1] In conversation with the Editors.

and left the Private Office to go to the Whips' Office. I was even having to run errands myself, as we were so short-staffed. Had we been fully staffed, Watson would never even have got as far as Hacker's Private Office without an appointment. I left a typist to arrange an appointment for Watson to see Hacker.

Apparently, after I left the room, Brough of Manpower Planning telephoned to say he had missed his train from Newcastle, and could not keep his appointment. Watson overheard, realised that Hacker was free at that moment, and walked straight into his office.

And because there were no other Private Secretaries, due to the economy drive, no one stopped him. And no one warned the Minister that he was meeting Watson instead of Brough.

No greater mishap could have occurred.

December 22nd

Today, everything collapsed in ruins. Total disaster.

I was expecting Mr Brough of Manpower Planning (NE Region) at 3 p.m. A man walked into my office and naturally I assumed he was Brough.

'Mr Brough?' I said.

'No,' he said, 'my name's Ron Watson. Mr Brough has had to cancel the meeting.'

Naturally, I assumed that Watson had been sent by Brough, and had come instead. So I interrupted, thanked him for coming and asked him to sit down and said, 'Look, Mr Watson, before we start there's one point I have to emphasise. This simply must not get out. If the unions were to hear of this all hell would break loose.'

'I see,' he said.

'Of *course* there are going to be redundancies,' I continued. 'You can't slim down a giant bureaucracy without getting rid of people. Ultimately, lots of people.'

He asked me if I wouldn't be holding discussions with the unions first.

I continued to dig my own grave. 'We'll go through the usual charade of consultation first,' I said, blithely unaware of the impending catastrophe, 'but you know what trades unionists are like. Just bloody-minded, and as thick as two short planks.' How could I have spoken like this to a total stranger?

'All of them?' he asked politely.

I was surprised by this question. I thought he should know, after all, he had to negotiate with them. 'Pretty well,' I said. 'All they're interested in is poaching members from each other or getting themselves on the telly – and they can never keep their big mouths shut.'

I remember quite clearly every word that I spoke. Each one is branded on my heart. Furthermore, it's all written down in front of me – in an interview that Watson gave to the *Standard* as soon as he left my office.

Then the man asked me about drivers and transport service staff, specifically. 'They'll be the first to go,' I said. 'We're wasting a fortune on cars and drivers. And they're all on the fiddle anyway.'

It was at this moment that Watson revealed that he was not Mr Brough's deputy, but was in fact the General Secretary of the Civil Service Transport and Associated Government Workers. And he had come to my office to check that there was no truth in the rumours about redundancies for his members!

Oh my God! . . .

December 24th

Yesterday and today there has been an acute shortage of Christmas cheer.

All the Civil Service drivers are on strike. I arrived yesterday morning, having read all about the strike in the press. All the papers quoted Ron Watson quoting me: 'Of course there's going to be redundancies. Lots.'

I asked Bernard how he could have let this happen.

'CBE, Minister,' he replied, unhappily.

I wasn't sure what he meant. Could I have been awarded the CBE? – or could *he*?

He explained. 'Can't Be Everywhere'. Another idiotic Civil Service abbreviation. 'In normal circumstances . . .' he petered out. After all, we both knew how this tragedy had occurred.

Bernard reminded me of all my appointments for today. An office Christmas party, some meetings – nothing of any consequence. I spent the day dodging the press. I wanted to discuss the situation with Sir Humphrey, but apparently he was unavailable all day.

Annie and I were invited to the French Embassy's Christmas party, at 8 p.m. I asked Bernard to get me my car – and then realised, as I spoke, that there were no drivers. I told him to call Annie, to get her to bring our car in to collect me.

Bernard had already thought of that, but apparently our car had been giving trouble all day and Annie wanted to take it to the garage. I got hold of her and told her the garage would wait – the car would get us from Whitehall to Kensington okay.

Annie came for me, we set off in our evening clothes.

Yet again I was wrong and the bloody car broke down in Knightsbridge. In the rush hour. In the pouring rain. I tried to fix it. I was wearing my dinner jacket. I asked Annie for the umbrella, she said I had it. I knew she had it. We shouted at each other, she got out and slammed her door and walked away, and I was left with the car blocking all of Harrods' Christmas rush hour traffic with horns blaring and drivers yelling abuse at me.

I got to the French Embassy an hour and a half late, soaked to the skin and covered in oil. I had three or four glasses of champagne right away – well, who wouldn't in the circumstances? I needed them!

When I left, not drunk exactly, but a bit the worse for wear, I must admit, I dropped my keys in the gutter beside the car. Then they fell down a grating, so I had to lie down to try and reach them, and some bastard from the press was there.

This morning I had a frightful hangover. I felt tired and sick. The press had really gone to town over my alleged drunkenness. They really are unbelievably irresponsible nowadays.

Mr Economy falls down in gutter after champagne party

Another paper's headline was HACKER TIRED AND EMOTIONAL AFTER EMBASSY RECEPTION.

Sir Humphrey read it aloud, and remarked that it was slightly better, perhaps, than the first.

'Better?' I asked.

'Well . . . different, anyway,' said Sir Humphrey.

I asked if anyone had said anything beyond 'tired and emotional'. Bernard informed me that William Hickey said I was 'overwrought'. I didn't mind that quite so much, until Sir Humphrey added – for clarification – 'overwrought as a newt, actually'.

By now I felt that it could not get any worse. But I was wrong. Bernard produced today's lead story from the *Daily Telegraph*, which, astonishingly and horrifyingly, claimed that *I* was recruiting extra staff to the DAA.

Hacker recruits 400 new Civil Servants

By our political staff

In a so-called "economy drive" James Hacker, the Minister for Administrative Affairs, has recruited four hundred more Civil Servants.

I demanded an explanation from Sir Humphrey. And he had one ready, of course.

'Minister, you *asked* for these extra people. You demanded a complete study, a survey, facts and figures. These measures cannot be taken by non-people. If you create more work, more people have to be employed to do it. It's common sense.'

While I was taking this on the chin, he came in with another right hook to the head. 'And if you persist with your Bureaucratic Watchdog Office, there'll be at least another four hundred new jobs there as well.'

I was shattered. My head was aching, I felt sick, my career seemed to be in ruins, I was being pilloried in the press and the only idea of mine that I've managed to push through since I've been here had now to be abandoned.

Yet, throughout, from my first day here, all the permanent officials appear to have been doing their best to help me in every possible way. So are they completely inept? Or am I? Are they pretending to help while secretly obstructing my every move? Or are they incapable of understanding a new approach to the Department's work? Do they try to help me by pushing me towards the Ministry's policy? Is there a difference between the Minister's policy and the Ministry's policy? Why am I asking so many questions to which there is no known answer? How deep is the ocean, how high is the sky? [*Irving Berlin – Ed.*]

There was silence in the office. I didn't know what we were going to do about the four hundred new people supervising our economy drive or the four hundred new people for the Bureaucratic Watchdog Office, or anything! I simply sat and waited and hoped that my head would stop thumping and that some idea would be suggested by someone sometime soon.

Sir Humphrey obliged. 'Minister . . . if we were to end the economy drive and close the Bureaucratic Watchdog Office we could issue an immediate press announcement that you had axed eight hundred jobs.' He had obviously thought this out carefully in advance, for at this moment he produced a slim folder from under his arm. 'If you'd like to approve this draft. . . .'

I couldn't believe the impertinence of the suggestion. Axed eight hundred jobs? 'But no one was ever doing these jobs,' I pointed out incredulously. 'No one's been appointed yet.'

'Even greater economy,' he replied instantly. 'We've saved eight hundred redundancy payments as well.'

'But . . .' I attempted to explain '. . . that's just phony. It's dishonest, it's juggling with figures, it's pulling the wool over people's eyes.'

'A government press release, in fact,' said Humphrey. I've met some cynical politicians in my time, but this remark from my Permanent Secretary was a real eye-opener.

I nodded weakly. Clearly if I was to avoid the calamity of four hundred new people employed to make economies, I had to give up the four hundred new people in my cherished Watchdog Office. An inevitable *quid pro quo.* After all, politics is the art of the possible. [*A saying generally attributed to R. A. Butler, but actually said by Bismarck (1815–98) in 1867, in conversation with Meyer von Waldeck: 'Die Politik ist die Lehre von Möglichen' – Ed.*]

However, one vital central question, the question that was at the root of this whole débâcle, remained completely unanswered. 'But Humphrey,' I said. 'How are we actually going to slim down the Civil Service?'

There was a pause. Then he said: 'Well . . . I suppose we could lose one or two of the tea ladies.'

4
Big Brother

January 4th
Nothing of interest happened over Christmas. I spent the week in the constituency. I went to the usual Christmas parties for the constituency party, the old people's home, the general hospital, and assorted other gatherings and it all went off quite well – I got my photo in the local rag four or five times, and avoided saying anything that committed me to anything.

I sensed a sort of resentment, though, and have become aware that I'm in a double-bind situation. The local party, the constituency, my family, *all* of them are proud of me for getting into the Cabinet – yet they are all resentful that I have less time to spend on them and are keen to remind me that I'm nothing special, just their local MP, and that I mustn't get 'too big for my boots'. They manage both to grovel and patronise me simultaneously. It's hard to know how to handle it.

If only I could tell them what life is really like in Whitehall, they would know that there's absolutely no danger of my getting too big for my boots. Sir Humphrey Appleby will see to that.

Back to London today for a TV interview on *Topic*, with Robert McKenzie. He asked me lots of awkward questions about the National Data Base.

We met in the Hospitality Room before the programme was recorded, and I tried to find out what angle he was taking. We were a little tense with each other, of course. [*McKenzie used to call the Hospitality Room the Hostility Room – Ed.*]

'We are going to talk about cutting government extravagance and that sort of thing, aren't we?' I asked, and immediately realised that I had phrased that rather badly.

Bob McKenzie was amused. 'You want to talk about the government's extravagance?' he said with a twinkle in his eye.

'About the ways in which I'm cutting it down, I mean,' I said firmly.

'We'll get to that if we have time after the National Data Base,' he said.

I tried to persuade him that people weren't interested in the Data Base, that it was too trivial. He said he thought people were *very* interested in it, and were worried about Big Brother. This annoyed me, and I told him he couldn't trivialise the National Data Base with that sort of sensationalistic approach. Bob replied that as I'd just said it was trivial already, why not?

We left the Hospitality Room. In the studio, waiting for the programme to begin, a girl with a powder-puff kept flitting about and dabbing at my face and preventing me from thinking straight. She said I was getting a bit pink. 'We can't have that,' said Bob jovially, 'what would the *Daily Telegraph* say?'

Just before we started recording I remarked that I could well do without all those old chestnut questions like, 'Are we creating a Police State?'

In retrospect, perhaps this was a mistake.

[*We have found, in the BBC Archives, a complete transcript of Robert McKenzie's interview with James Hacker. It is printed overleaf – Ed.*]

BRITISH BROADCASTING CORPORATION

THIS SCRIPT WAS TYPED FROM A RECORDING NOT COPIED FROM AN ORIGINAL SCRIPT. BECAUSE OF THE RISK OF MISHEARING AND THE DIFFICULTY IN SOME CASES OF IDENTIFYING INDIVIDUAL SPEAKERS THE BBC CANNOT VOUCH FOR ITS COMPLETE ACCURACY.

TOPIC: JANUARY 4th INTERVIEW BETWEEN ROBERT MCKENZIE AND THE RT HON. JAMES HACKER MP

MCKENZIE: Good evening. Is Big Brother watching you ? To be more precise, did you know that the Government is building up a dossier on you ?

It's called by the harmless sounding name of "National Integrated Data Base". What it means is that at the press of a button any Civil Servant can inspect just about every detail of your life - your tax, your medical record, the car you drive, the house you live in, motoring offences, periods of unemployment, children's school records, the lot - and that Civil Servant may happen to be your next door neighbour.

Recently there has been mounting concern over this powerful totalitarian weapon that the computer revolution has put in the Government's hands. And the man who wields that weapon is the Minister for Administrative Affairs, the Rt Hon James Hacker MP.

Minister, are you laying the foundations of a police state in this country ?

HACKER: You know, I'm glad you asked me that question.

PAUSE

MCKENZIE: In that case, Minister, could we have an answer ?

- 1 -

BBC tv

BRITISH BROADCASTING CORPORATION

HACKER: (CONT) Yes, of course. I'm about to give you one, if I may. As I was saying, I'm glad you asked me that question. Because ... well, because it's a question that a lot of people are asking. And why ? Because ... well, because a lot of people want to know the answer to it. And let's be quite clear about this - without beating about the bush - the plain fact of the matter is that it is a very important question indeed and people have a right to know.

PAUSE

MCKENZIE: But Minister, you haven't given me an answer yet.

PAUSE

HACKER: I'm sorry, what was the question ?

MCKENZIE: How can I know that if I annoy you in this interview, you won't go back to your office, press a button and examine my tax returns, my hospital records, my police record ...

HACKER: Oh, come on Bob, you know as well as I do that's not the way we do things in this country. Impossible to organise, anyway.

MCKENZIE: Are you saying, Minister, you would like to do those things, but you are too incompetent as yet ?

- 2 -

BRITISH BROADCASTING CORPORATION

HACKER: (CONT) We're not incompetent. We could certainly check up on you if we wanted, that is, er, check up on people. Not you, of course, I don't mean you. But we're not interested in people. Er, that is, when I say we're not interested in people, I don't mean we're not interested in people, of course we are, I mean we're not interested in people in that way, if you know what I mean, in that we would never want to check up on ... people.

MCKENZIE: So what's the Data Base for, if it's not for checking up on people ?

HACKER: You know, that's a very interesting question. (PAUSE) Look, the point is, people have just been alarmed by one or two silly press articles. It's a computer, that's all, it's for storing up information and speeding up government business thus avoiding a massive expansion of clerical staff. Computers are good news.

MCKENZIE: But if you put information into it, you're going to want information out !

HACKER: Not necessarily.

MCKENZIE: So you're spending £25 million to store information you're never going to use ?

HACKER: No - yes - no, well - yes, no, there will be safeguards.

- 3 -

BRITISH BROADCASTING CORPORATION

MCKENZIE: (CONT) Such as ?

HACKER: Well, we'll be looking at a whole range of possibilities. But it's a complex and highly technical business, you know.

MCKENZIE: Well, perhaps I can help you. Let me read you an extract from an article written two years ago by the Editor of Reform. I think his name was Jim Hacker. The article was called: "Big Brother and the Not-So-Civil-Service". I quote: "if we are to protect the citizen from Government spying, three measures are urgent. One, no Civil Servant must have access to another department's files without specific signed authorisation from a Minister. Two, unauthorised snooping must be made a criminal offence. And three, every citizen should have the right to inspect his own personal file and get errors corrected." What do you think of those proposals, Mr Hacker ? Alarmist ?

HACKER: No, well, I stand by that, I mean, all these things must happen. Er, in due course.

MCKENZIE: Why not now ?

HACKER: Well, Rome wasn't built in a day. It's under review. But ... well, these things take time you know.

MCKENZIE: Mr Hacker, am I talking to the former Editor of Reform or a Civil Service Spokesman ?

- 4 -

BRITISH BROADCASTING CORPORATION

HACKER: (CONT) Well, we haven't talked yet about the safeguards. My new Bureaucratic Watch Dog Office, for instance, and ...

MCKENZIE: Mr Hacker it sounds as if we'll be needing a whole pack of watchdogs before very long. Thank you very much.

- 5 -

I thought I'd waffled a bit, but Bob told me I'd stonewalled beautifully. We went back to Hospitality for another New Year's drink. I congratulated him on finding that old article of mine – a crafty move. He said that one of his research girls had found it, and asked if I wanted to meet her. I declined – and said I'd just go back to my office and have a look at her dossier!

I watched the programme in the evening. I think it was okay. I hope Sir Humphrey is pleased, anyway.

January 7th

There was divided opinion in the office this afternoon about my TV appearance three days ago. The matter came up at a 4 p.m. meeting with Sir Humphrey, Bernard and Frank Weisel.

Humphrey and Bernard thought I'd been splendid. Dignified and suitable. But Frank's voice was particularly notable by its silence, during this chorus of praise. When I asked him what he thought, he just snorted like a horse. I asked him to translate.

He didn't answer me, but turned to Sir Humphrey. 'I congratulate you,' he began, his manner even a little less charming than usual. 'Jim is now perfectly house-trained.' Humphrey attempted to excuse himself and leave the room.

'If you'll excuse me, Mr Weasel . . .'

'Weisel!' snapped Frank. He turned on me. 'Do you realise you just say everything the Civil Service programmes you to say. What are you, a man or a mouth?'

Nobody laughed at his little pun.

'It may be very hard for a political adviser to understand,' said Sir Humphrey, in his most patronising manner, 'but I am merely a civil servant and I just do as I am instructed by my master.'

Frank fumed away, muttering, 'your master, typical stupid bloody phrase, public school nonsense,' and so forth. I must say, the phrase interested me too.

'What happens,' I asked, 'if the Minister is a woman? What do you call her?'

Humphrey was immediately in his element. He loves answering questions about good form and protocol. 'Yes, that's most interesting. We sought an answer to the point when I was a Principal Private Secretary and Dr Edith Summerskill was appointed Minister in 1947. I didn't quite like to refer to her as my mistress.'

He paused. For effect, I thought at first, but then he appeared to have more to say on the subject.

'What was the answer?' I asked.

'We're still waiting for it,' he explained.

Frank chipped in with a little of his heavy-duty irony. 'It's under review is it? Rome wasn't built in a day, eh Sir Humphrey? These things take time, do they?'

Frank is actually beginning to get on my nerves. The chip on his shoulder about the Civil Service is getting larger every day. I don't know why, because they have given him an office, he has free access to me, and they tell me that they give him all possible papers that would be of use to him. Now he's started to take out his aggressions on me. He's like a bear with a sore head. Perhaps he's still getting over his New Year's hangover.

Humphrey wanted to leave, so did I, but Bernard started to give me my diary appointments – and that started another wrangle. Bernard told me I was to meet him at Paddington at 8 a.m. tomorrow, because I was to speak at the Luncheon of the Conference of Municipal Treasurers at the Vehicle Licensing Centre in Swansea. Frank then reminded me that I was due in Newcastle tomorrow night to address the by-election meeting. Bernard pointed out to me that I couldn't do both and I explained this to Frank. Frank pointed out that the by-election was important to us, whereas the Swansea trip was just a Civil Service junket, and I explained this to Bernard. Bernard then reminded me that the Conference had been in my diary for some time and that they all expected me to go to Swansea, and I explained this to Frank and then Frank reminded me that Central House [*the party headquarters – Ed.*] expected me to go to Newcastle, but I didn't explain this to Bernard because by this time I was tired of explaining and I said so. So Frank asked Bernard to explain why I was double booked, Bernard said no one had told him about Newcastle, I asked Frank why he hadn't told Bernard, Frank asked me why *I* hadn't told Bernard, and I pointed out that I couldn't remember everything.

'I shall go to Swansea,' I said.

'Is that a decision, Minister?' asked Bernard.

'That's final,' I said.

Frank then played his trump card. 'The PM expects you to go to Newcastle,' he said. Why hadn't he said this till now, stupid man? I asked if he was sure. He nodded.

'Bernard, I think I'd better go to Newcastle,' I said.

'Is that a decision?' asked Frank.

'Yes, that's final,' I said. 'And now I'm going home.'

'Is *that* a decision?' asked Sir Humphrey. I wasn't sure whether or not he was asking for clarification or sending me up. I still find him completely baffling. Anyway, he continued: 'Minister, I think you've made the wrong decision, if I may say so. Your visit to Swansea is in the programme, it's been announced, you can't really get out of it.'

This was becoming impossible. They all seem to expect me to be in two places at once. I told them to find some way of getting me from Swansea to Newcastle – train, car, helicopter, I didn't care how – and I would fulfil both engagements. 'And now,' I announced, 'I'm going home – that's final!'

'Finally final?' asked Bernard.

His intentions are equally obscure.

As I left, Bernard gave Roy, my driver, four red boxes and asked me to be sure to do them tonight because of all the Committee papers for tomorrow and letters that have to go off before the weekend.

'And if you're a good boy,' said Frank in a rather poor imitation of Bernard's accent, 'your nanny will give you a sweetie.'

I really don't have to put up with all this aggravation from Frank. I'm stuck with these damn permanent officials, but Frank is only there at my express invitation. I may have to remind him of this, very soon.

When I got home Annie was packing. 'Leaving me at last?' I enquired jovially. She reminded me that it is our anniversary tomorrow and we have arranged to go to Paris.

I was appalled!

I tried to explain to her about the trips to Swansea and Newcastle. She feels that she doesn't want to spend her anniversary in Swansea and Newcastle, particularly not at a lunch for Municipal Treasurers at the Vehicle Licensing Centre. I can see her point. She told me to cancel my meetings, I said I couldn't, so she said she'd go to Paris without me.

So I phoned Bernard. I told him it was my wife's wedding anniversary – Annie said, 'yours too' – and mine too. Bernard made some silly joke about a coincidence. I told him I was going to Paris tomorrow, instead, and that it was final and that I knew I'd said it was final before but now this was really final – I told him he'd have to sort everything out. Then *he* talked for three minutes and when I rang off I was still going to Swansea and Newcastle tomorrow.

Those civil servants can talk you in or out of anything. I just don't seem to know my own mind any more.

Annie and I fumed in silence for a while, and finally I asked her the really important question of the day: had she seen me on my TV interview – (I'd been in London, she'd been down in the constituency).

'I saw someone who looked like you.'

I asked her what that was supposed to mean. She didn't answer.

'Frank said that I'm just a Civil Service mouthpiece,' I muttered resentfully.

Annie said, 'Yes.'

I was shocked. 'You mean . . . you agree?'

'Of course,' she said. 'You could have hired an actor to say it all for you. He'd have said it better. And while you're at it, why not just sign your letters with a rubber stamp or get an Assistant Secretary to sign them – they write them anyway.'

I tried to remain dignified. 'Assistant Secretaries do not write my letters,' I said. 'Under-Secretaries write them.'

'I rest my case, m'lud,' she said.

'You think I've become a puppet too?'

'I do. Maybe they should get Miss Piggy to do your job. At least she's prettier.'

I must say I was feeling pretty hurt and defeated. I sighed and sat on the bed. I honestly felt near to tears. Is this how a Cabinet Minister usually feels, I wondered, or am I just an abysmal failure? I couldn't see what was wrong, but something certainly was.

'I don't know what to do about it,' I said quietly. 'I'm just swamped by the volume of work. I'm so depressed.'

Annie suggested that, as we weren't going to Paris after all, we might at least go for a quiet little candlelit dinner on the corner. I told her that I couldn't, because Bernard had told me to work through three red boxes tonight.

Annie said something which changed my whole perception of my situation. She said, 'What do you mean, "Bernard's told me!"? When you edited *Reform* you were quite different – you went in, you told people what to do, demanded what you wanted, and you got it! What's changed? You're the same man – you're just allowing them to walk all over you.'

And, suddenly, I saw that it was true. She's right. That's why Frank has been getting at me too. Either I get them by the throat or they'll get me by the throat! It's the law of the jungle, just like in the Cabinet.

'How many articles did you blue-pencil and tear up in those days?' she asked.

'Dozens,' I remembered.

'And how many official papers have you torn up?'

'None,' I told her. 'I'm not allowed to.'

She smiled reproachfully at me, and I realised that I still hadn't broken out of this destructive pattern of behaviour.

'Not allowed to?' She held my hand. 'Darling, you're the Minister. You can do anything you like.'

She's right. I am. I can. And, somehow, all my officials have house-trained me. I see it now. Honestly, I'm so grateful to Annie, she has such remarkable common sense. Well, they're going to get quite a surprise. Suddenly, I can't wait to get to the office. My New Year Resolution is: Take Charge.

January 11th

Today was better.

But only a little better. *My* attitude was fine, but unfortunately *his* didn't seem to change all that much.

I summoned Humphrey to my office. I don't think he liked being summoned. Then I told him that Frank was absolutely correct, and Bob McKenzie too – the National Data Base has to be organised differently.

To my surprise, he agreed meekly. 'Yes Minister,' he murmured.

'We are going to have all possible built-in safeguards,' I went on.

'Yes Minister,' he murmured again.

'Right away,' I added. This took him by surprise.

'Er . . . what precisely do you mean, right away?'

'I mean right away,' I said.

'Oh I see, you mean *right away*, Minister.'

'Got it in one, Humphrey.'

So far, so good. But, having totally accepted at the start of the conversation that it was all to be different, he now started to chip away at my resolve.

'The only thing is,' he began, 'perhaps I should remind you that we are still in the early months of this government and there's an awful lot to get on with, Minister . . .'

I interrupted. 'Humphrey,' I reiterated firmly, 'we are changing the rules of the Data Base. Now!'

'But you can't, Minister,' he said, coming out into the open.

'I can,' I said, remembering my stern talk from Annie last night, 'I'm the Minister.'

He changed tactics again. 'Indeed you are, Minister,' he said, rapidly switching from bullying to grovelling, 'and quite an excellent

Minister at that, if I may say so.'

I brushed all the flannel aside. 'Never mind the soft soap, Humphrey,' I replied. 'I want all citizens to have the right to check their own file, and I want legislation to make unauthorised access to personal files illegal.'

'Very well,' said Sir Humphrey. 'It shall be done.'

This rather took the wind out of my sails. 'Right,' I said. 'Good,' I said. 'Then we go ahead,' I said, wondering what the catch was.

I was right. There was a catch. Sir Humphrey took this opportunity to explain to me that we can go ahead, if the Cabinet agrees, and take the matter to the Ministerial Committee, and then we can go ahead to the Official Committee. After that, of course, it's all plain sailing – straight to the Cabinet Committee! And then back to Cabinet itself. I interrupted to point out that we'd *started* with Cabinet.

'Only the policy, Minister,' explained Sir Humphrey. 'At this juncture Cabinet will have to consider the specific proposals.'

I conceded the point, but remarked that after going back to Cabinet we could then go ahead. Sir Humphrey agreed – but with the proviso that if Cabinet raises any questions, which it almost certainly would, the proposals would then have to go back to the Ministerial Committee, the Official Committee, the Cabinet Committee and the Cabinet again.

'I know all this,' I said brusquely. 'I'm assuming that Cabinet will raise no objections.' Sir Humphrey raised his eyebrows and visibly refrained from comment.

I didn't know all this at all, actually – the complex mechanics of passing legislation don't ever really become clear to you in Opposition or on the back benches.

'So after Cabinet, we go ahead. Right?'

'Yes,' he said, 'to the Leader of the House Committee. And then to Parliament – where there's the Committee stage of course.'

But suddenly the penny dropped. Suddenly I realised he was blurring the whole issue. A blindfold dropped away from my eyes, as if by magic. 'Humphrey,' I said, 'you're talking about legislation – but *I'm* talking about administrative and procedural changes.'

Sir Humphrey smiled complacently. 'If members of the public are to have the right to take legal action, then legislation is necessary and it will be very complicated.'

I had the answer to that. 'Legislation is not necessary in order for the citizen to be able to see his own file, is it?'

Sir Humphrey thought carefully about this. 'No-o-o-o,' he finally said, with great reluctance.

'Then we'll go ahead with that.' Round one to me, I thought.

But Sir Humphrey had not yet conceded even that much. 'Minister,' he began, 'we could manage that *slightly* quicker, but there are an awful lot of administrative problems as well.'

'Look,' I said, 'this must have come up before. This Data Base has been in preparation for years, it hasn't just materialised overnight – these problems must have been discussed.'

'Yes indeed,' he agreed.

'So what conclusions have been reached?' I asked.

Sir Humphrey didn't reply. At first I thought he was thinking. Then I thought he hadn't heard me, for some curious reason. So I asked him again: 'What conclusions have been reached?' a little louder, just in case. Again there was no visible reaction. I thought he'd become ill.

'Humphrey,' I asked, becoming a little concerned for his health and sanity, 'can you hear me?'

'My lips are sealed,' he replied, through unsealed lips.

I asked him what exactly he meant.

'I am not at liberty to discuss the previous government's plans,' he said. I was baffled.

'Why not?' I asked.

'Minister – would you like everything that you have said and done in the privacy of this office to be revealed subsequently to one of your opponents?'

I'd never thought of that. Of course, I'd be absolutely horrified. It would be a constant threat. I would never be able to speak freely in my own office.

Sir Humphrey knew that he'd scored a bull's-eye. He pressed home his advantage. 'We cannot give your political opponents ammunition against you – nor vice versa.'

Of course, I can see his point but there is one essential difference in this instance. I pointed out to Sir Humphrey that Tom Sargent was my predecessor, and he wouldn't mind. He's a very decent chap. After all, the Data Base is not a party political matter, politicians of all parties are united on this.

But Sir Humphrey wouldn't budge. 'It's the principle, Minister,' he said, and added that it just wouldn't be cricket.

This was a powerful argument. Naturally I don't want to do anything that's not cricket. So I suppose I'll never know what went on before I came here. I can't see a way round that.

So where have we got to? We've established that we don't need legislation to enable the citizen to see his own file, but that there are numerous unspecified admin. problems that have to be solved first.

One other thing occurred today. Bernard said that because of the adverse (Bernard called it 'not entirely favourable') press reaction to my appearance on *Topic*, the other network wants me to appear on their programme *World in Focus*. Funny how television is never interested when you've got an important announcement to make, but the moment some trivial thing goes wrong the phone never stops ringing. At first I told him to decline, but he said that if I don't appear they'll do the item anyway, and no one will be there to state my case.

I asked Humphrey what I was to say about safeguards for the Data Base, in view of our very limited progress today. 'Perhaps you could remind them, Minister, that Rome wasn't built in a day.'

Big help!

As I review the meeting, writing it all down for this diary, I now feel that I got absolutely nowhere today. But there must be *some* way to get Sir Humphrey and the DAA to do what I tell them.

[*In the light of Hacker's experience and frustrations, it is as well to remember that if a Whitehall committee is not positively stopped, it will continue. There could be a Crimea committee, for all we know. There is very probably a ration-book committee and an identity-card committee – Ed.*]

January 12th

Today, by a lucky chance, I learned a bit more about dealing with Sir Humphrey.

I bumped into Tom Sargent, in the House of Commons smoking room. I asked if I could join him, and he was only too pleased.

'How are you enjoying being in Opposition?' I asked him jocularly.

Like the good politician he is, he didn't exactly answer my question. 'How are you enjoying being in government?' he replied.

I could see no reason to beat about the bush, and I told him that, quite honestly, I'm not enjoying it as much as I'd expected to.

'Humphrey got you under control?' he smiled.

I dodged that one, but said that it's so very hard to get anything done. He nodded, so I asked him, 'Did *you* get anything done?'

'Almost nothing,' he replied cheerfully. 'But I didn't cotton on to his technique till I'd been there over a year – and then of course there was the election.'

It emerged from the conversation that the technique in question was Humphrey's system for stalling.

According to Tom, it's in five stages. I made a note during our conversation, for future reference.

Stage One: Humphrey will say that the administration is in its early months and there's an awful lot of other things to get on with. (Tom clearly knows his stuff. That is just what Humphrey said to me the day before yesterday.)

Stage Two: If I persist past Stage One, he'll say that he quite appreciates the intention, something certainly ought to be done – but is this the right way to achieve it?

Stage Three: If I'm still undeterred he will shift his ground from how I do it to *when* I do it, i.e. 'Minister, this is not the time, for all sorts of reasons.'

Stage Four: Lots of Ministers settle for Stage Three according to Tom. But if not, he will then say that the policy has run into difficulties – technical, political and/or legal. (Legal difficulties are best because they can be made totally incomprehensible and can go on for ever.)

Stage Five: Finally, because the first four stages have taken up to three years, the last stage is to say that 'we're getting rather near to the run-up to the next general election – so we can't be sure of getting the policy through'.

The stages can be made to last three years because at each stage Sir Humphrey will do absolutely nothing until the Minister chases him. And he assumes, rightly, that the Minister has too much else to do. [*The whole process is called Creative Inertia – Ed.*]

Tom asked me what the policy was that I'm trying to push through. When I told him that I'm trying to make the National Integrated Data Base less of a Big Brother, he roared with laughter.

'I suppose he's pretending it's all new?'

I nodded.

'Clever old sod,' said Tom, 'we spent years on that. We almost had a White Paper ready to bring out, but the election was called. I've done it all.'

I could hardly believe my ears. I asked about the administrative problems. Tom said there were none – all solved. And Tom guessed that my enquiries about the past were met with silence – 'clever bugger, he's wiped the slate clean'.

Anyway, now I know the five stages, I should be able to deal with Humphrey quite differently. Tom advised me not to let on that we'd had this conversation, because it would spoil the fun. He also warned me of the 'Three Varieties of Civil Service Silence', which would be Humphrey's last resort if completely cornered:

1 The silence when they do not want to tell you the facts: *Discreet Silence.*
2 The silence when they do not intend to take any action: *Stubborn Silence.*
3 The silence when you catch them out and they haven't a leg to stand on. They imply that they could vindicate themselves completely if only they were free to tell all, but they are too honourable to do so: *Courageous Silence.*

Finally Tom told me what Humphrey's next move would be. He asked how many boxes they'd given me for tonight: 'Three? Four?'

'Five,' I admitted, somewhat shamefaced.

'Five?' He couldn't hide his astonishment at how badly I was doing. 'Have they told you that you needn't worry too much about the fifth?' I nodded. 'Right. Well, I'll bet you that at the bottom of the fifth box will be a submission explaining why any new moves on the Data Base must be delayed – and if you never find it or read it they'll do nothing further, and in six months' time they'll say they told you all about it.'

There was one more thing I wanted to ask Tom, who really had been extremely kind and helpful. He's been in office for years, in various government posts. So I said to him: 'Look Tom, you know all the Civil Service tricks.'

'Not all,' he grinned, 'just a few hundred.'

'Right,' I said. 'Now how do you defeat them? How do you make them do something they do not want to do?'

Tom smiled ruefully, and shook his head. 'My dear fellow,' he replied, 'if I knew that I wouldn't be in Opposition.'

January 13th

I did my boxes so late last night that I'm writing up yesterday's discoveries a day late.

Tom had been most helpful to me. When I got home I told Annie all about it over dinner. She couldn't understand why Tom, as a member of the Opposition, would have been so helpful.

I explained to her that the Opposition aren't really the opposition. They're just called the Opposition. But, in fact, they are the opposition in exile. The Civil Service are the opposition in residence.

Then after dinner I did the boxes and sure enough, at the bottom of the fifth box, I found a submission on the Data Base. Not merely at the bottom of the fifth box – to be doubly certain the submission had somehow slipped into the middle of an eighty-page report on Welfare Procedures.

By the way, Tom has also lent me all his private papers on the Data Base, which he kept when he left office. Very useful!

The submission contained the expected delaying phrases: 'Subject still under discussion . . . programme not finalised . . . nothing precipitate . . . failing instructions to the contrary propose await developments.'

Annie suggested I ring Humphrey and tell him that I disagree. I was reluctant – it was 2 a.m., and he'd be fast asleep.

'Why should he sleep while you're working?' Annie asked me. 'After all, he's had you on the run for three months. Now it's your turn.'

'I couldn't possibly do that,' I said.

Annie looked at me. 'What's his number?' I asked, as I reached for our address book.

Annie added reasonably: 'After all, if it was in the fifth box you couldn't have found it any earlier, could you?'

Humphrey answered the phone with a curious sort of grunting noise. I had obviously woken him up. 'Sorry to ring you so late, you weren't in the middle of dinner, were you?'

'No,' he said, sounding somewhat confused, 'we had dinner some while ago. What's the time?'

I told him it was 2 a.m.

'Good God!' He sounded as though he'd really woken up now. 'What's the crisis?'

'No crisis. I'm still going through my red boxes and I knew you'd still be hard at it.'

'Oh yes,' he said, stifling a yawn. 'Nose to the grindstone.'

I told him I'd just got to the paper on the Data Base.

'Oh, you've found . . .' he corrected himself without pausing, 'you've read it.'

I told him that I thought he needed to know, straight away, that I wasn't happy with it, that I knew he'd be grateful to have a little extra time to work on something else, and that I hoped he didn't mind my calling him.

'Always a pleasure to hear from you, Minister,' he said, and I think he slammed down the phone.

After I rang off I realised I'd forgotten to tell him to come and talk about it before Cabinet tomorrow. I was about to pick up the phone when Annie said: 'Don't ring him now.'

I was surprised by this sudden show of kindness and consideration for Sir Humphrey, but I agreed. 'No, perhaps it is a bit late.'

She smiled. 'Yes. Just give him another ten minutes.'

January 14th

This morning I made a little more progress in my battle for control over Humphrey and my Department, though the battle is not yet won.

But I had with me my notes from the meeting with Tom Sargent, and – exactly as Tom had predicted – Sir Humphrey put his stalling technique into bat.

'Humphrey,' I began, 'have you drafted the proposed safeguards for the Data Base?'

'Minister,' he replied plausibly, 'I quite appreciate your intention and I fully agree that there is a need for safeguards but I'm wondering if this is the right way to achieve it.'

'It's my way,' I said decisively, and I ticked off the first objection in my little notebook. 'And that's my decision.'

Humphrey was surprised that his objection had been brushed aside so early, without protracted discussion – so surprised that he went straight on to his second stage.

'Even so Minister,' he said, 'this is not really the time, for all sorts of reasons.'

I ticked off number two in my notebook, and replied: 'It is the perfect time – safeguards have to develop parallel with systems, not after them – that's common sense.'

Humphrey was forced to move on to his third objection. Tom really has analysed his technique well.

'Unfortunately, Minister,' said Humphrey doggedly, 'we have tried this before, but, well . . . we have run into all sorts of difficulties.'

I ticked off number three in my little book. Humphrey had noticed this by now, and tried to look over my shoulder to see what was written there. I held the book away from him.

'What sort of difficulties?' I enquired.

'Technical, for example,' said Humphrey.

Thanks to a careful study of Tom's private papers, I had the answer ready. 'No problem at all,' I said airily. 'I've been doing some research. We can use the same basic file interrogation programme as the US State Department and the Swedish Ministry of the Interior. No technical problems.'

Sir Humphrey was getting visibly rattled, but he persisted. 'There are also formidable administrative problems. All departments are affected. An interdepartmental committee will have to be set up . . .'

I interrupted him in mid-sentence. 'No,' I said firmly. 'I think you'll find, if you look into it, that the existing security procedures are adequate. This can just be an extension. Anything else?'

Humphrey was gazing at me with astonishment. He just couldn't work out how I was so thoroughly in command of the situation. Was I just making a series of inspired guesses, he wondered. As he didn't speak for a moment, I decided to help him out.

'Legal problems?' I suggested helpfully.

'Yes Minister,' he agreed at once, hoping that he had me cornered at last. Legal problems were always his best bet.

'Good, good,' I said, and ticked off the last but one stage on my little list. Again he tried to see what I had written down.

'There is a question,' he began carefully, 'of whether we have the legal power . . .'

'I'll answer it,' I announced grandly. 'We have.' He was looking at me in wonderment. 'All personnel affected are bound by their service agreement anyway.'

He couldn't argue because, of course, I was right. Grasping at straws he said: 'But Minister, there will have to be extra staffing – are you sure you will get it through Cabinet and the Parliamentary Party?'

'Quite sure,' I said. 'Anything else?' I looked at my list. 'No, nothing else. Right, so we go ahead?'

Humphrey was silent. I wondered whether he was being discreet, stubborn or courageous. Stubborn, I think.

Eventually, *I* spoke. 'You're very silent,' I remarked. There was more silence. 'Why are you so silent, by the way?'

He realised that he had to speak, or the jig was up. 'Minister, you do not seem to realise how much work is involved.'

Casually, I enquired if he'd never investigated safeguards before, under another government perhaps, as I thought I remembered written answers to Parliamentary questions in the past.

His reply went rather as follows: 'Minister, in the first place, we've agreed that the question is not cricket. In the second place, if there had been investigations, which there haven't or not necessarily, or I am not at liberty to say if there have, there would have been a project team which, had it existed, on which I cannot comment, would now be disbanded if it had existed and the members returned to their original departments, had there indeed been any such members.' Or words to that effect.

I waited till the torrent of useless language came to a halt, and then

I delivered my ultimatum. I told him that I wanted safeguards on the use of the Data Base made available immediately. He told me it isn't possible. I told him it is. He told me it isn't. I told him it is. We went on like that ('tis, 'tisn't, 'tis, 'tisn't) like a couple of three-year-olds, glowering at each other, till Bernard popped in.

I didn't want to reveal that Tom had told me of the safeguards that were ready and waiting, because then I'd have no more aces up my sleeve.

While I contemplated this knotty problem, Bernard reminded me of my engagements: Cabinet at 10, a speech to the Anglo-American Society lunch, and the *World in Focus* interview this evening. I asked him if he could get me out of the lunch. 'Not really, Minister,' he answered, 'it's been announced. It's in the programme.'

And suddenly the penny dropped. The most wonderful plan formed in my mind, the idea of the century!

I told Humphrey and Bernard to be sure to watch me on TV tonight.

[*The transcript of Hacker's appearance that night on* World in Focus *follows. It contains his first truly memorable victory over his officials– Ed.*]

THIS IS AN UNCORRECTED TRANSCRIPT ONLY. NOT FOR CIRCULATION WITHOUT PROGRAMME CONTROLLER'S APPROVAL.

WORLD IN FOCUS - JANUARY 14th - HACKER INTERVIEW

PRESENTER And our man on the spot tonight is the Right Honourable Jim Hacker, Minister for Administrative Affairs, and the man at the heart of the Big Brother computer controversy. He's talking to Godfrey Finch.

FINCH Minister, as you know, there's been an outcry this week about the dossier that the Civil Service Bureaucracy is apparently starting to build up on every citizen in the country. It is rumoured that this is not your own policy, that you wish to have safeguards for the individual citizen, but that you are being totally frustrated every step of the way by the Civil Service machine.

HACKER You know Godfrey, there's a lot of nonsense talked about the Civil Service. It is actually a marvellous, efficient, professional organisation capable of tremendous effort and speed. It is full of talented, dedicated people who do all they can to help Government policies become law.

FINCH Thank you for the commercial, Minister. If we could start the programme now ?

<u>HACKER</u> The fact is, the Civil Service and I are in complete accord on this whole matter, and our proposals are now ready for publication.

I am happy to announce tonight that, from March 1st, every citizen of the UK will have the absolute right to inspect his personal file and to check any information that he or she has ever supplied to the Government.

Secondly, no Civil Servant will be allowed to examine personal files from another department without written authority from a Minister. And I shall be announcing, in the House next week, legislation enabling the citizens to take legal action against any Civil Servant who gains unauthorised access to his file.

<u>FINCH</u> Well ... that's, er ... well, that's very interesting and encouraging, Minister. Why did you not say so earlier and put people's minds at rest ?

<u>HACKER</u> Frankly, Godfrey, I didn't believe the Civil Service could meet those deadlines. But they've convinced me that they can. Indeed my Permanent Secretary is staking his reputation on it.

And, if not, heads will roll.

SIR BERNARD WOOLLEY RECALLS:[1]
Jim Hacker always gave me the credit for this brilliant ploy, because of the unintentional double meaning of my remark, 'it's been announced, it's in the programme'.

However, I personally believe that Hacker was inspired by Edward Heath's famous manoeuvre when he was Prime Minister and wanted – in the teeth of Civil Service opposition – to announce a new £10 Christmas bonus for the Old Age Pensioners. After many weeks of obstruction within Number Ten he simply appeared on *Panorama* and announced it as a *fait accompli.* It happened. It happened late, but it happened.

I well remember that Humphrey Appleby's face was a picture when Jim made his statement – especially at the moment when he said that his Permanent Secretary had staked his reputation on it.

He turned to me and said: 'It can't be done.' I made no reply.

Then he said to me: 'Well Bernard, what do you make of the Minister's performance?'

I was obliged to say that, in my opinion, it was checkmate.

January 15th

Today was my happiest day since I became a Minister.

'Did you see me on the box last night?' I asked Humphrey cheerfully as he gloomed into the office looking like Mr Sowerberry at a funeral.

'Of course,' he replied, tight-lipped.

Actually, it didn't matter whether he'd seen me or not, because my TV appearance was completely reported in this morning's press.

'How was I?' I asked innocently. 'Good?'

'A most remarkable performance, Minister, if I may say so,' he answered with studied ambiguity.

'You may, you may,' I said, affecting not to notice it.

'Minister, we have been working very hard all night, and I'm happy to be able to inform you that we have come up with some draft proposals that would enable you to achieve your desired objectives by the stated dates.'

In other words, he spent five minutes digging out from the files the proposals agreed last year when Tom was Minister.

'Well done, Humphrey,' I said ingenuously. 'You see, I told the nation how splendid you are and I was right. I had every confidence in you.'

'Quite so, Minister,' he said through clenched teeth.

[1] In conversation with the Editors.

He got out a folder containing his proposals.

'Are those your proposals?' I asked.

'Yes.'

'Here are mine,' I said, and produced a folder too.

'You have proposals too?' He was surprised.

I told Humphrey to read his proposed safeguards. Then I would read mine. And we would see how they compared.

Humphrey started reading. 'One – Personal Data – 1A. Safeguards must be applied with reference to . . .'

I could resist it no longer. Reading from my folder, I joined in, and together, in unison, we read: '. . . two criteria – the need to know and the right to know. 1.A(i) the need to know. Only those officials for whom the information was submitted may be deemed, prima facie, to have a need to know.'

We looked at each other.

'We seem to be of the same mind,' I remarked.

'Where did those proposals come from?' he demanded. I said nothing. After a few moments he repeated, 'Where did those proposals come from?'

'Humphrey,' I replied in a tone of slight reproof, 'my lips are sealed.'

5

The Writing on the Wall

January 18th

The help that I received from Tom Sargent in the matter of the National Data Base might seem unusual to those who are outside the extraordinary world of politics. Strange though it may seem to those members of the public who read numerous abusive speeches in which members of the two main political parties revile each other as incompetent, dishonest, criminally stupid and negligent, cross-party friendships are extremely common. In fact, it is much easier to be friends with a member of the opposite party than a member of one's own party – for one is not in direct personal competition for office with members of the Opposition in the way that one is with one's colleagues.

All my Cabinet colleagues and I were naturally in bitter competition with each other during our years in Opposition. In the last three months we've all been so busy trying to deal with the *real* opposition – the Civil Service – that we've not had any real time to do-down each other. But I have a hunch, from the recent atmosphere in Cabinet, that some political manoeuvring is in the air again.

There are still numerous other matters concerning me, about which I have also had a little time to reflect this weekend. I realised early on (in my first week as a Minister, in fact) that Open Government presents real problems. It was made clear to me that if people stop having secrets they stop having power.

In fact, paradoxically, government is more open when it is less open. Open Government is rather like the live theatre: the audience gets a performance. And it gives a response. But, like the theatre, in order to have something to show openly there must first be much hidden activity. And all sorts of things have to be cut or altered in rehearsals, and not shown to the public until you have got them right.

The drawback with all this is that it begs the question – which is that the Civil Service keeps secrets from Ministers. They say they don't, but I'm sure they do. I'm now all in favour of keeping secrets from the public of course, for the reasons I've just given, but it should be *my* privilege, as the people's elected representative, to decide when to keep the people in ignorance. It should not be up to the Civil Service to keep *me* in ignorance.

Unfortunately, it is pretty hard to get this across to them.

I have also learned a few general lessons. I must never show my hopes or fears to Humphrey, if I can avoid it – especially party fears. If you give away your political weaknesses, they'll destroy you. You have to keep them guessing.

I now realise that I should always get civil servants to commit themselves first. Never say, 'I think . . .', but always say, 'What do *you* think . . .?'

I've also learned about 'yes' and 'no'. You can always turn a 'no' into a 'yes' – but not vice versa. Furthermore, when you say 'no', let the Private Office say it for you – but when you say 'yes', pre-empt the Private Office and phone up yourself. That way, *they* get the blame and *I* get the credit.

In fact, the point about making your own phone calls is crucial. The whole system is designed to prevent you from doing anything yourself. As far as the Civil Service is concerned, you must never make a phone call, or sort out a problem. Woe betide any Minister who lifts the phone to try to sort out a foreign trade deal, for instance. Civil servants will come at you from all sides mouthing phrases like, 'it's an FCO matter . . . correct channels . . . policy hangs by a thread . . . you *do* realise, don't you? . . . what if something were to go wrong? . . . on your head be it, Minister!' and many others.

This is all very squashing to the morale of an important public figure such as myself. If you're not careful they'll eventually have you in such a state that you'll be frightened to phone Potters Bar.

Furthermore, everything that one does is carefully watched and supervised. Bernard listens in to all my phone calls, except the ones that I make on the private line. The theory is that he can make useful notes on my behalf, and is fully informed about my views and activities – true! But, as we know, information is a double-edged sword. [*It's no accident that most of the really powerful offices in the world are called 'Secretary' – Secretary of State, Permanent Secretary, General Secretary, Party Secretary, etc. 'Secretary' means the person who is entrusted with the secrets, the information no one else knows – the élite – Ed.*]

I must say, though, that I find it an invaluable way to pass on criticism of my permanent officials, knowing that Bernard is listening in to my every word!

Tonight, in one of my red boxes, there is a third redraft of a report to the Think-Tank on Civil Service overmanning. [*'Think-Tank' was the colloquial name of the Central Policy Review Staff – Ed.*] I'm still not pleased with it. I shall have a lot of questions to ask about it tomorrow morning.

January 19th

We had a meeting about the Think-Tank report. I told Humphrey that I still wasn't happy with it, and he obligingly offered to redraft it.

This hardly seems to be the answer. I pointed out that he had redrafted it three times already.

Bernard argued about this. 'That's not quite correct, Minister.'

I told him I could count. And that this was the third draft. 'Quite so,' he said. 'It has been drafted once and redrafted twice.' A typical piece of boring pedantic quibbling. Bernard has an idiotic obsession about using language with accuracy – it's fortunate he's not in politics.

I told him not to quibble, and Humphrey said placatingly he would be happy to redraft the report a third time. Of course he would. And a fourth time, and a fifth no doubt. 'And a sixth,' I went on. 'But it still won't say what *I* want it to say, it will say what *you* want it to say. And I want it to say what *I* want it to say.'

'What do you want it to say?' asked Bernard.

'We want it to say what you want it to say,' murmured Humphrey soothingly.

'I'm sure,' wittered Bernard, 'that the Department doesn't want you to say something that you don't want to say.'

I tried again. For the fourth time in as many weeks I explained the position. 'Six weeks ago the Think-Tank asked for our evidence on Civil Service overmanning. Three times I have briefed a group of civil servants in words of one syllable – and each time I get back a totally unintelligible draft which says the exact opposite of what I have told them to say.'

'With respect, Minister,' countered Sir Humphrey (untruthfully), 'how do you know it says the opposite if it is totally unintelligible?' He really is the master of the irrelevant question-begging answer.

'All I want to say,' I explained plaintively, 'is that the Civil Service is grossly overmanned and must be slimmed down.'

'I'm sure we all want to say that,' lied my Permanent Secretary.

'And that is what the report says.'

'No it doesn't.'

'Yes it does.'

Then we said, 'Oh no, it doesn't,' 'Oh yes, it does,' 'Oh no, it doesn't,' at each other for a while. Then I quoted phrases from the draft report at him. It says, for instance, that a phased reduction of about a hundred thousand people is 'not in the public interest'. Translation: it *is* in the public interest but it is not in the interest of the Civil Service. 'Public opinion is not yet ready for such a step,' it says. Translation: Public opinion is ready but the Civil Service is not! Then it goes on: 'However, this is an urgent problem and we therefore propose setting up a Royal Commission.' Translation: This problem is a bloody nuisance, but we hope that by the time a Royal Commission reports, four years from now, everyone will have forgotten about it or we can find someone else to blame.

[*Hacker was beginning to understand Civil Service code language. Other examples are:*

'I think we have to be very careful.' Translation: We are not going to do this.

'Have you thought through all the implications?' Translation: You are not going to do this.

'It is a slightly puzzling decision.' Translation: Idiotic!

'Not entirely straightforward.' Translation: Criminal.

'With the greatest possible respect, Minister . . .' Translation: Minister, that is the silliest idea I've ever heard – Ed.]

Humphrey could see no way out of this impasse. 'Minister, I can only suggest that we redraft it.' Brilliant!

'Humphrey,' I said, 'will you give me a straight answer to a straight question?'

This question took him completely by surprise, and he stopped to think for a brief moment.

'So long as you are not asking me to resort to crude generalisations or vulgar over-simplifications, such as a simple yes or no,' he said, in a manner that contrived to be both openly ingenuous and deeply evasive, 'I shall do my utmost to oblige.'

'Do you mean yes?' I asked.

A fierce internal struggle appeared to be raging within. 'Yes,' he said finally.

'Right,' I said. 'Here is the straight question.'

Sir Humphrey's face fell. 'Oh,' he said, 'I thought that was it.'

I persevered. 'Humphrey, in your evidence to the Think-Tank, are you going to support my view that the Civil Service is overmanned and feather-bedded or not? Yes or no! Straight answer!'

Could I have put this question any more plainly? I don't think so. This was the reply: 'Minister, if I am pressed for a straight answer I shall say that, as far as we can see, looking at it by and large, taking one thing with another, in terms of the average of departments, then in the last analysis it is probably true to say that, at the end of the day, you would find, in general terms that, not to put too fine a point on it, there really was not very much in it one way or the other.'

While I was still reeling from this, he added, no doubt for further clarification, 'As far as one can see, at this stage.'

I made one last attempt. 'Does that mean yes or no?' I asked, without much hope.

'Yes and no,' he replied helpfully.

'Suppose,' I said, 'suppose you *weren't* asked for a straight answer?'

'Ah,' he said happily, 'then I should play for time, Minister.'

Humphrey's never going to change. I certainly will never change him. Today I got nowhere fast. No, not even fast – I got nowhere, slowly and painfully! The conversation finished with Humphrey suggesting that I take the draft home and study it for the next couple of days, because I might then find that it does indeed say what I want it to say. An idiotic time-wasting suggestion, of course. He's just trying to wear me down.

'And if it doesn't say what I want it to say?' I asked testily.

Sir Humphrey smiled. 'Then we shall be happy to redraft it for you, Minister,' he said.

Back to square one.

January 20th

I have thought about yesterday's events very carefully. I do not propose to give this draft back to the Department for any more redrafting. I shall write it myself, and not return it until it is too late for them to change it.

I mentioned this to Bernard, and he thought it was a good idea. I told him in the strictest confidence, and I hope I can trust him. I'm sure I can.

[*Hacker reckoned without the pressures that the Civil Service can apply to its own people. Sir Humphrey enquired about the fourth draft report several times over the next two weeks, and observed that Bernard Woolley was giving evasive answers. Finally, Bernard was invited for a disciplinary drink at Sir Humphrey's Club in Pall Mall. We have found a memo about the meeting among Sir Humphrey's private papers – Ed.*]

B. W. came for a drink at the Club.

I questioned him about the Department's Report to the Think-Tank.

He said, 'You mean, the Minister's report?', a not-insignificant remark.

In answer to my questions as to why we had not yet had it returned to us, he suggested that I ask the Minister. A most unsatisfactory reply.

I explained that I had chosen to ask *him*. As he remained stubbornly silent, I observed that he did not seem to be replying.

'Yes and no,' he said. He knows full well that this is one of my favourite replies, and I felt obliged to tick him off for impertinence.

In answer to other questions, B.W. insisted that the Minister is doing his boxes conscientiously, but repeatedly refused to explain the delay over the draft report, merely advising me to enquire of the Minister as he (B.W.) was the Minister's *Private* Secretary.

He appeared to be anxious about his situation, and clearly had been put under some obligation by the Minister to treat some piece of information in strict confidence. I therefore decided to increase his anxiety considerably, to the extent that he would be obliged to find a way of either satisfying both myself and his Minister, and therefore showing that he is worthy to be a flyer [*'High Flyer' means young man destined for the very top of the Service – Ed.*] or of taking one side or the other, thereby revealing an inability to walk a tightrope in a high wind.

I therefore reminded him that he was an employee of the DAA. And, admirable though it is to be loyal to his Minister, an average Minister's tenure is a mere eleven months whereas Bernard's career will, he hopes, last until the age of sixty.

B.W. handled the situation with skill. He opted for asking me a hypothetical question, always a good idea.

He asked me: *If* a purely hypothetical Minister were to be unhappy with a departmental draft of evidence to a committee, and *if* the hypothetical Minister were to be planning to replace it with his own hypothetical draft worked out with his own political advisers at his party HQ, and *if* this Minister was planning to bring in his own draft so close to the final date for evidence that there would be no time to redraft it, and *if* the hypothetical Private Secretary were to be aware of this hypothetical draft – in confidence – should the hypothetical Private Secretary pass on the information to the Perm. Sec. of the hypothetical Department?

A good question. Naturally, I answered B.W. by saying that no Private Secretary should pass on such information, if given in confidence.

B. W. shows more promise than I thought. [*Appleby Papers 23/RPY/13c*]

February 1st

It is now two weeks since I decided to take over the Think-Tank report. My final redraft is going well. Frank and his chaps have been hard at work on it, and I've been burning the midnight oil as well. The situation seems to be infuriating Humphrey, which gives me some considerable pleasure.

Today he again asked me about my redraft of the redraft of the draft. 'What about the evidence to the Central Policy Review Staff?' he said.

'You mean the Think-Tank?' I said playing for time.

'Yes Minister.'

'Why do you want it?' I asked.

'So that we can redraft it.'

'That won't be necessary.'

'I think it will, Minister.'

'Humphrey,' I said firmly, 'drafting is not a Civil Service monopoly.'

'It is a highly specialised skill,' he replied, 'which few people outside the Service can master.'

'Nonsense,' I said. 'Drafts are easy. It's a game anyone can play.'

'Not without getting huffed,' he answered. Actually, he's quite witty, really.

I chuckled at his joke, and changed the subject. But he didn't let me get away with it. 'So can I have the draft back, please?' he persisted.

'Of course,' I said, with a smile. He waited. In vain.

'When, Minister?' he asked, trying to smile back, but definitely through clenched teeth.

'Later,' I said airily.

'But *when*?' he snarled through his smile.

'You always say we mustn't rush things,' I said irritatingly.

He then asked me for a straight answer! The nerve of it! However, as he had started to use my terminology, I answered him in his.

'In due course, Humphrey.' I was really enjoying myself. 'In the fullness of time. At the appropriate juncture. When the moment is ripe. When the requisite procedures have been completed. Nothing precipitate, you understand.'

'Minister,' he said, losing all traces of good humour. 'It is getting urgent.'

He was getting rattled. Great. My tactics were a triumph. 'Urgent?' I said blandly. 'You *are* learning a lot of new words.' I don't think I've ever been quite so rude to anyone in my life. I was having a wonderful time. I must try it more often.

'I hope you will forgive me for saying this,' began Sir Humphrey in his iciest manner, 'but I am beginning to suspect that you are concealing something from me.'

I feigned shock, surprise, puzzlement, ignorance – a whole mass of false emotions. 'Humphrey!' I said in my most deeply shocked voice, 'surely we don't have any secrets from each other?'

'I'm sorry, Minister, but sometimes one is forced to consider the possibility that affairs are being conducted in a way which, all things being considered, and making all possible allowances, is, not to put too fine a point on it, perhaps not entirely straightforward.' Sir Humphrey was insulting me in the plainest language he could manage in a crisis. Not entirely straightforward, indeed! Clearly, just as it's against the rules of the House to call anyone a liar, it's against the Whitehall code of conduct too.

So I decided to come clean at last. I told him that I have redrafted the redraft myself, that I'm perfectly happy with it, and that I don't want him to redraft it again.

'But . . .' began Sir Humphrey.

'No buts,' I snapped. 'All I get from the Civil Service is delaying tactics.'

'I wouldn't call Civil Service delays "tactics", Minister,' he replied smoothly. 'That would be to mistake lethargy for strategy.'

I asked him if we hadn't already set up a committee to investigate delays in the Civil Service. He concurred.

'What happened to it?' I asked.

'Oh,' he said, brushing the matter aside, 'it hasn't met yet.'

'Why not?' I wanted to know.

'There . . . seems to have been a delay,' he admitted.

It is vital that I make Humphrey realise that there is a real desire for radical reform in the air. I reminded him that the All-Party Select Committee on Administrative Affairs, which I founded, has been a great success.

This was probably an error, because he immediately asked me what it has achieved. I was forced to admit that it hasn't actually achieved anything *yet*, but I pointed out that the party is very pleased by it.

'Really?' he asked. 'Why?'

'Ten column inches in the *Daily Mail* last Monday, for a start,' I replied proudly.

'I see,' he said coldly, 'the government is to measure its success in column inches, is it?'

'Yes . . . and no,' I said with a smile.

But he was deeply concerned about my redraft of the draft report.

'Minister,' he said firmly, 'the evidence that you are proposing to submit is not only untrue, it is – which is much more serious – unwise.' One of Humphrey's most telling remarks so far, I think. 'We have been through this before: *the expanding Civil Service is the result of parliamentary legislation, not bureaucratic empire building.*'

I begin to think that Sir Humphrey really believes this.

'So,' I said, 'when this comes up at Question Time you want me to tell Parliament it's their fault that the Civil Service is so big?'

'It's the truth, Minister,' he insisted.

He can't seem to grasp that I don't want the truth, I want something I can tell Parliament.

I spelled it out to him. 'Humphrey, you are my Permanent Secretary. Are you going to support me?'

'We shall always support you as your standard-bearer, Minister – but not as your pall-bearer.'

There seemed to be a vaguely threatening air about these remarks. I demanded to know what he was actually *saying.* As I was becoming more and more heated, he was becoming icier and icier.

'I should have thought,' he pronounced, in his most brittle voice with excessive clarity of enunciation, somewhat reminiscent of Dame Edith Evans as Lady Bracknell, 'that my meaning was crystal-clear. Do not give such a report to a body whose recommendations are to be published.'

As always, he has completely missed the point. I explained that it is *because* the report is to be published that I am submitting the evidence. *I*, the Minister, am to be the judge of when to keep secrets, *not* the permanent officials.

I appeared to have silenced him completely. Then, after a rather long pause for thought, he enquired if he might make one more suggestion.

'Only if it's in plain English,' I replied.

'If you must do this damn silly thing,' he said, 'don't do it in this damn silly way.'

February 2nd

On the way to Number Ten this morning Bernard showed me the agenda for Cabinet. To my horror, I was informed that Cabinet was due to discuss my proposal to close down the Land Registry – or what was *described* as my proposal! I'd never heard of it till that moment. It is a scheme to transfer residual functions to the Property Services Agency. The idea is to reduce the number of autonomous government departments, in which there has been a 9¾% rise. Bernard told me I'd initialled it. God knows when – I suppose it must have been in a red box sometime over the last few weeks but I don't recall it. I've been working on the Think-Tank report and nothing else for the last week or more. Anyway, I can't remember every paper I struggle through at one or two a.m. – in fact, I can hardly remember any of them. There has to be a better system than this.

Bernard assured me that I didn't really need to know much about the proposal because his information on the grapevine, through the Private Office network, was that the proposal would go through on the nod.

[*Regrettably, this situation was not as uncommon as the reader might suppose. Because of both the pressure of time and the complexity of much legislation, Ministers frequently had to propose measures to Cabinet that they themselves either had not read or did not fully understand. Hence the distinction sometimes drawn between Ministerial policy, i.e. policies about which the Minister has strong personal views or commitments, and Ministry policy, i.e. most policy – Ed.*]

February 3rd

Today was the blackest day so far. Perhaps not only the blackest day since I became a Minister, but the blackest day since I went into politics.

I am deeply depressed.

However, I feel I must record the events of the day, and I'll do so in the order in which they occurred.

It appears that Sir Humphrey went to the usual weekly Permanent Secretaries' meeting this morning. It seems that he was ticked off by a couple of his colleagues when he revealed that I had written the draft report for the Think-Tank.

Humphrey complained to Bernard about my behaviour, it seems, and Bernard – who seems to be the only one I can totally trust – told me. Apparently Sir Frederick Stewart (Perm. Sec. of the FCO) actually said to Humphrey that once you allow a Minister to write a draft report, the next thing you know they'll be dictating policy.

Incredible!

It is true, of course. I have learned that he who drafts the document wins the day.

[*This is the reason why it was common Civil Service practice at this time to write the minutes of a meeting* BEFORE *the meeting took place. This achieves two things. First, it helps the chairman or secretary to ensure that the discussion follows the lines agreed beforehand and that the right points are made by somebody. And second, as busy men generally cannot quite remember what was agreed at meetings, it is extremely useful and convenient to lay it down in advance. Only if the conclusions reached at a meeting are radically different or diametrically opposed to what has been previously written in the minutes will the officials have to rewrite them. Thus it is that pre-written minutes can dictate the results of many meetings, regardless of what may be said or agreed by those actually present – Ed.*]

Sir Humphrey and Sir Frederick were discussing Humphrey's plan (*not* mine, I may add!) for reducing the number of autonomous government departments, when they encountered Dr Donald Hughes,[1] who overheard their conversation.

Hughes revealed that the Think-Tank recommendation accepted the idea of reducing the number of autonomous government departments. This news came as a profound shock to Sir Humphrey, because not all the Ministerial evidence has been taken – ours, for instance, has not!

However, it seems that they have reported unofficially, and clearly the report is not going to change now, no matter what we say. Dr Hughes explained to Sir Humphrey that the Central Policy Review Staff do not sully their elevated minds with anything as squalid as evidence from Ministers!

Sir Humphrey, at first, was not unhappy with Donald Hughes's news. Naturally, as an experienced civil servant, a proposal to reduce and simplify the administration of government conjured up in Humphrey's mind a picture of a large intake of new staff specifically to deal with the reductions.

However, this is not the plan at all. Humphrey informed me, at an urgently convened meeting at nine a.m. this morning [*Tautology – Ed.*] that Dr Donald Hughes had made these points:

1 That Jim Hacker is always seeking to reduce overmanning in the Civil Service.
2 That he is going to succeed, at last.
3 And that to facilitate this matter, the Treasury, the Home Office and the Civil Service Department have all proposed abolishing the Department of Administrative Affairs.
4 And that 'the PM is smiling on the plan' (his very words).

[1] Dr Donald Hughes was the Prime Minister's Senior Policy Adviser, brought into government from outside. Tough, intelligent, hard-bitten and with no love for senior civil servants.

Appalling! My job's at stake.

It seems that the PM is entranced by the idea, on the grounds that it is neat, clean, dramatic, and will be politically popular.

The plan is that all the DAA's functions will be subsumed by other departments.

And my fate? Apparently it is to be presented to the press and public that I have won through with a public-spirited self-sacrificing policy, and I'm to be kicked upstairs to the Lords.

Donald Hughes, rubbing salt in the wound, apparently described it as 'approbation, elevation and castration, all in one stroke'. It seems he suggested that I should take the title Lord Hacker of Kamikaze.

Apparently Hughes was very pleased with himself, and with this plan, presumably because of his own crusade against Civil Service extravagance, bureaucracy and waste. Ironically, I agree with him on all that – but not at the expense of *my* job, thank you very much.

This certainly confirms my instincts, that some political Cabinet in-fighting was due to start up again, and clearly we have a huge fight on our hands. Everyone's against us. The Perm. Secs of the Treasury, Home Office and Civil Service Department all stand to gain more power and influence. So do my Cabinet colleagues running those departments. And, of course, I always knew that the DAA was a political graveyard and that the PM might have been handing me a poisoned chalice – after all, I did run Martin's leadership campaign against the PM – whose motto, incidentally, is 'In Defeat, Malice – in Victory, Revenge!'

It seems that Donald Hughes, to do him justice, also pointed out that Humphrey would also be on the way out. 'There's a Job Centre in the Horseferry Road,' he had said maliciously. 'The number 19 stops right outside.'

This is the only remotely amusing thing I've heard in the last twenty-four hours. I shouldn't think Humphrey's been on a bus since he left Oxford.

So when Humphrey brought me up-to-date this morning, I was appalled. I could hardly believe it at first. I told Humphrey I was appalled.

'You're appalled?' he said. 'I'm appalled.'

Bernard said he was appalled, too.

And, there's no doubt about it, the situation is appalling.

I have no doubt that the situation is as described by Sir Humphrey as described by Donald Hughes. It rings true. And Humphrey, yesterday, saw the joint Departmental proposal made by the Treasury,

Home Office and Civil Service Department. And Hughes is very close to the PM too, so he must know what's going on.

I asked Humphrey if I'd get another job, whether or not I was sent to the Lords. And, incidentally, I shall definitely refuse a peerage if it is offered.

'There is a rumour,' replied Sir Humphrey gravely, 'of a new post. Minister with general responsibility for Industrial Harmony.'

This was the worst news yet. Industrial Harmony. That means strikes.[1]

From now on, every strike in Britain will be my fault. Marvellous!

I pondered this for some moments. My reverie was interrupted by Sir Humphrey enquiring in a sepulchral tone: 'Have you considered what might happen to *me*, Minister? I'll probably be sent to Ag. and Fish. The rest of my career dedicated to arguing about the cod quota.'

Bernard dared to smile a little smile, and Humphrey turned on him. 'And as for you, young man, if your Minister bites the dust your reputation as a flyer – such as it is – will be hit for six. You'll probably spend the rest of your career in the Vehicle Licensing Centre in Swansea.'

'My God,' said Bernard quietly.

We sat in silence, lost in our own tragic thoughts, for some considerable time. I heaved a sigh. So did Humphrey. Then Bernard.

Of course, the whole thing is Sir Humphrey's fault. Reducing the number of autonomous government departments was an idiotic proposal, playing right into the hands of our enemies. I said so. He replied that it was all my fault, because of my proposal to the Think-Tank to carry out the phased reduction of the Civil Service.

I pooh-poohed this as a ridiculous suggestion because the Think-Tank hasn't even *seen* our report yet. But Humphrey revealed that the Party sent an advance copy to the PM from Central House.

So perhaps we've both dropped ourselves in it. Anyway, there was no point in arguing about it, and I asked Humphrey for suggestions.

There was another gloomy silence.

'We could put a paper up,' he said finally.

'Up what?' I asked. Brilliant!

Humphrey asked me if *I* had any suggestions. I hadn't. We turned to Bernard.

'What do you think, Bernard?'

[1] Hacker was clearly right about this. On the same euphemistic principle, the Ministry of War was renamed the Ministry of Defence, and the Department responsible for unemployment was called the Department of Employment.

'I think it's appalling,' he repeated. A lot of use he is.

Then Humphrey proposed that we work together on this. This was a novel suggestion, to say the least. I thought his job was to work with me on all occasions. This seemed like an admission. Furthermore, his idea of our working together is generally that he tells me what to do, and I then do it. And look where it's got us!

However, I asked him what he had to suggest.

'With respect, Minister,' he began. This was too much. I told him not to use that insulting language to me ever again! Clearly he was about to imply that anything I had to say on the subject would be beneath contempt.

But Humphrey reiterated that he *really* meant that we should work together. 'I need you,' he said.

I must admit I was rather touched.

Then, to my utter astonishment, he suggested that we sent for Frank Weisel.

Humphrey is clearly a reformed character. Even though it's probably too late to matter!

'You see, Minister, if the Prime Minister is behind a scheme, Whitehall on its own cannot block it. Cabinet Ministers' schemes are easily blocked . . .' he corrected himself at once, '. . . redrafted, but the PM is another matter.'

In a nutshell, his scheme is to fight this plan in Westminster as well as Whitehall. Therefore he believes that Frank can help to mobilise the backbenchers on my behalf.

I suggested that Fleet Street might be of use, if Frank can get the press on our side. Humphrey blanched and swallowed, but to his credit agreed. 'If there is no other way, even Fleet Street . . .' he murmured.

February 4th

Frank was away yesterday. So we had the meeting with him today.

He'd just heard the news. We asked for his reaction. For the first time that I can remember, he was speechless. He just sat and shook his head sadly. I asked him what suggestions he had.

'I can't think of anything . . . I'm appalled,' he replied.

We all agreed that it was appalling.

So I took charge. 'We've got to stop flapping about like wet hens. We've got to do something to save the Department from closure. Frank, get through to the Whips' office to mobilise the backbenchers and Central House, to stop this before it starts.'

'I'm awfully sorry to quibble again, Minister, but you can't actually stop things before they start,' intervened Bernard, the wet-hen-in-chief. He's really useless in a crisis.

Frank pointed out that this idea of mine wasn't much good, as the scheme to abolish the DAA would probably be popular with backbenchers. So I pointed out that it was Humphrey's idea, anyway.

Bernard's overnight deliberations led him to propose a publicity campaign in the press, full-page ads praising the Department. He offered us some slogans: ADMINISTRATION SAVES THE NATION and RED TAPE IS FUN.

We just boggled at these ideas. So he then suggested RED TAPE HOLDS THE NATION TOGETHER.

Sometimes I really despair of Bernard.

There was a long pause, after which Humphrey remarked bleakly, 'There's no doubt about it, the writing's on the wall.'

None of us can see any real hope of averting catastrophe.

It's appalling!

February 5th

Life must go on, even while the Sword of Damocles hangs over us.

Today we had a meeting about the Europass. This was a completely new development. I've never even heard of it. Apparently there's been information about it in my boxes for the last couple of nights, but I've been too depressed and preoccupied to grasp anything I've read.

It seems that the Europass is a new European Identity Card, to be carried by all citizens of the EEC. The FCO, according to Humphrey, is willing to go along with the idea as a *quid pro quo* for a settlement over the butter mountain, the wine lake, the milk ocean, the lamb war, and the cod stink.

Apparently the PM wants me to introduce the necessary legislation.

I'm *horrified* by this.

Sir Humphrey was surprised at my reaction. He'd thought it was a good idea as I'm known to be pro-Europe, and he thinks that a Europass will simplify administration in the long run.

Frank and I tried to explain to the officials that for me to introduce such a scheme would be political suicide. The British people do not want to carry compulsory identification papers. I'll be accused of trying to bring in a police state, when I'm still not fully recovered from the fuss about the Data Base. 'Is this what we fought two world wars

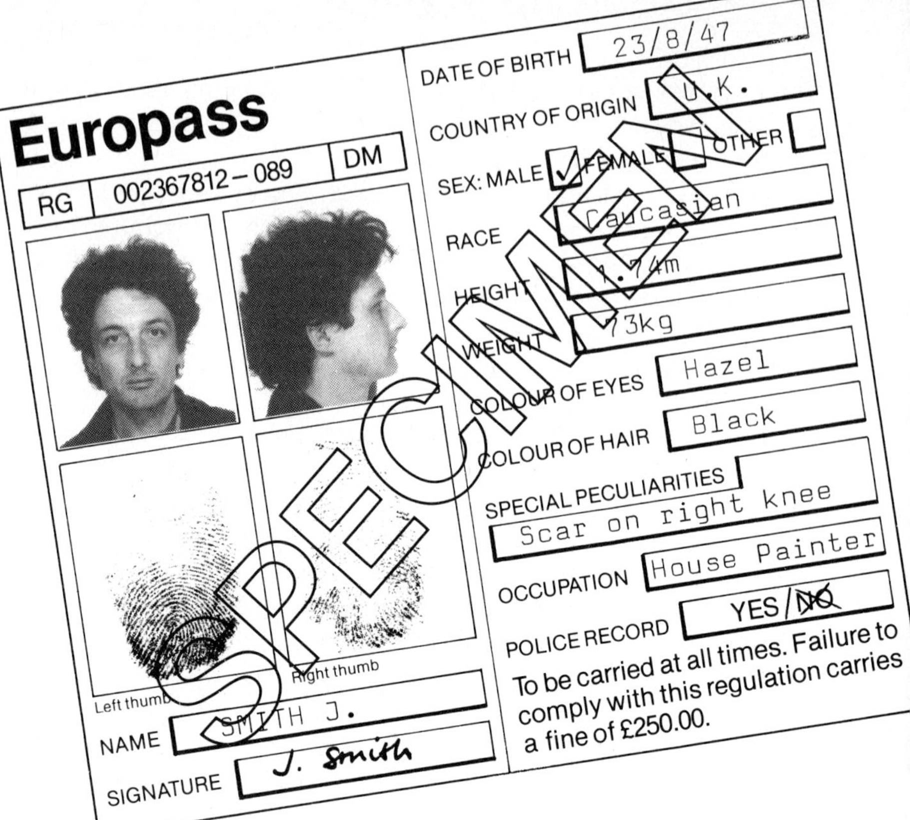

Europass

RG 002367812 – 089 DM

Left thumb

Right thumb

NAME SMITH J.

SIGNATURE J. Smith

DATE OF BIRTH 23/8/47

COUNTRY OF ORIGIN U.K.

SEX: MALE ✓ FEMALE OTHER

RACE Caucasian

HEIGHT 1.74m

WEIGHT 73kg

COLOUR OF EYES Hazel

COLOUR OF HAIR Black

SPECIAL PECULIARITIES Scar on right knee

OCCUPATION House Painter

POLICE RECORD YES / ~~NO~~

To be carried at all times. Failure to comply with this regulation carries a fine of £250.00.

SPECIMEN

for?' I can hear the backbenchers cry.

'But it's nothing more than a sort of driving licence,' said Humphrey.

'It's the last nail in my coffin,' said I.

'You might get away with calling it the Euroclub Express,' said Bernard. I told him to shut up or get out.

Frank asked why we had to introduce it, not the FCO? A good question.

'I understand,' explained Humphrey, 'that the PM did originally suggest that the FCO introduce the measure, but the Secretary of State for Foreign and Commonwealth Affairs suggested that it was a Home Office measure, and then the Home Office took the view that it is essentially an administrative matter. The PM agreed.'

Frank said, 'They're all playing pass the parcel.'

Can you blame them, when they can hear it ticking?

Humphrey then observed mournfully that the identity card bill would probably be the last action of our Department.

Frank and I, unlike the civil servants, were still puzzled that such a proposal as the Europass could even be seriously under consideration by the FCO. We can both see clearly that it is wonderful ammunition for the anti-Europeans. I asked Humphrey if the Foreign Office doesn't realise how damaging this would be to the European ideal?

'I'm sure they do, Minister,' he said. 'That's why they support it.'

This was even more puzzling, since I'd always been under the impression that the FO is pro-Europe. 'Is it or isn't it?' I asked Humphrey.

'Yes and no,' he replied of course, 'if you'll pardon the expression. The Foreign Office is pro-Europe because it is really anti-Europe. In fact the Civil Service was united in its desire to make sure the Common Market didn't work. That's why we went into it.'

This sounded like a riddle to me. I asked him to explain further. And basically, his argument was as follows: Britain has had the same foreign policy objective for at least the last five hundred years – to create a disunited Europe. In that cause we have fought with the Dutch against the Spanish, with the Germans against the French, with the French and Italians against the Germans, and with the French against the Italians and Germans. [*The Dutch rebellion against Philip II of Spain, the Napoleonic Wars, the First World War, and the Second World War – Ed.*]

In other words, divide and rule. And the Foreign Office can see no reason to change when it has worked so well until now.

I was aware of all this, naturally, but I regarded it as ancient history. Humphrey thinks that it is, in fact, current policy. It was necessary for us to break up the EEC, he explained, so we had to get inside. We had previously tried to break it up from the outside, but that didn't work. [*A reference to our futile and short-lived involvement in EFTA, the European Free Trade Association, founded in 1960 and which the UK left in 1972 – Ed.*] Now that we're in, we are able to make a complete pig's breakfast out of it. We have now set the Germans against the French, the French against the Italians, the Italians against the Dutch. . .and the Foreign Office is terribly happy. It's just like old times.

I was staggered by all of this. I thought that all of us who are publicly pro-Europe believed in the European ideal. I said this to Sir Humphrey, and he simply chuckled.

So I asked him: if we don't believe in the European ideal, why are we pushing to increase the membership?

'Same reason,' came the reply. 'It's just like the United Nations. The more members it has, the more arguments you can stir up, and the more futile and impotent it becomes.'

This all strikes me as the most appalling cynicism, and I said so.

Sir Humphrey agreed complacently. 'Yes Minister. We call it diplomacy. It's what made Britain great, you know.'

Frank, like the terrier that he is, wanted to continue worrying away at the problem of the Europass. 'How will the other EEC countries feel about having to carry identity papers? Won't they resist too?'

Sir Humphrey felt not. 'The Germans will love it, the French will ignore it, and the Italians and Irish will be too chaotic to enforce it. Only the British will resent it.' He's right, of course.

I must say that, to me, it's all beginning to look suspiciously like a plot to get rid of me. Frank doesn't subscribe to a conspiracy theory on this occasion, on the grounds that I'm to be got rid of *anyway* as my department is to be abolished.

But I've got a sneaking suspicion that the PM just wants to make absolutely sure. Frank told me not to be paranoid, but I think *he*'d be paranoid if everyone were plotting against him.

'We're on your side, Minister.' Sir Humphrey was trying to be comforting. Life is full of surprises!

Then I had an idea. I suddenly realised that Martin will be on my side. I can't imagine why I didn't think of it before. He's Foreign Secretary – and, to my certain knowledge, Martin is genuinely pro-Europe. (Humphrey calls him 'naïf'). Also I ran his campaign against the PM, and he only stands to lose if I'm squeezed out.

We've arranged a meeting with him on Monday, at the House. I can't think *how* he can help, exactly, but between us we may find some lever.

February 8th

All is well. The battle is won. My career, Humphrey's career, and the DAA have all been saved by a brilliant piece of political opportunism, of which I am extremely proud. Plus a little bit of luck, of course. But it's been a very satisfactory day.

We all gathered conspiratorially at Martin's office. He was full of his usual second-rate witticisms.

'You've done a Samson act, Jim.'

I, presumably, looked blank.

'You see, you wanted to reduce the Civil Service, and you've done it. You've pulled the whole superstructure down – and buried yourself.'

I didn't know whether I was supposed to smile, or congratulate him on his wit, or what.

Sir Humphrey, of course, couldn't wait to join the analogy game. 'A Pyrrhic victory,' he intoned mournfully, presumably to remind us all that he is a classicist.

'Any ideas?' I asked Martin.

He had none. So we all had another of our tremendous gloomy silences.

Frank, fortuitously as it turned out, continued worrying away at the puzzle of why the PM wanted to introduce a Europass. 'I don't understand it. It doesn't make sense. Why can't the PM see the damage it's going to do to the government?'

I agreed, and remarked that this Europass thing is the worst disaster to befall the government since I was made a member of the Cabinet. [*We don't think that Hacker actually meant what he seems to be saying here – Ed.*]

Martin was quite calm about the Europass. 'Everyone knows it won't happen,' he said.

Who does he mean by 'everyone'? I certainly didn't know it wouldn't happen – but then, I didn't even know it *would* happen till yesterday.

'The PM,' continued Martin, 'has to play along with it till after the Napoleon Prize is awarded.'

Apparently the Napoleon Prize is a NATO award, given once every five years. A gold medal, big ceremony in Brussels, and £100,000. The PM is the front runner. It's awarded to the statesman who has made the biggest contribution to European unity since Napoleon. [*That's if you don't count Hitler – Ed.*]

'The award committee meets in six weeks,' said Martin, 'and so obviously the PM doesn't want to rock the boat until it's in the bag.'

I think I caught Bernard mumbling to himself that you don't put boats in bags, but it was very quiet, I might have misheard, and he refused to repeat what he'd said which makes me think I didn't mishear at all.

'And,' said Martin, reaching the point at last, 'once the prize is won, the PM will obviously dump the Europass.'

I had this wonderful idea. I couldn't quite articulate it. It was slowly forming in the back of my mind. But first I needed some answers.

'Martin,' I asked. 'How many people know about the winner of the Napoleon Prize?'

'It's top secret,' he said. Naturally, I was disappointed. Top secret means that everyone knows.

But not this time, apparently. '*Top secret*, top secret,' said Martin.

I was now so excited that I was becoming incoherent. 'Don't you see?' I said. 'Backbenchers . . . leaks . . .'

A puzzled Humphrey asked me if I were referring to the Welsh Nationalist Party.

And at that moment God was on my side. The door opened, and in stepped Dr Donald Hughes. He apologised, and said he'd return later, but I stopped him. I told him that he was the very man I wanted to see, that I wanted his advice, and invited him to take a pew.

He pretended that he was eager to help me. But he warned that if it were a case of shutting stable doors after horses have bolted, even he would be powerless to help. I said, flatteringly, that I'm sure that he would not be powerless. I put it to him that I was in a serious moral dilemma – which, of course, I invented at that very moment.

My dilemma was this, I said. I told Hughes that I knew that a backbencher was planning to table a question to the PM about whether or not the Europass is to be adopted by Britain.

Hughes was immediately jumpy. 'Which backbencher? The Europass is top secret.'

'Like the winner of the Napoleon Prize?' I asked.

We eyed each other carefully – I wasn't entirely sure of my next move, but thankfully Bernard stepped in with an inspirational reply. 'I think the Minister means a hypothetical backbencher,' he said. Good old Bernard.

Hughes said that it was highly improbable that such a question would be asked.

I ignored that, and explained that if the question were to be asked, there were only two possible replies: if the PM says *yes* it would be damaging to the government in the country – but if the PM says *no* it would be even more damaging to the government in Europe. And to the PM personally – in view of the Napoleon Prize.

Hughes nodded, and waited. So I continued. 'Suppose a hypothetical Minister got wind of this hypothetical backbencher's question, in advance, what should he do?'

'The only responsible course for a loyal minister,' he said carefully, 'would be to see that the question was not tabled. That must be obvious.'

'It's a serious business trying to suppress an MP's question,' I said. Of course, he and I both knew that, as yet, there was no question and no such backbencher – but that there could be, if I chose to set it up.

'The only way to stop him,' I offered, 'might be to let the backbencher table a question asking the PM to squash rumours about the closure of the Department of Administrative Affairs.'

There it was. My offer of a deal. Out in the open. Hughes paused to consider, just for a few moments, in case he could see a way out. But there was none.

And, to his credit, he handled it superbly. At once out came all the appropriate phrases: 'But I'm sure . . . whatever made you think? . . . no question of anything but the fullest support . . .' etc.

Then Humphrey, who'd got the idea at last, moved in for the kill. 'But you said only a few days ago that the plan to abolish the Department had been put up and the PM was smiling on it.'

'Smiling *at* it,' said Donald Hughes smoothly. 'Smiling *at* it, not *on* it. The idea was ridiculous, laughable, out of the question. A joke.' Beautifully done – I take my hat off to him.

So I asked him for a minute from the PM's office, to be circulated to all departments within twenty-four hours, scotching the rumour. So that we could all share the joke.

'Do you really think it's necessary?' he asked.

'Yes,' replied Humphrey, Bernard, Frank, Martin and I. In unison.

Hughes said that in that case, he was sure it could be arranged, that it would be a pleasure, how much he'd enjoyed chatting to us all, excused himself and left. Presumably he hurried straight to Number Ten.

Game, set and match. One of my most brilliant performances. I am exceedingly pleased with myself.

Bernard asked, after Donald Hughes had gone, if Hughes can *really* fix it for us. 'Don't Prime Ministers have a mind of their own?' he asked.

'Certainly,' I said to Bernard. 'But in the words of Chuck Colson, President Nixon's henchman, when you've got them by the balls, their hearts and minds will follow.'

6
The Right to Know

February 9th
Today I had an environmental issue to deal with. A deputation of several environmentalists brought me a petition. Six fat exercise books, full of signatures. There must be thousands of signatures, if not hundreds of thousands.

They were protesting about my proposed new legislation to sort out all the existing confusions and anomalies in the present system – not that you can *call* it a system – which is a mess, a hotchpotch. Local authorities, tourist authorities, national parks, the National Trust, the Countryside Commission, the CPRE[1] are all backbiting and buckpassing and nobody knows where they are and nothing gets done. The sole purpose of the new legislation is to tidy all this up and make all these wretched committees work together.

I explained this to the deputation. 'You know what committees are?' I said. 'Always squabbling and procrastinating and wasting everyone's time.'

'*We* are a committee,' said one of them, an unprepossessing bespectacled female of indeterminate age but clear upper-middle-class Hampstead origins. She seemed rather offended.

I explained that I didn't mean *her* sort of committee; all that I was trying to do was create a new authority with clear simple procedures. Public money will be saved. It seems to me that it should be welcome to everyone.

However, these representatives of the Hampstead middle class were worried about some place called Hayward's Spinney. Apparently it is going to lose its protected status under the new scheme – like one or two other places – because it's simply not economic to administer it properly.

[1] The Council for the Protection of Rural England.

But it seems that Hayward's Spinney is regarded by some of these cranks as a vital part of Britain's heritage. 'The badgers have dwelt in it for generations,' spluttered an elderly upper-class socialist of the Michael Foot patrician ilk.

'How do you know?' I asked, simply out of curiosity.

'It said so in *The Guardian*,' said an intense young man in hobnail boots.

Some reason for believing anything! You've only got to be in public life for about a week before you start to question if the newspapers are even giving you today's date with any accuracy! However, the young man thrust a copy of *The Guardian* at me.

I looked at the story he had circled in red. Actually, what *The Guardian* said was: 'The bodgers have dwelt in it for in it for generators.'

I read it aloud, and laughed, but they appeared to have absolutely no sense of humour. Then the middle-aged lady in a brown tweed skirt that enveloped mighty hips demanded, 'How would you feel if you were going to have office blocks built all over your garden by a lot of giant badgers?'

Giant badgers? I tried not to laugh at this Monty Pythonesque vision, while another of these freaks continued self-righteously, 'There's nothing special about man, Mr Hacker. We're not above nature. We're all a part of it. Men are animals too, you know.'

Obviously I knew that already. I'd just come from the House of Commons.

Bernard helped me get rid of them after about ten minutes. I made no promises to them, and gave them the usual bromides about all views being taken into consideration at the appropriate stage. But I am concerned that no one in the Department warned me that unifying the administration of the countryside would mean removing special protected status from these blasted badgers. Not that I give a damn about badgers, but I have been allowed to tell Parliament and the press that no loss of amenity was involved.

I should take this matter up with Humphrey tomorrow.

I shall also take up the matter of why my time is being wasted with footling meetings of this kind, when I want to spend much more time meeting junior staff here, getting to know their problems, and generally finding out how to run the Department more efficiently.

[*We discovered a remarkable exchange of memos between Sir Humphrey Appleby and Bernard Woolley, written during this week – Ed.*]

**DEPARTMENT OF
ADMINISTRATIVE AFFAIRS**

From the Permanent Under-Secretary of State

B.W. ——

I gather that the Minister has been arranging for himself unsupervised meetings with junior members of the Department — Assistant Secretaries, Principals, and even right down to Higher Executive Officers. Please explain

A. 9/ii

DEPARTMENT OF ADMINISTRATIVE AFFAIRS

From the Private Secretary

Sir Humphrey

The Minister wishes to get to know members of the Department at all levels, and to understand what they do and why. B.W. Feb 9th

DEPARTMENT OF
ADMINISTRATIVE AFFAIRS

From the Permanent Under-Secretary of State

B.W. —

These meetings must be stopped at once. If the Minister talks to underlings he may learn things that we don't know ourselves. Our whole position could be undermined.

H.A. 10/ii

DEPARTMENT OF
ADMINISTRATIVE AFFAIRS

From the Private Secretary

Sir Humphrey

The Minister feels that such meetings increase our knowledge. He also has expressed a wish to run the Department better, as things are now going pretty well.

B.W. Feb. 10th

DEPARTMENT OF ADMINISTRATIVE AFFAIRS

From the Permanent Under-Secretary of State

B.W. —

I think you ought to be very careful. I am puzzled by your recent memos and am wondering if the Minister is being entirely straightforward. I am bound to say that you should give urgent and active consideration to this matter, and ask yourself if you have considered all the implications. Ministerial activities in this area are liable to have consequences which could be unfortunate, or even regrettable.

A.A.
11/ii

[*Translation: 'Considered all the implications' means 'You are making a complete balls-up of your job.' 'Consequences which could be unfortunate, or even regrettable' means 'You are in imminent danger of being transferred to the War Graves Commission' – Ed.*]

DEPARTMENT OF ADMINISTRATIVE AFFAIRS

From the Private Secretary

Sir Humphrey

I should be grateful for further advice on this matter.

B.W. Feb 11th

DEPARTMENT OF ADMINISTRATIVE AFFAIRS

From the Permanent Under-Secretary of State

B.W. — Please note the following points:

1. You refer to increased knowledge. Desirable and worthy though this ambition is, please remember that it is folly to increase your knowledge at the expense of your authority.
2. When a Minister actually starts to run his Department, things are not going pretty well. They are going pretty badly. It is not the Minister's job to run the Department. It is my job, for which I have had twenty-five years' training and practice.
3. If the Minister were allowed to run the Department we should have:
   (i) chaos
   (ii) innovations
   (iii) public debate
   (iv) outside scrutiny.
4. A Minister has three functions:
   (i) He is an Advocate. He makes the Department's actions seem plausible to Parliament and the public.
   (ii) He is Our Man in Westminster, steering our legislation through parliament. (N.B. Ours, not his.)
   (iii) He is our Breadwinner. His duty is to fight in Cabinet for the money we need to do our job.

PLEASE NOTE: It's not his function to review departmental procedures and practices with Principals and Higher Executive Officers.

HA. 12/ii

SIR BERNARD WOOLLEY RECALLS:[1]
Being rather young and green at this time, I was still somewhat puzzled about how to put Sir Humphrey's advice into practice, as the Minister made these diary appointments for himself and was getting thoroughly on top of his work.

I sought a meeting with Sir Humphrey, and began it by attempting to explain that I couldn't prevent the Minister from doing what he wanted if he had the time.

Sir Humphrey was thunderously angry! He asked me why the Minister had free time. He told me to ensure that the Minister *never* had free time, and that it was my fault if he had. My job was to create activity. The Minister must make speeches, go on provincial visits, foreign junkets, meet deputations, work through mountains of red boxes, and be forced to deal with crises, emergencies and panics.

If the Minister made spaces in his diary, I was to fill them up again. And I was to make sure that he spent his time where he was not under our feet and would do no damage – the House of Commons for instance.

However, I do recall that I managed to redeem myself a little when I was able to inform Sir Humphrey that the Minister was – even as we spoke – involved in a completely trivial meeting about preserving badgers in Warwickshire.

In fact, he was so pleased that I suggested that I should try to find some other threatened species with which to involve the Minister. Sir Humphrey replied that I need not look far – Private Secretaries who could not occupy their Ministers were a threatened species.

February 10th

This morning I raised the matter of the threatened furry animals, and the fact that I told the House that no loss of amenity was involved.

Sir Humphrey said that I'd told the House no such thing. The speech had contained the words: 'No *significant* loss of amenity.'

I thought this was the same thing, but Sir Humphrey disabused me. 'On the contrary, there's all the difference in the world, Minister. Almost anything can be attacked as a loss of amenity and almost anything can be defended as not a significant loss of amenity. One must appreciate the significance of *significant*.'

I remarked that six books full of signatures could hardly be called insignificant. Humphrey suggested I look inside them. I did, and to my utter astonishment I saw that there were a handful of signatures in each book, about a hundred altogether at the most. A very cunning ploy – a press photo of a petition of six fat books is so much more

[1] In conversation with the Editors.

impressive than a list of names on a sheet of Basildon Bond.

And indeed, the publicity about these badgers could really be rather damaging.

However, Humphrey had organised a press release which says that the relevant spinney is merely deregistered, not threatened; that badgers are very plentiful all over Warwickshire; that there is a connection between badgers and brucellosis; and which reiterates that there is no 'significant loss of amenity'.

We called in the press officer, who agreed with Humphrey that it was unlikely to make the national press except a few lines perhaps on an inside page of *The Guardian*. The consensus at our meeting was that it is only the urban intellectual middle class who worry about the preservation of the countryside because they don't have to live in it. They just read about it. Bernard says their protest is rooted more in Thoreau than in anger. I am beginning to get a little tired of his puns.

So we'd dealt satisfactorily with the problems of the animal kingdom. Now I went on to raise the important fundamental question: Why was I not told the full facts before I made the announcement to the House?

Humphrey's reason was astonishing. 'Minister,' he said blandly, 'there are those who have argued – and indeed very cogently – that on occasion there are some things it is better for the Minister not to know.'

I could hardly believe my ears. But there was more to come.

'Minister,' he continued unctuously, 'your answers in the House and at the press conference were superb. You were convinced, and therefore convincing. Could you have spoken with the same authority if the ecological pressure group had been badgering you?'

Leaving aside this awful pun, which in any case I suspect might have been unintentional despite Humphrey's pretensions to wit, I was profoundly shocked by this open assertion of his right to keep me, the people's representative, in ignorance. Absolutely monstrous. I told him so.

He tried to tell me that it is in my best interests, a specious argument if ever I heard one. I told him that it was intolerable, and must not occur again.

And I intend to see that it doesn't.

February 16th

For the past week Frank Weisel and I have been hard at work on a plan to reorganise the Department. One of the purposes was to have assorted officials at all levels reporting to me.

Today I attempted to explain the new system to Sir Humphrey, who effectively refused to listen.

Instead, he interrupted as I began, and told me that he had something to say to me that I might not like to hear. He said it as if this were something new!

As it happens, I'd left my dictaphone running, and his remarks were recorded for posterity. What he actually said to me was: 'Minister, the traditional allocation of executive responsibilities has always been so determined as to liberate the Ministerial incumbent from the administrative minutiae by devolving the managerial functions to those whose experience and qualifications have better formed them for the performance of such humble offices, thereby releasing their political overlords for the more onerous duties and profound deliberations that are the inevitable concomitant of their exalted position.'

I couldn't imagine why he thought I wouldn't want to hear that. Presumably he thought it would upset me – but how can you be upset by something you don't understand a word of?

Yet again, I begged him to express himself in plain English. This request always surprises him, as he is always under the extraordinary impression that he has done so.

Nevertheless, he thought hard for a moment and then, plainly, opted for expressing himself in words of one syllable.

'You are not here to run this Department,' he said.

I was somewhat taken aback. I remarked that I think I am, and the public thinks so too.

'With respect,' he said, and I restrained myself from punching him in the mouth, 'you are wrong and they are wrong.'

He then went on to say that it is *his* job to run the Department. And that my job is to make policy, get legislation enacted and – above all – secure the Department's budget in Cabinet.

'Sometimes I suspect,' I said to him, 'that the budget is all you really care about.'

'It is rather important,' he answered acidly. 'If nobody cares about the budget we could end up with a Department so small that even a Minister could run it.'

I'm sure he's not supposed to speak to me like this.

However, I wasn't upset because I'm sure of my ground. 'Humphrey,' I enquired sternly, 'are we about to have a fundamental disagreement about the nature of democracy?'

As always, he back-pedalled at once when seriously under fire. 'No,

Minister,' he said in his most oily voice, giving his now familiar impression of Uriah Heep, 'we are merely having a demarcation dispute. I am only saying that the menial chore of running a Department is beneath you. You were fashioned for a nobler calling.'

Of course, the soft soap had no effect on me. I insisted on action, now! To that end, we left it that he would look at my reorganisation plan. He promised to do his best to put it into practice, and will set up a committee of enquiry with broad terms of reference so that at the end of the day we can take the right decisions based on long-term considerations. He argued that this was preferable to rushing prematurely into precipitate and possibly ill-conceived actions which might have unforeseen repercussions. This seems perfectly satisfactory to me; he has conceded the need for wide-ranging reforms, and we might as well be sure of getting them right.

Meanwhile, while I was quite happy to leave all the routine paperwork to Humphrey and his officials, from now on I was to have direct access to *all* information. Finally, I made it clear that I never again wished to hear the phrase, 'there are some things it is better for a Minister not to know.'

February 20th

Saturday today, and I've been at home in the constituency.

I'm very worried about Lucy. [*Hacker's daughter, eighteen years old at this time – Ed.*] She really does seem to be quite unbalanced sometimes. I suppose it's all my fault. I've spent little enough time with her over the years, pressure of work and all that, and it's obviously no coincidence that virtually all my successful colleagues in the House have highly acrimonious relationships with their families and endlessly troublesome adolescent children.

But it can't all be my fault. *Some* of it must be her own fault! Surely!

She was out half the night and came down for a very late breakfast, just as Annie and I were starting an early lunch. She picked up the *Mail* with a gesture of disgust – solely because it's not the *Socialist Worker*, or *Pravda*, I suppose.

I had glanced quickly through all the papers in the morning, as usual, and a headline on a small story on an inside page of *The Guardian* gave me a nasty turn. HACKER THE BADGER BUTCHER. The story was heavily slanted against me and in favour of the sentimental wet liberals – not surprising really, every paper has to pander to its typical reader.

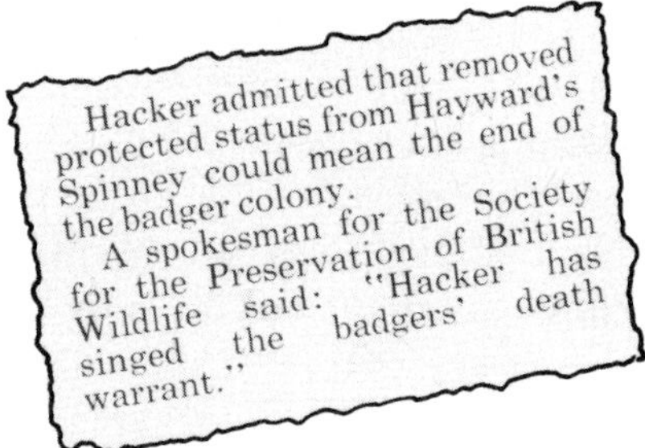
Hacker admitted that removed protected status from Hayward's Spinney could mean the end of the badger colony.
A spokesman for the Society for the Preservation of British Wildlife said: "Hacker has singed the badgers' death warrant."

Good old *Grauniad.*

I nobly refrained from saying to Lucy, 'Good afternoon' when she came down, and from making a crack about a sit-in when she told us she'd been having a lie-in.

However, I *did* ask her why she was so late home last night, to which she replied, rather pompously, 'There are some things it is better for a father not to know.' 'Don't *you* start,' I snapped, which, not surprisingly, puzzled her a little.

She told me she'd been out with the trots. I was momentarily sympathetic and suggested she saw the doctor. Then I realised she meant the Trotskyites. I'd been slow on the uptake because I didn't know she was a Trotskyite. Last time we talked she'd been a Maoist.

'Peter's a Trot,' she explained.

'Peter?' My mind was blank.

'You've only met him about fifteen times,' she said in her most scathing tones, the voice that teenage girls specially reserve for when they speak to their fathers.

Then Annie, who could surely see that I was trying to work my way through five red boxes this weekend, asked me to go shopping with her at the 'Cash and Carry', to unblock the kitchen plughole, and mow the lawn. When I somewhat irritably explained to her about the boxes, she said they could wait!

'Annie,' I said, 'it may have escaped your notice that I am a Minister of the Crown. A member of Her Majesty's Government. I do a *fairly* important job.'

Annie was strangely unsympathetic. She merely answered that I have twenty-three thousand civil servants to help me, whereas she had none. 'You can play with your memos later,' she said. 'The drains need fixing now.'

I didn't even get round to answering her, as at that moment Lucy stretched across me and spilled marmalade off her knife all over the cabinet minutes. I tried to scrape it off, but merely succeeded in buttering the minutes as well.

I told Lucy to get a cloth, a simple enough request, and was astounded by the outburst that it provoked. 'Get it yourself,' she snarled. 'You're not in Whitehall now, you know. "Yes Minister" . . . "No Minister" . . . "Please may I lick your boots, Minister?"'

I was speechless. Annie intervened on my side, though not as firmly as I would have liked. 'Lucy, darling,' she said in a tone of mild reproof, 'that's not fair. Those civil servants are always kowtowing to Daddy, but they never take any real notice of him.'

This was too much. So I explained to Annie that only two days ago I won a considerable victory at the Department. And to prove it I showed her the pile of five red boxes stuffed full of papers.

She didn't think it proved anything of the sort. 'For a short while you were getting the better of Sir Humphrey Appleby, but now they've snowed you under again.'

I thought she'd missed the point. I explained my reasoning: that Humphrey had said to me, *in so many words*, that there are some things that it's better for a Minister not to know, which means that he hides things from me. Important things, perhaps. So I have now insisted that I'm told *everything* that goes on in the Department.

However, her reply made me rethink my situation. She smiled at me with genuine love and affection, and said:

'Darling, how did you get to be a Cabinet Minister? You're such a clot.'

Again I was speechless.

Annie went on, 'Don't you see, you've played right into his hands? He must be utterly delighted. You've given him an open invitation to swamp you with useless information.'

I suddenly saw it all with new eyes. I dived for the red boxes – they contained feasibility studies, technical reports, past papers of assorted committees, stationery requisitions . . . junk!

It's Catch-22. Those bastards. Either they give you so little information that you don't know the facts, or so much information that you can't *find* them.

You can't win. They get you coming and going.

February 21st

The contrasts in a Minister's life are supposed by some people to keep you sane and ordinary and feet-on-the-ground. I think they're making me schizoid.

All week I'm protected and cosseted and cocooned. My every wish is somebody's command. (Not on matters of real substance of course, but in little everyday matters.) My letters are written, my phone is answered, my opinion is sought, I'm waited on hand and foot and I'm driven everywhere by chauffeurs, and everyone addresses me with the utmost respect as if I were a kind of God.

But this is all on government business. The moment I revert to party business or private life, the whole apparatus deserts me. If I go to a party meeting, I must get myself there, by bus if necessary; if I go home on constituency business, no secretary accompanies me; if I have a party speech to make, there's no one to type it out for me. So every weekend I have to adjust myself to doing the washing up and unblocking the plughole after five days of being handled like a priceless cut-glass antique.

And this weekend, although I came home on Friday night on the train, five red boxes arrived on Saturday morning in a chauffeur-driven car!

Today I awoke, having spent a virtually sleepless night pondering over what Annie had said to me. I staggered down for breakfast, only to find – to my amazement – a belligerent Lucy lying in wait for me. She'd found yesterday's *Guardian* and had been reading the story about the badgers.

'There's a story about you here, Daddy,' she said accusingly.

I said I'd read it. Nonetheless she read it out to me. 'Hacker the badger butcher,' she said.

'Daddy's read it, darling,' said Annie, loyally. As if stone-deaf, Lucy read the whole story aloud. I told her it was a load of rubbish, she looked disbelieving, so I decided to explain in detail.

'One: I am not a badger butcher. Two: the badger is not an endangered species. Three: the removal of protective status does not necessarily mean the badgers will be killed. Four: if a few badgers have to be sacrificed for the sake of a master plan that will save Britain's natural heritage – tough!'

Master plan is always a bad choice of phrase, particularly to a generation brought up on Second World War films. 'Ze master plan, mein Führer,' cried my darling daughter, giving a Nazi salute. 'Ze end justifies ze means, does it?'

Apart from the sheer absurdity of a supporter of the Loony Left having the nerve to criticise someone *else* for believing that the end justifies the means – which I don't or not necessarily, anyway – she is really making a mountain out of a ridiculous molehill.

'It's because badgers haven't got votes, isn't it?' This penetrating question completely floored me. I couldn't quite grasp what she was on about.

'If badgers had votes you wouldn't be exterminating them. You'd be up there at Hayward's Spinney, shaking paws and kissing cubs. Ingratiating yourself the way you always do. Yuk!'

Clearly I have not succeeded in ingratiating myself with my own daughter.

Annie intervened again. 'Lucy,' she said, rather too gently I thought, 'that's not a very nice thing to say.'

'But it's true, isn't it?' said Lucy.

Annie said: 'Ye-e-es, it's true . . . but well, he's in politics. Daddy *has* to be ingratiating.'

Thanks a lot.

'It's got to be stopped,' said Lucy. Having finished denouncing me, she was now instructing me.

'Too late.' I smiled nastily. 'The decision's been taken, dear.'

'I'm going to stop it, then,' she said.

Silly girl. 'Fine,' I said. 'That should be quite easy. Just get yourself adopted as a candidate, win a general election, serve with distinction on the back benches, be appointed a Minister and repeal the act. No problem. Of course, the badgers might be getting on a bit by then.'

She flounced out and, thank God, stayed out for the rest of the day.

[*Meanwhile, Bernard Woolley was becoming increasingly uneasy about keeping secrets from the Minister. He was finding it difficult to accustom himself to the idea that civil servants apply the 'need to know' principle that is the basis of all security activities. Finally he sent a memo to Sir Humphrey, asking for a further explanation as to why the Minister should not be allowed to know whatever he wants to know. The reply is printed opposite – Ed.*]

DEPARTMENT OF ADMINISTRATIVE AFFAIRS

From the Permanent Under-Secretary of State

B.W. -

This country is governed by ministers making decisions from the various alternative proposals which we offer them.

If they had all the facts, they would see many other possibilities, some of which would not be in the public interest. Nonetheless, they might formulate their own plans instead of choosing from the two or three which we put up.

So long as we formulate the proposals, we can guide them towards a correct decision.

We in the Service are not foolish or misguided enough to believe that there is one single correct solution to any problem. However, it is our public duty to guide the Minister towards what we like to call "the common ground".

In order to guide the Minister towards the common ground, key words should be inserted with a proposal to make it attractive:

Ministers will generally accept proposals which contain the words simple, quick, popular, and cheap.

Ministers will generally throw out proposals which contain the words complicated, lengthy, expensive and controversial.

Above all, if you wish to describe a proposal in a way that guarantees that a Minister will reject it, describe it as courageous.

Remember, guiding ministers in this fashion is what has made Britain what she is today.

AA. 22/ii

[*It is worth examining Sir Humphrey Appleby's choice of words in this memo. The phrase 'the common ground', for example, was much used by senior civil servants after two changes in government in the first four years of the 1970s. It seemed to mean policies that the Civil Service can pursue without disturbance to the party in power. 'Courageous' as used in this context is an even more damning word than 'controversial'. 'Controversial' only means 'this will lose you votes'. 'Courageous' means 'this will lose you the election' – Ed.*]

February 22nd

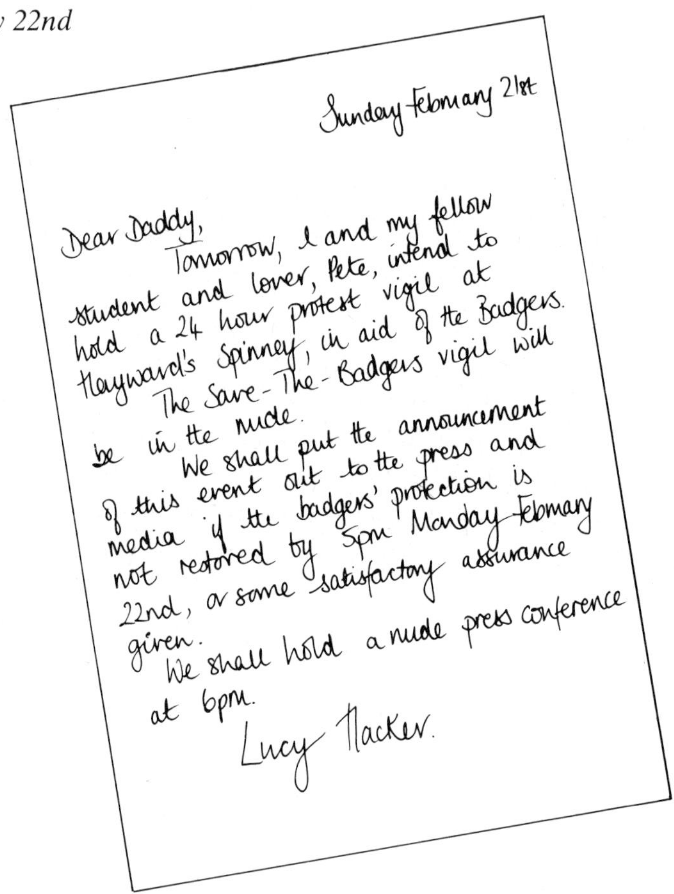

Sunday February 21st

Dear Daddy,

Tomorrow, I and my fellow student and lover, Pete, intend to hold a 24 hour protest vigil at Hayward's Spinney, in aid of the Badgers.

The Save-The-Badgers vigil will be in the nude.

We shall put the announcement of this event out to the press and media if the badgers' protection is not restored by 5pm Monday February 22nd, or some satisfactory assurance given.

We shall hold a nude press conference at 6pm.

Lucy Hacker.

[*The above letter was found by Bernard Woolley when he opened Hacker's boxes in the office on Monday 22 February. The envelope was addressed to 'Daddy' but rules state that Private Secretaries open every letter of every classification up to and including* TOP SECRET, *unless specifically marked* PERSONAL. *This was a letter not marked*

PERSONAL. *Hacker's diary continues – Ed.*]

This afternoon seemed to last an eternity. I think I've more or less got over the slings and arrows of outrageous fortune, but it was one of the worst afternoons of my political life so far. However, I shall relate it from the start. Firstly, there was Jak's cartoon in the *Standard.*

Then, on my return from Cabinet Committee after lunch, Bernard and Humphrey edged into the office looking extremely anxious. I asked if anything was wrong.

For the next four minutes they appeared to speak in riddles.

'Shall we say, a slight embarrassment,' said Sir Humphrey.

'How slight?' I asked.

First he rambled on about not wishing to overstate the case or suggest that there was any cause for undue alarm, but nevertheless . . . etc. etc. I told him to get on with it, he told me he had a confession to make, and I told him to make a clean breast of it.

'Not the happiest of phrases, in the circumstances,' he replied enigmatically. I still hadn't the foggiest idea what he was talking about, although it was soon to become only too clear.

But Humphrey couldn't find a way to tell me the bad news. Extraordinary. First he said there was to be a twenty-four-hour protest vigil in Hayward's Spinney, conducted by a girl student and her boyfriend. I could see no problem in two irresponsible layabouts trying – and failing – to attract attention to themselves.

And like an idiot, I said so. (If there's one lesson I learned today it is not to shoot from the hip. Wait until you know the full facts before giving *any* response, if you don't want to finish up looking like a proper Charlie.)

But I got an attack of verbal diarrhoea. 'Nobody's interested,' I said. 'Everyone's fed up with these ghastly students. They're just exhibitionists, you know.'

'In this case,' remarked Sir Humphrey, suddenly becoming less enigmatic, 'they seem to have something to exhibit. It is to be a nude protest vigil.'

This did seem to present a problem. It would clearly attract considerable press interest, and could even get onto the front pages of the tabloids. Regrettably, however, Humphrey hadn't given me the full picture, so I went on and on talking, making myself seem more idiotic every minute. 'Really, I don't know what gets into these students. Appalling. Quite shameless. And it's their parents' fault. Don't bring them up properly, let them run wild and feed them all this trendy middle-class anti-establishment nonsense.' Then I wittered on about the lack of authority nowadays, and how all this student anarchy is a shocking indictment of their parents' lack of discipline.

At this point Humphrey was kind enough to reveal to me that the student's name was Miss Hacker. For a moment I thought it was a coincidence. And then the penny dropped. I've never felt so foolish in my whole life. I'm sure (at least I *think* I'm sure) that Humphrey didn't intend to make any humiliation as complete as possible. But he succeeded. And I'll get him for it one day!

After I picked myself up off the floor, I expressed the hope that the press might not think it worth going all the way to Warwickshire. Even as I spoke I knew I was talking rubbish – for a story like this the press would go all the way to the South Pole.

Humphrey and Bernard just looked pityingly at me, and then showed me the letter.

I noted that Lucy was giving out the press release at five p.m. Very professional. Misses the evening papers, which not too many people read, and therefore makes all the dailies. She's learned *something* from being a politician's daughter.

Then Bernard said that he thought he'd better mention that Lucy was ringing up in ten minutes, from a call-box, for an answer.

I asked how we could kill the story. Silence from them both. 'Advise me,' I said.

'What about a bit of parental authority and discipline?' suggested Sir Humphrey. I told him not to be silly.

'If you could make her listen to reason . . .' volunteered Bernard.

I explained to him that she is a sociology student.

'Oh I see,' he said sadly.

Another long pause for thought. Then I suggested calling the police.

Humphrey shook his head, and composed the inevitable headline: MINISTER SETS POLICE ON NUDE DAUGHTER.

'I'm not sure that *completely* kills the story, Minister,' he said.

We sat in one of our tragic silences. Occasional sighs filled the room. Then Humphrey suddenly perked up. 'What if . . .' he said.

'Yes?' I said hopefully.

'What if . . .' he said again, '. . . I looked at the files?'

I'm ashamed to say that I completely lost my temper with him. 'Bloody marvellous!' I shouted. 'Is that what you get over thirty thousand a year for? My daughter's about to get herself all over the front page of the *Sun* and probably page three as well, and all you can think of is the *files*! Brilliant!'

He waited till I finished yelling. 'Nevertheless . . .' he said.

'They're all out there,' said Bernard, quickly indicating the Private Office. Humphrey disappeared as fast as he could, before I could shout at him again.

Bernard and I gazed at each other in despair. 'I wonder what sort of angle they'll take?' I said.

'Wide angle, I should think.' I glared at him. 'Oh, I see what you mean. Sorry.'

All I could think of was the fun the Opposition was going to have with this, next time I had to face questions in the House. 'Does the proud father want to make a statement?' 'Is the Minister's family getting too much exposure?' 'Did the Minister try to conduct a cover-up?' Or even: 'Does the Minister run the Department of Administrative Affairs any better than he runs his family?'

I mentioned the last question to Bernard, because it is my Achilles' heel. I added bitterly that I supposed Bernard would want me to tell the world that Sir Humphrey runs the Department.

Bernard seemed genuinely shocked.

'Certainly not, Minister, not I,' he said indignantly. 'I am your Private Secretary.'

'You mean,' I enquired disbelievingly, 'that when the chips are down, you'll be on my side, not Humphrey's?'

Bernard answered very simply: 'Minister, it is my job to see that the chips stay up!'

[*This is, in fact, a precise definition of the Private Secretary's role – Ed.*]

At that moment Lucy rang in. She was in a call-box. I grabbed the phone. First I tried bluffing. 'I got your little note,' I said, trying to laugh it off. 'You know, for a moment I was taken in. I thought it was serious.' My little laugh sounded false even to me.

'It is serious,' she replied coldly. 'Pete and I are just going to ring the Exchange Telegraph and Press Association, and then we're off to the Spinney.'

Then I grovelled. I begged her to think of the damage to me. She replied that it was the badgers who were going to be exterminated, not I.

She's quite wrong about that! This could have been the end of a promising career.

It was clear that she was about to go ahead with her dreadful plan, because I couldn't change my policy on her account, when Humphrey came running through the door waving a file. I've never seen him run before. He was burbling on about a new development and asked if he could speak to Lucy.

He took the phone, opened the file and began to explain his finding. 'I have just come upon the latest report from the Government's Wildlife Inspectors. It throws a new light on the whole issue.'

He went on to explain that, apparently, there is *no* badger colony in Hayward's Spinney. Apparently the wording of the report says: 'The last evidence of badger habitation – droppings, freshly-turned earth, etc. – was recorded eleven years ago.'

Lucy was plainly as astonished as Bernard and I. I was listening in on my other phone. So was Bernard, on his. She asked how come the newspaper had said badgers were there. Humphrey explained that the story about the poor badgers had been leaked to the press, untruthfully, by a local property developer.

Lucy was immediately willing to believe Humphrey. As far as the Trots are concerned, property developers are Satan's representatives on earth. She asked for the explanation.

'The Local Authority have plans to use the Spinney to build a new College of Further Education, but the developer wants to buy it for offices and luxury flats.'

'But,' interrupted Lucy, 'if it's protected, he can't.'

'No,' agreed Sir Humphrey, 'but nor can the Council. And he knows that, if they can't, they'll spend the money on something else. Then, in twelve months, he'll move in, show that there's no badgers after all, get the protection removed and build his offices.'

From the complete silence, I could tell that Lucy was profoundly shocked. Then Humphrey added: 'It's common practice among property developers. Shocking isn't it?'

I had no idea Humphrey felt this way about property developers. I had thought he rather liked them.

Lucy asked Humphrey if there was any wildlife at all in the Spinney.

'Yes, there is some,' said Humphrey, looking through the file. 'It's apparently been used as a rubbish dump by people from Birmingham, so there are lots of rats.'

'Rats,' she said quietly. Lucy hates rats.

'Yes, thousands of them,' said Humphrey and added generously, 'Still, I suppose they're wildlife too, in their way.' He paused and then remarked: 'It would be a pity to play into the developer's hands, wouldn't it?'

'I suppose it would,' she answered. Clearly the Save-the-Badgers vigil was off!

Humphrey added, with great warmth and total hypocrisy: 'But do let me say how much I respect your views and commitment.'

She didn't ask to speak to me again. She just rang off. The crisis was over as suddenly as it had begun. There was no way she was going to conduct a nude love-in with lots of rats in the vicinity – other than the press, of course.

I congratulated Humphrey profusely. 'It was nothing, Minister,' he said self-effacingly, 'it was all in the files.'

I was amazed by the whole thing. What a cunning bastard that property developer must be. I asked Humphrey to show me the report.

Suddenly he became his old evasive self. He told me it wasn't awfully interesting. Again I asked to see it. He held it behind his back like a guilty schoolboy.

Then I had an extraordinary insight. I asked him if the story were true. He claimed he didn't understand my question. So I asked him, again, clearly, if there had been one word of truth in that amazingly convenient story which he had just told Lucy.

He eyed me, and then enquired slowly and carefully: 'Do you really want me to answer that question, Minister? Don't answer hastily.'

It was a good question. A very good question. I could think of no advantage in knowing the truth, if my suspicions were correct. And a huge disadvantage – I would be obliged to be dishonest with Lucy, something I have never done and will never do!

'No,' I said after a few moments, 'um, Humphrey, don't bother to answer.'

'Quite so,' he said, as smug as I've ever seen him. 'Perhaps you would care to note that there *are* some things that it is better for a Minister not to know.'

7

Jobs for the Boys

[*At the beginning of March Jim Hacker came within a hair's-breadth of involving himself in a scandal that would have rocked the government and brought an ignominious and premature end to his political career. Ironically Hacker would have found himself taking responsibility for events with which he had no real connection or involvement – but for which, as Minister, he would have been answerable – Ed.*]

March 2nd

I arrived at the office in a rather good mood today. I'd done all my boxes. I was feeling thoroughly on top of the job. I'd handled all my PQs [*Parliamentary Questions – Ed.*] rather well yesterday, given a good speech last night at a dinner, and was looking forward to a broadcast that I'm due to make tomorrow. All splendid publicity. I find that people are at last beginning to know who I am, as a result of the high profile I've been managing recently.

I asked Bernard what the broadcast discussion would be about. NATO, I thought. Bernard said that, in fact, it would be about co-partnership in industry.

I knew it was something like that. Some sort of partnership, at any rate.

The discussion would contain the usual compulsory BBC ingredients – one politician, one employer and one trades unionist.

I noticed that the trades unionist in question was Joe Morgan, who had been the TUC representative on the Solihull project. I remarked that this was good, because it meant we could talk about the project on the air.

To my surprise, this rather non-controversial remark was greeted with much anxiety by Sir Humphrey.

'Minister, you're not proposing to refer to the Solihull project on the air?'

'I certainly am,' I said. 'It's a shining example of a successful collaboration between government and private industry.'

'Why do you say that?' he asked.

For a moment, I couldn't think why. Then I remembered. 'Because you said it was,' I pointed out. 'Why? Have you changed your mind?'

'No,' he said carefully, 'but . . . I would be much happier if you omitted such references from the broadcast.'

'Why?' I asked.

He said it was premature. I pointed out that work started on the project six months ago, so it could not possibly be described as premature.

'Precisely,' he said, 'rather out of date in fact.'

Remarkable! Premature *and* out of date?

Humphrey amended this foolishness instantly. He simply meant 'untimely', he claimed. So again, I asked him *why*?

'What I mean is, don't you think it will be rather uninteresting to the general public?' he whined.

I couldn't see why. It's an example of partnership in industry that is really happening. Now. *Extremely* interesting. I said so.

Humphrey seemed to be getting desperate. 'Quite so, Minister,' he said. 'It is *so* interesting, in fact, that there is a danger that it will obscure the main point that you wanted to make on the broadcast.'

'What is my main point?' I asked, suddenly unable to remember.

Humphrey also seemed to go blank. 'Bernard, what is the Minister's main point?'

Bernard reminded us. 'That private projects are more socially responsible with government money, and government projects are more efficient with private investment.'

This was precisely my main point. And reference to the Solihull project will obviously underline it. Humphrey really is a wet blanket. He just goes around stirring up apathy.

But he was still not satisfied. 'Minister,' he persisted. 'I must advise you very seriously with all the earnestness at my command that you do not refer to the Solihull project on the air tomorrow.'

Again I asked why? Again he dodged. But, by now, I had guessed. 'Could it be,' I enquired coldly, 'that you are planning to take all the credit for this scheme at next month's European Convention of Government Administration?'

Humphrey said, 'I beg your pardon?' – in other words, he didn't deny it! So I knew I was right. And I really tore him off a strip.

'Your keynote speech will be well reported, won't it? Well, let me explain some facts of life, Humphrey. Politicians are the ones who are ultimately responsible to the people, and it is we who get the credit. Not civil servants.'

Humphrey intervened. He assured me that he would be only too happy for me to take the credit for this project, as long as it wasn't tomorrow. Liar!

I brushed this procrastination aside. 'Humphrey,' I told him firmly, 'I am not going to fall for it. I am going to make all the political capital I can out of this Solihull project – I know a good thing when I see one.'

[*Hacker was completely mistaken. Sir Humphrey Appleby was trying to hush up all references to the Solihull project, with very good reason. Later that day Bernard Woolley, who had realised that there was more to this situation than met Hacker's eye, sought an interview with Sir Humphrey – Ed.*]

SIR BERNARD WOOLLEY RECALLS:[1]

It was clear to me that Sir Humphrey Appleby was engaged in a cover-up of one sort or another. However, I was adamant that I needed to be fully informed about this matter, as it did not seem possible for a £74 million building project on a nine-acre site in the middle of one of our largest cities to be swept under the carpet. Even if the brush were to be wielded by Sir Humphrey Appleby.

Sir Humphrey told me that he intended to try to use the Official Secrets Act. I remarked that I couldn't see how the project could be kept secret, as it was so big.

'It's a big secret,' replied Sir Humphrey.

I could also see no way to invoke the Official Secrets Act, when everybody knew about the project. I was young and green and had not yet fully realised that the Official Secrets Act is not to protect secrets but to protect officials.

Sir Humphrey attempted to explain his evasiveness by saying that, as the Minister had not enquired into the background of the Solihull project, he didn't wish to know. And it was, of course, standard Civil Service practice not to bother a Minister with information about which he had not enquired.

I took my courage in both hands, and indicated that I might hint to the Minister that I believed that there was a scandal connected with the Solihull project. Naturally, I made it clear to Sir Humphrey that I might *not* do so were I myself to be put more fully in the picture.

Sir Humphrey then came clean, rather reluctantly. I learned that the Solihull project had been set up by Sir Humphrey, acting for the DAA in partnership with Michael Bradley of Sloane Enterprises. This had happened long before my promotion to the Private Office.

Subsequently the Solihull Report came in, containing a paragraph casting

[1] In conversation with the Editors.

doubt on the financial soundness of Sloane Enterprises and Mr Bradley. [*'Casting doubt on the financial soundness' means that Bradley was probably about to go bankrupt' – Ed.*]

However, by the time the Report came out, Sir Humphrey was so committed to Bradley that it seemed a better risk to him to see the project through.

Now that I knew the full facts I was in an invidious position. Naturally I could not tell the Minister something that I had learned in confidence from the Perm. Sec. Equally, I had a duty to prevent my Minister involving himself in this matter if I could. It seemed that all I could do was to remonstrate with Sir Humphrey.

I explained that if the Minister knew the full facts he would certainly not be so foolish as to broadcast them. But Sir Humphrey insisted that as a matter of principle, Ministers should never know more than they need to know. Like secret agents. Because they may be captured and tortured.

'By terrorists?' I asked.

'By the BBC,' he replied. He also explained that the situation was not lost. The bank was dithering about whether or not to foreclose – a potential disaster. He was to have lunch that week with the Bank's Chairman, Sir Desmond Glazebrook. So, meanwhile, there must be no mention of the Solihull project on the air or to the press.

I was getting exceedingly worried about my part in what appeared to be a cover-up. I explained this to the Perm. Sec., who insisted that this was not a cover-up, it was responsible discretion exercised in the national interest to prevent unnecessary disclosure of eminently justifiable procedures in which untimely revelation would severely impair public confidence.

This sounded even worse than I thought – like Watergate! However, Sir Humphrey explained to me that Watergate was quite different. Watergate happened in America.

March 4th

Today I did the broadcast on the Solihull project, about which I am beginning to feel a little uneasy.

I drove with BW [*Bernard Woolley – Ed.*] to BH [*Broadcasting House – Ed.*]. I asked Bernard if I had correctly diagnosed Sir Humphrey's reasons for not wanting me to mention the Solihull project on the air. This question seemed to cause Bernard considerable anguish, but he merely shook his head slowly and sadly.

So I said to him: 'What is Humphrey's real reason for not wanting me to mention it?'

Bernard opted for answering my question with a question, i.e. not answering – 'Did you not think he gave six or seven very convincing reasons, Minister?'

'No,' I said. 'Did you think that?'

He ducked that question too. 'I'm sure,' he said evasively, 'that Sir Humphrey knows what he's doing.'

I'm sure he does. I only wish that *I* knew what Sir Humphrey is doing!

I decided to approach it another way. I feel, and I don't think I'm mistaken, that Bernard has a certain sense of loyalty towards me. So I asked him what he advised me to do.

This put him into a frightful state. 'Well,' he said, panicking, 'it's not for *me* to advise, Minister, but if it were, I would be obliged to advise you that you would be well advised to follow Sir Humphrey's advice.'

'Why?' I asked.

'Well,' he dithered. 'It's just that, well, um, certain projects have certain aspects which, with sensitive handling, given reasonable discretion, when events permit, there is no prima facie reason why, with appropriate give and take, if all goes well, in the fullness of time, um, when the moment is ripe, um, um . . .'

'Bernard!' I interrupted him. 'You're blathering, Bernard.'

'Yes Minister,' he agreed wretchedly.

'Why are you blathering, Bernard?' I enquired.

'It's my job, Minister,' he replied, and hung his head.

Clearly he is keeping something from me. But what? Foolishly, perhaps out of spite, I resolved to talk about the project on the air and get the matter – whatever it is – out in the open.

But I now wonder if this was a mistake.

Anyway, we recorded the broadcast and I talked, at some length, with some enthusiasm, about the Solihull project.

[*We have obtained the transcript of the broadcast discussion, and reproduce overleaf the relevant pages. Those taking part were Hacker, Joe Morgan — General Secretary of the Commercial and Administrative Workers Union – and Sir George Conway, Chairman of International Construction Ltd – Ed.*]

BBC Radio

HACKER: (CONT) and I should just like to point out that there is a perfect example of what can be done. It's going on up in Solihull now. Government money and private investment in real partnership.

MORGAN: Claptrap.

HACKER: No, no, it, um, excuse me Joe, it seems to me to be symbolic of everything this Government is working for. I've taken a great deal of personal interest in the Solihull Project.

CONWAY: Words.

HACKER: No, it's not just words, it's actually there in bricks and mortar. Concrete proof, if I can use that phrase, that our policy really works in practice. And there is...

PRESENTER: Thank you Minister. One last word, Sir George?

CONWAY: I'd just like to repeat that there's nothing wrong with the principle of partnership provided, provided, that there's no interference in management decisions from the State or the work force.

PRESENTER: Thank you, Sir George. Joe Morgan?

- 3 -

BBC Radio

MORGAN: (CONT) Dear, oh dear, oh dear. We all know that Sir George Conway is talking out-of-date capitalist claptrap. If partnership is to mean anything at all it must mean an equal partnership of unions, government and industry. In that order.

PRESENTER: Minister - a final word?

HACKER: Yes, well, I think basically we're all pretty much in agreement. Fundamentally. Aren't we? We all realise that if only we can work together we can forge a new Britain. And I'm delighted to have had this chance to talk about it with two of the principal forge...principal participants.

PRESENTER: Thank you. The Right Honourable James Hacker M.P., Minister for Administrative Affairs, was talking with Sir George Conway, Chairman of International Construction Ltd and Joe Morgan, General Secretary of the Commercial and Administrative Workers Union.

- 4 -

I didn't have time to go for a drink in the Hostility Room afterwards, but as I was leaving Joe Morgan buttonholed me.

'Oh,' he said, as if spontaneously, 'I hope you don't mind me mentioning this, Mr Hacker, but I wonder if you'd be able to put in a word for my members' claim for a special Birmingham allowance?'

I naturally pointed out to him that I cannot conduct trades union negotiations in a BBC studio. Furthermore, it is a matter for the Department of Employment.

Then he made a curious remark. 'I was thinking, see,' he said, 'that after this broadcast people might start asking questions about the Solihull project, wanting to know more about it, you understand?'

'I hope they do,' I said, stubbornly. Well, I do!

Then he said. 'But, as we know . . .' and he winked, '. . . there are some things . . .' he winked again '. . . better not found out.' Then he tapped the side of his nose with his forefinger and winked again. 'I'm sure we understand each other.'

He grinned and winked again. I began to suspect that he was trying to tell me something. But what? Or – and the more probable explanation suddenly flashed into my mind – he knows something and *he thinks I know too*. But whatever it is, *I don't*!

I played for time. I watched him wink again and asked him if he had something in his eye. 'Only a gleam,' he replied cheerfully.

I must have looked awfully blank. But he must have thought I was an awfully good poker player. He continued: 'Come off it, Hacker, we've got you by the short and curlies. I'm asking ten per cent below London Allowance, and we'll settle for thirty per cent below. Give you the credit for beating us down.'

'There's not going to be a Birmingham Allowance,' I said abstractedly, my mind racing. 'You'd better resign yourself to that.'

'If anyone's going to have to resign,' countered Morgan, 'it's not going to be me.'

Resign? What was the man hinting at?

'What do you mean?' I asked.

'The Solihull project, of course. I could hardly believe it when you took all the credit for it in the broadcast. Great courage of course.' Courage – how did that dreadful word get into the discussion? 'But whatever possessed you?'

I didn't know what he was on about. Cheerfully he burst into verse:

'Cannons to the right of him
Cannons to the left of him.
Into the Valley of Death rode Mr Hacker.'

I can't think what he was talking about. I'm getting very worried indeed.

[*It appears that Sir Humphrey Appleby met Sir Desmond Glazebrook for lunch at a club in Pall Mall on the same day as Hacker's broadcast. Most unusually, Sir Humphrey kept no notes and made no memos as a result of that meeting. This omission – which broke the habit and training of a lifetime in Whitehall – indicates that Sir Humphrey was profoundly frightened that the matter discussed at this meeting should ever become public knowledge.*

Fortunately, however, a letter came to light many years later, sent by Sir Desmond on 5 March, the next day, to his wife who was wintering in Barbados – Ed.]

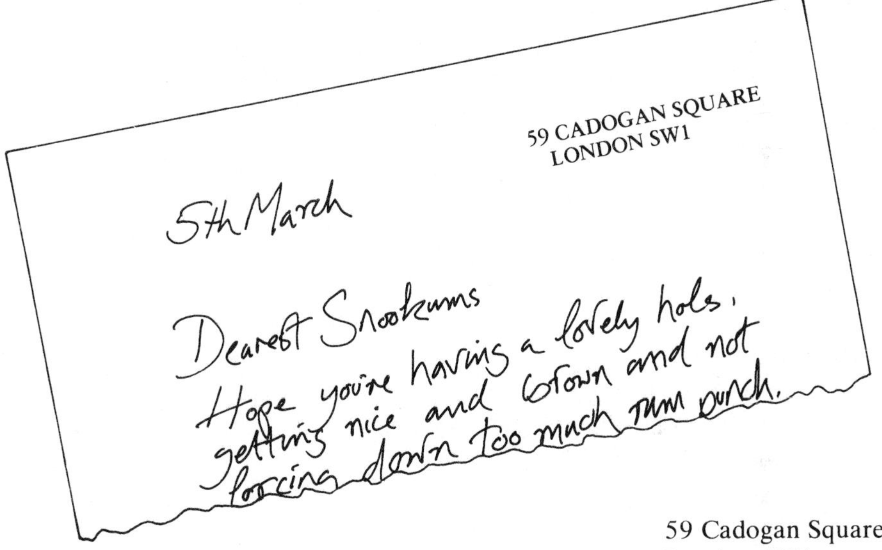

59 CADOGAN SQUARE
LONDON SW1

5th March

Dearest Snookums
Hope you're having a lovely hols, getting nice and brown and not forcing down too much rum punch.

59 Cadogan Square
London SW1

Dearest Snookums [*Lady Glazebrook – Ed.*]

Hope you're having a lovely hols, getting nice and brown and not forcing down too much rum punch.

Things are going quite well here. I made a little progress towards getting a couple of good quangos for my retirement, at lunch yesterday with old Humphrey Appleby, Perm. Sec. at the DAA. [QUANGO – *an acronym for Quasi-Autonomous Non-Governmental Organisation – Ed.*]

He's got a bit of a problem at work. He's got into bed with some idiot whiz-kid financier called Bradley, on a building project in Solihull. It seems that the whiz-kid has taken the money and run, leaving old Humphrey holding the bag. Anyway, I couldn't follow all the details because I'd had rather too much of the claret but, to cut a long story short, as Bradley can't pay his bills Humphrey wants our bank to take over the contract. He promised me that HMG would turn it all into a successful and profitable venture and all that bullshit. Whoever heard of the government being involved in a successful and profitable venture? Does he think I was born yesterday?

Naturally, I'd be perfectly happy to help good old Humph. out of a jam – it can't cost me anything, of course, since I'm retiring next year. But I told him that it's up to the Board and it could go either way. He swallowed that, I think, or pretended to anyway. I naturally chose that moment to remark that I was hoping to hear news of the new Ministry Co-Partnership Commission. I'm after the Chairmanship – £8000 a year part-time – just the thing to boost my meagre pension, don't you think, Snookums?

To my astonishment he told me that my name was on a *shortlist* for a couple of quangos. Shortlist, mark you! Bloody insult. Quangos can't suddenly be in short supply, no government ever cuts quangos without instantly replacing them with others. [*At this time there were about 8000 paid appointments within the gift of Ministers to Quangos, at a cost to the taxpayer of £5 million per year – Ed.*]

Humphrey, of course, pretended it was difficult to find me a quango, rather as I'd pretended that it was difficult for the bank to find his money.

He went through the most extraordinary routine. He mentioned the Advisory Committee of Dental Establishments, and asked if I knew anything about teeth. I pointed out that I was a banker. As I knew nothing about teeth, he then ruled out the Milk Marketing Board. Can't quite see the connection myself.

He offered the Dumping at Sea Representations Panel, asking if I lived near the sea. I asked if Knightsbridge was near enough – but apparently not. So it seems I'm out of the running for the Clyde River Purification Board too.

Then, with every bit of the meal, Humphrey had a new idea. Rump steak suggested to him the Meat Marketing Board; but I don't know a damn thing about meat. The fact that I eat it is not quite a close enough connection. So the Meat and Livestock Commission was ruled out too. *I'd* ordered Dover Sole, it reminded H. of the White Fish Authority. And, as the veg. arrived, he suggested the Potato Marketing Board, the Governors of the National Vegetable Research Station, the National Biological Standards Board, or the Arable Crops and Forage Board.

With the wine he suggested the Food and Drink Training Board. When I asked for mustard he mentioned the Food Additives and Contaminants Committee, and when we saw a Steak Diane being flambéed at the next table he offered the Fire Services Examination Board, the British Safety Council, and the St John's Ambulance.

Of course, all of this was to make his point that he too was demanding a *quid pro quo*. But it was rather humiliating because after all this he asked me rather querulously: if I knew nothing about *any* of these quangos, what *did* I know about? I was forced to explain that there was nothing I knew about particularly – after all, I'm a banker. It's not required.

Then he asked me if there were any minority groups that I could represent. I suggested bankers. We are definitely in a minority. He didn't seem to think that was the answer.

He explained to me that the ideal quango appointee is a black, Welsh, disabled woman trades unionist. He asked me if I knew one of them, but I don't.

I remarked that women are not a minority group and nor are trades unionists. Humphrey agreed, but explained that they share the same paranoia which is, after all, the distinguishing feature of any minority group.

So at the end of this whole rigmarole he was basically saying that my quango chances boil down to his Ministry's Industry Co-Partnership Commission, the Chairmanship of which is within the gift of his Minister.

It sounds ideal, actually. There's lots of papers but Old Humph. made it quite clear that it's not awfully necessary to read them; that, in fact he'd be delighted if I didn't bother so that I wouldn't have too much to say at the monthly meetings.

So it looks like we'll be scratching each other's backs. I'll have a word with my board, he'll have a word with his Minister, and I'll see you on the beach next week.

Your loving
Desi-pooh.

March 5th

Had a very worrying conversation with Roy, my driver, today. Didn't see him after recording the broadcast yesterday, because I was given a relief driver.

Roy asked me how the recording went. I said it had gone very well, that I'd talked about government partnership with industry, and that there was a most interesting project going on up in the Midlands.

I assumed he wouldn't have heard of it. I was wrong.

'You don't mean the Solihull project, sir?'

I was astonished. 'Yes,' I said. 'You've heard of it.'

Roy chuckled.

I waited, but he said nothing. 'What are you laughing at?' I asked.

'Nothing, sir,' he said. Then he chuckled again.

He'd obviously heard something.

'What have you heard?' I asked.

'Nothing. Really.'

I could see his face in the rear-view mirror. He was smiling. I didn't like it.

He was obviously laughing at some aspect of the Solihull project. But what? For some reason, I felt a need to defend it. To my *driver*? I must be cracking up. But I said, 'We regard it as a shining example of a successful collaboration between government and private enterprise.'

Roy chuckled again. He was really getting on my nerves.

'Roy, what's so funny?' I demanded. 'What do you know about all this?'

'No more than you might pick up on about thirty journeys between the DAA and Mr Michael Bradley's Office, 44 Farringdon Street, and 129 Birmingham Road, Solihull,' he replied.

'Thirty journeys?' I was astonished. 'Who with?'

'Oh,' said Roy cheerfully, 'your predecessor, sir, and Sir Humphrey, mostly.' He chuckled again. I could have killed him. What's so bloody funny, I'd like to know? 'Very cheerful they were on the first few trips. They kept talking about shining examples of successful collaboration and suchlike. Then . . .', he paused for effect, '. . . then the gloom started to come down, if you know what I mean, sir?'

Gloom? What did he mean, gloom? 'Gloom?'

'Well, no, not gloom, exactly,' said Roy and I relaxed momentarily. 'More like desperation really.'

My own mood was also moving inexorably from gloom to desperation. 'Desperation?' I asked.

'Well,' said Roy. 'You're the one who knows the background, aren't you, sir?'

I nodded. 'Yes I am.' I suppose I must have been a trifle unconvincing because my damn driver chuckled again.

'Was there . . . um . . . any . . . er . . . any particular bit of the background you were thinking of?' I tried to ask in a casual sort of way, still in a state of total mental chaos.

'No,' Roy said firmly. 'I mean, when something's fishy, it's just fishy isn't it? You don't know which particular bit the smell's coming from.'

'Fishy?' Did he know more than he was letting on? *What's* fishy?

'Well,' continued Roy helpfully, 'I mean, I don't really know do I? For all I know Mr Bradley may be quite kosher, despite everything Sir Humphrey said about him. Still, you'd know more about all that than I do, sir. I'm just the driver.'

Yes, I thought bitterly. What do I know? I'm just the bloody Minister.

March 7th
I've spent the weekend wondering if I can get any more information out of Roy. Does he know more, or has he told me everything he knows? Perhaps he can find out more, on the driver's network. Information is currency among the drivers. They leak all over the place. On the other hand, perhaps he'll trade the information that *I* don't know anything at all about the Solihull project – which could be very damaging to me, couldn't it?

But the question is, how to find out if Roy knows any more without losing face myself. (Or losing any *more* face.) I've heard that drivers can be silenced with an MBE – can I get more information with the hint or promise of an MBE? But how would I drop the hint?

These are foolish and desperate thoughts. First I'll try and get the truth out of my Permanent Secretary. Then I'll try my Private Secretary. Only then will I turn to my driver.

It occurs to me, thinking generally around the problems that I've encountered in the last six months, that it is not possible to be a good Minister so long as the Civil Service is allowed complete control over its own recruitment. Perhaps it *is* impossible to stop the Civil Service appointing people in its own likeness, but we politicians ought to try to stop it growing like Frankenstein.

This whole matter of the Solihull project – which I am determined to get to the bottom of – has reminded me how incomplete is my picture of my Department's activities. We politicians hardly ever know if information is being concealed, because the concealment is concealed too. We are only offered a choice of options, *all* of which are acceptable to the permanent officials, and in any case they force decisions on us the way magicians force cards on their audience in the three-card trick. 'Choose any card, choose my card.' But somehow we always choose the card they want us to choose. And how is it managed that we never seem to choose a course of action that the Civil Service doesn't approve? Because we're too busy to draft any of the documents ourselves, and he who drafts the document wins the day.

In fact, the more I think about it, the more the Department appears to be an iceberg, with nine-tenths of it below the surface, invisible, unknown, and deeply dangerous. And I am forced to spend my life manicuring the tip of this iceberg.

My Department has a great purpose – to bring administration, bureaucracy and red tape under control. Yet everything that my officials do ensures that not only does the DAA not achieve its purpose, but that it achieves the opposite.

Unfortunately, most government departments achieve the opposite of their purpose: the Commonwealth Office lost us the Commonwealth, the Department of Industry reduces industry, the Department of Transport presided over the disintegration of our public transport systems, the Treasury loses our money – I could go on for ever.

And their greatest skill of all is the low profile. These so-called servants of ours are immune from the facts of life. The ordinary rules of living don't apply to civil servants: they don't suffer from inflation, they don't suffer from unemployment, they automatically get honours.

Jobs are never lost – the only cuts are in planned recruitment. I have found out that there were just two exemptions to the 1975 policy of a mandatory five per cent incomes policy – annual increments and professional fees: annual increments because that is how civil servants get pay rises, and professional fees on the insistence of parliamentary Counsel, the lawyers who drafted the legislation. Otherwise the legislation would never have been drafted!

So what have I learned after nearly six months in office? Merely, it seems, that I am almost impotent in the face of the mighty faceless bureaucracy. However, it is excellent that I realise this because it means that they have failed to house-train me. If I were house-trained I would now believe a) that I am immensely powerful, and b) that my officials merely do my bidding.

So there is hope. And I am resolved that I shall not leave my office tomorrow until I have got right to the bottom of this strange mystery surrounding the Solihull project. There must be *some* way of finding out what's going on.

March 8th

Today was a real eye-opener.

I hadn't seen Sir Humphrey for some days. We met, at my request, to discuss the Solihull project. I explained that I had talked rather enthusiastically about the project on the air, but I am now having second thoughts.

'Any particular reason?' asked Sir Humphrey politely.

I didn't beat about the bush. 'Humphrey,' I said, 'is everything all right with the Solihull project?'

'I believe the building works are proceeding quite satisfactorily, Minister,' he replied smoothly.

I patiently explained that that was not quite what I meant. 'What is going on?' I asked.

'Building is going on, Minister,' he reported.

'Yes,' I said trying to keep my temper, 'but . . . something is up, isn't it?'

'Yes indeed,' he replied. At last I'm getting somewhere, I thought. I relaxed.

'What is up?' I said.

'The first floor is up,' said Sir Humphrey, 'and the second is almost up.'

I began to show my annoyance. 'Humphrey, please! I'm talking about the whole basis of the project.'

'Ah,' replied my Perm. Sec. gravely. 'I see.'

'What can you tell me about that?'

'Well, as I understand it, Minister . . .' here it comes, I thought, the truth at last, '. . . the basis is an aggregate of gravel and cement on six feet of best builder's rubble.'

Does he take me for a complete fool?

'Humphrey,' I said sternly, 'I think you know I am talking about the finance.'

So then he rabbited on about our contract with the construction company, and the usual stage payments, and all sorts of useless rubbish. I interrupted him.

'What is it,' I demanded, 'that I don't know?'

'What do you mean, precisely?' was his evasive reply.

In a state of mounting hysteria, I tried to explain. 'I don't know. It's just that . . . there's something I don't know, and I don't know because I can't find the right question to ask you because I don't know what to ask. What is it that I don't know?'

Sir Humphrey feigned innocence.

'Minister,' he said, '*I* don't know what you don't know. It could be almost anything.'

'But,' I persisted, 'you are keeping things from me, aren't you?'

He nodded.

'*What*?' I was nearly at boiling point by now. He smiled patronisingly at me. It was quite intolerable. He explained that it is the Department's duty to protect the Minister from the great tide of irrelevant information that beats against the walls of the Department day after day.

This was not the answer I was seeking. I stood up, and made one last attempt at explaining my problem – just in case he didn't fully understand it. 'Look Humphrey,' I began, 'there is something about the Solihull project that I know I don't know, and I know *you* know. I know *Bernard* knows. *Joe Morgan* knows. For heaven's sake, even my *driver* knows. It's only poor old Joe Soap here who has to stand up and talk about it in front of the British people who hasn't got a clue what's going on.'

Humphrey just stared at me. He said nothing. So I tried to spell it out for him.

'Humphrey,' I said, resisting the temptation to tear out my hair. Or his hair. 'Will you please answer one simple question?'

'Certainly Minister,' he said. 'What is it?'

'*I don't know*!' I yelled. 'You tell me and I'll ask it!'

March 10th

Today seemed to last an eternity. Ruin stared me in the face.

It began with another meeting with Humphrey. The atmosphere was distinctly frosty – Frank Weisel was there too, wanting to discuss his new paper about quangos.

I wasn't a bit interested in discussing quangos today, which seem to have no immediate relevance to my current problems, though it was full of stuff about 'ending the scandal of ministerial patronage' and 'jobs for the boys'. Humphrey described it as 'most imaginative' which Frank interpreted as a sign of approval. Frank hasn't yet learned that 'original' and 'imaginative' are two of Humphrey's most damning criticisms.

Frank's scheme was to hand over all quango appointments to a Select Committee of Parliament. 'Get the best men for the jobs instead of old chums, party hacks, and you scratch my back and I'll scratch yours,' he explained with his usual charm.

It seemed to me that it was a good plan, and I suggested we put it forward for legislation.

'It's certainly a novel proposal,' remarked Humphrey. 'Novel' – that's the other killer!

But Humphrey went on to explain his view that there was no sense in upsetting the current system when it is working smoothly.

Smoothly? I'd never heard such nonsense. Only this morning I'd received a proposal for the Chairmanship of the new Industrial Co-partnership Commission, the latest quango. And whose name was being put up? Sir Desmond Glazebrook, of all people. 'He's never worked in industry,' I said to Humphrey, 'he's never met a trades unionist, and he's said a whole lot of nasty things about this government – is this the kind of suggestion a smoothly working system comes up with?'

'But he would be an excellent Chairman,' said Sir Humphrey.

'He's an ignorant buffoon,' I explained carefully.

'Nonetheless,' said Sir Humphrey, 'an excellent Chairman.'

I told Humphrey that I drew the line at Glazebrook. I absolutely refused to appoint him. Over my dead body, I declared.

There was silence in the office for some moments. Then Sir Humphrey said, 'Minister, before you make your *final* decision I think there is something that you ought to see.'

And he produced a Ministry file. On the cover was written SOLIHULL PROJECT – TOP SECRET. Why top secret? I opened it. I saw why. Bradley, our Department's partner, owed £7½ million, was going bankrupt, and the entire project was in imminent danger of collapse.

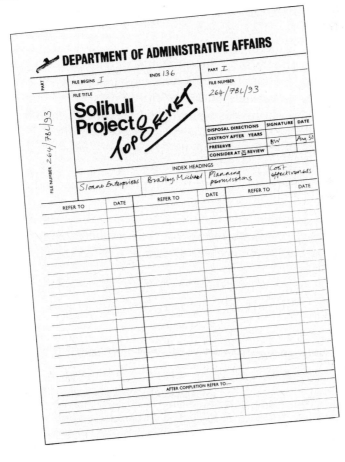

DEPARTMENT OF ADMINISTRATIVE AFFAIRS

PART | FILE BEGINS I | ENDS 136 | PART I

FILE NUMBER 264/7BL/93

FILE TITLE

Solihull Project TOP SECRET

DISPOSAL DIRECTIONS	SIGNATURE	DATE
DESTROY AFTER YEARS		
PRESERVE	BW	Aug 30
CONSIDER AT 1st/2nd REVIEW		

INDEX HEADINGS

Sloane Enterprises | Bradley, Michael | Planning permissions | Cost effectiveness

FILE NUMBER 264/7BL/93

REFER TO	DATE	REFER TO	DATE	REFER TO	DATE

AFTER COMPLETION REFER TO:—

I was aghast. Absolutely aghast. I asked Humphrey why I hadn't been told any of this and he wittered on idiotically about how he was deeply conscious of the heavy burdens of my office. It seems to me that he's made them quite a lot heavier in the last few days.

'If this comes out,' I said weakly, 'it will be all over the front pages. A public scandal. A disaster.'

'Appalling,' added Bernard. He's always such a comfort!

Then for a moment, Frank gave me a tiny ray of hope. 'Hold on, Jim.' He grabbed the file. 'Look, this report is dated before the election. You're in the clear.'

'Unfortunately,' murmured Humphrey, 'under the convention of Ministerial responsibility, the blame must fall . . .'

Frank interrupted him. 'But everyone will know it wasn't Jim.'

'Quite so.' Sir Humphrey shook his head mournfully. 'But the principle of democratic accountability requires the occasional human sacrifice – Crichel Down and all that.[1] When the pack is baying for blood . . . isn't that so, Minister?'

I couldn't speak.

Frank was undeterred. 'Surely he has only to point to the dates?'

'Ah, well,' Sir Humphrey put on his most pious expression, 'a lesser man might try to wriggle out of it. But there is only one honourable course. As the Minister is well aware.' He gazed at me sorrowfully and shook his head again. I felt I was at my own funeral.

'Don't you think Frank might have a point?' I asked, determined to fight to the last.

'Yes,' said Bernard, 'except that in that broadcast, which goes out . . .'

'Today,' I interjected.

'. . . today,' continued Bernard, 'you publicly identified yourself with the success of the project. In fact, it'll be on the air any minute now.'

We all gaped at each other. Then Bernard rushed for the radio.

I shouted, 'Bernard, get on to the BBC and stop it.'

[1] The Crichel Down affair in 1954 was possibly the last example of a Minister accepting full responsibility for a scandal within his Department, about which he did not know and could not have known. Nevertheless, Sir Thomas Dugdale, then Minister of Agriculture and Fisheries, accepted that as the Minister he was constitutionally responsible to Parliament for the wrong actions of his officials, even though their actions were not ordered by him and would not have been approved by him. He resigned, was kicked upstairs to the Lords and a promising career came to an end. No Minister since then has been – depending on your point of view – either so scrupulous or so foolish.

Humphrey said, 'I wish you luck, Minister, but – well, you know what the BBC are like.'

'Yes,' I agreed, 'but surely in a case like this, a crisis, an emergency, a scandal . . .'

'Yes,' he nodded, 'if you put it like that, they might move it to peak listening time. And then repeat it. And film it for *Panorama*.'

'I'll order them to cancel it,' I said.

'MINISTER TRIES TO CENSOR BBC,' said Humphrey, gloomily dreaming up headlines again.

I could see his point, of course. It was obviously hopeless. I was just about to suggest asking them very, very nicely when Bernard hurried in holding a transistor, and out of it came my voice saying all those dreadful things about government money and private investment in a real partnership, and how I took such a great personal interest in the Solihull project and how it is symbolic of everything this government is working for – concrete proof that our policy really works in practice.

I switched it off. I couldn't bear to listen to it. We gazed at each other, bleakly, in silence.

I waited. Nobody spoke.

Eventually I did.

'Humphrey,' I asked quietly, 'why did you let me say all that?'

'Minister,' he assumed his I'm-just-a-humble-civil-servant manner, 'I can only advise. I did advise. I advised most strongly. But when an adviser's advice is unheeded . . .'

He petered out, only too aware that he'd kept some rather vital information back from me.

'Advise me now,' I said coldly.

'Certainly Minister.' He thought for a moment. 'Now, it is possible Bartletts Bank will take over from Sloane Enterprises, and all will be well.'

The bank! I'd never thought of that. It seemed too good to be true!

'But . . .' said Humphrey.

Clearly it *was* too good to be true.

'But . . . the bank is hesitant. However, the Director in charge is retiring next year and is anxious for some appointment. The Chairmanship of a quango, for instance.'

I could see no problem at all. 'Give him one,' I said immediately. 'Give him that one you were proposing that fool Desmond Glazebrook for. Who is the Director in charge, anyway?'

'Desmond Glazebrook,' explained Humphrey.

Suddenly it all became clear.

I felt I had to leave a decent pause before I said that actually he's not such a bad chap really.

Frank was extraordinarily slow on the uptake. 'He's always attacking the government,' he said angrily.

I explained to Frank that it does us good to appoint our opponents occasionally. It's democratic – statesmanlike.

Frank seemed unimpressed with this point of view, and he argued and argued till finally I just told him to shut up.

I asked Humphrey who else knew about this wretched Solihull Report. Only Joe Morgan, Humphrey told me – which suddenly explained his confident claim for a Birmingham Allowance. Blackmail!

And it occurred to me at that moment that Desmond Glazebrook might need a *Deputy* Chairman, one with real experience of industry. A trades unionist, perhaps. I mentioned it to Humphrey, who thought it was an awfully good idea, and he immediately suggested Joe Morgan. *I* thought *that* was an awfully good idea.

'It takes two to quango, Minister,' smiled Humphrey, and we got them both on the phone right away.

Frank watched us in silence, and when we'd had brief chats with Desmond and Joe he had an absolutely amazing outburst – 'This is exactly what I've been talking about,' he shouted, even louder than usual. 'This is what's wrong with the system. Jobs for the boys. *Quid pro quo.* Corruption.' I couldn't believe my ears, Frank accusing *me* of corruption. What an idea! He's obviously going off his rocker.

'What about my quango abolition paper?' he yelled, going red in the face.

'Very good Frank,' I said smoothly. 'Imaginative. Ingenious.'

'Novel,' added Humphrey.

Then Frank announced that he wouldn't let me suppress it. As if I would do such a thing! Me, suppress papers? I'm a democrat, a believer in open government. Frank must be raving mad.

'I'll get it to Cabinet through someone else,' he threatened at the top of his not inconsiderable voice. 'I'll get it adopted as party policy. You'll see.'

He marched to the door. Then he stopped, and turned. He had a beatific smile on his face. I didn't like the look of it one bit. Whenever Frank smiles you know that something very nasty is about to happen. 'The press,' he said softly. 'The press. If the press were to get hold of this . . .'

And suddenly, I had a brainwave. 'Frank,' I said gently, 'I've been thinking. Changing the subject completely, of course, but have *you* ever thought about serving on a quango?'

'Oh no,' he replied, smiling his most unpleasant smile, 'you're not corrupting me!'

I explained patiently that nothing could be further from my thoughts. My idea is that, even better than abolishing the quango system, would be to make it work. And that if we set up a commission to supervise and report on the composition and activities of all quangos, it could be the answer. It could have very senior people, most Privy Councillors. I know that Frank has always secretly fancied himself hob-nobbing with Privy Councillors. I explained that such a body would need some really able people, people who have studied quangos, people who know the abuses of the system. 'And in view of your knowledge, and concern,' I finished, 'Humphrey suggested your name.'

'Privy Councillors?' said Frank, hypnotised.

'It's up to you, of course,' I added, 'but it would be a great service to the public. How do you feel?'

'You're not going to change my opinions, you know,' replied Frank thoughtfully. 'There is such a thing as integrity.'

Humphrey and I both hastened to agree with Frank on the importance of integrity, and we pointed out that it was, in fact, his very integrity that would make him such a good member of this quango.

'Mind you,' Humphrey said, instinctively aware of Frank's enormous sense of guilt which needs constant absolution and aware also of his deep commitment to the puritan work ethic, 'it would be very hard work. I'm sure that service in this super-quango would involve a great deal of arduous foreign travel, to see how they manage these matters in other important government centres – Japan, Australia, California, the West Indies . . .'

'Tahiti,' I added helpfully.

'Tahiti,' agreed Sir Humphrey.

'Yes,' said Frank with an expression of acute suffering on his face, 'it *would* be arduous, wouldn't it?'

'*Very* arduous,' we both said. Several times.

'But serving the public's what it's all about, isn't it?' asked Frank hopefully.

Humphrey and I murmured, 'serving the public, exactly' once or twice.

Then Frank said, 'And what about my quango paper?'

I told him it would be invaluable, and that he should take it with him.

And Humphrey offered to keep a copy on the files – with the Solihull Report.

8
The Compassionate Society

March 13th

Having effectively squashed the awful scandal that was brewing over the Solihull project, but having done a deal with Frank Weisel on the little matter of his suggested reforms in the quango system as a price for extricating myself from the appalling mess that Humphrey had got me into, I decided this weekend to consider my various options.

First of all it has become clear that Frank has to go. He really is very uncouth and, valuable as he was to me during my days in opposition, I can see that he lacks the subtlety, skill and discretion that my professional advisers display constantly.

[*The contradiction inherent in these two paragraphs indicates the state of mental confusion in which Hacker now found himself about Sir Humphrey after five months in Whitehall – Ed.*]

However, having despatched the self-righteously incorruptible Frank the day before yesterday on his arduous fact-finding mission to review important centres of government – California, Jamaica, and Tahiti – I already feel a load off my mind as one significant source of pressure on me is lifted. I felt free and easy for the first time in months, as if I had actually gained time yesterday.

I am now able to draw some conclusions about the Civil Service in general and Sir Humphrey in particular. I begin to see that senior civil servants in the open structure[1] have, surprisingly enough, almost as brilliant minds as they themselves would claim to have. However, since there are virtually no goals or targets that can be achieved by a civil servant personally, his high IQ is usually devoted to the avoidance of error.

Civil servants are posted to new jobs every three years or so. This

[1] The 800 people with the rank of Under-Secretary and above.

is supposed to gain them all-round experience on the way to the top. In practice, it merely ensures that they can never have any personal interest in achieving the success of a policy: a policy of any complexity takes longer than three years to see through from start to finish, so a civil servant either has to leave it before its passage is completed or he arrives on the scene long after it started. This also means you can never pin the blame for failure on any individual: the man in charge at the end will say it was started wrong, and the man in charge at the beginning will say it was finished wrong.

Curiously the Civil Service seem to approve of this system. They don't like civil servants to become emotionally involved in the success or failure of policies. Policies are for Ministers. Ministers or Governments stand or fall by them. Civil servants see themselves as public-spirited impartial advisers attempting to implement, with total impartiality, whatever policy the Minister or the Government see fit.

Except that they *don't*, do they? There's the rub.

Because Permanent Secretaries are always trying to steer Ministers of all parties towards 'the common ground'. [*In other words, the Department's policy – a policy they have some hope of being able to pursue uninterrupted, whichever party is in power – Ed.*]

Afterthought: considering that the avoidance of error is their main priority, it is surprising how many errors they make!

March 14th

Today, Sunday, has been spent going through my boxes and mugging up on my PQs [*Parliamentary Questions – Ed.*] for tomorrow.

I take PQs very seriously, as do all Ministers with any sense. Although the voters are mainly aware of a Minister's activities through the newspapers and television, his real power and influence still stems from the House of Commons. A Minister cannot afford to make an idiot of himself in the House, and will not last long if he doesn't learn to perform there adequately.

One day a month this ghastly event takes place. PQs are the modern equivalent of throwing the Christians to the lions, or the medieval ordeal by combat. One day a month I'm on First Order, and some other Minister from some other Department is on Second Order. Another day, vice versa. [*There's also Third Order but no one knows what it's there for because it's never been reached – Ed.*]

The Sundays and Mondays before I'm on First Order are absolute bloody anguish. I should think they're anguish for the civil servants too. Bernard has an Assistant Private Secretary employed full-time on getting answers together for all possible supplementaries. Legions of civil servants sit around Whitehall exercising their feverish imaginations, trying to foretell what possible supplementaries could be coming from the backbenchers. Usually, of course, I can guess the political implications of a PQ better than my civil servants.

Then, when the gruesome moment arrives you stand up in the House, which is usually packed as it's just after lunch and PQs are considered good clean fun because there's always a chance that a Minister will humiliate himself.

Still, I'm reasonably relaxed this evening, secure in the knowledge that, as always, I am thoroughly prepared for Question Time tomorrow. One thing I'm proud of is that, no matter how Sir Humphrey makes rings round me in administrative matters,[1] I have always prided myself on my masterful control over the House.

March 15th

I can hardly believe it. PQs today were a disaster! A totally unforeseen catastrophe. Although I did manage to snatch a sort of Pyrrhic victory from the jaws of defeat. I came in bright and early and went over all the possible supplementaries – I thought! – and spent lunchtime being tested by Bernard.

The first question was from Jim Lawford of Birmingham South-West who had asked me about the government's pledge to reduce the number of administrators in the Health Service.

I gave the prepared reply, which was a little self-congratulatory – to the civil servants who wrote it, of course, not to me!

[*We have found the relevant exchange in Hansard, and reprint it overleaf – Ed.*]

[1] A sign of growing awareness here from Hacker.

The Minister of Administrative Affairs (Mr. James Hacker): The Government has already achieved a reduction of 11·3% in administrative and clerical staff and is actually pursuing further economies. And in view of low pay and low morale and the fact that our health administrators are constantly under attack, I would like to take this opportunity to congratulate them on the vital contribution they make to the smooth running of the Health Service.

Mr. Lawford: I'm sure the house will welcome the Minister's tribute. I am aware it was actually written for him by his health administrators, but all the same he read it out beautifully. [Opposition laughter] But would the Minister explain how his assurance to the House squares with this minute from his own department. I quote: "We are concerned at the increase of 7% in Administrative and Clerical staff. However, if data processing staff were reclassified from 'administrative' to 'technical' [HON. MEMBERS: "Oh!"] if secretarial staff in hospitals were redesignated as 'ancillary workers' [HON. MEMBERS: "Oh!"] and if the base of comparison was changed from the financial to the calendar year, then the figures would show a fall of 11·3%." Would the Minister care to comment on this shabby deception?

Hon. Members: Answer! Answer!

Somebody had leaked this wretched paper to Lawford. He was waving it about with a kind of wild glee, his fat face shining with excitement. Everyone was shouting for an answer. Humphrey – or somebody – had been up to his old tricks again, disguising an increase in the numbers of administrative and secretarial staff simply by calling them by some other name. But a rose by any other name is still a rose, as Wordsworth said. [*In fact, Shakespeare said 'A rose by any other name would smell as sweet.' But Hacker was an ex-journalist and Polytechnic Lecturer – Ed.*] This looked like it was going to be a real political stink. And a stink by any other name is still a stink. [*Or a stink by any other name would smell as bad? – Ed.*] Had it stayed secret, it would have been seen as a brilliant manoeuvre to pass off an increase of staff by 7% as a decrease of 11.3% – but when leaked, it suddenly comes into the category of a shabby deception. What's more, an *unsuccessful* shabby deception – quite the worst kind!

I stalled rather well in the circumstances:

Hon. Members: Answer! Answer!

Mr. James Hacker: I have no knowledge of the document which the Honourable Member is brandishing. [Opposition jeers and cries of "why not?"]

Mr. Lawford: I will happily give the date and file reference to the Minister in exchange for an assurance that he will set up a full independent enquiry.

[Opposition cheers.]

Mr. Hacker: I will be very happy to look into the matter. [Opposition cries of "cover-up", "resign" and "whitewash".]

Thank God one of my own backbenchers came to my rescue. Gerry Chandler asked me if I could reassure my friends that the enquiries would not be carried out by my own Department but by an independent investigator who would command the respect of the House. I was forced to say that I was happy to give that assurance.

So I just about satisfied the House on that one. However, I shall have to have a very serious talk about the whole matter with Humphrey and Bernard tomorrow. I don't mind the deception, but allowing me to look ridiculous at Question Time is simply not on!

It's not even in *their* interest – I wasn't able to defend the Department, was I?

March 16th

This morning started none too well, either.

Roy [*Hacker's driver, and like all drivers, one of the best-informed men in Whitehall – Ed.*] picked me up as usual, at about 8.30. I asked him to drive me to the Ministry, as I was to spend all morning on Health Service administration.

He started needling me right away.

'Chap just been talking about that on the radio,' he said casually. 'Saying the trouble with the health and education and transport services is that all the top people in government go to private hospitals and send their kids to private schools . . .'

I laughed it off, though I sounded a little mirthless, I fear. 'Very good. Comedy programme, was it?'

This egalitarian stuff, though daft, is always a little dangerous if it's not watched very carefully.

'And they go to work in chauffeur-driven cars,' added my chauffeur.

I didn't deign to reply. So he persisted.

'Don't you think there's something in it? I mean, if you and Sir Humphrey Appleby went to work on a number 27 . . .'

I interrupted him. 'Quite impracticable,' I explained firmly. 'We work long enough hours as it is, without spending an extra hour a day waiting at the bus stop.'

'Yes,' said Roy. 'You'd have to make the bus service much more efficient, wouldn't you?'

'We certainly would,' I said, trying to dismiss the subject quickly.

'Yes,' said Roy. 'That's what he was saying, see?' The man should be a television interviewer.

'Same with the Health Service,' Roy continued inexorably. 'You a member of BUPA, sir?'

It was none of his bloody business. But I didn't say so. Instead, I smiled sweetly and asked if there was anything on the radio.

'*Yesterday in Parliament*, I think sir,' he replied, reaching for the switch.

'No, no, no, don't bother, don't bother,' I shrieked casually, but too late. He switched it on, and I was forced to listen to myself.

Roy listened with great interest. After it got to Second Order he switched it off. There was a bit of an awkward silence.

'I got away with it, didn't I?' I asked hopefully.

Roy chuckled. 'You were lucky they didn't ask you about that new St Edward's Hospital,' he said jovially.

'Why?'

'Well . . .' he smacked his lips. 'They finished building it fifteen months ago – and it's still got no patients.'

'I suppose,' I said, 'the DHSS haven't got enough money to staff it.'

'Oh, it's got *staff*,' said Roy. 'Five hundred administrators. Just no patients.'

Could this be true? It hardly seemed possible.

'Who told you this?' I asked cautiously.

'The lip.'

'The lip?'

[*The slang word used by drivers to describe he who knows the most – Ed.*]

'My mate Charlie,' he explained. 'He knows all right. He's the driver for the Secretary of State for Health.'

When I got to the office I summoned Humphrey at once. I told him straight out that I was appalled by yesterday's debate.

'So am I, Minister,' Humphrey said. I was slightly surprised to find him agreeing so vehemently.

'The stupidity of it . . . the incompetence,' I continued.

'I agree,' said Humphrey. 'I can't think what came over you.'

I blinked at him. 'I beg your pardon?'

'To concede a full *independent* enquiry . . .'

So that was it. I stopped him dead in his tracks. 'Humphrey!' I said magisterially. 'That is not what I am talking about.'

Sir Humphrey looked puzzled. 'But you mentioned stupidity and incompetence.'

'Yours, Humphrey!' I roared. '*Yours*!'

Now it seemed to be his turn to be astounded. '*Mine*, Minister?' He was incredulous.

'Yes. Yours. How could you drop me in it like that?'

To be fair, he personally hadn't dropped me in it. But his precious Department had. Humphrey, however, seemed disinclined to apologise.

'A small omission from the brief. We can't foresee everything.' Then his face resumed an expression of pure horror. 'But to concede a full independent enquiry . . .'

I'd had enough of this. 'I didn't particularly want an enquiry either,' I pointed out. 'But if you're drowning and somebody throws you a rope, you grab it.'

'It was not a rope,' replied Sir Humphrey. 'It was a noose. You should have stood up for the Department – that is what you are here for.'

That may be what *Humphrey* thinks I'm here for. As a matter of fact, it's nice to know he thinks I'm here for *something*. But I knew that if I didn't stop him he would give me a little lecture on Ministerial Responsibility.

The Doctrine of Ministerial Responsibility is a handy little device conceived by the Civil Service for dropping the Minister in it while enabling the mandarins to keep their noses clean. It means, in practice, that the Civil Service runs everything and takes all the decisions, but when something goes wrong then it's the Minister who takes the blame.

'No, Humphrey, it won't do,' I interjected firmly before he could go any further. 'I prepared myself thoroughly for Question Time yesterday. I mugged up all the Questions and literally dozens of supplementaries. I was up half Sunday night, I skipped lunch yesterday, I was thoroughly prepared.' I decided to say it again. '*Thoroughly prepared*!' I said. 'But nowhere in my brief was there the slightest indication that you'd been juggling the figures so that I would be giving misleading replies to the House.'

'Minister,' said Humphrey in his most injured tones, 'you said you wanted the administration figures reduced, didn't you?'

'Yes,' I agreed.

'So we reduced them.'

Dimly I began to perceive what he was saying. 'But . . . you only reduced the *figures*, not the actual number of administrators!'

Sir Humphrey furrowed his brow. 'Of course.'

'Well,' I explained patiently, 'that was not what I meant.'

Sir Humphrey was pained. 'Well really, Minister, we are not mind-readers. You said reduce the figures, so we reduced the figures.'

This was obvious nonsense. He knew perfectly well what I'd meant, but had chosen to take my instructions literally. It was because of this sort of Civil Service foolishness and unhelpfulness that this country is literally bleeding to death.

[*We assume that Hacker did not literally mean literally – Ed.*]

'How did it get out?' I demanded. 'Another leak. This isn't a Department, it's a colander.' I was rather pleased with that little crack. Sir Humphrey ignored it, of course. 'How can we govern responsibly,' I continued, 'if backbenchers are going to get all the facts?' There was another silence. Naturally. There was no answer to that one. 'Anyway,' I concluded, 'at least an enquiry gives us a little time.'

'So does a time bomb,' observed my Permanent Secretary.

So I waited to see if he had a disposal squad up his sleeve. Apparently not.

'If only you'd said we'd have a departmental enquiry,' he complained, 'then we could have made it last eighteen months, and finally said that it revealed a certain number of anomalies which have now been rectified but that there was no evidence of any intention to mislead. Something like that.'

I allowed myself to be diverted for a moment. 'But there *was* an intention to mislead,' I pointed out.

'I never said there wasn't,' Sir Humphrey replied impatiently. 'I merely said there was no evidence of it.'

I think I was looking blank. He explained.

'The job of a professionally conducted internal enquiry is to unearth a great mass of no evidence. If you say there was no intention, you can be proved wrong. But if you say the enquiry found no *evidence* of an intention, you can't be proved wrong.'

This is a most interesting insight into one of the Civil Service's favourite devices. In future I'll know what is *really* meant by a departmental enquiry. Even a full departmental enquiry. That would presumably mean that an even greater mass of no evidence had been unearthed for the occasion.

However I had to deal with the matter in hand, namely that I had agreed to an independent enquiry. 'Couldn't we,' I suggested thoughtfully, 'get an independent enquiry to find no evidence?'

'You mean, rig it?' enquired Sir Humphrey coldly.

This man's double standards continue to amaze me.

'Well . . . yes!'

'Minister!' he said, as if he was deeply shocked. Bloody hypocrite.

'What's wrong with rigging an independent enquiry if you can rig an internal one, I should like to know?' Though I already know the answer – you might get *caught* rigging an independent enquiry.

'No, Minister, in an independent enquiry everything depends on who the Chairman is. He absolutely has to be sound.'

'If he's sound,' I remarked, 'surely there's a danger he'll bring it all out into the open?'

Sir Humphrey was puzzled again. 'No, not if he's sound,' he explained. 'A sound man will understand what is required. He will perceive the implications. He will have a sensitive and sympathetic insight into the overall problem.'

He *was* suggesting that we rig it, in fact. He just likes to wrap it up a bit.

'Ah,' I said. 'So "sound" actually means "bent"?'

'Certainly not!' He was too quick with his denial. Methinks Sir Humphrey doth protest too much. 'I mean,' he tried again, 'a man of broad understanding . . .'

I decided to short-circuit the process by making some suggestions.

'Then what about a retired politician?'

'. . . and unimpeachable integrity,' added Humphrey.

'Oh I see.' I paused to think. 'What about an academic or a businessman?'

Sir Humphrey shook his head.

'Okay,' I said, knowing that he had someone in mind already. 'Out with it. Who?'

'Well, Minister, I thought perhaps . . . a retired civil servant.'

I saw his point. 'Good thinking, Humphrey.' It's wonderful what years of training can do for you!

'Sir Maurice Williams could be the man,' he went on.

I wasn't too sure about this. 'You don't think he might be too independent?'

'He's hoping for a peerage,' said Humphrey quietly, with a smile. He appeared to think he was producing an ace from up his sleeve.

I was surprised. 'This won't give him one, will it?'

'No, but the right finding will give him a few more Brownie points.'

Brownie points. This was a new concept to me. Humphrey explained that they all add up until you get the badge. This seems to make sense.

'Right,' I said decisively. 'Sir Maurice it is.' Thank God I find it so easy to take decisions.

'Thank you, Brown Owl,' smiled Humphrey, and left the room. He's really quite a pleasant fellow when he gets his way, and perhaps his idea will get us out of the embarrassment of an independent enquiry actually revealing anything – whether it be something we didn't know ourselves and should have known, or something we knew perfectly well and didn't want others to know we had known.

Of course, I realise on reflection that there is a third, and more real, possibility – that an independent enquiry would reveal something that Humphrey knew and I didn't know and that he didn't want me to know and that I would look an idiot for not knowing.

Like what happened yesterday, in other words.

So perhaps it's just as well to follow his advice, until the day dawns when I know some embarrassing information that he doesn't.

March 17th

A long meeting with Bernard Woolley today.

First of all, he was concerned about the Cuban refugees. Naturally. I'm concerned about them too. There's a whole row brewing in Parliament and the press about the government's refusal to help them.

I tried to point out that it's not my fault the Treasury won't give us the cash.

I can't beat the Treasury. No one can beat the Treasury.

I've decided to do nothing about the refugees because there's nothing I can do. However, Bernard and I had a more fruitful and revealing conversation about the new St Edward's Hospital that Roy had tipped me off about yesterday. It seemed at first as though Roy was misinformed.

'You asked me to find out about that alleged empty hospital in North London,' began Bernard.

I nodded.

'Well, as I warned you, the driver's network is not wholly reliable. Roy has got it wrong.'

I was very relieved. 'How did you find out this good news?' I asked.

'Through the Private Secretaries' network.'

This was impressive. Although the Private Secretaries' network is sometimes a little slower than the drivers' network, it is a great deal more reliable – in fact almost one hundred per cent accurate.

'And?'

Bernard explained that at this hospital there are only 342 administrative staff. The other 170 are porters, cleaners, laundry workers, gardeners, cooks and so forth.

This seemed a perfectly reasonable figure. So I asked how many medical staff.

'Oh, none of *them*,' replied Bernard casually, as if that were perfectly obvious in any case.

I wasn't sure I'd heard right. 'None?' I asked, cautiously.

'None.'

I decided to clarify a thing or two. 'We are talking about St Edward's *Hospital*, aren't we, Bernard?'

'Oh yes,' he answered cheerfully. 'It's brand-new, you see,' he added as if that explained everything.

'How new?'

'Well,' he said, 'it was completed eight months ago, and fully staffed, but unfortunately there were government cutbacks at that time and there was, consequently, no money left for the medical services.'

My mind was slowly boggling. 'A brand-new hospital,' I repeated quietly, to make sure I had not misheard, 'with five hundred administrative staff and no patients?'

I sat and thought quietly for a few moments.

Then Bernard said helpfully, 'Well, there is one patient, actually, Minister?'

'One?' I said.

'Yes – the Deputy Chief Administrator fell over a piece of scaffolding and broke his leg.'

I began to recover myself. 'My God,' I said. 'What if I'd been asked about this in the House?' Bernard looked sheepish. 'Why didn't I know? Why didn't you tell me?'

'I didn't know either.'

'Why didn't you know? Who *did* know? How come this hasn't got out?'

Bernard explained that apparently one or two people at the DHSS knew. And they have told him that this is not unusual – in fact, there are several such hospitals dotted around the country.

It seems there is a standard method of preventing this kind of thing leaking out. 'Apparently it has been contrived to keep it looking like a building-site, and so far no one has realised that the hospital is operational. You know, scaffolding and skips and things still there. The normal thing.'

I was speechless. 'The normal thing?' I gasped. [*Apparently, not quite speechless – Ed.*]

'I think . . .' I was in my decisive mood again, '. . . I *think* I'd better go and see it for myself, before the Opposition get hold of this one.'

'Yes,' said Bernard. 'It's surprising that the press haven't found out by now, isn't it?'

I informed Bernard that most of our journalists are so amateur that they would have grave difficulty in finding out that today is Thursday.

'It's actually Wednesday, Minister,' he said.

I pointed to the door.

[*The following Friday Sir Humphrey Appleby met Sir Ian Whitchurch, Permanent Secretary of the Department of Health and Social Security, at the Reform Club in Pall Mall. They discussed St Edward's Hospital. Fortunately, Sir Humphrey made a note about this conversation on one of his special pieces of margin-shaped memo paper. Sir Humphrey preferred to write in margins where possible, but, if not possible, simulated margins made him feel perfectly comfortable – Ed.*]

Ian was understandably concerned about Hacker's sudden interest in St Edward's Hospital. I explained that my Minister was greatly concerned that the Hospital contained no patients. We shared a certain sense of amusement on this point. My Minister was making himself faintly ridiculous. How can a hospital have patients when it has no nursing staff?

Ian was understandably concerned about Hacker's sudden interest in St Edward's Hospital.

[*We can infer from this note that Mr Bernard Woolley – as he then was – mentioned the matter of St Edward's Hospital to Sir Humphrey, although when we challenged Sir Bernard – as he now is – on this point he had no recollection of doing so – Ed.*]

I explained that my Minister was greatly concerned that the hospital contained no patients. We shared a certain sense of amusement on this point. My Minister was making himself faintly ridiculous. How can a hospital have patients when it has no nursing staff?

Ian quite rightly pointed out that they have great experience at the DHSS in getting hospitals going. The first step is to sort out the smooth-running of the place. Having patients around would be no help at all – they'd just get in the way. Ian therefore advised me to tell Hacker that this is the run-in period for St Edward's.

However, anticipating further misplaced disquiet in political circles, I pressed Ian for an answer to the question: How long is the run-in period going to run? I was forced to refer to my Minister's agreeing to a full independent enquiry.

Ian reiterated the sense of shock that he had felt on hearing of the independent enquiry. Indeed, I have no doubt that his shock is reflected throughout Whitehall.

Nevertheless, I was obliged to press him further. I asked for an indication that we are going to get some patients into St Edward's *eventually*.

Sir Ian said that if possible, we would. He confirmed that it is his present intention to have some patients at the hospital, probably in a couple of years when the financial situation has eased up.

This seems perfectly reasonable to me. I do not see how he can open forty new wards at St Edward's while making closures elsewhere. The Treasury wouldn't wear it, and nor would the Cabinet.

But knowing my Minister, he may not see things in the same light. He may, *simply* because the hospital is treating no patients, attempt to shut down the whole place.

I mentioned this possibility to Ian, who said that such an idea was quite impossible. The unions would prevent it.

It seemed to me that the unions might not yet be active at St Edward's, but Ian had an answer for that – he reminded me of Billy Fraser, the firebrand agitator at Southwark Hospital. Dreadful man. He could be useful.

Ian's going to move him on, I think. [*Appleby Papers 19/SPZ/116*]

[*Perhaps we should point out that Hacker would not have been informed of the conversation described above, and Sir Humphrey's memo was made purely as a private aide-mémoire – Ed.*]

March 22nd

Today I had a showdown with Humphrey over Health Service Administration.

I had a lot of research done for me at Central House [*Hacker's party headquarters – Ed.*] because I was unable to get clear statistics out of my own Department. Shocking!

They continually change the basis of comparative figures from year to year, thus making it impossible to check what kind of bureaucratic growth is going on.

'Humphrey,' I began, fully armed with chapter and verse, 'the whole National Health Service is an advanced case of galloping bureaucracy.'

Humphrey seemed unconcerned. 'Certainly not,' he replied. 'Not galloping. A gentle canter at the most.'

I told him that instances of idiotic bureaucracy flood in daily.

'From whom?'

'MPs,' I said. 'And constituents, and doctors and nurses. The public.'

Humphrey wasn't interested. 'Troublemakers,' he said.

I was astonished. 'The public?'

'They are some of the worst,' he remarked.

I decided to show him the results of some of my researches. First I showed him a memo about stethoscopes. [*As luck would have it, Hacker kept copies of all the memos to which he refers in his diary. These give us a fascinating insight into the running of the National Health Service in the 1980s – Ed.*]

Royal United Hospital

STETHOSCOPE REQUISITION

Because of the current supply situation it is not possible to issue you with the extra stethoscopes you have applied for.

We are, however, in a position to supply you with longer tubes for your existing stethoscopes.

Purchasing Dept

Sir Humphrey saw nothing strange in this and commented that if a supply of longer tubes was available it was right and proper to make such an offer.

Bernard then went so far as to suggest that it could save a lot of wear and tear on the doctors – with sufficiently long tubes for their stethoscopes, he suggested, they could stand in one place and listen to all the chests on the ward.

I hope and pray that he was being facetious.

Then I showed Humphrey the memos from St Stephen's about toilet rolls and the mortuary.

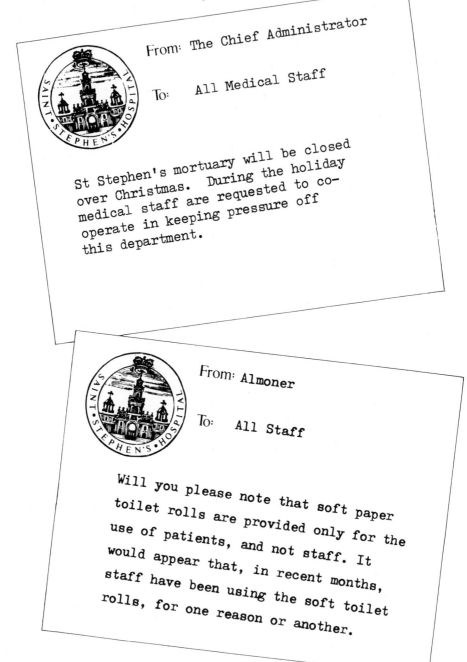

From: The Chief Administrator

To: All Medical Staff

St Stephen's mortuary will be closed over Christmas. During the holiday medical staff are requested to co-operate in keeping pressure off this department.

From: Almoner

To: All Staff

Will you please note that soft paper toilet rolls are provided only for the use of patients, and not staff. It would appear that, in recent months, staff have been using the soft toilet rolls, for one reason or another.

Sir Humphrey brushed these memos aside. He argued that the Health Service is as efficient and economical as the government allows it to be.

So I showed him a quite remarkable document from the Director of Uniforms in a Regional Health Authority:

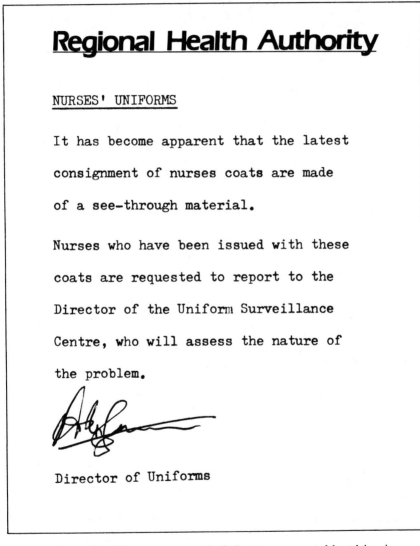

Regional Health Authority

NURSES' UNIFORMS

It has become apparent that the latest consignment of nurses coats are made of a see-through material.

Nurses who have been issued with these coats are requested to report to the Director of the Uniform Surveillance Centre, who will assess the nature of the problem.

Director of Uniforms

Humphrey had the grace to admit he was amazed by this piece of nonsense. 'Nice work if you can get it,' he said with a smile.

I saved my trump card till last. And even Humphrey was concerned about the Christmas dinner memo:

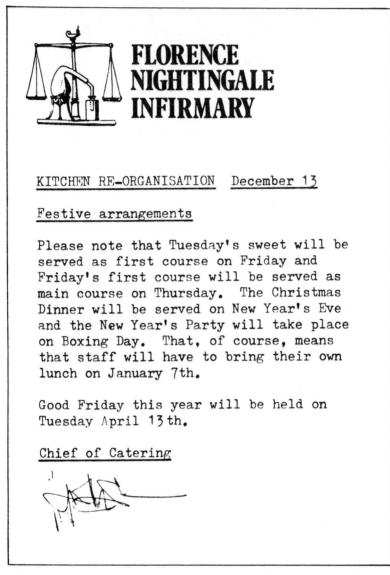

KITCHEN RE-ORGANISATION December 13

Festive arrangements

Please note that Tuesday's sweet will be served as first course on Friday and Friday's first course will be served as main course on Thursday. The Christmas Dinner will be served on New Year's Eve and the New Year's Party will take place on Boxing Day. That, of course, means that staff will have to bring their own lunch on January 7th.

Good Friday this year will be held on Tuesday April 13th.

Chief of Catering

Humphrey did at least admit that something might be slightly wrong if we are paying people throughout the NHS to toil away at producing all this meaningless drivel. And I learned this morning that in ten years the number of Health Service administrators has gone up by 40,000 and the number of hospital beds has gone down by 60,000. These figures speak for themselves.

Furthermore the annual cost of the Health Service has gone up by one and a half billion pounds. In real terms!

But Sir Humphrey seemed pleased when I gave him these figures. 'Ah,' he said smugly, 'if only British industry could match this growth record.'

I was staggered! 'Growth?' I said. 'Growth?' I repeated. Were my ears deceiving me? 'Growth?' I cried. He nodded. 'Are you suggesting that treating fewer and fewer patients so that we can employ more and more administrators is a proper use of the funds voted by Parliament and supplied by the taxpayer?'

'Certainly.' He nodded again.

I tried to explain to him that the money is only voted to make sick people better. To my intense surprise, he flatly disagreed with this proposition.

'On the contrary, Minister, it makes *everyone* better – better for having shown the extent of their care and compassion. When money is allocated to Health and Social Services, Parliament and the country feel cleansed. Absolved. Purified. It is a sacrifice.'

This, of course, was pure sophism. 'The money should be spent on patient care, surely?'

Sir Humphrey clearly regarded my comment as irrelevant. He pursued his idiotic analogy. 'When a sacrifice has been made, nobody asks the Priest what happened to the ritual offering after the ceremony.'

Humphrey is wrong, wrong, wrong, wrong! In my view the country *does* care if the money is misspent, and I'm there as the country's representative, to see that it isn't.

'With respect,[1] Minister,' began Humphrey, one of his favourite insults in his varied repertoire, 'people merely care that the money is not *seen* to be misspent.'

I rejected that argument. I reminded him of the uproar over the mental hospital scandals.

Cynical as ever, he claimed that such an uproar proved his point. 'Those abuses had been going on quite happily for decades,' he said. 'No one was remotely concerned to find out what was being done with their money – it was their sacrifice, in fact. What outraged them was being told about it.'

I realised that this whole ingenious theory, whether true or false, was being used by Humphrey as a smokescreen. I decided to ask a straight question.

'Are we or aren't we agreed that there is no point in keeping a hospital running for the benefit of the staff?'

[1] Meaning without respect.

Humphrey did not give a straight answer.

'Minister,' he admonished, 'that is not how I would have expressed the question.'

Then he fell silent.

I pointed out that that was how I had expressed it.

'Indeed,' he said.

And waited.

Clearly, he had no intention of answering any straight question unless it was expressed in terms which he found wholly acceptable.

I gave in. 'All right,' I snapped, 'how would you express it?'

'At the end of the day,' he began, '*one* of a hospital's prime functions is patient care.'

'One?' I said. 'One? What else?'

He refused to admit that I had interrupted him, and continued speaking with utter calm as if I had not said a word. 'But, until we have the money for the nursing and medical staff, that is a function that we are not able to pursue. Perhaps in eighteen months or so . . .'

'Eighteen months?' I was appalled.

'Yes, perhaps by then we may be able to open a couple of wards,' he said, acknowledging finally that I had spoken.

I regard this as so much stuff and nonsense. I instructed him to open some wards at once – and more than a couple.

He countered by offering to form an interdepartmental committee to examine the feasibility of monitoring a proposal for admitting patients at an earlier date.

I asked him how long that would take to report.

'Not long, Minister.'

'How long?'

I knew the answer before he gave it – 'Eighteen months,' we said in unison.

'Terrific!' I added sarcastically.

'Thank you,' he replied, charmingly unaware. It's hopeless.

So I made a new suggestion. 'I suggest that we get rid of everyone currently employed at the hospital and use the money to open closed wards in other hospitals.'

[*As Sir Humphrey had predicted, Hacker was prepared to shut down the whole hospital – Ed.*]

'And when we can afford it,' I added sarcastically, 'we'll open St Edward's with *medical staff*! If you would be so kind.'

Humphrey then argued that if we closed the hospital now we

would delay the opening of it *with patients* for years. 'You talk,' he said accusingly, 'as if the staff have nothing to do, simply because there are no patients there.'

'What *do* they do?' I asked.

Humphrey was obviously expecting this question. He promptly handed me a list. A list comprising all the administrative departments and what they do – with or without patients. Extraordinary.

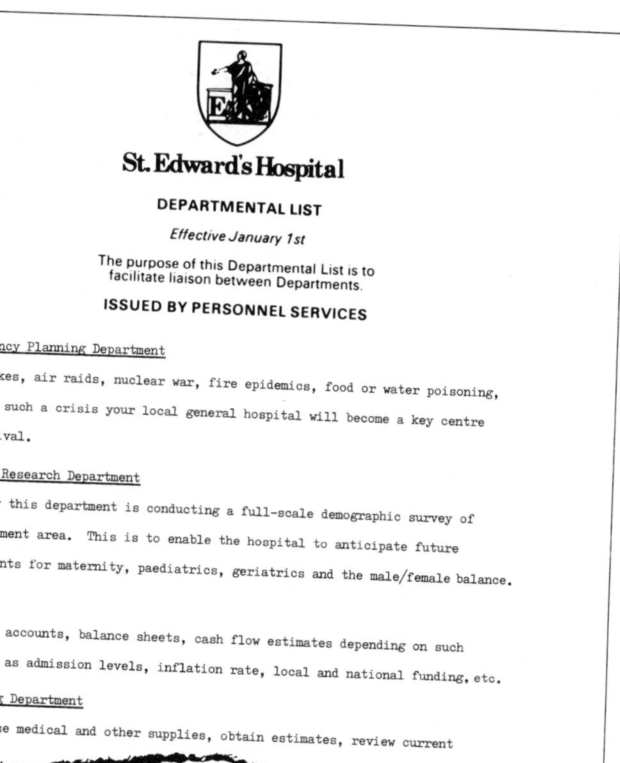

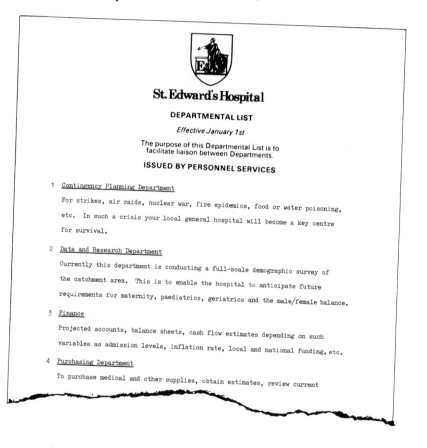

St. Edward's Hospital

DEPARTMENTAL LIST

Effective January 1st

The purpose of this Departmental List is to facilitate liaison between Departments.

ISSUED BY PERSONNEL SERVICES

1 Contingency Planning Department

For strikes, air raids, nuclear war, fire epidemics, food or water poisoning, etc. In such a crisis your local general hospital will become a key centre for survival.

2 Data and Research Department

Currently this department is conducting a full-scale demographic survey of the catchment area. This is to enable the hospital to anticipate future requirements for maternity, paediatrics, geriatrics and the male/female balance.

3 Finance

Projected accounts, balance sheets, cash flow estimates depending on such variables as admission levels, inflation rate, local and national funding, etc.

4 Purchasing Department

To purchase medical and other supplies, obtain estimates, review current

1. *Contingency Planning Department*
For strikes, air raids, nuclear war, fire epidemics, food or water poisoning, etc. In such a crisis your local general hospital will become a key centre for survival.

2. *Data and Research Department*
Currently this department is conducting a full-scale demographic survey of the catchment area. This is to enable the hospital to anticipate future requirements for maternity, paediatrics, geriatrics and the male/female balance.

3. *Finance*
Projected accounts, balance sheets, cash flow estimates depending on such variables as admission levels, inflation rate, local and national funding etc.

4. *Purchasing Department*
To purchase medical and other supplies, obtain estimates, review current and future catalogues and price lists.

5. *Technical Department*
For evaluating all proposed equipment purchases and comparing cost-effectiveness.

6. *Building Department*
To deal with the Phase Three building plans, the costing, the architectural liaison, and all other work necessary to complete the final phase of the hospital by 1994.

7. *Maintenance*
Maintenance of both the hospital structure itself, and the highly complex and expensive medical and technical equipment contained therein.
As an economy measure, this department also includes the Cleaning Department.

8. *Catering*
This department is self-explanatory.

9. *Personnel*
A very busy department, dealing with leave, National Health Insurance, and salaries. Naturally this department contains a number of staff welfare officers, who are needed to look after over 500 employees.

10. *Administration*
The typing pool, desks, stationery, office furniture and equipment, liaison between departments, agreeing on routine procedures.

I couldn't tell as I read this (and tonight I still can't) if Humphrey was playing a practical joke. Department 10 contains administrators to administrate other administrators.

I read it carefully, then I studied his face. He appeared to be serious.

'Humphrey,' I said, very slowly and carefully. 'There-are-no-patients! That-is-what-a-hospital-is-for! Patients! Ill-people! Healing-the-sick!'

Sir Humphrey was unmoved. 'I agree, Minister,' he said, 'but nonetheless all of these vital tasks listed here must be carried on with or without patients.'

'Why?' I asked.

He looked blank. 'Why?'

'Yes. Why?' I repeated.

'I don't understand,' he said.

I tried to rack my brains, to see how else I could put it. I finally gave up.

'Why?' I asked.

'Minister,' he said, 'would you get rid of the Army just because there's no war?'

A completely specious argument, and I told him so. He asked me how I would define specious. I dodged the question, and hurriedly pointed out that hospitals are different. Hospitals must get results!

At last I appeared to have shocked him. He was completely shaken out of his complacency.

'Minister,' he said earnestly, 'we don't measure our success by results, but by activity. And the activity is considerable. And productive. These 500 people are seriously overworked – the full establishment should be 650.' He opened his briefcase. 'May I show you some of the paperwork emanating from St Edward's Hospital?'

That was the *last* thing I wanted to see.

'No you may not,' I replied firmly. 'Enough is enough. Sack them all.'

He refused point-blank. He said it was impossible. He repeated that if we lost our administrators the hospital would *never* open. So I told him just to sack the ancillary workers. He said the unions wouldn't wear it.

I compromised. I instructed him to sack half the administrators and half the ancillary workers. I told him to replace them with medical staff and open a couple of wards. I also told him that it was my last word on the subject.

He tried to keep the discussion going. I wouldn't let him. But he seemed worryingly complacent about the whole situation, and as he left he said he would have a word with the Health Service unions. He held out little hope that such a solution were possible.

I'm beginning to feel like Alice in Wonderland.

[*Later that week Sir Humphrey Appleby had a meeting with Brian Baker, the General Secretary of the Confederation of Administrative Unions. It seems to have taken place privately, over a glass of sherry, after another meeting in Sir Humphrey's office. Most unusually, Sir Humphrey appears to have made no notes, memos or references to the meeting, not even in his private diary. This suggests that he regarded the discussion as potentially highly embarrassing. Fortunately, however, Brian Baker referred to this secret discussion at the next meeting of his Union's National Executive, and his account of it appears in the minutes – Ed.*]

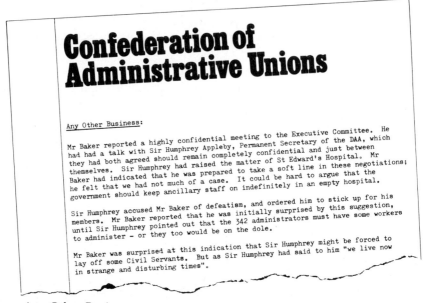

Confederation of Administrative Unions

Any Other Business:

Mr Baker reported a highly confidential meeting to the Executive Committee. He had had a talk with Sir Humphrey Appleby, Permanent Secretary of the DAA, which they had both agreed should remain completely confidential and just between themselves. Sir Humphrey had raised the matter of St Edward's Hospital. Mr Baker had indicated that he was prepared to take a soft line in these negotiations; he felt that we had not much of a case. It could be hard to argue that the government should keep ancillary staff on indefinitely in an empty hospital.

Sir Humphrey accused Mr Baker of defeatism, and ordered him to stick up for his members. Mr Baker reported that he was initially surprised by this suggestion, until Sir Humphrey pointed out that the 342 administrators must have some workers to administer - or they too would be on the dole.

Mr Baker was surprised at this indication that Sir Humphrey might be forced to lay off some Civil Servants. But as Sir Humphrey had said to him "we live now in strange and disturbing times".

Any Other Business:

Mr Baker reported a highly confidential meeting to the Executive Committee. He had had a talk with Sir Humphrey Appleby, Permanent Secretary of the DAA, which they had both agreed should remain completely confidential and just between themselves. Sir Humphrey had raised the matter of St Edward's Hospital. Mr Baker had indicated that he was prepared to take a soft line in these negotiations; he felt that we had not much of a case. It could be hard to argue that the government should keep ancillary staff on indefinitely in an empty hospital.

Sir Humphrey accused Mr Baker of defeatism, and ordered him to stick up for his members. Mr Baker reported that he was initially surprised by this suggestion, until Sir Humphrey pointed out that the 342 administrators must have some workers to administer – or they too would be on the dole.

Mr Baker was surprised at this indication that Sir Humphrey might be forced to lay off some civil servants. But as Sir Humphrey had said to him 'we live now in strange and disturbing times'.

Mr Baker asked if Sir Humphrey would support the union if we took industrial action. Sir Humphrey pointed out that he is charged with keeping the wheels of government in motion, and could not possibly countenance a show of solidarity.

Nevertheless, he hinted that he would not come down heavy on a widespread and effective show of opposition from our members.

Mr Baker wanted to know where the Minister stood on this matter. Sir Humphrey explained that the Minister does not know his ACAS from his NALGO.

Mr Baker then indicated that, if he was to cause effective disruption, he needed some active help and support from Sir Humphrey. What with the hospital empty for fifteen months and no hope of opening any wards for another year or more, he informed Sir Humphrey that our members were resigned and apathetic.

Sir Humphrey asked if Billy Fraser was resigned or apathetic. At first Mr Baker thought Sir Humphrey did not realise that Fraser is at Southwark Hospital. But Sir Humphrey indicated that he could soon be transferred to St Edward's.

The Assistant General Secretary commented that this is good news. We can do much to improve our members' pay and conditions at St Edward's if there is some real shop-floor militancy to build on.

Finally, Mr Baker reported that Sir Humphrey escorted him out of the door, offering good wishes to his fraternal comrades and singing 'we shall overcome'.

The Executive Commitee urged Mr Baker to keep a close eye on Sir Humphrey Appleby in all future negotiations because of the possibility either that he's a traitor to his class or that he's going round the twist.

Brian Baker, General Secretary of the Confederation of Administrative Unions, relaxing after a successful meeting of his National Executive Committee (Reproduced by kind permission of his grandson)

[*Hacker's diary continues – Ed.*]

March 25th

Today I paid an official visit to St Edward's Hospital. It was a real eye-opener.

The Welcoming Committee – I use the term in the very broadest sense, because I can hardly imagine a group of people who were less welcoming – were lined up on the steps.

I met Mrs Rogers, the Chief Administrator, and an appalling

Glaswegian called Billy Fraser who rejoices in the title of Chairman of the Joint Shop Stewards Negotiating Committee. Mrs Rogers was about forty-five. Very slim, dark hair with a grey streak – a very handsome Hampstead lady who speaks with marbles in her mouth.

'How very nice to meet you,' I said to Fraser, offering to shake his hand.

'I wouldn't count on it,' he snarled.

I was shown several empty wards, several administrative offices that were veritable hives of activity, and finally a huge deserted dusty operating theatre suite. I enquired about the cost of it. Mrs Rogers informed me that, together with Radiotherapy and Intensive Care, it cost two and a quarter million pounds.

I asked her if she was not horrified that the place was not in use.

'No,' she said cheerfully. 'Very good thing in some ways. Prolongs its life. Cuts down running costs.'

'But there are no patients,' I reminded her.

She agreed. 'Nonetheless,' she added, 'the essential work of the hospital has to go on.'

'I thought the patients were the essential work of the hospital.'

'Running an organisation of five hundred people is a big job, Minister,' said Mrs Rogers, beginning to sound impatient with me.

'Yes,' I spluttered, 'but if they weren't here they wouldn't be here.'

'What?'

Obviously she wasn't getting my drift. She has a completely closed mind.

I decided that it was time to be decisive. I told her that this situation could not continue. Either she got patients into the hospital, or I closed it.

She started wittering. 'Yes, well, Minister, in the course of time I'm sure . . .'

'Not in the course of time,' I said. '*Now*. We will get rid of three hundred of your people and use the savings to pay for some doctors and nurses so that we can get some patients in.'

Billy Fraser then started to put in his two penn'orth.

'Look here,' he began, 'without those two hundred people this hospital just wouldn't function.'

'Do you think it's functioning now?' I enquired.

Mrs Rogers was unshakeable in her self-righteousness. 'It is one of the best-run hospitals in the country,' she said. 'It's up for the Florence Nightingale award.'

I asked what that was, pray.

'It's won,' she told me proudly, 'by the most hygienic hospital in the Region.'

I asked God silently to give me strength. Then I told her that I'd said my last word and that three hundred staff must go, doctors and nurses hired, and patients admitted.

'You mean, three hundred jobs lost?' Billy Fraser's razor-sharp brain had finally got the point.

Mrs Rogers had already got the point. But Mrs Rogers clearly felt that this hospital had no need of patients. She said that in any case they couldn't do any serious surgery with just a skeleton medical staff. I told her that I didn't care whether or not she did serious surgery – she could do nothing but varicose veins, hernias and piles for all I cared. But *something* must be done.

'Do you mean three hundred jobs lost,' said Billy Fraser angrily, still apparently seeking elucidation of the simple point everybody else had grasped ten minutes ago.

I spelt it out to him. 'Yes I do, Mr Fraser,' I replied. 'A hospital is not a source of employment, it is a place to heal the sick.'

He was livid. His horrible wispy beard was covered in spittle as he started to shout abuse at me, his little pink eyes blazing with class hatred and alcohol. 'It's a source of employment for my members,' he yelled. 'You want to put them out of work, do you, you bastard?' he screamed. 'Is that what you call a compassionate society?'

I was proud of myself. I stayed calm. 'Yes,' I answered coolly. 'I'd rather be compassionate to the patients than to your members.'

'We'll come out on strike,' he yelled.

I couldn't believe my eyes or ears. I was utterly delighted with that threat. I laughed in his face.

'Fine,' I said happily. 'Do that. What does it matter? Who can you harm? Please, do go on strike, the sooner the better. And take all those administrators with you,' I added, waving in the direction of the good Mrs Rogers. 'Then we won't have to pay you.'

Bernard and I left the battlefield of St Edward's Hospital, I felt, as the undisputed victors of the day.

It's very rare in politics that one has the pleasure of completely wiping the floor with one's opponents. It's a good feeling.

March 26th

It seems I didn't quite wipe the floor after all. The whole picture changed in a most surprising fashion.

Bernard and I were sitting in the office late this afternoon congratulating ourselves on yesterday's successes. I was saying, rather smugly I fear, that Billy Fraser's strike threat had played right into my hands.

We turned on the television news. First there was an item saying that the British Government is again being pressured by the US Government to take some more Cuban refugees. And then – the bombshell! Billy Fraser came on, and threatened that the whole of the NHS in London would be going on strike tonight at midnight if we laid off workers at St Edward's. I was shattered.

[*We have been fortunate to obtain the transcript of the television news programme in question, and it is reproduced below – Ed.*]

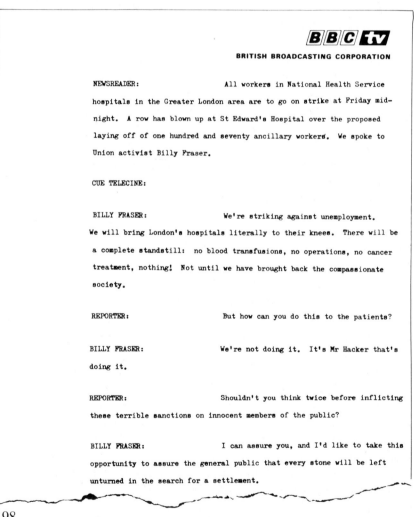

BRITISH BROADCASTING CORPORATION

NEWSREADER: All workers in National Health Service hospitals in the Greater London area are to go on strike at Friday midnight. A row has blown up at St Edward's Hospital over the proposed laying off of one hundred and seventy ancillary workers. We spoke to Union activist Billy Fraser.

CUE TELECINE:

BILLY FRASER: We're striking against unemployment. We will bring London's hospitals literally to their knees. There will be a complete standstill: no blood transfusions, no operations, no cancer treatment, nothing! Not until we have brought back the compassionate society.

REPORTER: But how can you do this to the patients?

BILLY FRASER: We're not doing it. It's Mr Hacker that's doing it.

REPORTER: Shouldn't you think twice before inflicting these terrible sanctions on innocent members of the public?

BILLY FRASER: I can assure you, and I'd like to take this opportunity to assure the general public that every stone will be left unturned in the search for a settlement.

Humphrey came in at that moment.

'Oh,' he said, 'you're watching it.'

'Yes,' I said through clenched teeth. 'Humphrey, you told me you were going to have a word with the unions.'

'I did,' he replied. 'But well, what can I do?' He shrugged helplessly. I'm sure he did his best with the unions. But where has it got us?

I asked him what we were supposed to do now.

But Humphrey had come, apparently, on a different matter – of equal urgency. Another bombshell, in fact!

'It looks as if Sir Maurice Williams' independent enquiry is going to be unfavourable to us,' he began.

I was appalled. Humphrey had promised me that Williams was sound. He had told me that the man wanted a peerage.

'Unfortunately,' murmured Sir Humphrey, embarrassed, looking at his shoes, 'he's also trying to work his peerage in his capacity as Chairman of the Joint Committee for the Resettlement of Refugees.'

I enquired if there were more Brownie points in refugees than in government enquiries.

He nodded.

I pointed out that we simply haven't got the money to house any more refugees.

Then came bombshell number three! The phone rang. It was Number Ten.

I got on the line. I was told rather sharply by a senior policy adviser that Number Ten had seen Billy Fraser on the six o'clock news. By 'Number Ten' he meant the PM. Number Ten hoped a peace formula could be found very soon.

As I was contemplating this euphemistic but heavy threat from Downing Street, Humphrey was still rattling on about the boring old Cuban refugees. Sir Maurice would be satisfied if we just housed a thousand of them, he said.

As I was about to explain, yet again, that we haven't the time or the money to open a thousand-bed hostel . . . the penny dropped!

A most beautiful solution had occurred to me.

A thousand refugees with nowhere to go. A thousand-bed hospital, fully staffed. Luck was on our side after all. The symmetry was indescribably lovely.

Humphrey saw what I was thinking, of course, and seemed all set to resist. 'Minister,' he began, 'that hospital has millions of pounds' worth of high-technology equipment. It was built for sick British, not healthy foreigners. There is a huge Health Service waiting list. It would be an act of the most appalling financial irresponsibility to waste all that investment on . . .'

I interrupted this flow of hypocritical jingoistic nonsense.

'But . . .' I said carefully, 'what about the independent enquiry? Into our Department? Didn't you say that Sir Maurice's enquiry was going to come down against us? Is that what you want?'

He paused. 'I see your point, Minister,' he replied thoughtfully.

I told Bernard to reinstate, immediately, all the staff at St Edward's, to tell Sir Maurice we are making a brand-new hospital available to accommodate a thousand refugees, and to tell the press it was my decision. Everyone was going to be happy!

Bernard asked me for a quote for the press release. A good notion.

'Tell them,' I said, 'that Mr Hacker said that this was a tough decision but a necessary one, if we in Britain aim to be worthy of the name of . . . the compassionate society.'

I asked Humphrey if he was agreeable to all this.

'Yes Minister,' he said. And I thought I detected a touch of admiration in his tone.

9
The Death List

March 28th
It's become clear to me, as I sit here for my usual Sunday evening period of contemplation and reflection, that Roy (my driver) knows a great deal more than I realised about what is going on in Whitehall.

Whitehall is the most secretive square mile in the world. The great emphasis on avoidance of error (which is what the Civil Service is really about, since that is their only real incentive) also means that avoidance of publication is equally necessary.

As Sir Arnold is reported to have said some months ago, 'If no one knows what you're doing, then no one knows what you're doing *wrong*.'

[*Perhaps this explains why government forms are always so hard to understand. Forms are written to protect the person who is in charge of the form – Ed.*]

And so the way information is provided – or withheld – is the key to running the government smoothly.

This concern with the avoidance of error leads inexorably to the need to commit everything to paper – civil servants copy *everything*, and send copies to all their colleagues. (This is also because 'chaps don't like to leave other chaps out', as Bernard once explained to me.) The Treasury was rather more competent before the invention of Xerox than it is now, because its officials had so much less to read (and therefore less to confuse them).

The civil servants' hunger for paper is insatiable. They want all possible information sent to them, and they send all possible information to their colleagues. It amazes me that they find the time to do anything other than catch up with other people's paperwork. If indeed they do.

It is also astonishing that so little of this vast mass of typescript ever becomes public knowledge – a very real tribute to Whitehall's talent for secrecy. For it is axiomatic with civil servants that information should only be revealed to their political 'masters' when absolutely necessary, and to the public when absolutely unavoidable.

But I now see that I can learn some useful lessons from their methods. For a start, I must pay more attention to Bernard and Roy. I resolve today that I will not let false pride come between Roy and me – in other words, I shall no longer pretend that I know more than my driver does. Tomorrow, when he collects me at Euston, I shall ask him to tell me anything that he has picked up, and I shall tell him that he mustn't assume that Ministers know more secrets than drivers.

On second thoughts, I don't need to tell him that – he knows already!

As to the Private Secretaries' grapevine, it was most interesting to learn last week that Sir Humphrey had had a wigging from Sir Arnold. This will have profoundly upset Humphrey, who above all values the opinions of his colleagues.

For there is one grapevine with even more knowledge and influence than the Private Secretaries' or the drivers' – and that is the Permanent Secretaries' grapevine. (Cabinet colleagues, of course, have a hopeless grapevine because they are not personal friends, don't know each other all that well, and hardly ever see each other except in Cabinet or in the Division Lobby.)

This wigging could also, I gather, affect his chances of becoming Secretary to the Cabinet on Arnold's retirement, or screw up the possibility of his finding a cushy job in Brussels.

Happily, this is not my problem – and, when I mentioned it to my spies, both Bernard and Roy agreed (independently) that Sir Humphrey would not be left destitute. Apart from his massive index-linked pension, a former Permanent Secretary is always fixed up with a job if he wants it – Canals and Waterways, or *something*.

As for Bernard, I have recently been impressed with his loyalty to me. He seems to be giving me all the help he possibly can without putting his own career at risk. In fact, I am almost becoming concerned about the amount of rapport, decency and goodwill that exists between us – if he exhibits a great deal more of these qualities he will almost certainly be moved elsewhere. There may come a time when the Department feels that the more use he is to *me* the less use he is to *them*.

March 29th
I was sitting at my desk this afternoon going through some letters when Bernard sidled in holding something behind his back.

'Excuse me, Minister,' he said. 'There's something in the press about you that I think you ought to see.'

I was pleased. 'About me? That's nice.'

Bernard looked bleak. 'Well . . .' he swallowed, 'I'm afraid it's in *Private Eye*.'

Trembling, I took the offending rag and held it away from me with my forefinger and thumb. I didn't have the courage to open it. Normally the press officer brings you your own press cuttings. If he'd given his job to Bernard, it meant terrible news. No prizes for guessing which, in the case of *Private Eye*.

'They're . . . um . . . exposing something,' said Bernard.

Panic thoughts flashed through my mind. In that instant my whole life passed before me. Was it that IOS Consultancy, I wondered? Or that character reference I wrote for Dr Savundra? Or that wretched party at John Poulson's?

I didn't even dare mention them to Bernard. So I put a good face on it. 'Well,' I said, chin up, 'what have they made up about me to put in their squalid little rag?'

'Perhaps you'd better read it yourself,' he said.

So I did.

It was acutely embarrassing.

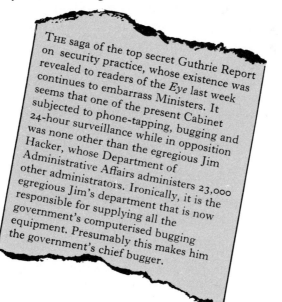

THE saga of the top secret Guthrie Report on security practice, whose existence was revealed to readers of the *Eye* last week continues to embarrass Ministers. It seems that one of the present Cabinet subjected to phone-tapping, bugging and 24-hour surveillance while in opposition was none other than the egregious Jim Hacker, whose Department of Administrative Affairs administers 23,000 other administrators. Ironically, it is the egregious Jim's department that is now responsible for supplying all the government's computerised bugging equipment. Presumably this makes him the government's chief bugger.

I sent for Humphrey at once. I had to establish whether or not this lie was true.

One aspect of this squalid little story puzzled me in particular – 'What does egregious mean?' I asked Bernard.

'I think it means "outstanding" . . . in one way or another,' he explained.

That's okay, *if* that's what it means, but it seems a little too generous for *Private Eye*. I must remember to look it up sometime.

Humphrey arrived, was shown the piece, and actually had the temerity to laugh at the bugger joke.

'Is this true?' I demanded.

'Oh absolutely not, Minister,' he replied firmly. I was relieved for a moment, until he went on, 'It's only one of their little jokes. I don't think that anyone actually supposes that you are a bu . . . I mean . . . that is . . .'

I exploded. 'Humphrey, I'm not talking about that tasteless little joke. I'm asking you if the gist of this story is true – was I once under surveillance and am I now responsible for the bugging equipment?'

'Surely . . .' said Humphrey evasively, and how well I recognise the tactics by now! 'Surely you don't believe what you read in that squalid little rag?'

[*'Squalid little rag' was clearly Whitehall general slang usage for* Private Eye *at about this time – Ed.*]

I asked him again. Was it accurate?

Sir Humphrey again declined to give a straight answer. 'I don't think we should take it too seriously, Minister,' he replied suavely.

I saw red. I told him that I regard this as an outrageous and intolerable intrusion into my privacy. If he didn't see anything wrong with it, I certainly did. And I propose to take it very seriously indeed. I reminded Humphrey that the article stated that I, a free citizen, and furthermore an MP, have been under total surveillance. Surveillance is an attack on democracy. I asked Humphrey if he was aware that it contravenes the European Convention on Human Rights.

He remained calm. 'Surveillance,' he said, 'is an indispensable weapon in the battle against organised crime.'

I was incredulous. That's no reason for bugging me, a politician. 'Humphrey,' I asked, 'are you describing politicians as organised crime?'

He smiled. 'Well . . . disorganised crime too,' he joked. I was not amused. He realised that he was going too far, and hastily started to repair the damage. 'No, seriously, Minister . . .'

I cut him short. I reminded Humphrey of my own track record, one which made this situation particularly awkward for me.

'While I was editor of *Reform* I wrote a leader criticising this kind of intrusion. Furthermore, I started a nationwide petition against bureaucratic busybodies snooping and phone-tapping. And *now* I learn,' I continued angrily, ' – from *Private Eye*, please note, and not from you – that *I*, of *all* people, am in charge of the whole technical side of it.' It was all profoundly embarrassing.

Sir Humphrey merely nodded.

I asked the inevitable question.

'Why didn't you tell me about this?'

'Because,' came the inevitable answer, 'you didn't ask.'

'Well,' I said, 'thank God for the free press. Thank God for at least one brave, open and fearless journal in this country.'

Bernard started to remind me that I had previously described it differently, but I stopped him. However, I took the opportunity to explain to him that he really must sharpen up his political antennae. He needs to learn to adjust more flexibly to a developing situation.

He took my point, I think – I hope!

The next question inevitably raised by these revelations concerns the tapes and/or transcripts that must have been made of my bugged conversations. Where are they?

'I imagine,' said Humphrey carelessly, as if it didn't really matter all that much, 'that they must have been put into a report.'

'And who got those reports?' I wanted to know.

'I imagine that the Home Secretary gets . . . got them.' He corrected himself quickly. But not quickly enough.

'*Gets* them?' I shrieked. 'You mean it's *still going on*?'

He tried to pacify me, but without success. 'No, Minister, not you, not now. *Now* he will be getting reports on current members of Her Majesty's Opposition.'

The mechanics were still unclear to me. 'Who gives these reports to the Home Secretary?' I demanded.

He shrugged. 'MI5, presumably.'

'You seem very calm about all this.'

He smiled. He was really getting right up my nose, the complacent . . . [*expletive deleted – Ed.*]

I certainly wasn't calm about it. I threw one of my real fits. I denounced the whole business. 'It is *horrifying*,' I insisted. 'A British citizen – in my case, a *distinguished* British citizen – one who has dedicated his life to the service of his fellow countrymen . . . and all the time those gloating, faceless bureaucrats are listening to his every word. All his private calls. His rows with his wife. His shouting matches with his daughter. His private arrangements with his accountant.' Perhaps I'd gone too far – maybe the room was bugged! 'Not that I have anything I'd be ashamed to reveal, my life is an open book.'

'Quite, quite,' agreed both Humphrey and Bernard.

'But it's the principle of the thing!'

I stopped. I waited. The ball was in his court. Surely Sir Humphrey would have something to say. But no explanation or justification was forthcoming.

Sir Humphrey just sat there, head sympathetically inclined to one side, listening, for all the world like a Freudian psychoanalyst who has been sitting at the head of a couch listening to the rantings and ravings of a neurotic patient.

After he'd said nothing for quite a long time, I realised that he *didn't* realise that the ball was in his court.

'Why?' I asked.

Sir Humphrey jumped, and focused his eyes in my direction. 'Why what?' he replied. 'Why surveillance, or why you?'

'Both.'

'In any case,' he smiled blandly, 'it's the same answer.'

My blood boiled. 'Then why,' I snapped, 'did you split it into two questions?'

There was no reply to that.

[*Sir Humphrey could hardly explain to Hacker that he did not want to risk answering a question that Hacker had not asked – Ed.*]

Then Humphrey began his general explanation. 'I should have thought it was perfectly obvious. Before the election it was rumoured that you might be appointed Secretary of State for Defence. If the PM were to consider giving you Defence, you can surely see that it would be in the national interest for MI5 to satisfy itself that you were not a security risk?'

'But my privacy was invaded,' I pointed out.

He smiled his smuggest smile. 'Better than your country being invaded, Minister.'

I must say, I could see that point. There was a valid argument there.

But I was sure that Humphrey had never experienced the feeling that I was feeling. And democracy is about the feelings and rights of the individual – that's what distinguishes a democracy from a dictatorship.

I said to him: 'Have *you* ever been under surveillance, Humphrey?'

He was astounded. 'Me?'

'You. You, Humphrey.'

He got on to his highest horse. 'I am a civil servant,' he said, as if that absolutely closed the discussion.

'So were Burgess and Maclean, and Philby,' I observed.

He was rattled, but he swiftly produced a counter-argument. 'They were not Permanent Secretaries! One becomes a Permanent Secretary only after a lifetime of personal responsibility, reliability and integrity. The most rigorous selection procedures winnow out all but the most upright, honourable and discreet of public servants.'

I noted the emphasis on 'discreet'. The secrecy thing again, here openly acknowledged. I also noted that in giving this glowing description of Permanent Secretaries he thought that he was, in fact, describing himself. And I also noted that he had begged the question: even if Permanent Secretaries are never security risks, Humphrey said that he had *never* been bugged. But he hasn't been a Permanent Secretary all his life, has he?

As Humphrey had described the qualities of Permanent Secretaries in a way that argued that they need not be subject to surveillance, I inquired how he felt about Ministers. It was as I expected.

'Ministers,' he said, 'have a whole range of dazzling qualities including . . . um . . . well, including an enviable intellectual suppleness and moral manoeuvrability.'

I invited him to explain himself.

'You can't trust Ministers,' he said bluntly. I was appalled at his rudeness. 'I'm being quite candid now,' he added unnecessarily. Bloody insolent, I'd call it. 'I don't mean, by the way, that we can't trust *you*, Minister – of course we can. But in general terms Ministers, unlike civil servants, are selected completely at random – by Prime Ministerial whim, in recognition of doubtful favours received, or to avoid appointing someone of real ability who might become a threat – not *you*, of course, Minister. *You* can certainly be trusted. *You* might almost be a civil servant yourself.'

[*Sir Humphrey almost certainly meant this as a compliment. Indeed, the ultimate compliment. However, Hacker should certainly have taken this as a hint that he might be house-trained. Regrettably, he allowed the flattery to get the better of him – Ed.*]

I was mollified. I didn't think he was bullshitting.

I let him continue. 'Minister, would you trust every one of your Cabinet colleagues never to betray a confidence?'

I couldn't really give an answer to that, without appearing somewhat disloyal to my Cabinet colleagues.

'And what about all the Opposition Front Bench?' he asked.

That was an easy one. 'You certainly can't trust that lot,' I exclaimed.

'Quite so,' he said, checkmating me neatly, 'and *you* were on the Opposition Front Bench at the time.'

It has always been hard to win this kind of argument with Humphrey. But he's into winning arguments – whereas I'm into getting things done!

So I cut the discussion short. I made my decision. Which is to stop all surveillance. It's a matter of principle.

He countered by informing me that this is a Home Office matter, and in many cases not within our purview.

This didn't bother me. I can certainly make it much more difficult in future. If I'm responsible for the apparatus, I intend to make myself responsible for some proper democratic safeguards for us all (before the apparatus can be used).

'Are you perhaps going to suggest,' he enquired sarcastically, 'that people will not be able to be put under secret surveillance until they've signed a form saying that they agree to it?'

I rose above it. 'No,' I said gently but firmly, 'I propose that we shall have a Select Committee of both Houses chaired by a Law Lord to decide on every application. And no surveillance will be allowed to go on for more than two weeks without reapplying.'

Then I told him to set the wheels in motion.

He argued no further, but took his leave of me in a very frosty manner.

I was full of ideas today. After Humphrey had stalked out I told Bernard to send a minute to each member of the Cabinet.

I also thought of planting a question from one of our backbenchers to the Home Secretary. Something like: *Will the Home Secretary assure the House that none of his Cabinet colleagues has ever been placed under government surveillance?* That will shake him. And it will bring the matter out into the open. We'll see if it's just a Home Office matter! I think not!

Finally, I asked Bernard to make an appointment for me to meet Walter Fowler of the *Express* for a quick drink in Annie's Bar at the

House, later this week.

'What for?' Bernard wanted to know.

'First law of political indiscretion,' I replied. 'You always have a drink before you leak.'

[*Walter Fowler was the Lobby Correspondent of the* Express. *This meant that he would probably have been their political editor or head of the paper's political staff. The Lobby was a uniquely British system, the best way yet devised in any democracy for taming and muzzling the press.*

This is because it is hard to censor the press when it wants to be free, but easy if it gives up its freedom voluntarily.

There were in the 1980s 150 Lobby Correspondents, who had the special privilege of being able to mingle with MPs and Ministers in the Lobby behind both chambers of Parliament. As journalists, however, they were – quite properly – not allowed to sit down on the leather-covered benches. Neither were they allowed to report anything they saw – e.g. MPs hitting one another – nor anything they overheard.

You may ask: who stipulated what they were not allowed to do? Who made all these restrictions? Answer: The lobby correspondents themselves!

In return for the freedom of access to Ministers and MPs, they exercised the most surprising and elaborate self-censorship.

The Lobby received daily briefings from the Prime Minister's Press Secretary at Number Ten Downing Street, and weekly briefings from the Leader of the House and the Leader of the Opposition. All these briefings were unattributable.

The Lobby correspondents argued that, in return for their self-censorship, they would learn infinitely more about the government, its motives, and its plans. The politicians loved the Lobby system because they could leak any old rubbish, which the Lobby would generally swallow whole. As they had heard it in confidence, they believed it must be true.

We believe, with the advantage of hindsight, that the Lobby was merely one example of the way in which the British establishment dealt with potential danger or criticism – it would embrace the danger, and thus suffocate it.

The Lobby certainly discouraged political journalists from going out and searching for a story, as they only had to sit on their bottoms in Annie's Bar (the bar exclusively reserved for the press, with the highest alcoholic consumption of any of the thirteen bars within the Palace of Westminster – which was saying something!) and a 'leak' would come their way.

Finally, a word on leaks. Because there was no free access to information in Whitehall, everybody leaked. Everybody knew there was no other way to make the wheels go round.

Equally, everybody pretended that leaking was 'not on', 'not cricket', 'below board' or underhand in the same way. This is because discretion is the most highly valued talent in Whitehall. Even above 'soundness'. Or perhaps discretion is the ultimate indication that you are 'sound'!

Whenever a 'leak' occurred there would be cries of moral indignation, and a leak inquiry would be set up by the Prime Minister. Such enquiries seldom reported at the end, for fear of the embarrassing result – most leaks came from 'Number Ten' (a euphemism), most budget leaks from 'Number Eleven' (another euphemism) – Ed.]

March 30th

I met Walter Fowler in Annie's Bar, as arranged, and leaked my plans for curtailing surveillance.

Walter seemed a little sceptical. He said it was a worthy cause but I'd never see it through. This made me all the more determined. I told him that I intended to see it through, and to carry the Home Office on this matter in due course. I asked him if it would make a story – I knew it would, but journalists like to feel that their opinions are valuable.

Walter confirmed it would make a story: 'MINISTER FIGHTS FOR PHONE-TAP SAFEGUARDS – yes, there's something there.' He wheezed deeply and drank two-thirds of a pint of special.

I asked where they'd run it. He thought fairly high up on the Home News Page. I was slightly disappointed.

'Not on page one?'

'Well . . .' said Walter doubtfully. 'Can I attribute it? MINISTER SPEAKS OUT!'

I squashed that at once.

'So where did I get the story?' asked Walter plaintively. 'I presume I can't say it was "officially announced" or a "government spokesman"?'

I told him he presumed right.

We silently pondered the other options.

'How about "sources close to the Minister"?' he asked after a minute or two.

'Hopeless,' I pointed out, 'I don't want *everybody* to know I told you. Isn't it possible for you to do a "speculation is growing in Westminster . . ."?'

Walter shook his head sadly. 'Bit weak,' he said, and again he wheezed. He was like an old accordion. He produced a vile-looking pipe from his grubby pockets and stuffed tobacco into the bowl with a stubby forefinger that had a thick black line of dirt under the nail.

I watched fascinated. 'What about "unofficial spokesman",' I suggested, just before the first gust of smoke engulfed me.

'I've used that twice this week already,' replied Walter, contentedly polluting the atmosphere of central London. I choked quietly.

It was true. He had used it twice this week. I'd noticed. 'Cabinet's leaking like a sieve, isn't it?'

He nodded. 'Yes – um . . .' he poured some more bitter past his nicotine-stained molars into his smoking mouth, '. . . could we attribute it to a leading member of the sieve?' I looked at him. 'Er . . . Cabinet?' he corrected himself hastily.

I shook my head.

'How would you like to be an "informed source"?' he offered.

That seemed a good idea. I hadn't been an informed source for some weeks.

'Okay,' I said. 'That's what I'll be.'

Walter chuckled. 'Quite a joke, isn't it?'

'What?' I asked blankly.

'Describing someone as "informed", when his Permanent Secretary is Sir Humphrey Appleby.'

He bared his yellow teeth at me. I think it was a smile. I didn't smile back – I just bared my teeth at him.

March 31st

Annie came up to London today from the constituency.

So this evening I told her about the surveillance we'd been under. I thought she'd be as indignant as me. But she didn't seem to care.

I tried to make her grasp the extent of the wrongdoing. 'Everything we said on the phone, everything we said to each other – all recorded. Transcribed. It's humiliating.'

'Yes, I see . . .' she said thoughtfully, 'it is a little humiliating that someone at MI5 knows just how boring our life is.'

'What?'

'All will be revealed,' she said. 'Or has already been revealed. That what you talk about at home is what you talk about in public –

the gross national product, the public sector borrowing requirement, the draft agenda for the party conference . . .'

I explained that I didn't mean *that.* I meant that all our private family talk had been overheard.

'Oh dear, yes,' said Annie. 'I hadn't thought of that . . . "Have you got the car keys?" . . . "No, I thought *you* had them" . . . "No, I gave them to you" . . . My God, that could bring the government down!'

'Annie.' I was cross. 'You're not taking this seriously.'

'Whatever gives you that idea?'

'You still haven't grasped how our privacy has been intruded upon. They might have heard what we say to each other . . . in bed.'

'Would it matter?' she asked, feigning surprise. 'Do you snore in code?'

I think she was trying to tell me something. Only last week she caused me great embarrassment when she was interviewed in some juvenile woman's magazine. They asked her if the earth moved when she went to bed with me. 'No,' she'd replied, 'not even the bed moves.'

Perhaps this was part of a campaign.

It was. She went on. 'Look, it's the Bank Holiday weekend coming up. Why don't we go away for a long weekend, two or three days, like we used to?'

My first thought was that I couldn't. Then I thought: why not? And I couldn't think of a reason. After all, even statesmen need holidays. I agreed.

'Let's go to Kingsbury Down,' she said.

'Fine,' I said. 'Where is it?'

She stared at me. 'Only where we spent our honeymoon, darling.' Funny, I'd forgotten the name of the place. I tried to remember what it looked like.

'It's where you first explained to me your theory about the effect of velocity of circulation on the net growth of the money supply.'

I remembered it well. 'Oh yes, I know the place then,' I said.

Annie turned towards her bedside lamp. 'Did you get that, boys?' she muttered into it.

[*A startling development took place on the following day. The Special Branch contacted Sir Humphrey Appleby and Bernard Woolley with the news that a terrorist hit list had been discovered, and Jim Hacker's name appeared on it as a potential target.*

The list apparently was drawn up by a group calling itself the International Freedom Army – Ed.]

SIR BERNARD WOOLLEY RECALLS:[1]
We could not imagine who on earth could possibly want to assassinate the Minister. He was so harmless.

Nevertheless, Sir Humphrey Appleby and I were fully agreed that it was not possible to take risks with the Minister's life, and so the whole paraphernalia of security would have to be brought out to protect him.

[*Hacker's diary continues – Ed.*]

April 2nd
Bernard greeted me like a mother hen this morning. He asked after my health with an earnest and solicitous attitude.

I thought perhaps it was because I was a little late at the office. I hadn't slept too well – 'I feel like death,' I remarked.

Bernard whispered to Sir Humphrey, 'Perhaps that's just as well,' a comment which I did not understand at the time but which I now regard as having been in the poorest of taste.

I was actually rather cheerful. My leak had worked. A story had appeared in the *Express*: HACKER MOVES TO CURB PHONE TAPS. I was described as an informed source, as agreed, and Walter had not taken a by-line – the story was 'from our Political Staff'.

Sir Humphrey wondered audibly where they'd got the information, and stared at me. Naturally I admitted nothing.

[*It has been said that the ship of state is the only type of ship that leaks from the top – Ed.*]

'Anyway,' I added, 'this leak only confirms my determination to act on this matter.'

Humphrey asked me if I'd considered all the implications. This is generally the Civil Service way of asking me if I realised that I was talking rubbish. In this case, as it was to turn out, I had *not* quite considered all the implications.

So I replied that free citizens have a right to privacy. An absolute right.

How could I have said such a thing?

But I didn't know then what I knew just five minutes later. Those bastards hadn't told me.

'Suppose . . .' suggested Sir Humphrey smoothly, 'suppose MI5 had reason to suspect that these "free citizens" were, shall we say to take a purely hypothetical example, planning to assassinate a Minister of the Crown?'

[1] In conversation with the Editors.

I made a little speech. I spoke of the freedom of the British people, and how this is more important than the lives of a few Ministers. I said that freedom is indivisible, whereas Ministers are expendable. 'Men in public life must expect to be the targets of cranks and fanatics. A Minister has the duty to set his own life at naught, to stand up and say "Here I am, do your worst!" and not cower in craven terror behind electronic equipment and secret microphones and all the hideous apparatus of the police state.' Me and my big mouth.

Sir Humphrey and Bernard looked at each other. The former tried to speak but I made it clear that I would brook no arguments.

'No Humphrey, I don't want to hear any more about it. You deal in evasions and secrets. But politicians in a free country must be seen to be the champions of freedom and truth. Don't try and give me the arguments in favour of telephone tapping – I can find them in Stalin's memoirs.'

'Actually,' quibbled Bernard, 'Stalin didn't write any memoirs. He was too secretive. He was afraid people might read them.'

Humphrey succeeded in interrupting us.

'Minister,' he insisted, 'you *must* allow me to say one more thing on this matter.'

I told him that he might say one sentence, but he should keep it brief.

'The Special Branch have found your name on a death list,' he said.

I thought I must have misheard.

'What?' I said.

'The Special Branch have found your name on a death list,' he repeated.

This made no sense. A death list? Why me?

'A death list?' I asked. 'What do you mean, a death list?'

'An assassination list,' he said.

He really is a fool. 'I know what you mean by a death list,' I said, 'but . . . what do you mean?'

Sir Humphrey was now as baffled as I.

'I don't know how I can express it more clearly, Minister,' he said plaintively.

Obviously, I wanted him to explain things like what the list was, where it came from, why I was on it – my mind was racing with dozens of unanswered questions, that's why I was so inarticulate.

Sir Humphrey tried to answer what he thought I was asking him.

'To put it absolutely bluntly, Minister, confidential investigations have revealed the existence of certain documents whose provenance is currently unestablished, but whose effect if realised would be to create a cabinet vacancy and precipitate a by-election.'

I didn't know what he meant. I asked him.

'You are on a death list, Minister.'

We were going round in circles. 'Who . . . ?' I spluttered, 'What . . . ?'

'Ah,' he said. 'I see. It is the International Freedom Army. A new urban guerrilla group, apparently.'

My bowels were turning to water. 'But what have they got against me?' I whispered.

Bernard reminded me of the vague rumours recently of a Cabinet reshuffle, and that my name has been mentioned in one or two of the papers in connection with the Ministry of Defence.

I asked who they could be, these urban guerrillas. Bernard and Humphrey just shrugged.

'Hard to say, Minister. It could be an Irish splinter group, or Baader-Meinhof, or PLO, or Black September. It could be home-grown loonies – Anarchists, Maoists. Or it might be Libyans, Iranians, or the Italian Red Brigade for all we know.'

'In any case,' added Bernard, 'they're all interconnected really. This could simply be a new group of freelance killers. The Special Branch don't know where to start.'

That was *very* encouraging, I must say! I couldn't get over the cool, callous, unemotional way in which they were discussing some maniacs who were trying to kill me.

I tried to grasp at straws.

'There's a *list* of names, is there? You said a list? Not just me?'

'Not just you, Minister,' Sir Humphrey confirmed.

I said that I supposed that there were hundreds of names on it.

'Just three,' said Humphrey.

'Three?'

I was in a state of shock. I think. Or panic. One of those. I just sat there unable to think or speak. My mouth had completely dried up.

As I tried to say something, anything, the phone rang. Bernard answered it. Apparently somebody called Commander Forest from Special Branch had come to brief me.

Bernard went to get him. As he left he turned to me and said in a kindly fashion: 'Try looking at it this way, Minister – it's always nice to be on a shortlist. At least they know who you are.'

I gave him a withering look, and he hurried out.

Sir Humphrey filled in the background. The Special Branch had apparently informed the Home Secretary (the usual procedure) who recommended detectives to protect me.

I don't see how they can protect me. How can detectives protect me from an assassin's bullet? Nobody can. Everybody knows that.

I said this to Humphrey. I suppose I hoped he'd disagree – but he didn't. 'Look at it this way,' he responded. 'Even if detectives cannot protect anyone, they do ensure that the assassin is brought to justice. After the victim has been gunned down.'

Thanks a lot!

Bernard brought in Commander Forest. He was a tall thin cadaverous-looking individual, with a slightly nervous flinching manner. He didn't really inspire confidence.

I decided that I had to put on a brave show. Chin up, stiff upper lip, pull myself together, that sort of thing. I'd been talking a lot about leadership. Now I had to prove to them – and myself – that I was officer material.

I smiled reassuringly at the Commander, as he offered to brief me on the standard hazards and routine precautions. 'I don't really have to take these things too seriously, do I?' I asked in a cavalier manner.

'Well, sir, in a sense, it's up to you, but we do *advise* . . .'

I interrupted. 'Look, I can see that some people might get into a frightful funk but, well, it's the job, isn't it? All in a day's work.'

Commander Forest gazed at me strangely. 'I admire your courage, sir,' he said as if he really thought I were a raving idiot.

I decided I'd done enough of the stiff upper lip. I'd let him speak. 'Okay, shoot,' I said. It was an unfortunate turn of phrase.

'Read this,' he said, and thrust a Xeroxed typescript into my hand. 'This will tell you all you need to know. Study it, memorise it, and keep it to yourself.'

[*The Museum of the Metropolitan Police at New Scotland Yard has kindly lent us a copy of 'Security Precautions', the document handed to Hacker. It is self-explanatory – Ed.*]

SECURITY PRECAUTIONS

Assassination hazards fall broadly into four categories:
i) BULLETS
ii) BOMBS
iii) POISONS
iv) ACCIDENTS so-called
There is also the possibility of gassing, throttling, stabbing, drowning, garotting and ritual disembowelling, but most of these are comparatively infrequent in the UK

i) BULLETS
Snipers can be found in various locations
(a) a high building
(b) a car travelling beside your car
(c) Stealing up close to you in a crowd
(d) at your front door, as an unexpected caller
(e) in a parked van, concealing a marksman
(f) thrusting a revolver through your car window
etc. etc

Precautions
(a) Avoid crowds
(b) Keep away from windows
(Bullet-proof net curtains will be provided at your home and your office)
(c) Never answer your own front door
(d) Keep your car window up, windows and doors locked while you are driving
(e) Never draw up at traffic lights on the pavement side
(f) If a car pulls across in front of you, do *not* ram it in the middle. *Aim for one of the axles and sweep it aside*

N.B. Initially, Special Branch Police Officers will not only answer your front door for you, but will give all available protection and cover: alarms, 24-hour patrols by your local constituency police force, special locks, phone taps,
– etc

ii) BOMBS
(a) Car bombs – use regulation issue mirror at the end of a long pole, in order to check thoroughly the underside of your chassis each morning, and on any occasion on which the car has been left unattended

(b) Letter/parcel bombs – never open any yourself
N.B. For the time being all your mail will be redirected

iii) POISON
(a) *Gifts* of food and drink, chocolates, sweets, etc. – treat with suspicion
(b) Check milk bottle tops in the morning for hypodermic holes
(c) Avoid strangers approaching you with umbrellas – (the ferrule jabbed in the calf/thigh method)

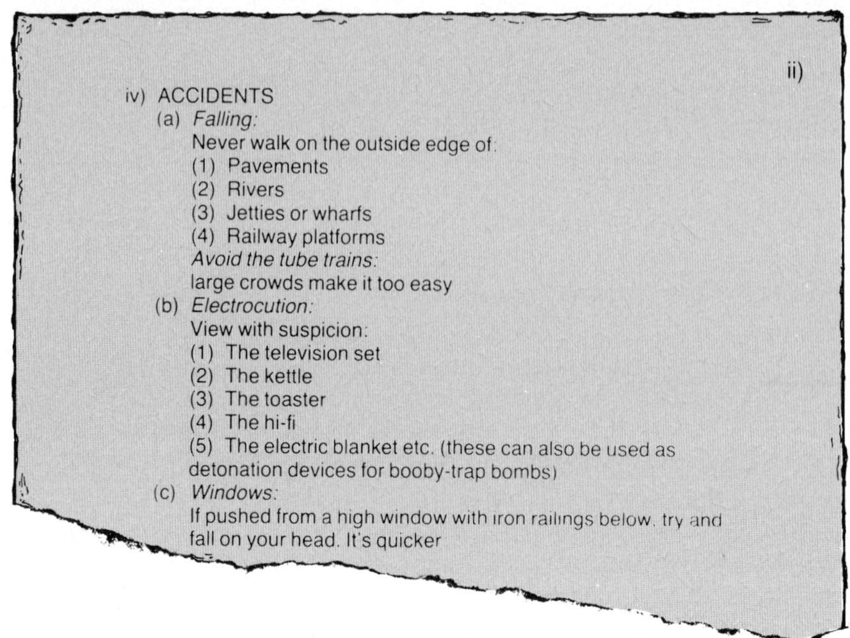
ii)

iv) ACCIDENTS
(a) *Falling:*
Never walk on the outside edge of:
(1) Pavements
(2) Rivers
(3) Jetties or wharfs
(4) Railway platforms
Avoid the tube trains:
large crowds make it too easy
(b) *Electrocution:*
View with suspicion:
(1) The television set
(2) The kettle
(3) The toaster
(4) The hi-fi
(5) The electric blanket etc. (these can also be used as detonation devices for booby-trap bombs)
(c) *Windows:*
If pushed from a high window with iron railings below, try and fall on your head. It's quicker

I read the document through. It seemed to me as though I had little chance of survival. But I must continue to have courage.

After Commander Forest had left, I asked Humphrey how the police would find these terrorists before they found me. That seems to be my only hope.

Sir Humphrey remarked that telephone tapping and electronic surveillance of all possible suspects is the best way of picking these bastards up.

'But,' he added cautiously, 'that does incur intolerable intrusion upon individual privacy.'

I carefully considered the implications of this comment.

And then I came to the conclusion. A slightly different conclusion, although I think that perhaps he had misunderstood what I'd been saying earlier.

I explained that, on the other hand, if the people's elected representatives are to represent the people, it follows that any attack on these elected representatives is, *in itself*, an attack on freedom and democracy. The reason is clear. Such threats strike at the very heart of the people's inalienable democratic right to be governed by the leaders of their choice. Therefore, the safety of these leaders must be protected by every possible means – however much we might regret the necessity for doing so or the measures that we may be forced to take.

I explained all this to Humphrey. He was in complete agreement – although I didn't care for his choice of words. 'Beautifully argued, Minister,' he replied. 'My view exactly – or else you're a dead duck.'

April 5th

Today there was a slight embarrassment.

My petition arrived.

The petition against phone tapping and electronic surveillance, the one that I started a year and a half ago when I was in opposition and Editor of *Reform*. Bernard wheeled into the office a huge office trolley loaded with piles of exercise books and reams of paper. It now has two and a quarter million signatures. A triumph of organisation and commitment, and what the hell do I bloody well do with it?

It is now clear to me – now that I have the *full* facts which you cannot get when in opposition, of course – that surveillance is an indispensable weapon in the fight against organised terror and crime.

Bernard understood. He offered to file the petition.

I wasn't sure that filing it was the answer. We had acknowledged receipt from the deputation – they would never ask to see it again. And they would imagine that it was in safe hands since I'm the one who began it all.

I told him to shred it. 'Bernard,' I said, 'we must make certain that no one ever finds it again.'

'In that case,' replied Bernard, 'I'm sure it would be best to file it.'

[*This situation was not without precedent.*

In April 1965 the Home Secretary told the House of Commons that 'no useful purpose' would be served by reopening the enquiry into the Timothy Evans case. This was despite a passionate appeal from a leading member of the Opposition front bench, Sir Frank Soskice, who said: 'My appeal to the Home Secretary is most earnest. I believe that if ever there was a debt due to justice and to the reputation both of our own judicial system and to the public conscience . . . that debt is one the Home Secretary should now repay.'

Interestingly enough, a general election had occurred between the launching and the presenting of the petition. Consequently the Home Secretary who rejected Sir Frank Soskice's impassioned appeal – and petition – for an enquiry was Sir Frank Soskice – Ed.]

April 11th
I've just had the most awful Easter weekend of my life.

Annie and I went off on our quiet little weekend together just like we used to.

Well – almost like we used to. Unfortunately, half the Special Branch came with us.

When we went for a quiet afternoon stroll through the woods, the whole place was swarming with rozzers.

They kept nice and close to us – very protective, but impossible for Annie and me to discuss anything but the weather. They all look the other way – *not*, I hasten to add, out of courtesy or respect for our privacy, but to see if they could spot any potential attacker leaping towards me over the primroses.

We went to a charming restaurant for lunch. It seemed as though the whole of Scotland Yard came too.

'How many for lunch?' asked the head waiter as we came in.

'Nine,' said Annie acidly. The weekend was not working out as she'd expected.

The head waiter offered us a nice table for two by the window, but it was vetoed by a sergeant. 'No, that's not safe,' he muttered to me, and turned to a colleague, 'we've chosen that table over there for the target.'

Target!

So Annie and I were escorted to a cramped little table in a poky little corner next to the kitchen doors. They banged open and shut right beside us, throughout our meal.

As we sat down I was briefed by one of the detectives. 'You sit here. Constable Ross will sit over there, watching the kitchen door – that's your escape route. We don't *expect* any assassins to be among the kitchen staff as we only booked in here late morning. I'll sit by the window. And if you do hear any gunshots, just dive under the table and I'll take care of it.'

I'm sure he meant to be reassuring.

I informed him that I wasn't a bit worried. Then I heard a loud report close to my head, and I crashed under the table.

An utterly humiliating experience – some seconds later I stuck my head out and realised that a champagne bottle had just been opened for the next table. I had to pretend that I'd just been practising.

By this time, with all this talk of escape routes, assassins in the kitchen and so forth, I'd gone right off my food. So had Annie. And our appetites weren't helped by overhearing one of the detectives at the next table order a spaghetti Bolognese followed by a T-bone steak with beans, peas, cauliflower and chips – and a bottle of Château Baron Philippe Rothschild 1961, no less!

He saw us staring at him, beamed, and explained that his job really took it out of him.

We stuck it for nearly two days. We went to the cinema on Saturday evening, but that made Annie even more furious. She'd wanted to see *La Cage aux Folles* but in the end we went to a James Bond film – I knew that none of the detectives liked foreign films, and it didn't seem fair to drag them along to a French film with subtitles.

Annie was black with rage because I'd put their choice first. When she put it like that, I saw what she meant. I hated the Bond film anyway – it was all about assassination attempts, and I couldn't stand it.

The detectives were very fed up with us when we walked out halfway through it.

Finally, back in our hotel, lying in the bed, rigid with tension, unable to go to the loo without being observed, followed and overheard, we heard the following murmured conversation outside the bedroom door.

'Are they going out again?'

'No, they've turned in for the night.'

'Is the target in there now?'

'Yeah – target's in bed with his wife.'

'They don't seem to be enjoying their holiday, do they?'

'No. Wonder why.'

We decided to get up and go home then and there.

But did we find peace and quiet? You bet we didn't. When we got to Birmingham at 1.45 a.m. on Sunday morning, the front garden was knee-deep in the local bluebottles, all wanting to show that they were doing their bit. The flowerbeds were trampled underfoot, searchlights playing constantly on all sides of the house, Alsatians baring their teeth and growling . . . Bedlam!

So now we lay in our *own* beds, still rigid with tension, still unable to go to the loo without some flat-foot examining it first, still with detectives knocking on the bedroom door and barging straight in while saying, 'May I just check your windows sir,' but with the additional pleasures of dogs barking and searchlights lighting up the whole room at intervals of twenty-nine seconds.

I told Annie, pathetically trying to make the best of it all, that she'd soon get used to being a famous man's wife. She didn't say anything. I think she'd almost rather be a famous man's widow.

Thank God we still weren't subject to surveillance at home.

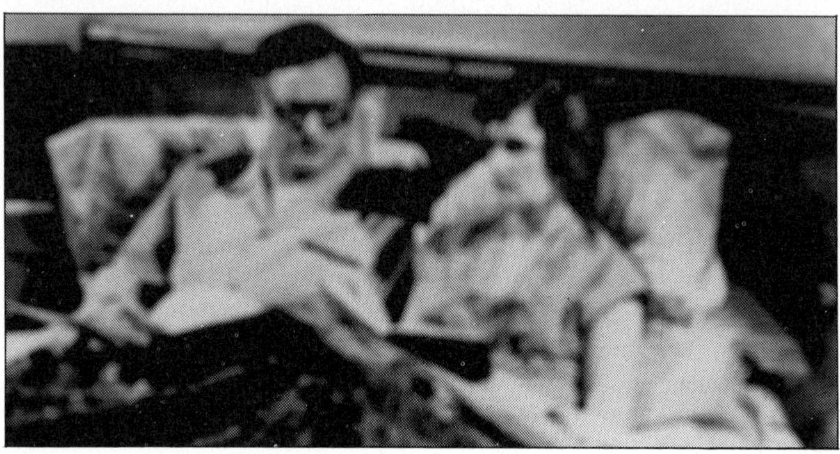

Secret photo (released by the Special Branch at New Scotland Yard after the passing of the Freedom of Information Act, 1994) showing Mr and Mrs Hacker in bed at their home on 12 April.

April 13th

Easter Monday I slept all day, since it's impossible to sleep at night.

Today I was back in the office and trying to handle a difficult interview with the dreadful Walter Fowler, who had somehow got wind of the petition. He seemed to find it extraordinary that I had now suppressed the petition that I started the year before last. Of course, he didn't know that my changed circumstances had made me see the whole matter of surveillance in a fresher and clearer way.

'I don't follow,' he complained. 'You say you're out to stop bugging and phone tapping. And now you get this petition. Two and a quarter million signatures. A terrific boost to your case. And you won't even give me a quote saying you welcome it?'

I made an unshakeable resolve to stay silent. Anything I said was liable to be quoted. You can't ever trust the press.

'What about making a promise to implement its main recommendations?'

I realised that I had to break my unshakeable resolve. 'Well you see Walter,' I began in most condescending manner, 'things aren't that simple.'

'Why not?' he asked.

'Security considerations,' I said.

'There always were,' he said. 'But you said yourself that "security" is the last excuse of a desperate bureaucrat.'

Irritating bastard. I resolved to stay silent again.

Then Walter said: 'Okay. I think I'll make it an even bigger story. MINISTER REJECTS HIS OWN PETITION.'

My resolve shook again. 'Steady on, Walter,' I blurted out, 'don't be silly.'

'Are you accepting the petition or rejecting it?' he asked, giving me a simple choice.

'No,' I replied carefully.

Then it transpired that he *did* know all my circumstances. 'My Editor wants me to ask if being on the Freedom Army death list has altered your views in any way.'

Of course it has! Obviously! I'd be a complete fool if it hadn't.

'Certainly not,' I said. 'What an absurd idea! Never have occurred to me till you mentioned it just now.'

He didn't believe me but he couldn't prove anything. 'But how else am I to explain this sudden change of tune?'

I was getting a bit desperate by then, but thank God Bernard knocked on the door and appeared. Saved by the bell. He told me Humphrey wanted a word with me.

Humphrey came in. Walter didn't leave till I asked him if he minded. And he didn't leave the building – he just said he'd wait outside till we'd finished.

Humphrey asked me if I'd had a good weekend. Sadistic bastard. He must have known what my weekend would be like, with half the Special Branch present – all those romantic rozzers with Smith and Wessons under their armpits.

He nodded sympathetically. 'The burdens of office,' he said.

'This can't go on!' I said. Why can't I keep my big mouth shut?

'I'm glad you said that,' he replied smoothly, 'because it isn't going to.' My jaw dropped open. 'We've just heard from the Special Branch that your protection is being withdrawn.'

Withdrawn? I was appalled. I thought he'd misunderstood me. I asked why?

'The police have suffered an acute personnel establishment shortfall.'

I was about to ask if anybody was hurt, when I realised what he meant. Short-staffed. He meant short-staffed! And because the police were short-staffed they were going to allow me to be killed? I was horrified.

'There is a much more real and dangerous threat to the Soviet Premier at the Chequers meeting tomorrow,' he continued.

Much more real and dangerous? More real and dangerous to *him*, maybe. I searched desperately for an argument for them to protect me rather than him. 'He's Russian,' I said. 'I'm British!'

Then Sir Humphrey revealed further reasons why my protection was to be withdrawn.

'In fact, Minister, the Special Branch are confident that the threat to your life has diminished.'

Naturally I was anxious to know how they could be so bloody confident.

'Surveillance, Minister. They overheard a conversation.' Humphrey seemed reluctant to tell me. I told him to spit it out, that I had a right to know, and that I wanted a straight answer!

He nodded, and then went into his normal mumbo-jumbo. God knows what he said, I couldn't unravel it.

SIR BERNARD WOOLLEY RECALLS:[1]
I recall what Sir Humphrey said because I minuted it at the time. He explained that in view of the somewhat nebulous and inexplicit nature of Hacker's remit and the arguably marginal and peripheral nature of Hacker's influence on the central deliberations and decisions within the political process, there would be a case for restructuring their action priorities in such a way as to eliminate Hacker's liquidation from their immediate agenda.

[*Hacker's diary continues – Ed.*]

So I asked him to put it into English. He then said that the Freedom Army had apparently decided that I wasn't really important enough for it to be worth assassinating me.

He put it as gently as he could, I could see that. Even so, it was a bit of a blow. Not that they'd decided not to assassinate me, of course, but a bit of a blow to my pride nonetheless.

I asked Humphrey what he thought of this new situation. 'I don't agree with them, of course,' he said.

'You mean,' I asked, 'you think I *should* be assassinated?'

'No, no.'

'You mean, I'm not important enough?'

'Yes. *No*! I mean you *are* important enough but they shouldn't assassinate you anyway.' He breathed a sigh of relief.

Anyway, it seemed I was off the hook, and perhaps that's all to the good. I mean, there's no point in being important but dead, is

[1] In conversation with the Editors.

there? But, if even terrorist loonies doubt my value to the government, there's clearly some image-building to be done right away.

Bernard then asked me if I'd finish my interview with Walter Fowler. Of course, I was delighted to.

He was ushered in, and I opened up right away. I told Bernard to bring the petition along on the trolley, so that Walter could see how big it was.

Bernard said, 'The petition? But I thought you said . . .'

'Yes I did,' I interrupted hastily. 'Could you get it, Bernard?' He still looked blank. 'Antennae, Bernard,' I explained.

The penny dropped. 'Ah. Yes. Indeed, Minister,' he said quickly. 'You mean, I'm to get the petition that you said you were so pleased with?'

The boy's learning.

Walter demanded an answer to his various questions. I told him to sit down. Then I told him that I welcomed the petition, warmly. That it is not just something you sweep under the carpet.

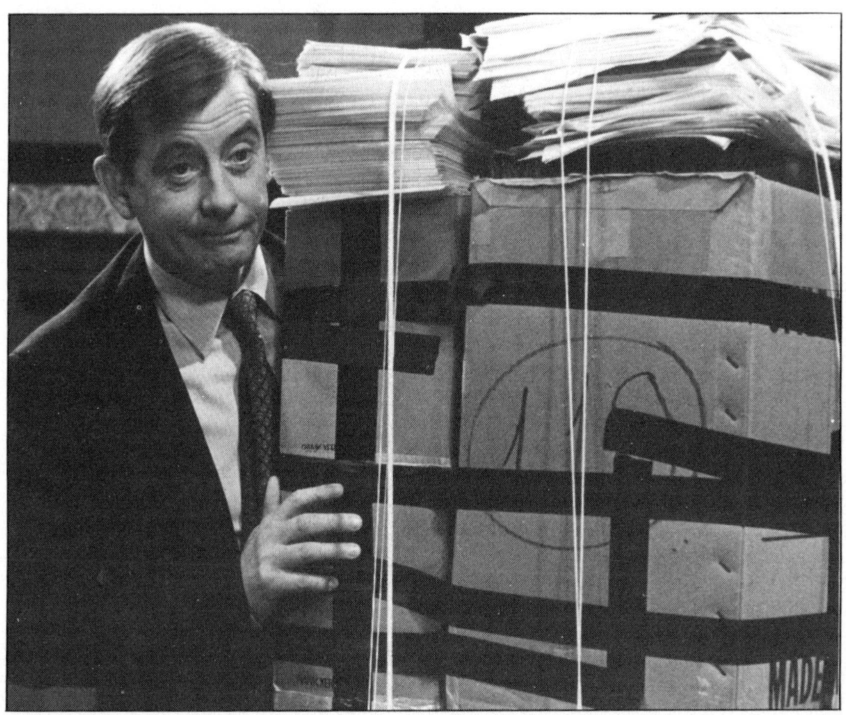

Bernard Woolley receiving the petition and wondering how to sweep it under the carpet (DAA Archives)

'And as for death lists,' I concluded. 'Well – Ministers are dispensable, but freedom is indivisible. Isn't that so, Humphrey?'

'Yes Minister,' replied my smiling Permanent Secretary, dead on cue.

10
Doing the Honours

April 23rd

I had a very unsatisfactory meeting today, with assorted secretaries – Deputy Secretaries, Under-Secretaries, and Assistant Secretaries.

I asked about economies in accommodation, in stationery acquisition, in parks and forestry commission administration, in data processing equipment, in the further education budget.

As always I was met with the usual vague and regretful murmurs of 'No Minister,' 'Afraid not Minister,' 'Doesn't seem possible, Minister,' 'Sadly it cannot be, Minister,' 'We have done the utmost possible, Minister,' 'Pared to the bone, Minister, alas!' and so forth.

I reflected aloud that at least the Universities are not going to cost us quite so much, now that overseas students are to pay fees that cover the full cost of their education here.

'Unless,' someone said, 'you make the exceptions which have been proposed to you.'

Nobody else at the meeting had been prepared to make exceptions. I couldn't see why I should. I remarked that as it seemed the only available saving at the moment we had no choice but to hang on to it.

As the meeting broke up Bernard reminded me again that the Honours Secretary at Number Ten had been asking if I had approved our Department's recommendations for the Honours List.

Curiously this was about the eighth time Bernard had asked me. I enquired sarcastically if honours were really the most important subject in the whole of the DAA.

Bernard replied, without any apparent awareness of my sarcasm, that they were indeed the most important subject for the people on the list. 'They're never off the phone,' he said pathetically. 'Some of them don't seem to have slept for about three nights.'

I was mildly surprised. I thought it was all a formality. 'Ministers never veto Civil Service honours, do they?' I asked.

'Hardly ever. But it's theoretically possible. And they're all getting worried by the delay.'

I suddenly realised that Bernard had just told me that people *knew* they were on the list. How? The file is marked *strictly confidential.*

He shook his head sadly at me when I mentioned it. 'Oh Minister,' he replied, and smiled at me in a kindly fashion.

I was amused and embarrassed at my naïveté. But all that energy that goes into worrying about honours . . . If only they'd put a quarter of it into cutting expenditure. I asked Bernard how I could get this Department to want economies in the way they wanted OBEs and KCBs and so on.

A gleam came into Bernard's eye. 'Well,' he said, with a slightly mischievous air that I'd never noticed before. 'I've been thinking . . .' Then he hesitated.

'Go on.'

'No, no, no.'

'What was it?'

'No. Nothing, Minister.'

I was on tenterhooks. I knew he had something up his sleeve. 'Come on Bernard,' I ordered, 'spit it out.' Bernard did not spit it out. Instead, he tentatively explained that it was not his place, and he wouldn't suggest this, and he couldn't *possibly* recommend it, but '. . . well . . . suppose you were to refuse to recommend any honours for Civil Servants who haven't cut their budgets by five per cent per annum?'

'Bernard!'

He retreated immediately.

'Oh, I'm so sorry, do forgive me, Minister, I knew I shouldn't have . . .'

'No, no,' I said, hastily reassuring him. Bernard has great ideas but he needs much more confidence. 'It's brilliant!'

And indeed it is a brilliant idea. I was cock-a-hoop. It's our only hold over the civil servants. Ministers can't stop their pay rises, or their promotion. Ministers don't write their reports. Ministers have no real disciplinary authority. But Bernard is right – I can withhold honours! It's brilliant!

I congratulated him and thanked him profusely.

'You thought of it, Minister!'

I didn't get the point at first. 'No, you did,' I told him generously.

'No, *you* did,' he said meaningfully. '*Please!*'

I understood. I nodded, and smiled reassuringly.

He looked even more anxious.

[*Some days later Sir Humphrey Appleby was invited to dine at the High Table of his alma mater, Baillie College, Oxford. He refers to the dinner and subsequent discussion in his private diary – Ed.*]

Had an excellent high table dinner at Baillie, followed by a private chat over the port and walnuts, with the Master and the Bursar. Clearly they were worried about the cuts. Sir William [*Sir William Guthrie, the Master – Ed.*] was looking somewhat the worse for wear – and the worse for port. His face was red, his hair is now quite white but his eyes were still the same clear penetrating blue. Rather patriotic, really. Christopher [*Christopher Venables, the Bursar – Ed.*] still looked like the precise ex-RAF officer that he had been in the days before he became a don – tall, neat, and meticulous in manner and speech.

I asked the Master how he was feeling. He replied that he was feeling very old. But he smiled. 'I'm already an anomaly, I shall soon be an anachronism, and I have every intention of dying an abuse.' Very droll!

Guthrie and Venables started out by telling me that they intended to sell the rest of the rather delicious 1927 Fonseca[1] which we were drinking. Baillie has a couple of pipes left and the Bursar told me they'd fetch quite a bit. I couldn't think what they were talking about. I was astounded. Excellent shock tactics, of course. Then they told me that if they sold all the paintings and the silver, they could possibly pay off the entire mortgage on the new buildings.

They think – or want me to think – that Baillie College is going to the wall.

It transpired that the trouble is the government's new policy of charging overseas students the full economic rate for their tuition. Baillie has always had an exceptional number of overseas students.

The Bursar tells me that they cannot charge the full economic fee of £4000 per annum. Hardly anyone will pay it.

He says he has been everywhere! All over the USA, raising funds, trying to sell the idea of an Oxford education to the inhabitants of Podunk, Indiana, and Cedar Rapids, Iowa.

But the competition is cut-throat. Apparently Africa is simply crawling with British Professors frantically trying to flog sociology courses to the natives. And India. And the Middle East.

I suggested that they do the obvious thing – fill up the vacancies with British students.

This idea met with a very cold response. 'I don't think that's awfully funny, Humphrey,' the Master said.

He explained that home students were to be avoided at all costs! *Anything* but home students!

[1] Vintage port.

The reason is simple economics. Baillie only gets £500 per head for the UK students. Therefore, it would have to take four hundred home students to replace a mere fifty foreigners. The number of students at a tutorial would quadruple. The staff/student ratio would go from one in ten to one in thirty-four.

I see their point. This could be the end of civilisation as we know it. It would certainly be the end of Baillie College as we know it. There would be dormitories. Classrooms. It would be indistinguishable from Wormwood Scrubs or the University of Sussex.

And Hacker is the Minister who has the authority to change it. I had not realised the implications of all this, it being a DES [*Department of Education and Science – Ed.*] decision. Ours not to reason why, ours just to put the administrative wheels in motion.[1]

[*Although Sir Humphrey, and Jim Hacker, were responsible for the implementation of these cuts, characteristically the Department of Education and Science had made them without consulting any of the other interested departments – the Foreign Office, or the Department of Health and Social Security or the Department of Administrative Affairs – Ed.*]

I suggested that we must persuade Hacker of the special and unique importance of Baillie College. He should be invited to dinner at High Table and the case explained to him.

The Master was noticeably worried about Hacker – he was concerned whether he was of the intellectual calibre to understand the case.

I pointed out that the case is intelligible to anyone of the intellectual calibre of Winnie-the-Pooh.

They asked me if Hacker *is* of the intellectual calibre of Winnie-the-Pooh. Clearly they've had dealings with politicians before.

I was able to reassure them on that point. I'm *fairly* sure that he is of the intellectual calibre of Winnie-the-Pooh. On his day.

I left Oxford convinced that I must find a way to get Baillie recognised as a special institution (like Imperial College) for the extraordinary work that they do. [*A well-chosen adjective! As this episode in Hacker's life is fundamentally concerned with honours – deserved or undeserved, earned or unearned – we felt that at this point it might be of interest to the reader to know the principal honours conferred on the antagonists:*

Sir William Guthrie, OM, FRS, FBA, Ph.D, MC, MA (Oxon)
Group Captain Christopher Venables, DSC, MA
Sir Humphrey Appleby, KCB, MVO, MA (Oxon)
Bernard Woolley, MA (Cantab)
The Rt Hon. James Hacker, PC, MP, BSc. (Econ)
Sir Arnold Robinson, GCMG, CVO, MA (Oxon) – Ed.]

[1] In fact, the size of Oxford University is limited by the University Grants Committee. Baillie might not even have been allowed to take more home students, except by taking them from other colleges. The other colleges would be unlikely to agree to this, because it would put them in jeopardy.

April 28th

This morning Humphrey badgered me again.

'Two things,' he said. 'First, there is the matter of the Departmental recommendations for the Honours List.'

I told him we'd leave that on one side for a bit.

He became very tense and twitchy. I tried not to show amusement. He told me we can't leave it as we are getting dangerously close to the five weeks.

[*All recipients of honours are notified at least five weeks before promulgation. Theoretically it gives them time to refuse. This is rare. In fact, the only time a civil servant is known to have refused a knighthood was in 1496. This was because he already had one – Ed.*]

I decided that I would not yet give my approval to the Department's Honours List, because I've been doing some research. [*Hacker almost certainly meant that a party research assistant had been doing some research and he had read the report – Ed.*] I have found that twenty per cent of all honours go to civil servants. The rest of the population of this country have to do something extra to get an honour. Over and above their ordinary work, for which they get paid. You or I have to do something special, like work with mentally-handicapped children for twenty-seven years, six nights a week – then we might get an MBE. But Civil Service knighthoods just come up with the rations.

These honours are, in any case, intrinsically ridiculous – MBE, for instance, according to *Whitaker's Almanack*, stands for Member of the Most Honourable Order of the British Empire. Hasn't anyone in Whitehall noticed that we've lost the Empire?

The civil servants have been having it both ways for years. When Attlee was PM he got £5000 a year and the Cabinet Secretary got £2500. Now the Cabinet Secretary gets more than the PM. Why? Because civil servants used to receive honours as a compensation for long years of loyal public service, for which they got poor salaries, poor pensions and few perks.

Now they have salaries comparable to executives in the most successful private enterprise companies (guess who's in charge of the comparability studies), inflation-proof pensions, chauffeur-driven cars – and they *still* get automatic honours.

[*Hacker was right. The civil servants were undoubtedly manipulating the honours system to their own advantage. Just as incomes policies have always been manipulated by those that control them: for instance, the 1975 Pay Policy provided exemptions for Civil Service increments and lawyers' fees. Needless to say, the policy was drafted by civil servants and parliamentary draftsmen, i.e. lawyers.*

The problem is, quis custodiet ipsos custodes?[1] – *Ed.*]

So how can civil servants possibly understand the way the rest of us live, if they are immune to the basic threats to economic well-being faced by the rest of us: inflation and unemployment?

And how did the civil servants get away with creating these remarkably favourable terms of service for themselves? Simply by keeping a low profile. They have somehow managed to make people feel that discussing the matter at all is in rather poor taste.

But that cuts no ice with me. I believe in action now!

I asked Humphrey how he accounted for twenty per cent of honours going to the Civil Service.

'A fitting tribute to their devotion to duty,' he said.

It's a pretty nice duty to be devoted to, I thought.

Humphrey continued: 'Her Majesty's civil servants spend their lives working for a modest wage and at the end they retire into obscurity. Honours are a small recompense for a lifetime of loyal, self-effacing discretion and devoted service to Her Majesty and to the nation.'

A pretty speech. But quite ridiculous. 'A modest wage?' I queried.

'Alas, yes.'

I explained to Humphrey, since he appeared to have forgotten, that he earned well over thirty thousand a year. Seven and a half thousand more than me.

He agreed, but insisted that it was still a relatively modest wage.

'Relative to whom?' I asked.

He was stuck for a moment. 'Well . . . Elizabeth Taylor for instance,' he suggested.

I felt obliged to explain to Sir Humphrey that he was in no way relative to Elizabeth Taylor. There are important differences.

'Indeed,' he agreed. 'She did not get a First in Greats.'[2]

Then, undaunted and ever persistent, he again asked me if I had approved the list. I made my move.

'No Humphrey,' I replied pleasantly, 'I am not approving any honour for anyone in this Department who hasn't earned it.'

[1] Translation: who guards the guards? A quotation from Juvenal's *Satires* and not, as is commonly supposed in political circles, from juvenile satires.

[2] The Oxford term for the second part of the classics degree course.

Humphrey's face was a wonderful study in blankness.

'What do you mean, earned it?'

I explained that I meant earned it. In other words, having done something to deserve it.

The penny dropped. He exploded. 'But that's *unheard* of,' he exclaimed.

I smiled serenely. 'Maybe so. But my new policy is to stop all honours for all civil servants who fail to cut their department's budgets by five per cent a year.'

Humphrey was speechless.

So after a few moments I said: 'May I take it that your silence indicates approval?'

He found his voice fast. 'You may *not*, Minister.' He was deeply indignant. 'Where did you get this preposterous idea?'

I glanced at Bernard, who studied his right shoe-lace intently. 'It came to me,' I said.

Humphrey was spluttering incoherently. 'It's ridiculous. It's out of the question. It's unthinkable.' Now that Humphrey had found his voice there was no stopping him. 'The whole idea . . . strikes at the whole root of . . . this is the beginning of the end . . . the thin end of the wedge . . . Bennite solution. [*Perhaps it was the word 'wedge' that reminded him of Benn – Ed.*] Where will it end? The abolition of the monarchy?'

I told him not to be silly. This infuriated him even more.

'There is *no reason*,' he said, stabbing the air with his finger, 'to change a system which has worked well in the past.'

'But it hasn't,' I said.

'We have to give the present system a fair trial,' he stated. This seemed quite reasonable on the face of it. But I reminded him that the Most Noble Order of the Garter was founded in 1348 by King Edward III. 'Surely it must be getting towards the end of its trial period?' I said.

So Humphrey tried a new tack. He said that to block honours pending economies might create a dangerous precedent.

What he means by 'dangerous precedent' is that if we do the right thing now, then we might be forced to do the right thing again next time. And on that reasoning nothing should ever be done at all. [*To be precise: many things may be done, but nothing must ever be done for the first time – Ed.*]

I told him I wasn't going to budge on my proposal. He resorted to barefaced lies, telling me that he was fully seized of my aims and had taken them on board and would do his best to put them into practice.

So I asked him point blank if he would put my policy into practice. He made me his usual offer. I know it off by heart now. A recommendation that we set up an interdepartmental committee with fairly broad terms of reference so that at the end of the day we would be in a position to think through all the implications and take a decision based on long-term considerations rather than rush prematurely into precipitate and possibly ill-conceived action that might well have unforeseen repercussions. [*In other words: No! – Ed.*]

I wasn't prepared to be fobbed off with this nonsense any longer. I told him I wanted *action now*. He went pale. I pointed out that, in my case, honours are fundamentally unhealthy. Nobody in their right mind can want them, they encourage sycophancy, snobbery and jealousy. 'And,' I added firmly, 'it is not fair that civil servants get them all.'

Humphrey argued again. 'We *have* done something to deserve them. We are *civil servants*,' he said.

'You just like having letters to put after your name to impress people,' I sneered. 'You wouldn't impress people if they knew what they stood for: KCB? Knight Commander of the Most Noble Order of the Bath? Bloody daft. They'd think you were a plumber. I think they should shove the whole lot down the Most Noble Order of the Plughole.'

Humphrey wasn't at all amused. 'Very droll,' he said condescendingly. 'You like having letters after your name too,' he continued. 'PC,[1] MP. And your degree – BSc.Econ., I think,' he sneered and slightly wrinkled up his elegant nose as if there were a nasty smell underneath it.

'At least I earned my degree,' I told him, 'not like your MA. At Oxford they give it to you for nothing, when you've got a BA.'

'Not for nothing. For four guineas,' he snapped spitefully.

I was tired of this juvenile bickering. And I had him on the run. I told him that I had made my policy decision and that was the end of it. 'And what was your other point?' I enquired.

Humphrey was in such a state of shock about the Honours List that he had forgotten his other point. But after a few moments it came back to him.

It seems that Baillie College, Oxford, will be in serious trouble over the new ruling on grants for overseas students.

[1] Privy Counsellor.

Humphrey said that nothing would please Baillie more than to take British students. Obviously that's true. But he explained that Baillie has easily the highest proportion of foreign students and that the repercussions will be serious at the schools of Tropical Medicine and International Law. And the Arabic Department may have to close down completely.

I'm sympathetic to all this, but hard cases make bad law. I just don't see how it's possible for us to go on educating foreigners at the expense of the British taxpayer.

'It's not just foreigners, Minister,' explained Humphrey. 'If, for instance, our Diplomatic Service has nowhere to immerse its recruits in Arab culture, the results could be catastrophic – we might even end up with a pro-Israeli Foreign Office. And what would happen to our oil policy then?'

I said that they could send their diplomatic recruits elsewhere.

'Where else,' he demanded, 'can they learn Arabic?'

'Arabia?' I suggested.

He was stumped. Then Bernard chipped in. 'Actually, Minister, Baillie College has an outstanding record. It has filled the jails of the British Empire for many years.'

This didn't sound like much of a recommendation to me. I invited Bernard to explain further.

'As you know,' he said, 'the letters JB are the highest honour in the Commonwealth.'

I didn't know.

Humphrey eagerly explained. 'Jailed by the British. Gandhi, Nkrumah, Makarios, Ben-Gurion, Kenyatta, Nehru, Mugabe – the list of world leaders is endless and contains several of our students.'

Our students? He had said *our* students. It all became clear.

I smiled benignly. 'Which college did you go to, Humphrey?'

'Er . . . that is quite beside the point, Minister.'

He wasn't having a very good day. 'I like being beside the point, Humphrey,' I said. 'Humour me. Which college did you go to? Was it Baillie, by any strange coincidence?'

'It so happens,' he admitted with defiance, 'that I am a Baillie man, but that has nothing to do with this.'

I don't know how he has the face to make such a remark. Does he really think I'm a complete idiot? At that moment the buzzer went and saved Humphrey from further humiliation. It was the Division Bell. So I had to hurry off to the House.

On my way out I realised that I had to ask Bernard whether I was to vote 'aye' or 'no'.

'No,' he replied and began to explain. 'It's an Opposition Amendment, the second reading of . . .'

But I had left by then. The man's a fool. It doesn't matter what the debate *is*, I just don't want to go through the wrong door.

[*Meanwhile, rumours about Hacker's plan to link economies with honours had travelled fast along the two major Whitehall grapevines – the private secretaries' and the drivers'. It was only a matter of hours before news reached Sir Arnold Robinson, the Secretary to the Cabinet. Sir Humphrey was asked to drop in for a chat with Sir Arnold, and an illuminating interview followed – illuminating not only for Sir Humphrey, but also for historians who learn that although the Cabinet Secretary is theoretically* primus inter pares[1] *he is in reality very much* primus. *It seems that all Permanent Secretaries are equal, but some are more equal than others.*

The notes that Sir Arnold made on Sir Humphrey's report have been found among the Civil Service files at Walthamstow and were of course released some years ago under the Thirty-Year Rule.

Sir Humphrey never saw these notes, because no civil servant is shown his own report, except in wholly unusual circumstances – Ed.]

Staff Report (Cont.) **CR36**

7. LONG TERM POTENTIAL

At present, he/~~she~~ seems

	unlikely to progress further	☑	1
or	to have potential to rise about one grade but probably no further	☐	2
or	to have potential to rise two or three grades	☐	3
or	to have exceptional potential	☐	4

8. GENERAL REMARKS

Please provide any additional relevant information here, drawing attention to any particular strengths or weaknesses

Told Appleby that I was a little bit worried about this idea of his Minister's, linking Honours to economies.

Appleby said that he could find no effective arguments against this plan.

I indicated that we would regard it as the thin end of the wedge, a Benn-ite solution. I asked where it would end?

[1] First among equals.

Told Appleby that I was a little bit worried about this idea of his Minister's, linking Honours to economies.

Appleby said that he could find no effective arguments against this plan.

I indicated that we would regard it as the thin end of the wedge, a Bennite solution. I asked where it would end?

Appleby replied that he shared my views and had emphasised them to the Minister. He added, somewhat strangely, that the scheme was 'intolerable but yet irresistible'.

I took a dim view. I informed Appleby that, while I was not in any sense reprimanding him, I wanted his assurance that this plan would not be put into practice.

He looked very shaken at the mention of no reprimand. [*Civil Service Code: the mere mention of a reprimand so high up the ladder is severe and deeply wounding criticism. It suggests that the Cabinet Secretary was flying in the face of the 'Good Chap Theory' – the theory that states that 'A Good Chap Does Not Tell A Good Chap What A Good Chap Ought To Know.' Sir Arnold was implying that Sir Humphrey was not a sufficiently good chap – Ed.*]

Appleby was unable to give me the assurance I required. He merely voiced a hope that Hacker would not be acting on this plan.

I was obliged to point out that hopes are not good enough. If honours were linked to economies in the DAA, the contagion could spread throughout government. To every department.

Again I invited him to say that we could count on him to scotch the scheme. He said he would try. Feeble! I was left with no alternative but to warn him most seriously that, although I was quite sure he knew what he was doing, this matter could cause others to reflect upon whether or not he was sound.

The poor chap seemed to take that very hard, as well he might!

Before I terminated the interview I mentioned that the Master of Baillie, our old college, had been on the phone, and that I was sure Appleby would make sure Hacker treated Baillie as a Special Case.

Appleby seemed no more confident on this matter either, although he said he had arranged for Hacker to be invited to a Benefactor's Dinner.

I congratulated him on his soundness in this matter, which didn't seem to cheer him up a great deal. I begin to think that Appleby is losing his grip – on Hacker at least.

Perhaps Appleby is not an absolutely first-rank candidate to succeed one as Cabinet Secretary. Not really able in every department. Might do better in a less arduous job, such as chairman of a clearing bank or as an EEC official.

A.R.

[*It is interesting to compare Sir Arnold's report with Sir Humphrey's own account of this interview – Ed.*]

Went over to see Arnold at the Cabinet Office. We got on very well, as usual. He was very concerned about Hacker's idea of linking honours to economies, and almost as concerned about the future of Baillie College. I was on a sticky wicket, but on the whole I think I was able to reassure him that I'm handling these difficult problems as well as anybody could reasonably expect. [*Appleby Papers 31/RJC/638*]

[*Hacker's diary resumes – Ed.*]
May 4th
Today was the Benefactor's Dinner at Baillie College, Oxford, which was, I think, an unqualified success.

For a start, on the way up to Oxford I learned a whole pile of useful gossip from young Bernard.

Apparently Sir Humphrey was summoned by the Cabinet Secretary yesterday and, according to Bernard, got the most frightful wigging. The Cabinet Secretary really tore him off a strip, because of Bernard's brilliant scheme linking economies to honours.

Interestingly, Bernard continues to refer to it as *my* scheme – on this occasion, because we were in the official car and of course Roy [*the driver – Ed.*] was quietly memorising every word we said, for future buying and selling. No doubt he can sell news of Sir Humphrey's wigging for quite a price in the drivers' pool, though, it should be worth several small leaks in exchange, I should think. So Roy should have some useful snippets in two or three days, which I must remember to extract from him.

I asked Bernard how the Cabinet Secretary actually goes about giving a wigging to someone as high up as Humphrey.

'Normally,' Bernard informed me, 'it's pretty civilised. But this time, apparently, it was no holds barred. Sir Arnold told Sir Humphrey that he wasn't actually reprimanding him!'

'*That* bad?'

'He actually suggested,' Bernard continued, 'that some people might not think Sir Humphrey was sound.'

Roy's ears were out on stalks.

'I see,' I said, with some satisfaction. 'A real punch-up.'

Sir Arnold was so bothered by this whole thing that I wondered if he had a personal stake in it. But I couldn't see why. I presumed he must have his full quota of honours.

I asked Bernard if Arnold already had his G. Bernard nodded. [*You get your G after your K. G is short for Grand Cross. K is a Knighthood. Each department has its own honours. The DAA gets the Bath – Sir Humphrey was, at this time, a KCB, and would have been hoping for his G – thus becoming a Knight Grand Cross of the Bath.*

In the FCO the Honours are the Cross of St Michael and St George – CMG, KCMG, and GCMG. The Foreign Office is not popular throughout the rest of the Civil Service, and it is widely held that the CMG stands for 'Call Me God', the KCMG for 'Kindly Call Me God' and the GCMG for 'God Calls Me God' – Ed.]

However, Bernard revealed that although Sir Arnold has indeed got his G, there are numerous honours to which he could still aspire: a peerage, for instance, an OM [*Order of Merit – Ed.*] or a CH [*Companion of Honour – Ed.*], the Order of the Garter, the Knight of the Thistle, etc.

I asked him about the Knight of the Thistle. 'Who do they award the Thistle to, Scotsmen and donkeys?' I enquired wittily.

'There is a distinction,' said Bernard, ever the diplomat.

'You can't have met the Scottish nationalists,' I replied, quick as a flash. I wasn't bothered by Roy's flapping lugs. 'How do they award the Thistle?' I asked.

'A committee sits on it,' said Bernard.

I asked Bernard to brief me about this High Table dinner. 'Does Humphrey *really* think that I will change government policy on University Finance as a result?'

Bernard smiled and said he'd heard Baillie College gives a very good dinner.

We got to Oxford in little over an hour. The M40 is a very good road. So is the M4, come to think of it. I found myself wondering why we've got two really good roads to Oxford before we got any to Southampton, or Dover or Felixstowe or any of the ports.

Bernard explained that nearly all of our Permanent Secretaries were at Oxford. And most Oxford Colleges give you a good dinner.

This seemed incredible – and yet it has the ring of truth about it. 'But did the Cabinet let them get away with this?' I asked.

'Oh no,' Bernard explained. 'They put their foot down. They said there'd be no motorway to take civil servants to dinners in Oxford unless there was a motorway to take Cabinet Ministers hunting in the Shires. That's why when the M1 was built in the fifties it stopped in the middle of Leicestershire.'

There seemed one flaw in this argument. I pointed out that the M11 has only just been completed. 'Don't Cambridge colleges give you a good dinner?'

'Of course,' said Bernard, 'but it's years and years since the Department of Transport had a Permanent Secretary from Cambridge.'

[*It is most interesting to compare Hacker's account of the dinner with Sir Bernard Woolley's recollections of the same event. First, Hacker's version - Ed.*]

The dinner itself went off perfectly.

I knew they wanted to discuss their financial problems, so when we reached the port and walnuts I decided to open up Pandora's box, let the cat out of the bag and get the ball rolling. [*Hacker never really learned to conquer his mixed metaphor problem – Ed.*] So I remarked that, for a college on the edge of bankruptcy we had not had a bad little dinner. In truth, of course, we'd had a wildly extravagant banquet with four courses and three excellent wines.

The Master countered by informing me that the Fitzwalter Dinner is paid for by a specific endowment – Fitzwalter was a great sixteenth-century benefactor.

The Bursar added that most nights I'd find them eating Mother's Pride[1] and processed cheese.

I remarked that what they need is a twentieth-century benefactor and this innocent remark produced a long lecture on the different types of University benefactors. Isaac Wolfson, apparently, is only the third man in history to have a college named after him at Oxford and Cambridge. Jesus and St John being the first two.

'Benefactors achieve some sort of immortality,' said the Bursar. 'Their names are kept alive and honoured for centuries. Sir William de Vere, whose name was inscribed on a sconce, directed a Baronial army away from Baillie in the fifteenth century – he had the soldiers quartered at St George's College instead.'

I didn't want to appear ignorant, but I ventured a comment that I didn't actually know there was a St George's College. 'There isn't,' said the Bursar, 'not any more.'

We all chuckled.

Then the Bursar told me about Henry Monkton.

'The Monkton Quad is named after him. He stopped Cromwell from melting down the college silver to pay for the New Model Army.'

Humphrey added:

'Told them that the silver was much better quality at Trinity, Cambridge.'

More chuckles all round. Then the Master pointedly remarked that it now looked as if there'd be no college left to remember these

[1] Brand name of popular packaged sliced loaf, not of the kind customarily consumed at High Table.

benefactors. Unless the problem of the overseas students can be solved.

They all looked at me and waited. I'm used to this kind of pressure, but naturally I wanted to help if I could. So I explained that one *always* tries to help and that politicians only go into politics out of a desire to help others. I explained that I'm an idealist. And, in case they were under the impression that all this talk of honouring benefactors might persuade me to help Baillie in some way, I pointed out that any honour is irrelevant to me – after all, there's not much point in having your name on a silver sconce when you're six feet under.

Humphrey changed the conversation abruptly at that moment, and started asking when the University awards its honorary doctorates. The Master said that the ceremony isn't for a few months but the Senate makes its final selection in a matter of weeks.

I don't think that it was entirely coincidental that Humphrey mentioned this matter at this juncture.

[*The ceremony in question takes place each June. A large luncheon is given in the Codrington Library of All Souls, followed by an afternoon reception. The degrees are given in a Latin ceremony, in the Sheldonian. All the speeches are in Latin. The Chancellor of the University was, at this period, that arch-manipulator of politicians and, with Sir Harold Wilson, Joint Life President of the Society of Electoral Engineers: Mr Harold Macmillan, as he then was (later Earl of Stockton) – Ed.*]

Humphrey, the Master, and the Bursar were – I realised – hinting at an offer. Not an unattractive one. I've always secretly regretted not being an Oxbridge man, as I am undoubtedly of sufficient intellectual calibre. And there must be very few LSE men who've ever had an honorary degree from Oxford.

The Master dropped another hint. Very decorously. He said that there was still one honorary doctorate of Law to decide, and that he and his colleagues were wondering whether it should go to a judge or to someone in government!

I suggested that someone in government might be more appropriate. Perhaps as a tribute to the Chancellor of the University. I know that I argued it rather brilliantly, because they were so enthusiastic and warm in response to me – but I can't actually remember precisely how I put it.

Exhausted by the intellectual cut and thrust of the evening, I fell asleep in the car going home.

SIR BERNARD WOOLLEY RECALLS:[1]

Having seen Hacker's account of this dinner, and his behaviour at it, I'm afraid to say that it is rather inaccurate and self-serving.

By the time we had reached the port Hacker was, not to put too fine a point on it, embarrassingly drunk.

The Master, Sir Humphrey and several of the dons set about persuading him that he would acquire a certain immortality if he became a college benefactor – in other words, if he made Baillie a special case in the matter of overseas students. A typical Oxford 'you scratch my back, I'll scratch yours' offer.

Hacker's reference to the conversation about Wolfson and Jesus Colleges is less than complete. When told that Wolfson is the only man, other than Jesus and St John, to have a college named after him at both Oxford and Cambridge, he looked glassy-eyed and blank. 'Jesus?' he asked. The Bursar actually felt called upon to clarify it. 'Jesus *Christ*, that is,' he explained.

When Hacker remarked that he wanted to help he was pouring himself a glass of port. His actual words, I clearly recall, were 'Yes, well, one would certainly like to help oneself . . . I mean, help one's friends, that is, help the college . . . not for the honours of course . . .'. He was completely transparent.

The Master and Bursar chimed in with suitable bromides like 'Perish the thought,' 'Ignoble suggestion,' and so forth.

Hacker then gave us all that guff about how he was in politics to help others, and how he wasn't interested in honours – but when the honorary doctorates were mentioned he got so excited he cracked a walnut so hard that pieces of shell were flying across High Table like shrapnel.

Then came his final humiliation.

By the time the matter was raised as to whether the last remaining honorary doctorate (if indeed it were so) should go to a judge or a politician, it was clear that the academics were playing games with Hacker.

He was too drunk to see that they were merely amusing themselves. I well remember the appalling drunken speech he launched into. It is forever etched on my memory.

He began by saying 'Judge? You don't want to make a judge a doctor of law. Politicians,' he said, 'are the ones who make the laws. And pass the laws,' he added, apparently unaware of the tautology. 'If it wasn't for politicians, judges wouldn't be able to do any judging, they wouldn't have any laws to judge, know what I mean? They'd all be out of work. Queues of unemployed judges. In silly wigs.'

I remember that argument well because the idea of unemployed judges in silly wigs richly appealed to me, as it would to anyone who has had contact with the higher and more self-satisfied reaches of the legal profession. In fact, I have always been struck by the absurdity of judges ticking people off in court about their unsuitable appearance – women in trousers, for instance – while the judges themselves are in fancy dress.

[1] In conversation with the Editors.

Be that as it may, Hacker continued in the cringing self-pitying lachrymose manner that he only exhibited when completely sloshed.

'Anyway, it's easy for the judges,' he whined, 'they don't have to suck up to television producers. Don't have to lie to journalists. Don't have to pretend to like their Cabinet colleagues. Do you know something?' he cracked another walnut and a piece of deadly flying shell struck the Bursar just below the left eye. 'If judges had to put up with some of my Cabinet colleagues we'd have the death penalty back tomorrow. Good job too.'

By this time old Sir Humphrey was trying to stem the flow – but to no avail.

For Hacker pointed accusingly at Sir Humphrey. 'And I'll tell you another thing,' he said, sublimely unaware that nobody at the table wanted to hear another thing, 'I can't send you to prison.'

Humphrey was flummoxed by this remark.

Hacker looked around the table. 'I can't send him to prison,' he said, as if he had revealed a new extraordinary anomaly in the law. 'But if I were a judge, I could whiz old Humphrey off to the Scrubs, no trouble, feet wouldn't touch the ground, clang bang, see you in three years' time, one-third remission for good conduct.'

Everyone was now staring at Hacker, open-mouthed, as he paused for breath, slurped at his glass and some Fonseca 1927 dribbled slowly down his chin. Being academics, they had hardly ever seen a politician in action late at night. [*Hacker's behaviour, of course, would have passed unnoticed at the House of Commons, where it would have been accepted as quite normal – possibly, even better than average – Ed.*]

Hacker was still talking. Now he was unstoppable. 'But I can't do that to old Humphrey,' he raved incoherently. 'I have to listen to him – Oh God!' He looked at the ceiling, and seemed to be on the verge of tears. 'He goes *on* and *on*. Do you know, his sentences are longer than Judge Jeffreys'?' He guffawed. We stared at him. 'No, no, to sum up, politicians are much more deserving, you don't want to give your donorary hoctorates to judges . . . definitely not.'

Finally he ground to a halt. The Master hastily pulled himself together and tried to rearrange his features so that they expressed friendliness rather than disgust. He was only partially successful.

Nevertheless he managed to tell Hacker that he had argued the proposition beautifully, and that he now realised that the honour couldn't possibly go to a judge.

There were mutters of agreement all round, as the dons continued their embarrassing flattery of Hacker. No one really understands the true nature of fawning servility until he has seen an academic who has glimpsed the prospect of money. Or personal publicity.

They went on to say how wonderful it would be to see Hacker standing there, in the Sheldonian, wearing magnificent crimson robes, receiving the doctorate in front of a packed assembly of eminent scholars such as himself. Hacker belched, alcoholic fumes emanated from his mouth, his eyes went glassy, he clutched his chair so that he wouldn't fall on to the floor, and he smiled beatifically.

I have always remembered that night. I took one more step towards maturity as I realised that even the most rigorous academics have their price – and it's not as high as you'd think.

[*Hacker's diary continues – Ed.*]

May 5th

Had rather a headache this morning. I don't know why, it can't be a hangover as I didn't drink all that much last night. I couldn't have done or I wouldn't have been such a success.

We were due to have yet another meeting to examine the possibility of administrative cuts. But the outcome was sure to be the same as last time.

Humphrey popped into my office five minutes early, for a private word. Very good news. Apparently the Master of Baillie took Humphrey aside last night and asked him to sound me out, to see if I'd be interested in accepting an honorary doctorate of Law from the University.

I feigned surprise. In fact I wasn't at all surprised, as I knew what an impression I'd made on them last night.

Humphrey was at pains to point out that it was not an actual offer. Apparently, according to Humphrey, the Council of the Senate or somebody or other is now trying to square the honorary doctorate with my well-known hostility to honours.

This was a bit of a blow. I had to squash this nonsense at once. 'Don't be silly, Humphrey, that's quite different,' I explained.

'Not entirely, Minister,' he replied. 'It is a matter of accepting a doctorate without having done anything to earn it, as you yourself might put it in your refreshingly blunt fashion.'

'I'm a Cabinet Minister,' I responded with some indignation.

'Isn't that what you're paid for?' Smooth treacherous bugger.

'The point is,' I told him, 'one can't really refuse an honorary doctorate. I should have thought anyone could see that I would be insulting the DAA if I refused – because clearly I've been offered it as a sort of vote of confidence in the Department because I am, in fact, the titular head.'

Humphrey fell silent, having indicated again that it was not yet an offer. Clearly he had some sort of deal in mind. I waited. And waited.

Then the penny dropped. 'By the way, Humphrey,' I said breezily. 'Changing the subject *entirely*, I would like to do what I can to help Baillie College over this overseas student problem.'

Now it was Humphrey's turn to feign surprise. 'Oh, good,' he said, and smiled.

I explained quietly, however, that we need a reason. By which I meant a pretext. He was ready with one, as I knew he would be.

'No problem. I understand that the Palace has been under pressure from a number of Commonwealth leaders. We can't embarrass the Palace, so we'll have to redesignate Baillie as a Commonwealth Education Centre.'

Immediately I saw a chance for the deal that *I* wanted to do.

'But how will I find the money?' I asked, wide-eyed. 'You know how set I am on making five per cent cuts across the board. If we could achieve that . . . well, anything's possible.'

I reckoned that this was an offer he couldn't refuse. I was right. 'We *might* be able to achieve these cuts – ' this was a big step forward – 'and I can only speak for this Department, of course, as long as this absurd idea of linking cuts to honours were to be shelved.'

So there it was. A double *quid pro quo*. Out in the open.

The expenditure Survey Committee gathered around my conference table.

The minutes of the last meeting went through on the nod. Then we came to Matters Arising. The first was *Accommodation*. Sir Humphrey pre-empted the Assistant Secretary who usually spoke on this matter. As the young man opened his mouth to reply, I heard Humphrey's voice: 'I'm happy to say that we have found a five per cent cut by selling an old office block in High Wycombe.'

The Assistant Secretary looked mightily surprised. Clearly Humphrey had not forewarned him of the New Deal.

I was delighted. I said so. We moved straight on to number two: *Stationery Acquisition*.

A Deputy Secretary spoke up, after getting an unmistakeable eye signal and slight nod of the head from Humphrey. 'Yes, we'd discovered that a new stock control system will reduce expenditure this year.'

'By how much?' I asked.

The Deputy Secretary hesitated uncertainly. 'About five per cent, wasn't it?' said Humphrey smoothly.

The Dep. Sec. muttered his agreement.

'Good, good,' I said. 'Three: *Parks and Forestry Administration*?'

An Under-Secretary spoke, having caught on with the civil servant's customary speed to a change in the party line.

'If we delay the planned new computer installation, we can make a saving there.'

'Can we?' I said, pretending surprise. 'How much?'

They all pretended that they couldn't remember. Much consultation of paper and files.

A bright Principal spoke up: 'About five per cent?' he said, hopefully. We all nodded our approval, and assorted civil servants muttered 'Of that order.'

Humphrey pointed out that the saving in the computer installation would lead inevitably to a cut in *Data Processing*. I looked at him expectantly. 'By about five per cent,' he said.

'This is all very encouraging, Humphrey,' I said benevolently.

And after the meeting, at which everyone had somehow managed to come up with cuts of about five per cent, Humphrey took me aside for a quiet word.

'Minister, while I think of it, have you finished with the list of departmental recommendations to the Honours Secretary?'

'Certainly.' I was at my most obliging. 'There was no problem with any of them. Bernard will give it to you. All right, Humphrey?'

'Yes, Doctor,' he replied.

A fitting tribute. I look forward to the ceremony next June.

11
The Greasy Pole

[*There are times in a politician's life when he is obliged to take the wrong decision. Wrong economically, wrong industrially, wrong by any standards – except one. It is a curious fact that something which is wrong from every other point of view can be right politically. And something which is right politically does not simply mean that it's the way to get the votes – which it is – but also, if a policy gets the votes, then it can be argued that that policy is what the people want. And, in a democracy, how can a thing be wrong if it is what the people will vote for?*

The incident in question only came to light slowly. The first reference that we can find to it is not in Jim Hacker's diary, but in Steel Yourself, *the memoirs of that uniquely outspoken Chairman of the British Chemical Corporation, the diminutive Glaswegian industrialist and scientist, Sir Wally McFarland.*

McFarland was known for his plain language and his unwillingness to bow to government interference in his nationalised industry. He was an expert both on chemicals and on business management – and he believed (rightly) that Hacker knew little or nothing about either. His low regard for Hacker was matched only by his contempt for Sir Humphrey's skill in business. Like many businessmen, he believed that in commerce the Civil Service was not safe with a whelk stall – Ed.]

From Steel Yourself*:*

On 16 April I had a meeting with Sir Humphrey Appleby at the Department of Administrative Affairs. It was the umpteenth meeting on the subject of the manufacture of Propanol on Merseyside under licence from the Italian Government.

To my astonishment Sir Humphrey seemed to indicate that there might be a problem with the Minister, but his language was as opaque as usual and I could not be sure of this.

I asked him if he was havering [*Scottish word, meaning to be indecisive – Ed.*]. He denied it, but said that we cannot take the Minister's approval for granted.

This was and still is incomprehensible to me. The Italian government was offering us a massive contract to manufacture Propanol at our Merseyside plant. This contract meant saving a plant which we would otherwise have to close down. It meant taking people on, instead of laying them off. And it meant big export royalties. We'd been fighting for two years to win it against tough German and US competition. It seemed completely obvious that it *had* to go ahead.

Appleby raised some footling idiotic question about what the Minister might think. In my experience Ministers *don't* think. In my ten years as Chairman of the BCC I dealt with nineteen different Ministers. They never stopped to think, even if they possessed the basic intelligence necessary for thought – which several of them did not. As a matter of fact, they were usually too lazy to talk to me because they were usually talking to the trade union leaders and bribing them not to strike.

I told Appleby my views. He denied that trade union leaders were bribed. Naturally. It may not be technically bribery, but what else do you call conversations that amount to 'Have a quango, Tom. Have a knighthood, Dick. Have a peerage, Harry'?

Appleby said that the Minister was worried about the Propanol scheme. If so, why hadn't anything been said till now?

At this stage I – unwisely, perhaps – brushed aside suggestions that the Minister was worried. He'd never shown any real interest in the scheme, so he could know nothing about it. Naïvely, I assumed that his ignorance would prevent him interfering. And, in any case, all Ministers are worried. I never met a Minister who wasn't worried.

Ministers worry whenever you do anything that is bold. Anything that makes business sense. Anything that is *necessary*, in fact. If I had never done anything to worry any of those lily-livered, vote-grubbing, baby-kissing jellies the BCC would have gone down the tube ten years earlier than it did.

Appleby said that the Minister's worries centred on the fact that Propanol contained *Meta*dioxin. [*Dioxin was the chemical released in the accident at Seveso, Italy, some years earlier. It was believed to cause damage to the foetus – Ed.*] This was typical. *Meta*dioxin is completely different, an inert compound. It had a clean bill of health from the FDA [*Food and Drugs Administration – Ed.*] in Washington. And the Henderson Committee was about to approve it.

Nonetheless, I could see that Appleby, in all his ignorance of chemistry, was still a little worried. Or else he was reflecting Hacker's worries.

I added that the name metadioxin was now not in the proposal. The chemical was simply called Propanol, making it politically safe.

Our meeting concluded with Appleby offering assurances that the Minister was unlikely to raise any objections, as long as the matter was handled with tact. I offered to go along myself, and have a tactful word with Hacker, and persuade that egotistical blancmange that there could be no argument on the matter.

Appleby declined my offer, and answered that he would be able to manage without what he generously called my unique and refreshing brand of tact.

I was not so sure. And, again, I was locked out of the crucial meeting.

Why do governments continually hire experts to run nationalised industries on business lines, and then interfere every time you try to make a business decision?

[*Hacker's diary continues – Ed.*]

June 4th

This morning Humphrey gave me some wonderful news. Or what appeared to be wonderful news.

He handed me a paper which summarised a new industrial scheme for Merseyside. In a nutshell, the plan is to turn a run-down chemical plant into one of the most profitable units in the British Chemical Corporation. Overnight it will make the BCC into the largest manufacturer of Propanol in Europe.

The benefits would be immense: capital equipment to be made in British factories, additional rateable income for the Local Authority, new jobs on Merseyside, foreign exchange from the exports, it all seemed too good to be true.

I said so.

'But it *is* true, Minister,' said Sir Humphrey, beaming.

How could it be, I asked myself. *Then* I asked myself, what's the point of asking myself? So I asked Humphrey.

'How could it be?' I asked. 'What's the snag?'

'The snag?' repeated Humphrey.

'Yes,' I repeated. 'The snag. What is the snag?'

I knew there must be some snag.

'I don't think I quite follow what you mean, precisely?' Humphrey was playing for time, I could tell.

I formulated my worries even as I voiced them. 'Well . . . what I mean is, this Propanol stuff is an Italian product. So why don't they produce it in Italy?' Humphrey was silent. This was indeed suspicious. 'Why are they making us such a generous present?'

'There's no snag about this, Minister,' said Sir Humphrey. 'It's wonderful news.'

I could see that if it *were* wonderful news, it would indeed be wonderful news.

'Yes,' I agreed cautiously. 'It *is* wonderful news. Wonderful news, isn't it?' I said to Bernard, who was taking the minutes on my right.

He flashed a glance at Humphrey, then replied warily, 'Yes, wonderful news,' but he didn't sound at all carefree.

I knew I'd find out nothing more, just by asking in a generalised fashion about snags. So I thought hard, I tried to find the right question. Humphrey would never actually lie to me [*Well, hardly ever – Ed.*] and will give me the right answers if I can only think of the right questions.

'Good old Propanol,' I said playing for time. Then, quite suddenly, it came to me. 'What *is* Propanol?' I asked.

'It's rather interesting,' said Humphrey promptly. 'It used to be made with dioxin, until the Seveso explosion in Northern Italy. Then they had to stop making it. Now they've developed a safe compound called metadioxin, but of course the Italian factory is still sealed off. So they've asked the BCC to make it for them.'

'Ah,' the fog was beginning to lift. 'An ill wind, eh?'

'Quite so,' he agreed contentedly.

'But is this new stuff perfectly safe?'

'Perfectly,' he replied.

'Good,' I said. So I was no nearer. Or was I?

'Humphrey, are you givng me a categorical and absolute assurance that this stuff is not only safe, but one hundred per cent safe?'

'Yes, Minister.'

Okay, so what's up? Why do I smell danger somewhere in all this unequivocally good news? 'Have you anything else to add, Humphrey, which you might regret later if you don't say it now?'

'Well Minister, I suppose I should point out that some weak Ministers might have doubts, in view of the similarity of the names, but no one with any backbone would be deflected from such a beneficial project on such a flimsy pretext.'

So that's all that it was. The similarity of the names. Humphrey was right. I told him so in the most forthright terms. 'Absolutely! I know the sort of Minister you mean. Political jellyfish. Frightened of taking any decision that might upset someone. After all, every decision upsets *someone*. Government is about doing what's right, not doing what's popular. Eh, Humphrey?'

Humphrey was full of approval. 'I couldn't have expressed it better myself, Minister.' Conceited bugger. 'I'll tell Sir Wally to go ahead.'

This sounded a touch more hurried than usual. I stopped Humphrey as he walked to the door, and sought further reassurance.

'Um . . . this decision *will* be popular, though, won't it?'

'Very popular,' Humphrey replied firmly.

I *still* felt a certain nagging worry, somewhere in my bones. 'Humphrey, I just want to be clear on this. You're not asking me to take a courageous decision, are you?'

Humphrey was visibly shocked. 'Of *course* not, Minister,' he insisted. 'Not even a controversial one. What a suggestion!'

[*Readers of these diaries will doubtless recall that whereas a controversial decision will merely lose you votes, a courageous decision will lose you the election – Ed.*]

Nonetheless, if I let it go at this, if anything went wrong I knew I should have to carry the can. So I suggested that perhaps we might take this matter to Cabinet.

'In my opinion,' Humphrey answered revealingly, 'the less said about this the better.'

'Why?'

'Because,' he said patiently, 'although metadioxin is totally harmless, the name might cause anxiety in ignorant and prejudiced minds.'

I was about to tick him off for referring to my Cabinet colleagues in this way (right though he was!) when I realised that he was referring to Friends of the Earth and other crank pressure groups.

June 7th

The matter of the Propanol plant is still not fully agreed. Joan Littler, MP for Liverpool South-West, came to see me today.

I didn't even know she was coming. I checked with Bernard, who reminded me that not only is she the PM's PPS [*Parliamentary Private Secretary, the first – and unpaid – rung on the government ladder – Ed.*] but also that the new Propanol plant would be in her constituency.

I told Bernard to bring her in. To my surprise (well, not *quite* to my surprise) Humphrey appeared at the door and asked if he could join us.

She came in, and I introduced her to Humphrey. She's in her late thirties, quite attractive in a pulled-through-a-hedge-backwards Shirley Williams' sort of way, and her slightly soft feminine manner disguises a hard-nosed opportunist. And she has the PM's ear, of course.

There was something rather aggressive about her opening gambit.

'Look here, Jim, what's the British Chemical Corporation up to in my constituency?'

'Well . . .' I began.

Sir Humphrey interrupted. 'They will shortly be announcing a very exciting project involving new jobs and new investment.'

She nodded, and turned to me. 'Yes, but there are some very worrying rumours about this project.'

'Such as?' I enquired in my most helpful tone.

She eyed me carefully. 'Rumours about dangerous chemicals.'

I nodded. 'Yes, well,' I began, 'obviously all chemicals have some element of danger . . .'

Humphrey interrupted again. 'The Minister means that the rumours are completely unfounded and there is no cause for alarm.'

I nodded. It was a good reply.

She didn't seem to think so. 'All the same,' she persisted, 'can I have your assurance, Jim, that first of all there'll be a full public enquiry?'

This seemed, I must say, a perfectly reasonable request. 'Actually,' I began, 'there'd be no harm in having a public enquiry, it might be . . .'

Humphrey interjected. 'The Minister was about to say that there is absolutely no need for a public enquiry. The whole matter has been fully investigated already and a report will be published shortly.'

Humphrey, it seemed to me, was being a little high-handed. Clearly Joan thought so too.

'Listen,' she said forcefully, 'I came here to talk to Jim.'

And Humphrey, as charming as ever, replied, 'And indeed you are talking to him.'

'But he's not answering! You are!'

I could quite see her point. Humphrey's helpfulness will sometimes achieve the opposite effect from what it is designed to achieve. Unfortunately, he is insensitive to this.

'The Minister and I,' continued Sir Humphrey complacently, 'are of one mind.'

She was incensed. 'Whose mind? Your mind?' She turned on me. 'Listen, I've heard on the grapevine that this factory will be making the chemical that poisoned Seveso and the whole of Northern Italy.'

'That's not true,' I replied, before Humphrey could screw things up further. I explained that the chemical in Seveso was dioxin, whereas this is metadioxin.

'But,' she asserted, 'that must be virtually the same thing.'

I assured her that it was merely a similar name.

'But,' she insisted, 'it's the same name, with "meta" stuck on the front.'

'Ah yes,' I agreed, 'but that makes all the difference.'

'Why?' she asked. 'What does meta mean?'

Of course, I hadn't the slightest idea. So I was forced to ask Humphrey.

'Simple, Minister,' he explained. 'It means "with" or "after", or sometimes "beyond" – it's from the Greek, you know.'

[*Like all Permanent Secretaries, Sir Humphrey Appleby was a generalist. Most of them studied classics, history, PPE or modern languages. Of course you might expect the Permanent Secretary at the Department of Administrative Affairs to have a degree in business administration, but of course you would be wrong – Ed.*]

Then he went on to explain that metadioxin means 'with' or 'after' dioxin, depending on whether it's with the accusative or the genitive: with the accusative it's 'beyond' or 'after', with the genitive it's 'with' – as in Latin, where the ablative is used for words needing a sense of with to precede them.

Bernard added – speaking for the first time in the whole meeting – that of course there is no ablative in Greek, as I would doubtless recall.

I told him I recalled no such thing, and later today he wrote me a little memo, explaining all the above Greek and Latin grammar.

However, I hoped these explanations would satisfy Joan Littler. And that, like me, she would be unwilling to reveal the limits of her education. No such luck.

'I still don't understand,' she said disarmingly.

Humphrey tried snobbery. 'Oh dear,' he sighed, 'I should have thought that was perfectly clear.' It never works.

Her eyes flashed. 'What I insist on knowing,' she stated, 'is what is the actual difference between dioxin and metadioxin.'

I didn't know, of course. Humphrey sailed into the rescue. 'It's very simple,' he replied grandly. 'Metadioxin is an inert compound of dioxin.'

I hoped that that would be that. But no.

She looked at me for help. I, of course, was unable to give her any. So I looked at Humphrey.

'Um, Humphrey,' I said, bluffing madly, 'I *think* I follow that but, er, could you, er, just explain that a little more clearly?'

He stared at me, coldly. 'In what sense, Minister?'

I didn't know where to start. I was going to have to think of the right question again. But Joan said: 'What does inert mean?'

Sir Humphrey stared at her, silently. And in that glorious moment I suddenly realised that he had no idea what he was talking about either.

'Well,' he said eventually, 'inert means that . . . it's not . . . ert.'

We all stared at each other in silence.

'Ah,' said Joan Littler.

'Ah,' I said.

'Wouldn't 'ert a fly,' muttered Bernard. At least, I think that's what he said, but when I asked him to repeat it he refused and fell silent.

And again, Joan Littler persisted.

'But,' she pressed me, 'what does that mean in practical terms?'

'You mean, chemically?' I asked her. My degree is in economics.

'Yes, chemically,' she said.

Again, I turned to Humphrey. 'Yes,' I said, beginning to enjoy myself, 'what does it mean chemically, Humphrey?'

His eyes spun. Bluffing magnificently, he said in his most patronising voice, 'Well, I'm not sure that I can explain in layman's language, Minister.'

I called the bluff. 'Do you know *any* chemistry, Humphrey?' I enquired.

'Of course not, Minister. I was in the Scholarship form.'

[*At any English public school – 'public' meaning 'private', of course – the scholarship form would have meant the classics form. Indeed, if you went to a very good school indeed you might avoid learning any science at all – Ed.*]

'And while we're at it,' continued Joan Littler, 'what's a compound?'

'You don't know any chemistry either?'

'No,' she replied. 'Do you?'

Suddenly, this all seemed awfully funny. None of us knew *anything* about the matter we were discussing. Joan, Humphrey, Bernard and I, all charged with a vital decision on a matter of government policy – and you couldn't have found four people anywhere in the UK who understood less about it.

[*It is significant that none of those present thought of telephoning Sir Wally McFarland. But then, he was merely the expert, and the chairman of the Nationalised Industry in question – Ed.*]

I grinned, embarrassed, like a naughty schoolboy. 'We *ought* to know something about inert compounds, oughtn't we?'

Humphrey had no sense of humour about this, and he made a brave attempt at bluffing us again.

'A compound is . . . well, you know what compound interest is, surely?' he complained. Joan and I nodded. 'Compound interest is a jolly good thing to enjoy. Well, that's the sort of thing a compound is.'

I stared at him. Did he really think that would do? I looked at Joan. She was staring at him too. But reduced to silence for the first time. So I plunged in hopefully.

'Well,' I said, trying it on in the hope of bringing the discussion to a close, 'that's about it, then. To sum up, I think we're all of the same mind, basically in agreement, broadly speaking, about this. And we are happy to continue with its development.'

Littler spoke up. 'I've said no such thing.'

We were getting nowhere. So I tried to sum it up again. I pointed out that we had established that the only similarity between dioxin and metadioxin was in the name. She didn't seem to see it.

I searched desperately for an analogy, 'It's like Littler and Hitler,' I explained. 'We're not saying that you're like Hitler because your name sounds similar.'

I realised that I'd been less than tactful, but the words were out. She flared up. 'That's hardly the point,' she said angrily.

'Then what *is* the point?' But I knew already.

'The point is, this factory is in my constituency.'

Of course I could see why she was worried, but if Humphrey was telling me the truth she was worried unnecessarily. 'It's good for the constituency.' I said. 'More jobs. More money. The only people who could possibly be upset by this are a few cranky environmentalists. It can't cost us more than, on balance, a couple of hundred votes.'

'My majority,' she replied quietly, 'is ninety-one.'

I hadn't realised. She certainly had a point. I don't want to be responsible for jeopardising a government-held marginal, especially if the sitting MP is PPS to the PM.

She pressed home her argument. 'And don't forget that there are three government constituencies bordering onto mine – all marginal, all with majorities of well under two thousand.'

I didn't know what to say. While I considered the position, Sir Humphrey spoke up again. 'Miss Littler,' he began, 'may I intervene once more?' She nodded. 'The case for the BCC manufacturing Propanol is overwhelming – am I right, Minister?'

'Overwhelming,' I agreed.

'It will create jobs,' continued Humphrey fluently, 'it will increase income for the Local Authority, and it will secure profitable export orders.'

'Export orders,' I agreed.

'Furthermore,' he continued, 'the chemical has been declared safe by the FDA in Washington.'

'Washington,' I agreed.

'We are having,' he went on, 'a report prepared here *as well*. The Minister regards this scheme as being wholly to the advantage of your constituency and the country.'

I chimed in. 'And if the stuff is dangerous, I *promise* you I'll stop it being made here. But if the report shows it's harmless, that would be absurd, wouldn't it?'

She sat still for a moment, staring at me, then at Humphrey. Then she stood up. She said she wasn't satisfied. (I can't blame her. If it were my constituency, I'm not sure I'd be satisfied either.) She advised me to remember that the party made me an MP – and that I certainly can't go on being a Minister if our party loses the next election.

She's got a point there too.

Also, I have a nasty feeling that the PM will hear her point of view before the end of the week.

Humphrey looked at me after she left, obviously asking for a go-ahead. I told him that I would consider the matter further, and told Bernard to put all the relevant papers in my box to take home and study. Then the decision should become clear.

June 8th

I've studied all the Propanol papers and I still don't know what to do.

So I called a meeting with Humphrey to discuss the report on Propanol that we have commissioned. I've been wondering if it really will be conclusively in favour of Propanol, as Sir Humphrey and Sir Wally predict.

I asked if I should meet Professor Henderson, who is chairing the report, or writing it himself or something.

Humphrey said that there was no need for such a meeting. He is apparently a brilliant biochemist and was chosen with some care.

Naturally he was chosen with care. But to what end: to produce a report that backs Sir Wally and Sir Humphrey? Naturally he was.

But surely none of them would be foolish enough to cook up a report saying that metadioxin were safe if, in fact, it were dangerous. Naturally not. I think I'm going round in circles.

There was another possibility that I could raise though. 'Suppose he produces one of those cautious wait-and-see reports?'

'In that case,' said Sir Humphrey cheerfully, 'we don't publish it, we use the American report instead.'

I was completely torn. On the one hand, the scheme is a wonderful one – the jobs, the income etc. – if it works out safely! And I'm assured it will. But if there's an accident after I have given the go-ahead . . . The consequences would be too awful to contemplate.

'Is there any chance he'll produce a report saying the stuff's dangerous?' I wanted to know.

Humphrey was plainly baffled. 'No. No chance. It isn't dangerous,' he said.

He clearly is totally sincere on this issue. And yet he's suggesting we don't publish a cautious wait-and-see type report if that's what Henderson writes.

'Why would you consider suppressing the Henderson report?'

He was outraged. 'I would never suppress it, Minister. I merely might not publish it.'

'What's the difference?'

'All the difference in the world. Suppression is the instrument of totalitarian dictatorships. You can't do that in a free country. We would merely take a democratic decision not to publish it.'

That makes sense. But what would I say to the press and to Parliament, I wondered? That we had hoped the Henderson Committee would show we'd made the right decision but instead they've said we cocked it up, so we're pretending the report doesn't exist? I offered this suggestion to Humphrey.

He was not amused. 'Very droll, Minister,' he remarked.

So I asked Humphrey, 'What *would* I say, if I decided not to publish it?'

'There is a well-established government procedure for suppressing – that is, not publishing – unwanted reports.'

This was news to me. I asked how it was done.

'You discredit them,' he explained simply.

How? I made notes as he spoke. It occurred to me, that his technique could be useful for discrediting some of the party's more idiotic research papers.

Stage one: The public interest
1) You hint at security considerations.

2) You point out that the report could be used to put unwelcome pressure on government because it might be misinterpreted. [*Of course, anything might be misinterpreted. The Sermon on the Mount might be misinterpreted. Indeed, Sir Humphrey Appleby would almost certainly have argued that, had the Sermon on the Mount been a government report, it should certainly not have been published on the grounds that it was a thoroughly irresponsible document: the sub-paragraph suggesting that the meek will inherit the earth could, for instance, do irreparable damage to the defence budget – Ed.*]

3) You then say that it is better to wait for the results of a wider and more detailed survey over a longer time-scale.

4) If there is no such survey being carried out, so much the better. You commission one, which gives you even more time to play with.

Stage two: Discredit the evidence that you are not publishing
This is, of course, much easier than discrediting evidence that you *do* publish. You do it indirectly, by press leaks. You say:
(a) that it leaves important questions unanswered
(b) that much of the evidence is inconclusive
(c) that the figures are open to other interpretations
(d) that certain findings are contradictory
(e) that some of the main conclusions have been questioned
Points (a) to (d) are bound to be true. In fact, all of these criticisms can be made of a report without even reading it. There are, for instance, always *some* questions unanswered – such as the ones they haven't asked. As regards (e), if some of the main conclusions have not been questioned, question them! Then they have.

Stage three: Undermine the recommendations
This is easily done, with an assortment of governmental phrases:
(a) 'not really a basis for long-term decisions . . .'
(b) 'not sufficient information on which to base a valid assessment . . .'
(c) 'no reason for any fundamental rethink of existing policy . . .'
(d) 'broadly speaking, it endorses current practice . . .'
These phrases give comfort to people who have not read the report and who don't want change – i.e. almost everybody.

Stage four: If stage three still leaves doubts, then Discredit The Man Who Produced the Report

This must be done OFF THE RECORD. You explain that:

(a) he is harbouring a grudge against the government
(b) he is a publicity seeker
(c) he's trying to get his knighthood
(d) he is trying to get his chair
(e) he is trying to get his Vice-Chancellorship
(f) he used to be a consultant to a multinational company *or*
(g) he wants to be a consultant to a multinational company

June 9th

Today the Propanol plan reached the television news, damn it. Somehow some environmental group got wind of the scheme and a row blew up on Merseyside.

The TV newsreader – or whoever writes what the newsreader reads – didn't help much either. Though he didn't say that Propanol was dangerous, he somehow managed to imply it – using loaded words like 'claim'.

[*We have found the transcript of the BBC Nine O'Clock News for 9 June. The relevant item is shown overleaf. Hacker seems to have a reasonable point – Ed.*]

BRITISH BROADCASTING CORPORATION

NEWSREADER: Apparently Propanol contains metadioxin, which the BCC claims is completely harmless. It is, however, a compound of dioxin, which was the chemical released

CUE NEWS FILM OF SEVESO INCIDENT

after a factory explosion at Seveso in Northern Italy in July 1976, spreading a cloud of poisonous dust over a four mile radius. Because dioxin can cause irreversible damage to the human foetus as well as other serious diseases the entire village was evacuated and the villagers were not allowed to return home for nearly a year.

CUE FILM OF MERSEYSIDE PROTEST. Group of women with placards: "NO TO THE POISON FACTORY", "BABYKILLERS KEEP OUT", "LIVES BEFORE PROFITS".

Today a Merseyside group of protesters voice their opposition to the BCC scheme outside the factory gates.

LIVERPOOL WOMAN: I'll tell you what we're going to do. As far as I'm concerned, Sir Wally can take his poisonous chemicals somewhere else. My daughter's expecting a baby in three months and I'm not having my grandchild deformed for the sake of bloody Eyties[1] I can tell you that.

REPORTER: But they say metadioxin is harmless.

LIVERPOOL WOMAN: Oh yes. They said Thalidomide was harmless too, didn't they? Well if it's all that harmless, why aren't they Eyties making it in Italy, eh? Tell me that! If we had a government that cared about ordinary people, they'd never allow it.

END OF FILM

NEWSREADER: The BCC said tonight that a Government Report on the safety of Propanol was due to be published shortly by the Department of Administrative Affairs. Today, in Prague, the Government announced that due to ....

- 1 -

[1] Italians.

[*We asked an old BBC current affairs man how the News would have treated the item if they had been in favour of the scheme, and we reproduce his 'favourable' version to compare with the actual one – Ed.*]

NEWSREADER: Propanol contains metadioxin, a compound of the chemical dioxin which was released in the Seveso explosion in Italy in 1976. It is however an inert compound and chemical analysis has shown it to be completely harmless.

CUT TO FILM OF FACTORY SHOWING PLANT AND OFFICES

The news was welcomed today at the factory where Propanol will be manufactured. It had been scheduled for closure at the end of the year, but now it will be taking on more staff. The contract is for a minimum of five years.

CUE FILM OF FACTORY WORKER

FACTORY WORKER: This is great news. At last we've got some work we can get our teeth into. It's really put heart in the lads.

CUT TO SIR WALLY

SIR WALLY: Everyone's worked like mad for this contract. It will mean a lot of exports as well as a lot of jobs. We were up against the Germans and the Americans, so it's a real vote of confidence in the British chemical industry.

REPORTER: Isn't metadioxin potentially dangerous?

SIR WALLY: No, that's dioxin; metadioxin is about as dangerous as self-raising flour.

END OF FILM

NEWSREADER: A government report is to be published shortly which, it is understood, will confirm an earlier American enquiry which gives metadioxin a clean bill of health.

June 10th

I summoned Humphrey first thing this morning. I pointed out that metadioxin is dynamite.

He answered me that it's harmless.

I disagreed. 'It may be harmless chemically,' I said, 'but it's lethal politically.'

'It can't hurt anyone,' he insisted.

I pointed out that it could finish me off.

No sooner had we begun talking than Number Ten was on the phone. The political office. Joan Littler had obviously made sure that Number Ten watched the Nine O'Clock News last night.

I tried to explain that this was merely a little local difficulty, and there were exports and jobs prospects. They asked how many jobs: I had to admit that it was only about ninety – but well-paid jobs, and in an area of high unemployment.

None of this cut any ice with Number Ten – I was talking to the Chief Political Adviser, but doubtless he was acting under orders. There was no point in fighting this particular losing battle with the PM, so I muttered (as Humphrey was listening, and Bernard was probably listening-in) that I was coming round to their point of view, *i.e.* that there was a risk to three or four marginals.

I rang off. Humphrey was eyeing me with a quizzical air.

'Humphrey,' I began carefully, 'something has just struck me.'

'I noticed,' he replied dryly.

I ignored the wisecrack. I pointed out that there were perfectly legitimate arguments against this scheme. A loss of public confidence, for instance.

'You mean votes,' he interjected.

I denied it, of course. I explained that I didn't exactly mean votes. Votes in themselves are not a consideration. But *the public will* is a valid consideration. We are a democracy. And it looks as if the public are against this scheme.

'The public,' said Sir Humphrey, 'are ignorant and misguided.'

'What do you mean?' I demanded. 'It was the public who elected me.'

There was a pointed silence.

Then Sir Humphrey continued: 'Minister, in a week it will all have blown over, and in a year's time there will be a safe and successful factory on Merseyside.'

'A week is a long time in politics,' I answered.[1]

[1] Originally said by Mr Harold Wilson as he then was.

'A year is a short time in government,' responded Sir Humphrey.

I began to get cross. *He* may be in government. But I'm in politics. And the PM is not pleased.

Humphrey then tried to tell me that I was putting party before country. That hoary old cliché again. I told him to find a new one.

Bernard said that a new cliché could perhaps be said to be a contradiction in terms. Thank you, Bernard, for all your help!

I made one more attempt to make Humphrey understand. 'Humphrey,' I said, 'you understand nothing because you lead a sheltered life. I want to survive. I'm not crossing the PM.'

He was very bitter. And very insulting. 'Must you always be so concerned with climbing the greasy pole?'

I faced the question head on. 'Humphrey,' I explained, 'the greasy pole is important. I have to climb it.'

'Why?'

'Because,' I said, 'it's there.'

June 11th

Today there was an astonishing piece in *The Times*. A leak.

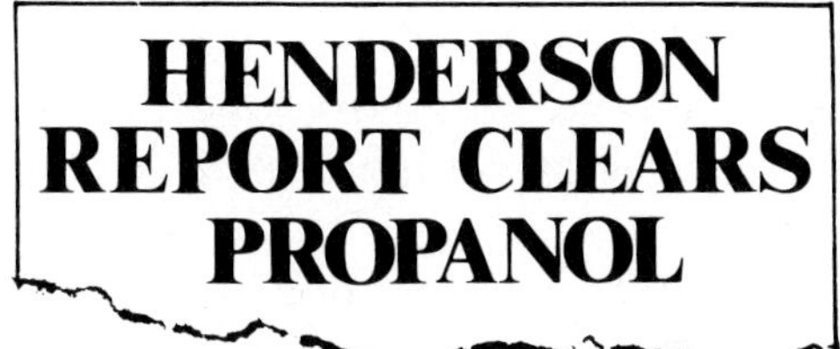

HENDERSON REPORT CLEARS PROPANOL

I was furious.

I asked Bernard how *The Times* knows the wording of the Henderson Report before I do.

'There's been a leak, Minister,' he explained.

The boy's a fool. Obviously there's been a leak. The question is, who's been leaking?

On second thoughts, perhaps he's not a fool. Perhaps he knows. And can't or won't tell.

'It's labelled "Confidential",' I pointed out.

'At least it wasn't labelled "Restricted",' he said.

[*RESTRICTED means it was in the papers yesterday. CONFIDENTIAL means it won't be in the papers till today – Ed.*]

I decided to put Bernard on the spot. 'Who leaked this? Humphrey?'

'Oh,' he said. 'I'm sure he didn't.'

'Are you?' I asked penetratingly.

'Well . . . he probably didn't.'

'No?' I was at my most penetrating.

'Well,' said Bernard with a sheepish smile, 'it *might* have been someone else.'

'These leaks are a disgrace,' I told him. 'And people think that it's politicians that leak.'

'It has been known, though, hasn't it?' said Bernard carefully.

'In my opinion,' I said reproachfully, 'we are much more leaked against than leaking.'

I then read *The Times* story carefully through. It contained a number of phrases that I could almost hear Humphrey dictating: 'Political cowardice to reject the BCC proposal' . . . 'Hacker has no choice', etc.

It was clear that, by means of this leak, Humphrey thinks that he has now committed me to this scheme.

Well, we shall see!

June 14th

I got my copy of the Henderson Report on Saturday, only a day after *The Times* got theirs. Not bad.

The Report gives me no way out of the Propanol scheme. At least, none that I can see at the moment. It says it's a completely safe chemical.

On the other hand, *The Times* commits me to nothing. It is, after all, merely an unofficial leak of a draft report.

Sir Wally McFarlane was my first appointment of the day. Humphrey came too – surprise, surprise!

And they were both looking excessively cheerful.

I asked them to sit down. Then Sir Wally opened the batting.

'I see from the press,' he said, 'that the Henderson Report comes down clearly on our side.'

I think perhaps he still thinks that I'm on his side. No, surely Humphrey must have briefed him. So he's pretending that he thinks that I'm still on his side.

I was non-committal. 'Yes, I saw that too.'

And I stared penetratingly at Humphrey.

He shifted uncomfortably in his seat. 'Yes, that committee is leaking like a sieve,' he said. I continued staring at him, but made no reply. There's no doubt that he's the guilty man. He continued, brazenly: 'So Minister, there's no real case for refusing permission for the new Plant now, is there?'

I remained non-committal. 'I don't know.'

Sir Wally spoke up. 'Look, Jim. We've been working away at this contract for two years. It's very important to us. I'm chairman and I'm responsible – and I tell you, as a chemist myself, that metadioxin is utterly safe.'

'Why do you experts always think you are right?' I enquired coldly.

'Why do you think,' countered Sir Wally emotionally, 'that the more *in*expert you are, the more likely *you* are to be right?'

I'm not an expert. I've never claimed to be an expert. I said so. 'Ministers are not experts. Ministers are put in charge precisely because they know nothing . . .'

'You admit that?' interrupted Sir Wally with glee. I suppose I walked right into that.

I persevered. 'Ministers know nothing *about technical problems*. A Minister's job is to consider the wider interests of the nation and, for that reason, I cannot commit myself yet.'

Sir Wally stood up, and lost his temper. (In the reverse order, I think.) 'Come off it, Hacker,' he exploded, 'this is the wrong decision and you know it. It is weak, craven and cowardly.'

Then I got angry. I stood up too. 'I am not a coward.'

'Sit down!' he whispered murderously. His eyes were flashing, and he looked quite ready for a physical punch-up. I decided that discretion was the better part of valour and sat down.

He was beside himself with rage. He was spitting all over my desk as he spoke. 'You think you'll lose a miserable few hundred votes from a few foolish ill-informed people in those constituencies? It's pathetic!'

'It's politics,' I explained.

'Exactly,' he agreed contemptuously, and walked to the door. Then he turned. 'I shall be telephoning the Secretary of State for Industry. I'm prepared to resign if you block this one.'

He stalked out.

We gazed at each other.

After a few moments Sir Humphrey spoke. 'How did you feel that went, Minister?' he enquired politely.

I refused to show my concern. As breezily as I could, I replied, 'We'll just have to get another chairman, that's all.'

Humphrey was incredulous. 'Get another? Get *another*? No one else on earth would take that job. *Nobody* wants to be chairman of a nationalised industry. It's instant ruin. They might as well accept the golden handshake on the day they start. It's only a matter of time.'

I still refused to show any concern. 'We'll find someone,' I said, with a confidence that I did not feel.

'Yes,' agreed Humphrey. 'Some useless nonentity or some American geriatric.'

'Not necessarily,' I replied.

'Oh no?' enquired Sir Humphrey. 'So how do you expect the DOI[1] to find a decent replacement when we've forced his predecessor to resign for taking a sound commercial decision which we blocked for political reasons?'

I could see no point in going through all that again. 'I have no choice,' I said simply.

Sir Humphrey tried flattery. 'Minister,' he wheedled. 'A Minister can do what he likes.'

'No,' I explained. 'It's the people's will. I am their leader. I must follow them. I have no guilty conscience. My hands are clean.'

Sir Humphrey stood up, coldly. 'I should have thought,' he remarked, 'that it was frightfully difficult to keep one's hands clean while climbing the greasy pole.'

Then *he* stalked out.

I really was winning friends and influencing people this morning.

I was left with good old faithful Bernard.

We sat and contemplated the various possibilities that could arise from the morning's débâcle. Clearly we had to avoid Wally making a public fuss. We had to stop him giving interviews on *Panorama* or making press statements accusing me of political interference.

I am really on the horns of a dilemma. If I stop the scheme, *The Times* and *The Daily Telegraph* will say that I'm a contemptible political coward. But if I let it go ahead the *Daily Mirror* and the *Sun* will say I'm murdering unborn babies. I can't win!

The only way out is if the Henderson Report had *any* doubt about the safety of metadioxin. But it hasn't. I've read it very carefully.

On the other hand – I've suddenly realised – no one else has read it. Because it's not quite finished. It's still only a *draft* report.

Tomorrow I'll talk to Bernard about this matter. Perhaps the answer is to meet Professor Henderson while there's still time.

[1] Department of Industry.

June 15th

This morning, at our daily diary session, I asked Bernard if Professor Henderson is a Cambridge man.

Bernard nodded.

'Which college is he at?' I asked casually.

'King's,' said Bernard. 'Why?'

I brushed it aside. 'Just curious – wondered if it was my old college.'

Mistake! 'Weren't you at LSE?' he asked.

'Oh yes, so I was,' I found myself saying. Feeble! I really must do better than that!

I asked Bernard to give me his file, and I asked for a Cambridge telephone directory.

Bernard spoke up bravely. 'Minister . . .' he began nervously, '. . . you do realise that . . . not that you have any such intention, of course . . . but, well, it would be most improper to try to influence an independent report of this nature.'

I agreed wholeheartedly that it would be most improper. Unthinkable, in fact. 'But I just thought that we might go and have tea with my old friend R. A. Crichton, Provost of King's.' I told Bernard to get him on the phone.

Bernard did so.

'And,' I added, 'who knows? Professor Henderson might easily drop in for tea with his Provost. That would be a happy coincidence, wouldn't it?'

Bernard thought for a split second, and agreed that it would be perfectly natural, if they were both at the same college.

'There's nothing improper about a coincidence, is there, Bernard?'

Deadpan, he replied: 'How can a coincidence be improper, Minister? Impropriety postulates intention, which coincidence precludes.'

Memo: I must learn to use longer words.

June 18th

I had a most satisfactory day up in Cambridge.

Tea with Crichton, my old friend at King's. Now a peer, and very relaxed in academic life.

I asked him how it felt, going from the Commons to the Lords.

'It's like being moved from the animals to the vegetables,' he replied.

By a strange coincidence Professor Henderson had been invited for tea. Crichton introduced us.

Henderson seemed slightly taken aback. 'I must say, I didn't expect to see the Minister,' he said. We both agreed that it was a remarkable coincidence.

Crichton looked astonished and asked if we knew each other. I explained that we'd never met, but that Henderson was writing a report for my Department.

Crichton said that this was quite a coincidence, and Henderson and I both agreed that it was an *amazing* coincidence.

After that we all settled down a bit and, over the Earl Grey, Henderson remarked that I must have been very happy with the draft of his report.

I assured him that I was delighted, absolutely delighted, and I complimented him on his hard work. He, with modesty – and truth – admitted that most of the hard work had been done by the FDA in Washington.

I asked him if he'd ever done a government report before. He said he hadn't. So I explained that his name will be attached to it forever. THE HENDERSON REPORT.

'A kind of immortality, really,' I added.

He seemed pleased. He smiled, and said he'd never thought of it like that before.

Then I went straight for the jugular. 'But,' I said casually, 'if anything were to go wrong . . .' And I paused.

He was instantly perturbed. 'Go wrong?' His little academic eyes blinked behind his big academic hornrims.

'I mean,' I said gravely, 'if metadioxin is not quite as safe as you say it is. It's your career – this is very courageous of you.'

Professor Henderson was now very concerned. Courageous was manifestly the last thing he ever wanted to be. He was also puzzled, and not quite getting my drift. 'I don't understand,' he said. 'None of the standard tests on metadioxin show any evidence of toxicity.'

I paused for effect. Then: 'None of the *standard* tests. Quite.'

I paused again, while he panicked silently.

'What do you mean?' he said in a high strangled voice that didn't quite seem to belong to this tall fellow with a high forehead and big feet.

I got out my little notebook to refresh my memory. 'Funnily enough,' I explained, 'I was just making a few notes in the train on the way up here. Of course, I'm not a biochemist, you understand, but I'm told that the FDA report leaves some important questions unanswered.'

He thought about this. 'Well . . .' he said finally, and stopped.

I went on: 'And that some of the evidence is inconclusive, that some of the findings have been questioned, and the figures are open to other interpretations.'

Henderson tried to make sense of all this. Then he said: 'But *all* figures are open to . . .'

I interrupted him. 'Absolutely! And that different results might come from a wider and more detailed study over a longer time scale.'

'Well, obviously . . .' he began.

'Yes,' I said firmly. 'You see. If something did go wrong – even in ten years' time, a delayed effect – well, the press would go straight to your report. And if it turned out you'd done laboratory trials for a multinational drug company . . .'

He was appalled. 'But that was fifteen years ago.'

'Fourteen,' I corrected him. (This immensely useful piece of information had been revealed by his file.) 'And you know what the press are like – "No smoke without fire." Even if there's no real basis. Could be a millstone round your neck.'

I could see that Henderson was wavering, so I piled on the pressure.

'The popular press would be merciless if anything *did* go wrong: DEATH AGONY OF HENDERSON REPORT VICTIMS'.

Henderson was quaking in his shoes. He was in a frightful state. 'Yes, yes, well, I, er, I don't know what to do. I mean. I can't change the evidence. Metadioxin is a safe drug. The report has to say so.'

He looked at me, desperately. I carefully did not fall into the trap. I was not going to make the elementary mistake of telling him what to put in his independent report.

'Quite,' I agreed. 'Quite. I can see you have no choice.'

And I left him.

As I strolled across the room to refill my cup of tea, I saw dear old Crichton slide into my chair and offer Henderson a buttered crumpet.

I knew what he was going to say. He was going to tell Henderson that it's only the phrasing of the Conclusion that you have to worry about. That's the only part the press ever reads.

At the moment it reads: 'On existing evidence, the Committee can see no reason not to proceed.'

I'm sure Crichton will suggest some excellent alternative. And I'm equally sure that Henderson will take his advice.

June 22nd

Victory.

I got the final version of the Henderson Report today. It's all exactly the same, but for the end paragraph, which has undergone the teeniest bit of redrafting.

> While the committee can see no reason not to proceed on the existing evidence, it should be emphasised that Metadioxin is a comparatively recent compound, and it would be irresponsible to deny that after further research its manufacture might be found to be associated with health risks.

I called Bernard at once, and told him to release the report to the press.

Then I cancelled all appointments for today, took a train to Liverpool where another protest meeting was due to take place, the press office notified the press, radio and television – and, in a glorious triumphant moment, I announced at the meeting, on television, to an enthusiastic cheering crowd that I would not be giving my approval for the BCC to manufacture Propanol.

I reckon that's four marginals won in the next general election.

When I got home tonight I saw Sir Wally on *Newsnight*. He made no mention of resignation – he couldn't, of course, he'd been completely outmanoeuvred.

He simply issued a statement in which he said that if the Henderson Report was correct to cast doubt on the safety of metadioxin it was obviously impossible to consider manufacturing it on Merseyside.

June 23rd

Sir Humphrey was angrier with me today than I've ever seen him.

'Do you feel like a hero?' he asked.

'Yes,' I replied. 'Number Ten will be delighted.'

'Probably one of the worst governmental decisions I have ever witnessed,' he snarled. I wasn't bothered by this open rudeness.

'Probably one of the best political decisions I've ever made,' I replied confidently.

Bernard was silent.

'What do *you* think, Bernard?' I asked cruelly.

Bernard looked desperate. 'I think . . . that, bearing everything in mind . . . and, ah . . . after due consideration and, well . . . um . . . considering all the implications and, ah, points of view, um, that, well, in other words, I am in fact, *bound* to say that . . . you looked awfully good on television, Minister.'

Having enjoyed watching Bernard wriggle, I turned back to Humphrey. 'Oh by the way,' I asked, 'can we manage a CBE for Henderson? Or a Vice-Chancellorship or something?'

Humphrey was appalled. 'Certainly not! He's completely unreliable and totally lacking in judgement. I still can't think why he suddenly cast doubt on his whole report in that final paragraph.'

'Because,' I replied without thinking, 'he has excellent judgement, enormous stature and great charm.' Then I realised what I'd said.

So did Humphrey. 'I thought you said you'd never met him.' Quick as a flash I replied, 'Intellectual stature.'

Humphrey was not fooled. 'And charm?' he enquired scathingly.

I was almost stumped. 'He . . . er . . . he writes with charm,' I explained unconvincingly. 'Doesn't he, Bernard?'

'Yes Minister,' replied Bernard dutifully.

Sir Humphrey's face was a picture.

12
The Devil You Know

July 1st

The EEC is really intolerably difficult to deal with. For months I have been working with the DAA to get the whole of the Civil Service to place one big central order for word-processing machines. This would replace the present nonsensical practice of every separate department in Whitehall ordering all different sorts of word-processors in dribs and drabs.

If we at the DAA placed one big central order for everyone, the sum of money would be so large it would enable UK manufacturers to make the right sort of investment in systems development.

For days now, we have been on the verge of success. Months of patient negotiations were about to pay off. I was all ready to make a major press announcement: I could see the headlines: HACKER'S MASSIVE INVESTMENT IN MODERN TECHNOLOGY. JIM'S VOTE OF CONFIDENCE IN BRITISH INDUSTRY. BRITAIN CAN MAKE IT, SAYS JIM.

And then, this morning, we got another bloody directive from the bloody EEC in bloody Brussels, saying that all EEC members *must* work to some niggling European word-processing standards. And therefore, we must postpone everything in order to agree plans with a whole mass of European Word Processing Committees at the forthcoming European Word Processing Conference in Brussels.

I called a meeting to discuss all this. I went through the whole story so far, and Sir Humphrey and Bernard just sat there saying, 'Yes Minister,' and 'Quite so Minister,' at regular intervals. Some help.

Finally, I got tired of the sound of my own voice. [*Was this a first? – Ed.*] I demanded that Humphrey contribute something to the discussion.

He sighed. 'Well, Minister, I'm afraid that this is the penalty we have to pay for trying to pretend that we are Europeans. Believe me, I fully understand your hostility to Europe.'

As so often happens, Humphrey completely missed the point. I tried to explain again.

'Humphrey,' I said slowly and patiently, 'I'm not like you. I am pro-Europe. I'm just anti-Brussels. You seem to be anti-Europe and pro-Brussels.'

He dodged the issue, and pretended that he had no opinions on the EEC. Duplicitous creep. 'Minister, I am neither pro nor anti anything. I am merely a Humble Vessel into which Ministers pour the fruits of their deliberations. But it can certainly be argued that, given the absurdity of the whole European idea, Brussels is in fact doing its best to defend the indefensible and make the unworkable work.'

I told Humphrey that he was talking through his hat and that although I didn't want to sound pompous the European ideal is our best hope of overcoming narrow national self-interest.

He told me that I didn't sound pompous – merely inaccurate.

So I explained yet again to the Humble Vessel that Europe is a community of nations united by a common goal.

He chuckled, and I asked if Bernard and I might share the joke.

He was laughing at the idea that the community was united. 'Look at it *objectively*,' he said. 'The game is played for national interests, and always was.'

I disagreed. I reminded him that we went into the EEC to strengthen the international brotherhood of free nations.

Humphrey chuckled again. It really was most disconcerting. Then he began to tell me his interpretation – which was even more disconcerting.

'We went in,' he said, 'to screw the French by splitting them off from the Germans. The French went in to protect their inefficient farmers from commercial competition. The Germans went in to cleanse themselves of genocide and apply for readmission to the human race.'

I told Humphrey that I was quite shocked by his appalling cynicism. I couldn't actually argue with what he said because I feel, somewhat uneasily, that there is a ring of truth about it. I said: 'At least the little nations are in it for selfless reasons.'

'Ah yes,' he replied. 'Luxembourg is in it for the perks – all that foreign money pouring into the capital of the EEC.'

'Nonetheless, it's a very sensible location for the capital,' I argued.

He smiled. 'With the administration in Brussels and the Parliament in Strasbourg?' It's like having London as the capital with the House of Commons in Swindon and the Civil Service in Kettering.'

'If this were true,' I said doggedly, 'the other countries wouldn't have been trying to join.'

'Such as?'

'Well, take the Greeks.'

Sir Humphrey settled back reflectively in his chair. 'Actually,' he mused, 'I find it difficult to take the Greeks. Open-minded as I am about foreigners, as well you know.' (His total lack of self-awareness took my breath away!) 'But what will the Greeks want out of it? – an olive mountain and a retsina lake.' He looked at my face, and added apologetically: 'Sorry, I suppose some of your best friends are Greek.'

I could stand no more of this cynical rubbish. I tried to broaden the discussion, to look at the real problems of the community.

'The trouble with Brussels,' I began, 'is not internationalism. It's too much bureaucracy.'

I got no further. Humphrey interrupted me again.

'But don't you see,' he insisted, 'that the bureaucracy is a consequence of the internationalism? Why else would an English Commissioner have a French Director-General immediately below him, an Italian Chef-du-Division reporting to the Frenchman, and so on down the line?'

I was forced to agree. 'I agree,' I said.

'It's the Tower of Babel,' he said.

I was forced to agree again.

'I agree,' I said.

'In fact, it's even worse than that – it's like the United Nations,' he added.

I could not but agree for the third time. 'I agree,' I said.

We both stopped talking and gazed at each other. Where had we reached? What had we decided? What next?

Bernard tried to help out. 'Then, perhaps, if I may interject, perhaps you are in fact in agreement.'

'No we're not!' we said, in unison.

That much was certain!

'Brussels is a shambles,' I said, pursuing my theme of how the bureaucracy destroys the bonds between nations. I reminded Humphrey that the typical Common Market official is said to have the organising capacity of the Italians, the flexibility of the Germans and the modesty of the French. He tops all that up with the imagination of the Belgians, the generosity of the Dutch, and the intelligence of the Irish. Finally, for good measure, he has the European spirit of Mr Anthony Wedgwood Benn.[1]

'And now,' I concluded, 'they are all trying to screw up our excellent word-processing plan which is wholly in Britain's interest and my interest.'

'Which are, of course,' added Humphrey, 'one and the same thing.'

I stared at him, and enquired if he was being sarcastic. He denied it. I accepted his denial (though doubtfully) and continued to explore my theory of what's wrong with Brussels.

'The reason that Brussels bureaucrats are so hopeless is not *just* because of the difficulty of running an international organisation – it's because it's a gravy train.'

'A what?' asked Bernard.

'A gravy train,' I repeated, warming to my theme. 'They all live off claret and caviar. Crates of booze in every office. Air-conditioned Mercedes and private planes. Every one of those bureaucrats has got his snout in the trough and most of them have got their front trotters in as well.'

Humphrey, as always, sprang to the defence of the bureaucrats. 'I beg to differ, Minister,' he said reproachfully. 'Brussels is full of hard-working public servants who have to endure a lot of exhausting travel and tedious entertainment.'

Terribly tedious, I thought to myself, working through all that smoked salmon and forcing down all that champagne.

'And in any case, Minister,' continued Humphrey, 'you're blaming the wrong people.'

What was he talking about? I'd lost track.

'I understand,' he went on, 'that it was one of your Cabinet colleagues who gave Brussels early warning of your plan for the bulk-buying of word-processors, which is why they have brought this directive out so quickly.'

No wonder I'd lost track. He'd gone back to the point of our conversation. He really is a confusing man to talk to.

And that was it, was it? Betrayed again! By a Cabinet colleague!

[1] A left-wing politician prominent in the 1970s and the early 1980s, a peer's son educated at Westminster and Oxford, chiefly remembered for his lisp, his staring eyes, and his earnest attempts to disguise his privileged background by drinking mugs of tea in workers' co-operatives.

[*Who else? – Ed.*] No prizes for guessing who it was – Basil Corbett! Bloody Basil Corbett! When I think about Basil Corbett I really warm to Judas Iscariot. [*Basil Corbett was another tall, patrician, lisping politician with staring eyes, usually seen smoking a pipe so that people would feel he was 'sound' – Ed.*]

'Corbett?' I asked, though I knew.

Humphrey inclined his head slightly, to indicate that it was indeed the Secretary of State for Trade and Industry who had put the boot in.

I couldn't contain my anger. 'He's a treacherous, disloyal, arrogant, opinionated, publicity-seeking creep.' Humphrey gazed at me and said nothing. I mistook his attitude. 'I'm sorry if that sounds harsh, Humphrey,' I added.

'On the contrary, Minister,' replied Humphrey, 'compared with what his Permanent Secretary says, that ranks as a generous tribute.'

I wonder why Corbett did this to me – ah well, time will tell, no doubt.

July 2nd

I didn't have to wait long for the answer. Today's *Standard* contained significant and potentially worrying news.

CABINET RESHUFFLE

By Our Political Staff

IT IS being rumoured that the Prime Minister will announce important cabinet changes before the end of the present session. Basil Corbett is rumoured to be

Basil Corbett again. Every time that man comes anywhere near me I get a sharp stabbing pain in the back.

And how come I didn't know about this impending reshuffle? How did they know? I asked Humphrey if it was true.

He was evasive, of course. 'Minister, I am only a humble civil servant. I do not move in such exalted circles as Cabinet Ministers and journalists.'

I persisted. 'Is this rumour true?'

'Yes.'

A straight answer! I was somewhat taken aback. 'How do you know,' I asked, 'if you don't move in such exalted circles?'

'I mean,' he explained, 'it is true that it is rumoured.'

I was worried and anxious. I still am. A reshuffle. This is full of all sorts of implications. I have hardly started on all the things that I planned to do when I got the DAA.

I started to explain this to Humphrey, who pointed out that I may not be moved in a reshuffle. I think he meant to be reassuring, but perhaps he was trying to tell me that my career is not moving forward – which it ought to be.

I asked him if that's what he meant. Again he was evasive. 'At least it wouldn't be moving backwards,' he said.

Backwards? I'd never even considered moving *backwards*! Perhaps he wasn't being evasive after all.

'Look,' I ventured cautiously. 'Tell me. I mean, I'm doing all right, aren't I?'

'Yes indeed, Minister,' he replied smoothly. 'You're doing all right.'

I couldn't quarrel with his words – well, my words, really! – but there seemed to be an air of doubt in his delivery of them.

So I turned to Bernard and said, more positively: 'We're doing all right, aren't we Bernard?'

'Yes Minister.'

That was all. No other words of encouragement seemed to be forthcoming.

I felt I had to justify myself. God knows why! 'Yes' I said. 'Yes. I mean, perhaps I'm not the *outstanding* success of the government, but I'm not a failure, am I?'

'No Minister,' said Bernard, a shade dutifully, I thought. I waited. I was damned if I was going to ask for any compliments. Eventually Bernard said, 'Um – you're doing . . . all right.'

But did he mean it?

And if so, *what* did he mean?

I seemed to be in the throes of an attack of verbal diarrhoea. 'After all,' I said, 'in some ways I've been rather successful. And if Martin goes to the Treasury there's an outside chance I might get the Foreign Office.'

I paused. Nobody spoke. After an eternity Humphrey said, with unmistakable doubt this time, 'Perhaps you might.'

'You don't sound very certain,' I accused him.

To his credit he stuck up for himself. 'I'm not certain, Minister,' he replied, looking me straight in the eye.

I panicked. 'Why not? What have you heard?'

He remained as unperturbed as ever. 'Nothing, Minister, I assure you. That's why I'm not certain.'

I picked up the offending newspaper, stared at it again, and cast it down to the floor.

'Well,' I asked bitterly, 'how does Bob Carver in the *Standard* know all about this reshuffle, if we don't?'

'Perhaps,' speculated Humphrey, 'he has the PM's ear.'

That's the obvious answer – I was forced to agree. 'Yes,' I said. 'Everyone knows that he's in the PM's pocket.'

Bernard perked up. 'Then the PM must have a rather large ear,' he said.

I gave him another withering glance.

I decided not to worry about it any further. I will say no more about it.

It's pointless to worry about it. There's nothing to worry about, anyway.

Yet.

So I briefly discussed the Word Processing Conference in Brussels. Humphrey wants us to go. But it *might* be before the reshuffle.

I asked Humphrey if he knew when the reshuffle would be. After all, it considerably affects the plans I might want to make.

Humphrey's reply was as little help as usual. Something like: 'I'm not privy to the Prime Minister's plans for the projected reshuffle, if indeed there is to be a reshuffle, and I am therefore unaware of any projected date, if indeed there is such a date, and so I think you must proceed on the assumption that the reshuffle will not have happened and make plans for you or your successor accordingly, if indeed you are to have a successor, which of course you may not.'

I decided to decline the invitation. Just in case. I've seen this happen before. This is no time to go on an idiotic foreign junket. One day you're out of your office, the next day you're out of office.

SIR BERNARD WOOLLEY RECALLS:[1]
I well remember that rather tense discussion. Hacker told us no less than six or seven times that he would not worry about the reshuffle, that it was pointless to worry about it and the matter was closed.

[1] In conversation with the Editors.

Then he bit his fingernails a lot.

As he left the office on the way to the Commons, I advised him not to let the reshuffle prey on his mind.

He was most indignant. 'It's not preying on my mind,' he said. 'I've stopped thinking about it.'

And as he left he stopped, turned to me and said: 'Bernard, I'll see you at six o'clock in the House of Shuffles – er, Cards – er, Commons.'

[*During the following week a meeting took place at the Athenaeum Club between Sir Humphrey Appleby, Sir Arnold Robinson (the Cabinet Secretary) and – joining them later – Bernard Woolley. Sir Humphrey wrote a memo, which we found in the DAA Personnel Files at Walthamstow – Ed.*]

Had a meeting with Arnold, who claimed he was unable to give me any details about the impending reshuffle. He said he was merely Cabinet Secretary, not the Political Editor of the *New Standard*.

However, he revealed that Brussels have asked if Hacker would be available for the next Commissionership. It seems it's his if he wants it. A good European and all that.

B.W. [*Bernard Woolley – Ed.*] joined us for coffee. Arnold asked how he felt about having a new Minister. To my astonishment, B.W. said he would be sorry.

Of course, Private Secretaries often feel a certain loyalty to their Ministers, but these feelings must be kept strictly under control. Admitting these sentiments to Sir Arnold is not good for B.W.'s career.

Then, compounding his error, he said that we would all miss Hacker because he was beginning to get a grip on the job.

I sent him home at once.

Subsequently I explained, in confidence, the following essential points on the subject of reshuffles. I told him to commit them to memory.

1) Ministers with a grip on the job are a nuisance because:
   (a) they argue
   (b) they start to learn the facts
   (c) they ask if you have carried out instructions they gave you six months ago
   (d) if you tell them something is impossible, they may dig out an old submission in which you said it was easy
2) When Ministers have gone, we can wipe the slate clean and start again with a new boy
3) Prime Ministers like reshuffles – keeps everyone on the hop
4) Ministers are the *only* people who are frightened of them

B.W. suggested that it would be interesting if Ministers were fixed and Permanent Secretaries were shuffled around. I think he only does it to annoy. He must realise that such a plan strikes at the very heart of the system that has made Britain what she is today.

Just to be safe I instructed B.W. to memorise the following three points:

Power goes with permanence
Impermanence is impotence
Rotation is castration

Talking of which, I think that perhaps Bernard should be given a new posting before too long.

[*The following day, Sir Humphrey received a crucial piece of information in a note from Sir Arnold – Ed.*]

10 DOWNING STREET

From the Cabinet Secretary

July 8th

Dear Humpy,

Don't get out the champagne too soon. If Hacker takes Brussels, I'm sorry to say that you may get B.C.[1]

Yours ever,

A.

[*Hacker was naturally in complete ignorance of the above information. His diaries continue opposite – Ed.*]

[1] Basil Corbett.

July 9th
Still no news of the reshuffle.

I've been sitting up till late, doing my boxes. Three of them, tonight.

The papers were still full of rumours about the reshuffle. Annie asked me tonight if they're true.

I told her I didn't know.

She was surprised. She thought I was bound to know, as I'm in the Cabinet. But that's the whole point – we'll be the last to know.

Annie suggested I ask the PM. But obviously I can't – it would make me look as though I were insecure.

The trouble is, I don't know whether it'll be good news. I explained this to Annie. 'I don't know whether I'll be going up or down.'

'Or just round and round, as usual,' she said.

I asked her if, quite seriously, she thought I'd been a success. Or a failure.

She said: 'I think you've done all right.'

'But is that good enough?'

'I don't know,' she said. 'Is it?'

'I don't know,' I replied. 'Is it?'

We sat and looked at each other. It's so hard to tell. I had a sudden thought.

'Perhaps the PM might think I'm becoming too successful. A possible challenge to the leadership.'

Annie looked up from her book, and blinked. 'You?' she asked.

I hadn't actually meant me, as such, though I wasn't all that pleased that she was *so* surprised.

'No,' I explained, 'Martin. But with my support. So if the PM is trying to repel boarders and if Martin can't be got rid of safely, which he can't, not the Foreign Secretary, then . . . I'm the obvious one to be demoted. Do you see? Isolate Martin.'

She asked where I could be sent. 'That's easy. Lord President, Lord Privy Seal, Minister for the Arts, Minister for Sport in charge of Floods and Droughts – there's no shortage of useless non-jobs. And Basil Corbett is out to get me,' I reminded Annie.

'He's out to get everyone,' she pointed out. That's true.

'He's a smooth-tongued, cold-eyed, hard-nosed, two-faced creep,' I said, trying to be fair.

She was puzzled. 'How is he so successful?'

'Because,' I explained, 'he's a smooth-tongued, cold-eyed, hard-nosed, two-faced creep.'

Also he's got a good television manner, a lot of grassroots party support (though *all* the MPs hate him), and he has somehow conned the public into believing he's sincere.

His biggest and best weapon is elbows. I've got to elbow Corbett out of the way, or else he'll elbow me. I explained to Annie that elbows are the most important weapon in a politician's armoury.

'Other than integrity,' she said.

I'm afraid I laughed till I cried. Tears rolled down my face. It took me five minutes to get my breath back – what made it even funnier was Annie staring at me, uncomprehending, as if I'd gone mad.

I didn't really get my breath back till the phone rang. To my enormous surprise it was Gaston Larousse – from Brussels.

'Good evening, Commissionaire,' I said. Perhaps I should have just said Commissioner.

He was calling me to enquire if I'd let my name go forward as a commissioner of the EEC. I told him I was honoured, that I'd have to think about it, thanked him for thinking of me, etc. I asked him if Number Ten knew about it. He was evasive, but eventually said yes.

[*Notes of this phone call discovered many years later among Gaston Larousse's papers suggest that he was not intentionally evasive. Hacker, presumably in an attempt to show that he was a linguist, enquired if* Numéro Dix *knew about the offer. Larousse did not initially equate* Numéro Dix *with Number Ten Downing Street – Ed.*]

What does this mean?

I discussed it with Annie. Obviously, it would mean living in Brussels, as she pointed out.

But what does it *mean*? *Really* mean? Is it a plot by Number Ten to ease me out? Or is it a coincidence? Is it a hint? Is the PM giving me a face-saving exit? If so, why hasn't Number Ten told me? Or is it nothing to do with the PM? Was the vacancy coming up anyway? And it's a great honour – isn't it? Why is my life always so full of unanswerable questions?

Then Annie thought of yet another question. 'Is it a good job?'

I shook my head. 'It's a terrible job. It would be curtains for me as far as British politics is concerned. Worse than getting a peerage. Complete failure. You're reduced to forming a new party to try and get back.'

Annie asked what the job involved.

I began to list it all. 'Well,' I told her, 'you're right in the heart of that ghastly European bureaucracy. It's one big gravy train: fifty thousand a year salary, twenty thousand pounds expense account. All champagne and lobsters. Banquets. Overseas visits. Luxury hotels. Limousines and chauffeurs and private aircraft and siestas after lunch and weekends on the beach at Knokke-le-Zoute . . .' I suddenly realised what I was saying. It's strange how you can talk and talk and not hear yourself – not hear the implications of what you're saying.

'Perhaps,' I finished, 'we should go over there and have a look.'

Annie looked hopeful. 'Why not?' she said. 'Sometimes I think we deserve a bit of failure.'

July 12th

Had an interesting conversation with Roy[1] this morning. Of course, he knew all about the reshuffle.

I assumed he'd read it in the *Standard* like me – but no, he first heard of it a couple of weeks ago. (Why didn't he tell *me*? He knows that I rely on him to keep me fully informed.)

But it seems he assumed I knew. *All* the drivers knew. They knew it from the PM's driver and the Cabinet Secretary's driver – apparently it's been an open secret.

Casually, I asked him what *he'd* heard – trying thereby to suggest that I had also heard things. Which I haven't, of course.

'Just the usual, sir,' he replied. 'Corbett's in line for promotion, the PM can't overlook him. And apparently old Fred – sorry guv, I mean the Employment Secretary – he's going to get the push. Kicked upstairs.'

He seemed utterly confident about this. I asked him how he knew.

'His driver's been reassigned.'

'And what's the gossip about me?'

'Nothing, sir.'

Nothing! Was he telling the truth? There must be *some* gossip about me. I'm in the bloody Cabinet, for God's sake.

'Funny, isn't it?' said Roy. 'My mates and I haven't known what to make of that.' He gave me a sly look in the rear-view mirror. ''Course, you'll know what's happening to you, won't you sir?'

He knew bloody well I've not the faintest idea. Or else he was trying to find out. More information to barter in the transport pool.

'Yes, of course,' I replied, vaguely. I should have left it at that, but it was like picking at a scab. ''Course, it's hard to tell about one-

[1] Hacker's driver.

self sometimes – you know, whether one's a success, or . . .' He didn't come to the rescue. I tried again. 'Do your mates, er . . .'

He interrupted me, somewhat patronisingly.

'They all think you've done all right, sir.'

Again!

July 14th

Yesterday was full of meetings. Cabinet, Cabinet Committee, three-line whip in the house – I got very little time with Bernard. Not enough for a real conversation.

But Bernard's always given me loyal support, he's a bright fellow, and I decided to seek his advice.

I told him, over a cup of tea this afternoon, that I'm in a bit of a quandary.

'There's this reshuffle on the cards,' I began.

He chuckled. I couldn't see why. Then he apologised. 'I'm so sorry, Minister, I thought you were making a . . . do go on.'

'To complicate matters, and I tell you this in complete confidence, Bernard, I've been approached about becoming one of Britain's EEC Commissioners in Brussels.'

'How very nice,' said Bernard. 'It's always a help to have an ace up one's sleeve in a shuffle.'

'But *is* it nice?' I seized upon his reply. 'That's my dilemma.' He said nothing. I asked him if he really thought that, as Minister at the DAA, I'd done all right.

I suppose I was hoping for high praise. 'Superbly' would have been a nice answer. As it was, Bernard nodded and said, 'Yes, you've done all right.'

It seems that no one is prepared to commit themselves further than that on the subject of my performance. It really is rather discouraging. And it's not my fault I've not been a glittering success, Humphrey has blocked me on so many issues, he's never really been on my side. 'Look, let's be honest,' I said to Bernard. '*All right* isn't good enough, is it?'

'Well . . . it's all right,' he replied carefully.

So I asked him if he'd heard any rumours on the grapevine. About me.

He replied, 'Nothing, really.' And then he added: 'Only that the British Commissioner in Europe sent a telegram to the FCO [*Foreign and Commonwealth Office – Ed.*] and to the Cabinet Committee on Europe, that the idea for you to be a Commissioner came from

Brussels but that it is – at the end of the day – a Prime Ministerial appointment. The Prime Minister has in fact discussed it extensively with the Secretary of State for Foreign Affairs and the Secretary to the Cabinet, and cleared the way for you to be sounded out on the subject. As it is believed at Number Ten that you might well accept such an honour, a colleague of yours has been sounded out about becoming our Minister here at the DAA.' He paused, then added apologetically, 'I'm afraid that's all I know.'

'No more than that?' I asked with heavy irony.

I then asked which colleague had been sounded out to replace me at the DAA. Bernard didn't know.

But I was really getting nowhere with my basic problem. Which is, if I don't go to Europe will I be pushed up, or down – or out!

July 15th

Rumours suggest that the reshuffle is imminent. The papers are full of it. Still no mention of me, which means the lobby correspondents have been told nothing one way or the other.

It's all very nerve-racking. I'm quite unable to think about any of my ministerial duties. I'm becoming obsessed with my future – or lack of it. And I must decide soon whether to accept or decline Europe.

I had a meeting with Sir Humphrey today. It was supposed to be on the subject of the Word Processing Conference in Brussels.

I opened it up by telling Humphrey that I'd changed my mind. 'I've decided to go to Brussels,' I said. I meant go and have a look, as I'd arranged with Annie. But Humphrey misunderstood me.

'You're not resigning from the Department of Administrative Affairs?' he asked. He seemed shocked. I was rather pleased. Perhaps he has a higher opinion of me than I realised.

I put him out of his misery. 'Certainly not. I'm talking about this Word Processing Conference.'

He visibly relaxed. Then I added, 'But I would like to see Brussels for myself.'

'Why?' he asked.

'Why not?' I asked him.

'Why not indeed?' he asked me. 'But why?'

I told him I was curious. He agreed.

Then I told him, preparing the ground for my possible permanent departure across the Channel, that I felt on reflection that I'd been a bit hasty in my criticisms of Brussels and that I'd found Humphrey's defence of it thoroughly convincing.

This didn't please him as much as I'd expected. He told me that he had been reflecting on *my* views, that he had found much truth and wisdom in my criticism of Brussels. (Was this Humphrey speaking? I had to pinch myself to make sure I wasn't dreaming.)

'You implied it was corrupt, and indeed you have opened my eyes,' he said.

'No, no, no,' I said hastily.

'Yes, yes,' he replied firmly.

I couldn't allow Humphrey to think that I'd said it was corrupt. I *had* said it, actually, but now I'm not so sure. [*We are not sure whether Hacker was not sure that he wanted to be quoted or not sure that Brussels was corrupt – Ed.*] I told Humphrey that he had persuaded *me*. I can now see, quite clearly, that Brussels is full of dedicated men carrying a heavy burden of travel and entertainment – they need all that luxury and the odd drinkie.

'Champagne and caviar?' enquired Sir Humphrey. 'Private planes, air-conditioned Mercedes?'

I reminded Humphrey that these little luxuries oil the diplomatic wheels.

'Snouts in the trough,' remarked Humphrey, to no one in particular.

I reproved him. 'That is not an attractive phrase,' I said coldly.

'I'm so sorry', he said. 'I can't think where I picked it up.'

I drew the discussion to a close by stating that we would all go to Brussels next week to attend this conference, as he had originally requested.

As he got up to leave, Humphrey asked me if my change of heart about Brussels was entirely the result of his arguments.

Naturally, I told him yes.

He didn't believe me. 'It wouldn't be anything to do with rumours of your being offered a post in Brussels?'

I couldn't let him know that he was right. 'The thought is not worthy of you, Humphrey,' I said. And, thinking of Annie and trying not to laugh, I added solemnly: 'There is such a thing as integrity.'

Humphrey looked confused.

[*Later that day Sir Humphrey had lunch with Sir Arnold Robinson, Secretary to the Cabinet, at their club. He made the following note in his private diary – Ed.*]

I told Arnold that I was most concerned about letting Corbett loose on the DAA. I would regard it as a disaster of the utmost magnitude.

Arnold said that he was unable to stop the move. The Prime Minister appoints the Cabinet. I refused to accept this explanation – we all know perfectly well that the Cabinet Secretary arranges reshuffles. I said as much.

Arnold acknowledged this fact but insisted that, if the PM is really set on making a particular appointment, the Cabinet Secretary must reluctantly acquiesce.

I remain convinced that Arnold keeps a hand on the tiller.

[*The matter rested there until Sir Humphrey Appleby received a memo from Sir Arnold Robinson, see overleaf – Ed.*]

A memo from Sir Arnold Robinson to Sir Humphrey Appleby:

10 DOWNING STREET

From the Cabinet Secretary

July 19th

Dear Humpy,

Have been considering your problem further. I think the only answer to your problem is for J.H. to turn Brussels down.

A.

A reply from Sir Humphrey Appleby:

DEPARTMENT OF
ADMINISTRATIVE AFFAIRS

From the Permanent Under-Secretary of State

Dear Arnold,

I think he's going to take Brussels. He says he believes in the European ideal! Extraordinary, isn't it? I fear he's been taken in by his own speeches.

Also, I fear he regards himself as not having been a total success at the D.A.A.

HA

19/vii

A reply from Sir Arnold:

10 DOWNING STREET

From the Cabinet Secretary

July 20th

Dear Humpy,

It's not been all that hot. Partly your fault. You've blocked him continually, albeit in the interests of good government.

I suggest that Hacker has a big success within the next couple of days.

A.

A reply from Sir Humphrey:

DEPARTMENT OF
ADMINISTRATIVE AFFAIRS

From the Permanent Under-Secretary of State

Arnold —

A big success? In the next two days? What sort of success?

HA

20/vii

A reply from Sir Arnold:

10 DOWNING STREET

From the Cabinet Secretary

July 21st

Humpy,

Anything, my dear chap. Just give me some sort of case to present to the P.M. for keeping Hacker at the D.A.A.

There is one other possibility for Corbett: Dept of Employment. Fred is definitely going, because he keeps falling asleep in Cabinet – I know they all do, but Fred has taken to nodding off while he's actually talking.

A.

July 22nd
I was still paralysed with indecision as today began.

At my morning meeting with Humphrey I asked if he had any news. He denied it. I know he had lunch with the Cabinet Secretary one day last week – is it conceivable that Arnold Robinson told him nothing?

'You must know something?' I said firmly.

Slight pause.

'All I know, Minister, is that the reshuffle will definitely be announced on Monday. Have *you* any news?'

I couldn't think what he meant.

'Of Brussels,' he added. 'Are you accepting the Commissionership?'

I tried to explain my ambivalence. 'Speaking with my Parliamentary hat on, I think it would be a bad idea. On the other hand, with my Cabinet hat on, I can see that it might be quite a good idea. But there again, with my European hat on, I can see that there are arguments on both sides.'

I couldn't believe the rubbish I could hear myself talking. Humphrey and Bernard might well have wondered which hat I was talking through at the moment.

They simply gazed at me, silent and baffled.

Humphrey then sought elucidation.

'Minister, does that mean you have decided you want to go to Brussels?'

'Well . . .' I replied, 'yes and no.'

I found that I was enjoying myself for the first time for days.

Humphrey tried to help me clarify my mind.

He asked me to list the pros and cons.

This threw me into instant confusion again. I told him I didn't really know what I think, thought, because – and I don't know if I'd mentioned this to Humphrey before, I think I *might* have – it all rather depends on whether or not I've done all right. So I asked Humphrey how he thought I'd done.

Humphrey said he thought I'd done all right.

So I was no further on. I'm going round and round in circles. If I've done all right, I mean *really* all right, then I'll stay because I'll be all right. But if I've only done all right, I mean only *just* all right, then I think to stay here wouldn't be right – it would be wrong, right?

Humphrey then appeared to make a positive suggestion. 'Minister,' he volunteered, 'I think that, to be on the safe side, you need a big personal success.'

Great, I thought! Yes indeed.

'A triumph, in fact,' said Humphrey.

'Like what?' I asked.

'I mean,' said Humphrey, 'some great personal publicity for a great personal and political achievement.'

I was getting rather excited. I waited expectantly. But suddenly Humphrey fell silent.

'Well . . .' I repeated, 'what have you in mind?'

'Nothing,' he said. 'I'm trying to think of something.'

That was a great help!

I asked what the purpose would be of this hypothetical triumph. He told me that Sir Arnold indicated that the PM would be unable to move me downwards if I had a triumph before the reshuffle.

That's obvious. What's even more worrying is the implication that there was no possibility of the PM moving me upwards.

I mentioned this. Humphrey replied that, alas! one must be a realist. I don't think he realised just how insulting he was being.

I told Humphrey I'd take Brussels, and brought the meeting to a close. I decided I'd call Brussels tonight and accept the post, and thus avoid the humiliation of being demoted in the Cabinet by pre-empting the PM.

I told Humphrey he could go, and instructed Bernard to bring me details of the European Word Processing standardisation plans, to which I would now be fully committed.

Then Humphrey had an idea.

He stood up, excitedly.

'Wait a minute,' he said, 'I have an idea. Supposing you were to ignore the EEC and publish your *own* plan for word-processing equipment, and place huge contracts with British manufacturers, immediately, today, tomorrow, well *before Monday*, thus ensuring more jobs in Britain, more investment, more export orders . . .'

He looked at me.

I tried to readjust my thoughts. Weren't we back at square one? This is what I'd been about to do before we got the directive from Brussels a couple of weeks ago. And Humphrey had told me that we had to comply with a Brussels directive.

'It's not a directive,' he now explained. 'It hasn't been ratified by the Conference. It's a request.'

I wondered, aloud, if we could really stab our partners in the back, and spit in their faces.

Bernard intervened. 'You can't stab anyone in the back while you spit in their face.' I suppose he was trying to be helpful.

The more I thought about it, the more I realised that Humphrey's scheme had a touch of real genius about it. Defying Brussels would be very popular in the country. It would be a big story. And it would prove that I had elbows.

I told Humphrey that it was a good idea.

'You'll do it?' he asked.

I didn't want to be rushed. 'Let me think about it,' I said. 'After all, it would mean giving up . . .' I didn't know how to put it.

'The trough?' he offered.

'No, that's *not* what I meant,' I replied coldly, though actually it was what I meant.

He knew it was anyway, because he said: 'When it comes to it, Minister, one must put one's country first.'

On the whole, I suppose I agree with that.

July 23rd

JIM FIXES THEM!
Big boost for Britain!

ADMINISTRATIVE AFFAIRS supremo Jim Hacker today gave the Common Market one in the eye. In a move that will be very popular throughout the country, he told our European partners that Britain would go it alone in information technology.

My repudiation of the EEC request had indeed proved to be a big story. A triumph, in fact. Especially as I accompanied it with a rather jingoistic anti-Brussels speech. The popular press loved it, but I'm afraid that I've irrevocably burned my boats – I don't think I'll be offered a Commissionership again in a hurry.

Let's hope it does the trick.

July 26th

The reshuffle was announced today. Fred was indeed kicked upstairs, Basil Corbett went to Employment, and I stayed where I am – at the DAA.

Humphrey popped in first thing, and told me how delighted he was that I was staying.

'I know I probably shouldn't say this, but I personally would have been deeply sorry to lose you.' He told me that he meant it most sincerely.

'Yes,' I said benignly, 'we've grown quite fond of each other really, haven't we, like a terrorist and a hostage.'

He nodded.

'Which of you is the terrorist?' asked Bernard.

'He is,' Humphrey and I said in unison, each pointing at the other.

Then we all laughed.

'By the way,' I asked, 'who would have had my job if I'd gone to Brussels?'

'I've no idea,' said Humphrey.

But Bernard said: 'Didn't you tell me it was to be Basil Corbett, Sir Humphrey?'

A bucket of cold water had been thrown over our temporary spirit of bonhomie. Humphrey looked more embarrassed than I've ever seen him. No wonder he would have been so sorry to lose me.

I looked at him for confirmation.

'Basil Corbett?' I asked.

'Yes Minister,' said Sir Humphrey. And he blushed.

13
The Quality of Life

[*Early in September Sir Humphrey Appleby started negotiations with the merchant bank of which Sir Desmond Glazebrook was the Chairman. Sir Desmond had been appointed Chairman of the Co-Partnership Commission in March by Hacker, at Appleby's instigation, in order to get them both off the hook of the Solihull Report scandal (see pages 149–70).*

In September Sir Humphrey was negotiating for a seat on the board of the bank when he retired three or four years hence. Sir Humphrey Appleby still had not received his G, nor had he sewn up a suitable retirement position for himself. Recent encounters with Sir Arnold Robinson (see Chapter 10) suggested that, although it was not impossible that he would become the next Secretary of the Cabinet, he was probably not the front-runner. He was known to be anti-Europe, so a Director-Generalship in Brussels seemed unlikely to be offered. He was therefore most anxious to ensure the seat on the board of Sir Desmond's bank – Ed.]

September 14th

Excellent coverage in the press today for my speech on the environment last night.

Headlines in a couple of the quality dailies: HACKER SPEAKS OUT AGAINST TOWER BLOCKS and MINISTER'S COURAGEOUS STAND ON HIGH BUILDINGS, though the latter does make me sound more like Harold Lloyd than a Minister of the Crown. Still, to be called courageous by a newspaper is praise indeed.

But all this coverage in the posh press, though nice, isn't worth all that much in votes. There was no coverage of my speech in the popular press. It's weeks since I had my photo in any of the mass-circulation dailies.

So I called in Bill Pritchard, the press officer, and asked his advice. He thought for a moment or two.

'Well,' he offered, 'the papers always like a photograph of a pretty girl.'

Brilliant. I pointed out that, although it may have escaped his notice, I did not qualify on that score. But he went on to suggest that I judge a bathing beauty contest, kiss the winner, that sort of thing. A cheap stunt really, and rather old hat. Besides, if my picture's going to be in the paper I'd like the readers to look at *me*.

Then he suggested animals and children. He pointed out that tomorrow's visit to a City Farm will almost certainly yield good publicity. Apparently it's to be covered by the *Mirror*, *Mail*, *Express*, *Sun*, and *Today* and *Nationwide*.

This is marvellous. Telly coverage is the best of all, of course. And an innocuous non-controversial venue like a City Farm can't possibly contain any hidden pitfalls.

Bill told me that Sue Lawley wanted to interview me. And that I was to be photographed with some baby donkeys at the *Sun*'s special request.

Sometimes I think he's got no sense at all! Even if the *Sun* has no ulterior motive (which I doubt) it would be a gift for *Private Eye* – JAMES HACKER WITH A CROWD OF OTHER DONKEYS or A MEETING OF THE INNER CABINET.

I refused. He offered little pigs instead. I don't think that my being photographed with a crowd of little pigs is any great improvement! That could give rise to SNOUTS IN THE TROUGH jokes.

I told Bill to pull himself together, and that I'd agree to be photographed with Sue Lawley or a nice woolly lamb. Positively no one else.

[*Politicians frequently try to avoid making public appearances that could give rise to jokes at their expense. For instance, when Harold Wilson was PM in the late 1960s some of his advisers suggested that perhaps he shouldn't go to* Fiddler on the Roof *as it might encourage jokes about his leadership style. He also avoided going to visit* A Month in the Country *as it was feared that this would give rise to dangerous speculation that he was going to the country, i.e. calling a general election – Ed.*]

At my diary session later this morning Bernard said that Sir Desmond Glazebrook wanted an urgent meeting with me tomorrow. He's a ridiculous old fool who keeps making speeches against the government. Unfortunately, I appointed him Chairman of the Co-Partnership Commission – I'd had no choice [*see Chapter 7 – Ed.*].

Glazebrook wants to talk to me about his forthcoming application to add some more storeys to his bank's proposed new office block.

Clearly he hasn't read this morning's papers!

This is just the sort of thing we have to stop. Someone has to speak out to save the environment. I shall do it, without fear or favour. It is the right thing to do. Also, it'll be very popular.

[*Bernard Woolley reported this conversation with Hacker to Sir Humphrey Appleby sometime later that day. He knew that Appleby was due to meet Sir Desmond Glazebrook for tea, to discuss the new high-rise building for the bank, and he felt obliged to let Sir Humphrey know the extent of the Minister's opposition to it.*

We found a report of this and of Appleby's meeting with Glazebrook among Sir Humphrey's private papers – Ed.]

B. reported to me that the Minister wanted to make a courageous stand on high buildings, for the press. I hope he has a head for heights. It seems that Hacker will do anything to get his picture in the papers.

Had tea with Sir Desmond, and reported that the matter did not look too hopeful. He was surprised. I remarked that, clearly, he had not read the *Financial Times* this morning.

'Never do,' he told me. I was surprised. He is a banker after all.

'Can't understand it,' he explained. 'It's too full of economic theory.'

I asked him why he bought it and carried it about under his arm. He explained that it was part of the uniform. He said it took him thirty years to understand Keynes's economics and just when he'd finally got the hang of it everyone started getting hooked on those new-fangled monetarist ideas. Books like *I want to be free* by Milton Shulman.

Presumably he means *Free To Choose* by Milton Friedman, but I share his feelings and doubts.

He asked me why they are all called Milton, and said he was still stuck on Milton Keynes. I corrected him: 'Maynard Keynes.' He said he was sure there was a Milton Keynes, I felt the conversation should be abandoned then and there, and I opened up his copy of the *FT* and showed him our Minister's speech to the Architectural Association last night in which he attacked skyscraper blocks. This speech has attracted much favourable publicity and must be reckoned a problem for us now.

Sir Desmond insisted that the bank's new block is not a skyscraper. Nonetheless, it has thirty-eight storeys on current plans, and he is asking for an extra six storeys.

The Minister, on the other hand, is talking about a maximum tolerable height of eight storeys.

The Minister is further encouraged by his party's manifesto, which contained a promise to prevent many more high-rise buildings. But this problem is more easily dealt with. I explained to Sir Desmond that there is an implicit pact offered to every Minister by his senior officials: if the

Minister will help us implement the opposite policy to the one to which he is pledged (which once he is in office he can see is obviously undesirable and/or unworkable) we will help him to pretend that he is in fact doing what he said he was going to do in his Manifesto.

[*We are indeed fortunate that Sir Humphrey's training as a civil servant – training to put everything down in writing – resulted in his recording for posterity these attitudes and skills which were undoubtedly Civil Service practice in the 1980s but which were kept secret because they were unacceptable constitutionally – Ed.*]

Desmond said that this was a reasonable compromise, in his opinion. So it is. Regrettably, reasonableness is not the first quality that springs to mind when one contemplates the average Minister. [*Hacker was a very average Minister – Ed.*]

Desmond tried to apply pressure to me. He dropped hints about our future plans together. I reassured Desmond that, although he would not get permission from Hacker this week and although it would be tricky, I was sure a way could be found to alter any adverse decision.

Desmond was puzzled. He thought a decision was a decision. I explained that a decision is a decision *only* if it is the decision you wanted. Otherwise, of course, it is merely a temporary setback.

Ministers are like small children. They act on impulse. One day they want something desperately, the next day they've forgotten they ever asked for it. Like a tantrum over a rice pudding – won't touch it today and asks for two helpings tomorrow. He understood this.

Desmond asked me if I intended to tell him that I refused to accept his decision. The man really is dense! I explained that, on the contrary, I shall start off by accepting Hacker's decision enthusiastically. Then I shall tell him to leave the details to me. [*Appleby Papers 97/JZD/31f*]

[*Hacker's diary continues – Ed.*]

September 15th

We had the urgent meeting with Sir Desmond Glazebrook today. It went off most satisfactorily and presented no problems, largely because it was preceded by a meeting between me and Sir Humphrey in which I ensured his full co-operation and support.

When Humphrey popped in for a quick word before the meeting he outlined Glazebrook's case for a tower block:

1) There are already several tower blocks in the area

2) Their International Division is expanding rapidly and needs space. And international work brings in valuable invisible exports

3) Banks need central locations. They can't move some of it elsewhere

4) It will bring in extra rate revenue for the city

This is a not unreasonable case. But, as I pointed out to Humphrey, it's a typical bank argument, money, money, money! What about the environment? What about the beauty?

Humphrey was impressed. 'Indeed Minister,' he agreed. 'Beauty. Quite.' He told Bernard to make a note of it.

I could see I was winning. 'And what about our children? And our children's children?'

Again he agreed, and told Bernard to be sure he make a note of 'children's children'.

'Who are you serving, Humphrey?' I asked. 'God or Mammon?'

'I'm serving you, Minister,' he replied.

Quite right. I told Bernard to show Glazebrook in, and Sir Humphrey said to me: 'Minister, it's entirely your decision. Entirely your decision.' I think he's getting the idea at last! That I'm the boss!

Desmond Glazebrook arrived with an architect named Crawford, complete with plans. They began by explaining that they would be making a formal application later, but they'd be grateful for any guidance that I could give them at this stage.

That was easy. I told them that I had grave misgivings about these tower blocks.

'Dash it, this is where we make our profits,' said Sir Desmond. 'Six extra storeys and we'll really clean up. Without them we'll only make a measly twenty-eight per cent on the whole project.'

I stared at him coldly. 'It's just profits, is it, Sir Desmond?'

He looked confused. 'Not *just* profits,' he said, 'it's profits!'

'Do you ever think of anything except money?' I asked him.

Again he looked completely blank. 'No. Why?'

'You don't think about beauty?'

'Beauty?' He had no idea what I was driving at. 'This is an office block, not an oil-painting.'

I persevered. 'What about the environment?' I enquired.

'Well . . .' he said, looking at Humphrey for help. Sir Humphrey, to his credit, gave him none. 'Well, I promise you we'll make sure it's part of the environment. I mean, it's bound to be, once it's there, isn't it?'

I had reached my decision. 'The answer's no,' I said firmly.

Crawford the architect intervened. 'There is just one thing, Minister,' he said timidly. 'As you will remember from the papers, similar permission has already been given for the Chartered Bank of New York, so to refuse it to a British bank. . . .'

I hadn't realised. Bernard or Humphrey should have briefed me more thoroughly.

I didn't answer for a moment, and Sir Desmond chipped in:

'So it's all right after all, is it?'

'No it's not,' I snapped.

'Why not, dammit?' he demanded.

I was stuck. I had to honour our manifesto commitment, and I couldn't go back on my widely-reported speech yesterday. But if we'd given permission to an American bank . . .

Thank God, Humphrey came to the rescue!

'The Minister,' he said smoothly, 'has expressed concern that a further tall building would clutter the skyline.'

I seized on this point gratefully. 'Clutter the skyline,' I repeated, with considerable emphasis.

'He is also worried,' continued Sir Humphrey, 'that more office workers in that area would mean excessive strain on the public transport system.'

He looked at me for support, and I indicated that I was indeed worried about public transport. Humphrey was really being most creative. Very impressive.

'Furthermore,' said Humphrey, by now unstoppable, 'the Minister pointed out that it would overshadow the playground of St James's Primary School here . . .' (he pointed to the map) 'and that it would overlook a number of private gardens, which would be an intrusion of privacy.'

'Privacy,' I agreed enthusiastically.

'Finally,' said Humphrey, lying through his teeth, 'the Minister also pointed out, most astutely if I may say so, that your bank owns a vacant site a short way away, which would accommodate your expansion needs.'

Sir Desmond looked at me. 'Where?' he asked.

I stabbed wildly at the map with my finger. 'Here,' I said.

Desmond looked closely. 'That's the river, isn't it?'

I shook my head with pretended impatience at his stupidity, and again Humphrey saved the day. 'I think the Minister was referring to *this* site,' he said, and pointed with precision.

Sir Desmond looked again.

'Is that ours?' he asked.

'It is, actually, Sir Desmond,' whispered Crawford.

'What are we doing with it?'

'It's scheduled for Phase III.'

Sir Desmond turned to me and said, as if I hadn't heard, 'That's scheduled for Phase III. Anyway,' he went on, 'that's at least four hundred yards away. Difficult for the Board to walk four hundred yards for lunch. And impossible to walk four hundred yards back afterwards.'

I felt that I'd spent enough time on this pointless meeting. I brought it to a close.

'Well, there it is,' I said. 'You can still put in your formal application, but that will be my decision, I'm sure.'

Bernard opened the door for Sir Desmond, who stood up very reluctantly.

'Suppose we design a different rice pudding?' he said.

I think he must be suffering from premature senility.

'Rice pudding?' I asked.

Humphrey stepped in, tactful as ever. 'It's er . . . it's bankers' jargon for high-rise buildings, Minister.'

'Is it?' asked Sir Desmond.

Poor old fellow.

After he'd gone I thanked Humphrey for all his help. He seemed genuinely pleased.

I made a point of thanking him *especially* because I know that he and Desmond Glazebrook were old chums.

'We've known each other a long time, Minister,' he replied. 'But even a lifelong friendship is as naught compared with a civil servant's duty to support his Minister.'

Quite right too.

Then I had to rush off to my public appearance at the City Farm.

Before I left, Humphrey insisted that I sign some document. He said it was urgent. An administrative order formalising government powers for temporary utilisation of something-or-other. He gave me some gobbledegook explanation of why I had to sign it rather than its being put before the House. Just some piece of red tape.

But I wish he wouldn't always try to explain these things to me when he can see I'm late for some other appointment.

Not that it matters much.

SIR BERNARD WOOLLEY RECALLS:[1]

Hacker was being thoroughly bamboozled by Sir Humphrey and was completely unaware of it.

[1] In conversation with the Editors.

The Administrative Order in question was to formalise government powers for the temporary utilisation of unused local authority land until development commences, when of course it reverts to the authority.

In answer to Hacker's question as to why it was not being laid before the House, Sir Humphrey gave the correct answer. He explained that if it were a statutory instrument it would indeed have to be laid on the table of the House, for forty days, assuming it were a negative order, since an affirmative order would, of course, necessitate a vote, but in fact it was not a statutory instrument nor indeed an Order in Council but simply an Administrative order made under Section 7, subsection 3 of the Environmental Administration Act, which was of course an enabling section empowering the Minister to make such regulations affecting small-scale land usage as might from time to time appear desirable within the general framework of the Act.

After he had explained all this, to Hacker's evident incomprehension, he added humorously, 'as I'm sure you recollect only too clearly, Minister.' Appleby really was rather a cad!

I must say, though, that even I didn't grasp the full significance of this move that afternoon. I didn't even fully comprehend, in those days, why Humphrey had persuaded Hacker to sign the document on the pretext that it was urgent.

'It was not urgent,' he explained to me later, 'but it was important. Any document that removes the power of decision from Ministers and gives it to us is important.'

I asked why. He rightly ticked me off for obtuseness. Giving powers of decision to the Service helps to take government out of politics. That was, in his view, Britain's only hope of survival.

The urgency was true in one sense, of course, in that whenever you want a Minister to sign something without too many questions it is always better to wait until he is in a hurry. That is when their concentration is weakest. Ministers are always vulnerable when they are in a hurry.

That is why we always kept them on the go, of course.

[*Hacker's diary for that day continues – Ed.*]

It's always hard to find something to make a speech about. We have to make a great many speeches, of course – local authority elections, by-elections, GLC elections, opening village fêtes or the new old people's home, every weekend in my constituency there's something.

We must try to have *something* to say. Yet it can't be particularly new or else we'd have to say it in the House first, and it can't be particularly interesting or we'd already have said it on TV or radio. I'm always hoping that the Department will cook up something for me to talk about, something that we in the government would have to be talking about anyway.

Equally, you have to be careful that, in their eagerness to find something, they don't cook up anything too damn silly. After all,

I've got to actually get up and say it.

Most civil servants can't write speeches. But they can dig up a plum for me (occasionally) and, without fail, they should warn me of any possible banana skins.

Today I planned to make a sort of generalised speech on the environment, which I'm doing a lot of recently and which seems to go down well with everyone.

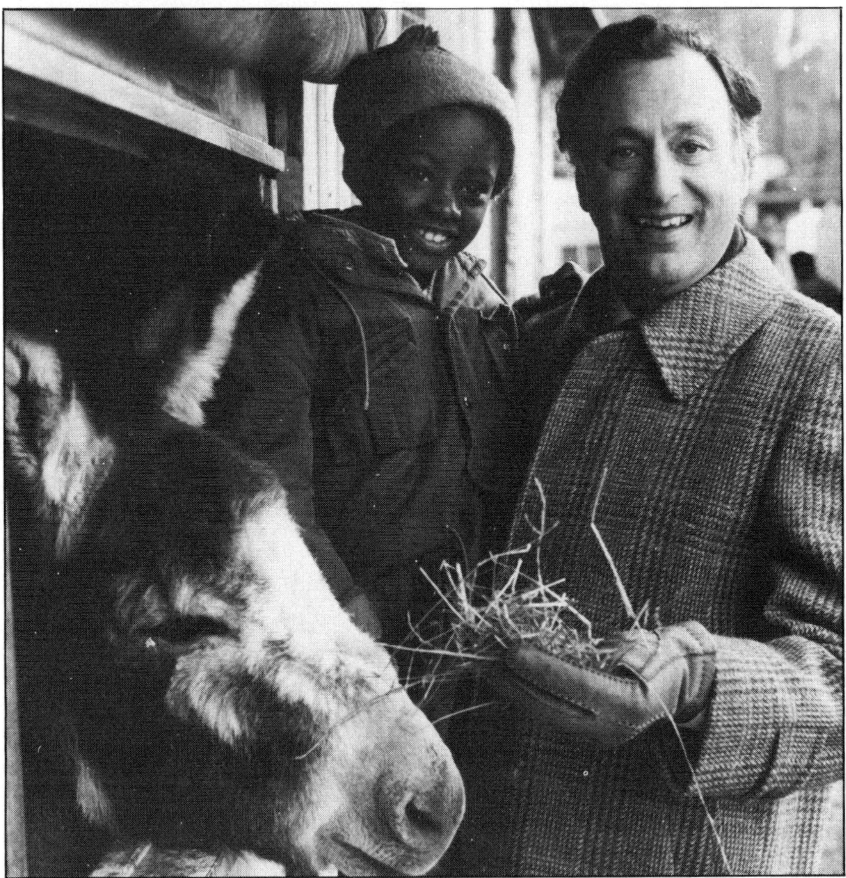

Hacker was persuaded to pose for the above photograph against his better judgement, because he was unwilling to appear 'a bad sport' in public. He subsequently had the photograph suppressed but it was released under the Thirty-Year Rule (DAA Archives)

At the City Farm we were met by a brisk middle-class lady called Mrs Phillips. She was the Warden of the City Farm. My party simply consisted of me, Bill Pritchard of the press office, and Bernard.

We were asked to drive up to the place two or three times in succession, so that the television crew could film us arriving.

The third time seemed to satisfy them. Mrs Phillips welcomed me with a singularly tactless little speech: words to the effect of 'I'm so grateful that you could come, we tried all sorts of other celebrities but nobody else could make it.'

I turned to the cameraman from the BBC and told him to cut. He kept filming, impertinent little man. I told him again, and then the director said cut so he finally did cut. I instructed the director to cut Mrs Phillips' tactless little speech right out.

'But . . .' he began.

'No buts,' I told him. 'Licence fee, remember.' Of course I said it jokingly, but we both knew I wasn't joking. The BBC is always much easier to handle when the licence fee is coming up for renewal.

I think he was rather impressed with my professionalism and my no-nonsense attitude.

We went in.

I realised that I didn't know too much about City Farms. Furthermore, people always like to talk about themselves and their work, so I said to Mrs Phillips – who had a piglet in her arms by this time – 'Tell me all about this.'

'This is a piglet,' she replied. Asinine woman. Or perhaps I should say piginine.[1]

I told her to tell me about the farm. She said that there are over fifty such City Farms, built on urban wasteland to give children who seldom see the countryside a chance to understand livestock and food production. A wonderful idea.

I was photographed with Mrs Phillips, meeting the staff, with the children and with the piglets. [*Everybody's a ham – Ed.*] Then it was time for my speech.

There was a moment of slight embarrassment when I realised Bernard had given me the wrong speech, but that was soon overcome.

SIR BERNARD WOOLLEY RECALLS:[2]
Slight embarrassment does not begin to describe the general reaction to Hacker's speech.

There was confusion over who had the copy of his speech, I or he. I distinctly remembered giving it to him. He denied it, and demanded I look in

[1] One of Hacker's rare jokes.
[2] In conversation with the Editors.

my briefcase. There was indeed a speech for him there. And he grabbed it and read it.

[*The speech has been found in the DAA archives, and we reprint it below – Ed.*]

DEPARTMENT OF
ADMINISTRATIVE AFFAIRS

It is a very great pleasure to be here with you all today. You know, things are changing fast. We live in a world of change. The silicon chip is changing our lives. The quality of life is becoming more and more important: the environment, conservation, the problems of pollution, the future of our children and our children's children, these are today's issues.

There is quite rightly an increasing concern about high-rise buildings and I'm happy to reassure all of you who are Members of the Architectural Association that

over

Yes, indeed, Hacker had insisted on reading the speech that we had put into my briefcase *after* his address to the Architectural Association on the issue of high-rise buildings.

There was an embarrassed pause, while I whispered to him that *he* had today's speech. He felt in his inside pocket, found the City Farm speech, and began to read.

Unfortunately, this only increased the already considerable embarrassment.

DEPARTMENT OF
ADMINISTRATIVE AFFAIRS

It is a very great pleasure to be here today at this City Farm. You know, things are changing fast. We live in a world of change. The silicon chip is changing our lives. The quality of life is becoming more and more important: the environment, conservation, the problems of pollution, the future of our children and our children's children, these are today's issues.

The City Farm is a welcome and important addition to the way of life for children in inner cities and we in the government feel they have a vital part to play in our children's educational and social life, and we shall do all we can to help this movement flourish.

Happy Birthday.

[*Hacker's diary continues – Ed.*]

After my speech I was interviewed by Sue Lawley for *Nationwide*, surrounded by kids and animals as previously arranged with Bill.

While they were positioning everyone for the cameras, Mrs Phillips asked me if she could really rely on my support. I told her that of course she could. She then explained that their lease was running out at the end of the year, and they needed to get it extended.

I couldn't involve myself too directly. I had gone there to get some personal publicity, and I'm not fully acquainted with all their circumstances. So I pointed out that this lease was not really within my sphere of influence, but that I would do what I could to help the

City Farm movement flourish. This I was careful to state only in the most general terms.

Then the interview began, just as a very grubby smelly child of indeterminate sex with a sticky lollipop in its mouth was placed on my knee. I tried to show pleasure instead of disgust – which I fear would have been my natural expression.

Sue Lawley asked Mrs Phillips the first question. 'Warden, I understand that the lease on this wonderful City Farm is due to run out at the end of the year.'

I could scarcely believe my ears as I heard Mrs Phillips reply: 'Yes, we have been very worried about this, but I've just had a word with the Minister, Mr Hacker, and he has indicated that he will make sure that the farm can carry on.'

I was startled and horrified, more so when Sue Lawley turned to me and asked how I was going to ensure the continuance of the City Farm.

I started out to qualify what Mrs Phillips had said, with the usual temporising phrases like 'let's be absolutely clear about this' and 'at the end of the day' and so forth, but somehow felt unable to deny what she'd said while the cameras were rolling. Instead, I heard myself saying, 'the quality of life is becoming more and more important. The environment, conservation, the problems of pollution, the future of our children and our children's children, these are today's issues.'

[*We have discovered the following series of memos that were exchanged, over the following few days, between Sir Frank Gordon, Second Permanent Secretary at the Treasury, and Sir Humphrey Appleby, see opposite – Ed.*]

A note from Sir Frank Gordon, Second Permanent Secretary of the Treasury:

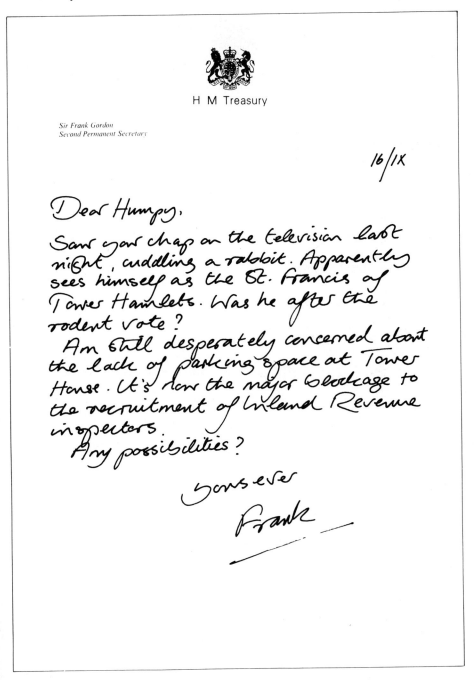

H M Treasury

Sir Frank Gordon
Second Permanent Secretary

16/IX

Dear Humpy,

Saw your chap on the television last night, cuddling a rabbit. Apparently sees himself as the St. Francis of Tower Hamlets. Was he after the rodent vote?

Am still desperately concerned about the lack of parking space at Tower House. It's now the major blockage to the recruitment of Inland Revenue inspectors.

Any possibilities?

Yours ever

Frank

A reply from Sir Humphrey Appleby:

DEPARTMENT OF
ADMINISTRATIVE AFFAIRS

From the Permanent Under-Secretary of State

Dear Frank,

The problem is solved. Two days ago I got the authority to use the 1½ acre local government site behind Tower House. The lease is running out, and there are no utilisation plans.

Official notification will follow in due course — the wheels are in motion.

Yours ever

Humpy

16/ix

A reply from Sir Frank:

H M Treasury

Sir Frank Gordon
Second Permanent Secretary

17/IX

Dear Humpy,

Do you mean you got an order under section 7 subsection 3?

Frank.

A reply from Sir Humphrey:

DEPARTMENT OF
ADMINISTRATIVE AFFAIRS

From the Permanent Under-Secretary of State

Dear Frank,

As our American Allies would say, affirmative. The site is currently used as a City Farm for schoolchildren. It is the very one visited by St Francis, indeed.

It can be argued that these places are unhygienic, a danger to public health etc.

I suggest you move quickly, before the lease is renewed.

Yours ever

Humpy. 17/ix

A reply from Sir Frank:

H M Treasury

Sir Frank Gordon
Second Permanent Secretary

20/IX

Dear Humpy,

Very grateful for the help. Won't it put St. Francis in a bit of a spot? Or is that what you wanted?

Frank

A reply from Sir Humphrey:

DEPARTMENT OF ADMINISTRATIVE AFFAIRS

From the Permanent Under-Secretary of State

Dear Frank,

Yes.

Yours ever

Humpy

20/ix

We also discovered a brief note to Sir Desmond Glazebrook, addressed to his home at Cadogan Square:

DEPARTMENT OF
ADMINISTRATIVE AFFAIRS

From the Permanent Under-Secretary of State

Dear Desmond,

I think I have found out how I can get the Minister to eat up his rice pudding.

Yours ever

H.

20/ix

[*Hacker's diary continues – Ed.*]

September 20th

For some reason they didn't run the story of my visit to the City Farm in the *Standard* last week.

But today I got a double-page spread. Wonderful. One photo of me with a duck, another with a small multiracial girl. Great publicity for me, and the Department.

I was busy discussing the possibilities of visiting other City Farms – in Birmingham, Manchester, Glasgow, Newcastle. Preferably in the Special Development Areas. [*The new euphemism for marginal constituencies – Ed.*]

This happy conversation was rudely interrupted by Bernard announcing that the wretched Mrs Phillips was outside in the Private Office, demanding to see me.

I couldn't see why. Then Bernard told me that it was announced this morning that the City Farm is being closed. This was a bombshell.

'The lease runs out at the end of the year and it's being turned into a car park,' Bernard told me. 'For Inland Revenue Inspectors.'

Bill and I both knew what the headlines would be. CHILDREN AND ANIMALS EVICTED BY TAXMEN. HACKER RENEGES ON TV PLEDGE. That sort of thing.

I told Bernard that it simply couldn't be allowed to happen. 'Which idiot authorised it?' I asked.

He stared unhappily at his shoes. 'I'm afraid, er, you did, Minister.'

It seems that the administrative order that I signed a couple of days ago, which Humphrey said was so urgent, gives government departments the power to take over local authority land. It's known as Section 7, subsection 3 in Whitehall.

I sent for Humphrey. I told Bernard to get him *at once*, pointing out that this is about the worst disaster of the century.

There *were* two World Wars, Minister,' said Bernard as he picked up the phone. I simply told him to shut up, I was in no mood for smartarse insubordination.

'Fighting on the beaches is one thing,' I snarled. 'Evicting cuddly animals and small children to make room for tax inspectors' cars is in a different league of awfulness.'

Humphrey arrived and started to congratulate me on my television appearance. What kind of a fool does he think I am? I brushed this nonsense aside and demanded an explanation.

'Ah yes,' he said smoothly. 'The Treasury, acting under Section 7, subsection 3 of the Environmental . . .'

'It's got to be stopped,' I interrupted brusquely.

He shook his head, and sighed. 'Unfortunately, Minister, it is a Treasury decision and not within our jurisdiction.'

I said I'd revoke the order.

'That, unfortunately,' he replied, shaking his head gloomily, 'is impossible. Or very difficult. Or highly inadvisable. Or would require legislation. One of those. But in any case it could not invalidate an action taken while the order was in force.'

As I contemplated this dubious explanation, Mrs Phillips burst in.

She was in full Wagnerian voice. 'I don't care if he's talking to the Queen and the Pope,' she shouted at some poor Executive Officer outside my door. She strode across the room towards me. 'Judas,' was her initial greeting.

'Steady on,' I replied firmly.

'You promised to support us,' she snarled.

'Well, yes, I did,' I was forced to admit.

'Then you must see that our lease is renewed.'

Sir Humphrey tried to intervene between us. 'Unfortunately, dear lady, it is not in my Minister's power to . . .'

She ignored him and said to me: 'Mr Hacker, you have given your word. Are you going to keep it?'

Put like that, I was in a bit of a spot. I did my best to blur the issue.

'Yes,' I said, 'in that, well, I shall certainly . . . you know, I didn't exactly give my word, that is, I shall explore all the avenues, make every effort, do all that is humanly possible —' Words to that effect.

Mrs Phillips was no fool. 'You mean no!' she said.

I was quite honestly stuck for a reply. I said 'No,' then that seemed a little unambiguous so I said 'No, I mean Yes,' then that seemed dangerous so I added that by no I didn't mean no, not definitely not, no.

Then – another bombshell! 'Don't say I didn't warn you,' she said. 'My husband is deputy features editor of the *Express*. Tomorrow morning your name will be manure. You will be roasted alive by the whole of the national press.'

The room fell silent after she swept out and slammed the door. An intense gloom had descended upon the assembled company – or upon me, anyway. Finally, Sir Humphrey found his voice: 'It falls to few people,' he said encouragingly, 'to be within twenty-four hours both St Francis and St Joan.'

I have got to stop this farm being closed. But how? Clearly I'm going to get no help from my Permanent Secretary.

September 21st

No story in the *Express* today, which was a slight relief. But I couldn't believe they'll let it pass.

And when I got to the office there was a message asking me to call that wretched rag.

Also, a message that Sir Desmond wanted to see me urgently. I suggested a meeting next week to Bernard, but it seemed that he was downstairs waiting! Astonishing.

So Bernard let him in. Humphrey appeared as well.

When we were all gathered, Glazebrook said he'd just had an idea. For nine storeys extra on his bank! I was about to boot him out when he explained that if they had nine more storeys the bank could postpone Phase III for seven years. This would leave a site vacant.

'So?' I was not getting his drift.

'Well,' he said. 'I was reading in the *Financial Times* a day or two ago about your visit to that City Farm. Thought it was a jolly good wheeze. And, you see, our Phase III site is only two hundred yards away from it, so you could use it to extend the farm. Or if they wanted to move . . . for any reason . . . it's actually a bit bigger . . . We thought of calling it the James Hacker Cuddly Animal Sanctuary . . .' (he and Humphrey exchanged looks) 'well, Animal Sanctuary anyway, and nine storeys isn't really very much is it?'

It was clear that they were in cahoots. But it was, unmistakably, a way out. If I gave them permission for a high-rise bank, they'd enable the City Farm to stay open.

It is incredible, I thought, that I should ever have thought that Humphrey would take my side against his old chum Glazebrook. And yet, Glazebrook is not really Humphrey's type. He must be holding something over Humphrey . . . I wonder what.

Meanwhile, I had to think up some valid reasons for approving the high-rise building – and quickly. The official application wouldn't be in for a while but in front of Bernard I felt I had to come up with some face-saving explanations. Fortunately, everyone pitched in.

'You know, Humphrey,' I began, 'I think the government has to be very careful about throttling small businesses.'

Bernard said, 'The bank's not actually a small business.'

'It will be if we throttle it,' I said firmly, squashing him. He looked puzzled. 'Bernard,' I said casually, 'what's one more skyscraper when there's so many already?'

'Quite so,' agreed Sir Humphrey.

'And let's announce it right away,' I continued.

So we all agreed that the high-rise building will cut both ways. It will create shade for the school. Extra revenue for the public transport system. And as for privacy – well, it could be fun for people in their gardens to look up and see what's going on in the offices. Couldn't it?

'After all,' I added meaningfully, 'some extraordinary things go on in offices, don't they Humphrey?'

He had the grace to smile. 'Yes Minister,' he agreed.

14

A Question of Loyalty

September 27th
I'm due to go to Washington tomorrow for an official visit. I should have thought that it wasn't strictly necessary for me to be away for a whole week but Sir Humphrey insists that it's of enormous value if I stay there for an appreciable time so as to get the maximum diplomatic benefit from it all.

I'm to address a conference on administration. One of the Assistant Secretaries, Peter Wilkinson, has written me an excellent speech. It contains phrases like 'British Government Administration is a model of loyalty, integrity and efficiency. There is a ruthless war on waste. We are cutting bureaucracy to the bone. A lesson that Britain can teach the world.' Good dynamic stuff.

However, I asked Humphrey yesterday if we could prove that all of this is true. He replied that a good speech isn't one where we can prove that we're telling the truth – it's one where nobody else can prove we're lying.

Good thinking!

I hope the speech is fully reported in the London papers.

SIR BERNARD WOOLLEY RECALLS:[1]
I well remember that Sir Humphrey Appleby was extremely keen for Hacker to go off on some official junket somewhere. Anywhere.

He felt that Hacker was beginning to get too much of a grip on the job. This pleased me because it made my job easier, but caused great anxiety to Sir Humphrey.

I was actually rather sorry to have missed the Washington junket, but Sir Humphrey had insisted that Hacker take one of the Assistant Private Secretaries, who needed to be given some experience of responsibility.

When he'd been away for five or six days I was summoned to Sir Humphrey's office. He asked me how I was enjoying having my Minister out of

[1] In conversation with the Editors.

the office for a week, and I – rather naïvely – remarked that it made things a little difficult.

It was instantly clear that I had blotted my copybook. That afternoon I received a memo in Sir Humphrey's handwriting, informing me of the benefits of ministerial absence and asking me to commit them to memory.

[*Fortunately Sir Bernard kept this memo among his personal papers, and we reproduce it here, written on Sir Humphrey's margin-shaped notepaper – Ed.*]

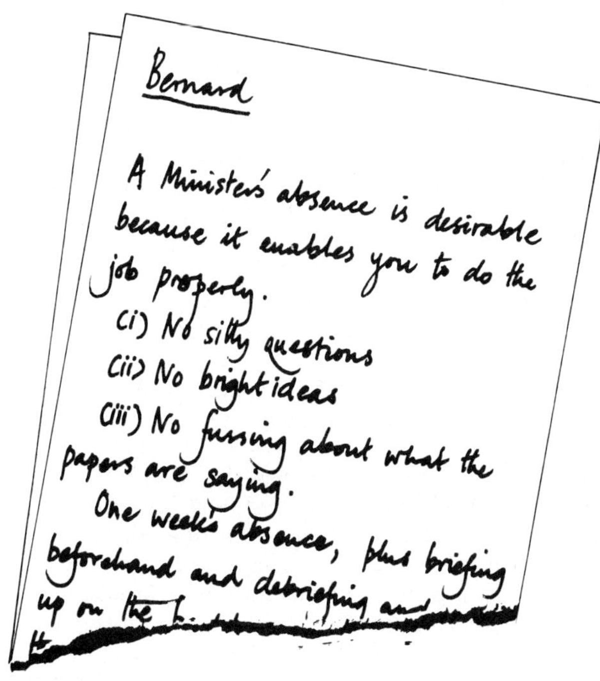

Bernard

A Minister's absence is desirable because it enables you to do the job properly.

(i) No silly questions
(ii) No bright ideas
(iii) No fussing about what the papers are saying.

One week's absence, plus briefing beforehand and debriefing and up on the

Bernard

A Minister's absence is desirable because it enables you to do the job properly.

(i) No silly questions
(ii) No bright ideas
(iii) No fussing about what the papers are saying.

One week's absence, plus briefing beforehand and debriefing and catching up on the backlog on his return, means that he can be kept out of the Department's hair for virtually a fortnight

Furthermore, a Minister's absence is the best cover for not informing the Minister when it is not desirable to do so – and for the next six months, if he complains of not having been informed about something, tell him it came up while he was away

[*Sir Bernard continued – Ed.*]

Anyway, the reason behind the increasing number of summit conferences that took place during the 1970s and 1980s was that the Civil Service felt that this was the only way that the country worked. Concentrate all the power at Number Ten and then send the Prime Minister away – to EEC summits, NATO summits, Commonwealth summits, anywhere! Then the Cabinet Secretary could get on with the task of running the country properly.

At the same meeting we discussed the speech that Peter had written for the Minister to deliver in Washington.

I suggested that, although Peter was a frightfully good chap and had probably done a frightfully good job on it in one way, there was a danger that the speech might prove frightfully boring for the audience.

Sir Humphrey agreed instantly. He thought that it would bore the pants off the audience, and it must have been ghastly to have to sit through it.

Nonetheless, he explained to me that it was an excellent speech. I learned that speeches are not written for the audience to which they are delivered. Delivering the speech is merely the formality that has to be gone through in order to get the press release into the newspapers.

'We can't worry about entertaining people,' he explained to me. 'We're not scriptwriters for a comedian – well, not a professional comedian, anyway.'

He emphasised that the value of the speech was that it said the correct things. In public. Once that speech has been reported in print, the Minister is committed to defending the Civil Service in front of Select Committees.

I sprang to the Minister's defence, and said that he defends us anyway. Sir Humphrey looked at me with pity and remarked that he certainly does so when it suits him – but, when things go wrong, a Minister's first instinct is to rat on his department.

Therefore, the Civil Service when drafting a Minister's speech is primarily concerned with making him nail his trousers to the mast. Not his colours, but his trousers – then he can't climb down!

As always, Sir Humphrey's reasoning proved to be correct – but, as was so often the case, he reckoned without Hacker's gift for low cunning.

[*Hacker's diary continues – Ed.*]

October 4th

I got back from Washington today. The visit was quite a success on the whole though I must say my speech didn't exactly thrill them. I mustn't leave speeches to the Department – they give me very worthy things to say but they're always so bloody boring.

I've been met by a huge backlog of work, piles of red boxes, half a ton of cabinet papers, hundreds of memos and minutes and submissions to catch up on.

And I doubt if I can ever really catch up on it because tomorrow I go in front of a Select Committee and I've got to try to read the redrafted paper on Establishment levels beforehand. Not only read it, but understand it. And not only understand it, but remember it. And it's been written by an Under-Secretary – therefore it's not in English, but in Under-Secretaryese.

Still, at least the press did report my speech, so that's all right.

Sir Humphrey popped in to welcome me home, and to brief me about the Select Committee.

'You do realise the importance of this hearing, don't you Minister?'

'Of course I do, Humphrey. The press will be there,' I explained.

[*Like many politicians, Hacker did not seem to believe in his own existence unless he was reading about himself in the newspapers – Ed.*]

'It's not just a question of the press,' he said. 'This is a scrutiny of the Department's future operation. If we were to emerge from the hearing as extravagant or incompetent . . .'

I interrupted him with a penetrating question. 'Are we extravagant or incompetent?'

'Of course not,' he replied with considerable indignation. 'But there are hostile MPs on the Committee. Especially the member for Derbyshire East.'

I hadn't realised that Betty Oldham was on the Committee.

Humphrey handed me a thick folder full of papers, with red and yellow and blue tags. 'I urge you to master this brief, Minister,' he said, and told me to ask if I found any problems.

I was fed up. I'm tired and jet-lagged today. I told him that I didn't want another brief on the Select Committee, I only just mastered one on the plane.

'What was in it?' he asked.

That was a bit embarrassing. I couldn't quite remember. I explained that it's rather hard to concentrate on the plane, as they keep trying to serve you drinks and show you movies and wake you up.

'I'm sure it's frightfully difficult to concentrate if you keep being woken up, Minister,' he said sympathetically. He added that this was the first and only brief containing possible questions from the Committee, all with the appropriate answers carefully presented to give the Department's position.

'Are they all absolutely accurate?' I wanted to know.

'It is carefully presented to give the Department's position,' he replied carefully.

'Humphrey,' I explained equally carefully. 'These Select Committees are very important. I can't be seen to mislead them.'

'You will not be seen to mislead them.'

I wasn't satisfied. I began to suspect that the brief was not strictly honest. I pressed him further.

'Is it the truth?'

'The truth and nothing but the truth,' he assured me.

'And the whole truth?'

'Of course not, Minister,' he replied with some impatience.

I was confused. 'So we tell them we're keeping some things secret, do we?'

He shook his head and smiled. 'Indeed not.'

'Why not?' I asked.

Sir Humphrey rose from his chair and announced magisterially: 'He that would keep a secret must keep it secret that he hath a secret to keep.' Then he left the room.

I was interested in the quotation, which struck me as rather profound. 'Who said that?' I asked Bernard.

Bernard looked puzzled. He stared at me, and then stared at the doorway through which Sir Humphrey had just walked.

'It was Sir Humphrey,' he said.

[*It is significant that Hacker was not at all shocked at the suggestion that he should conceal information from the Select Committee, or indeed tell lies to it. Such lies would be regarded in government circles as white lies. There are a number of issues about which a Minister automatically tells lies, and he would be regarded as foolish or incompetent if he told the truth. For instance, he would always deny an impending devaluation, or a run on the pound. And he would always give the impression that the UK had adequate and credible defences – Ed.*]

I sat at my desk feeling utterly washed out after a night with British Airways and a day with the Civil Service, and gazed at the enormous brief that I had to master in one day.

'Why,' I wondered aloud, 'are Ministers never allowed to go anywhere without their briefs?'

'It's in case they get caught with their trousers down,' Bernard replied rather wittily. At least, I *think* it was wit, but it might just have been a lucky chance.

He had kept my diary free for the whole day, so we were not interrupted. It emerged, as we went through it, that the submission that I'd read on the plane was a rehash of the report the Department produced last year. And the year before. And the year before that. Ever since 1867 probably. I pointed out to Bernard that the first sentence was enough to cure anybody of any desire to read the thing: 'The function of the DAA is to support and service the administrative work of all government departments.'

'Oh no,' he said, 'that bit's fascinating.'

I asked him how anyone could be fascinated by it.

'Well,' he said, 'if you look back to the first report in 1868, when Gladstone set up this Department's predecessor, you find that the first sentence is, 'The Department is responsible for the economic and efficient administration of government.'

'Ah,' I said, 'is that what it was for?'

'Yes,' said Bernard, 'but it proved a tough remit. They were responsible for every bit of waste and inefficiency. I suppose Gladstone meant them to be. So when it got too hot they did the usual.'

'What is "the usual"?' I asked.

It emerged that 'the usual' in Civil Service terms is to secure your budget, staff and premises and then quietly change your remit. In 1906 they changed the first sentence to 'The Department exists to *further* the efficient and economic administration of Government.' This removed the responsibility.

In 1931 they got it down to 'The Department exists to support all government departments in *their* pursuit of economic and efficient administration' which pushed the responsibility on to other departments. And by 1972 they had got rid of the embarrassing notions of economy and efficiency, and since then it has said 'The purpose of the DAA is to support and service the administrative work of all government departments.' The last vestige of the Department's real purpose removed in a mere one hundred and four years, and the Department itself one hundred and six times its original size.

I now see why Bernard is fascinated, but I still could hardly stay awake to the end of paragraph one. Perhaps it was just the jet-lag. Anyway, Bernard reminded me that the press will be there tomorrow – so I had no choice but to get down to it.

October 5th

I had my first experience of being grilled by a Select Committee today and I didn't like it one bit.

It all happens in a committee room at the House, a large gloomy

Gothic room with an air of Greyfriars school about it. I was made to feel a bit like Billy Bunter caught with his hands in someone else's tuckbox.

Along one side of a long table sit about nine MPs with the Chairman in the middle. On the Chairman's right is the secretary, a civil servant, who takes minutes. There are a few seats for the public and the press.

I was allowed to have Bernard with me, sitting slightly behind me of course, plus Peter Wilkinson and Gillian something-or-other from the Department. (*Assistant Secretaries – Ed.*)

I was allowed to make an opening statement. I'd done my homework well, and I reiterated everything that Sir Humphrey said in his submission: namely that the Department of Administrative Affairs is run to a high standard of efficiency and does indeed support and service the administrative work of all government departments.

Mrs Betty Oldham began the questioning. She tossed her red hair and smiled a thin, mirthless smile. Then she asked me if I'd heard of Malcolm Rhodes.

I hadn't. I said so.

She went on to inform me that he is an ex-Assistant Secretary from the DAA. I started to explain that as there are twenty-three thousand people working for the DAA I can hardly be expected to know them all, when she shouted me down (well, spoke over me really) and said that he was eased out, became a management consultant in America and has written a book.

She waved a pile of galley proofs at me.

'This is an advance proof,' she announced, with a glance at the press seats, 'in which Mr Rhodes makes a number of astounding allegations of waste of public money in the British Civil Service, particularly your Department.'

I was stumped. I really didn't know how to reply. I asked for a quick private word with my officials.

I turned to Bernard. 'Do we know anything about this?' I whispered urgently.

Peter said, 'I didn't know Rhodes had written a book.'

Gillian just said: 'Oh my God, oh my God!' That really filled me with confidence.

I asked who he was. Gillian said, 'A troublemaker, Minister.' Peter said he wasn't sound, the ultimate insult.

Bernard, who clearly knew even less about him than Peter and Gillian, asked what was in the book.

'We don't know.'

'Well, what do I say about it?' I whispered hysterically, aware that time was running out.

'Stall,' advised Peter.

That was a big help. I'd have to say *something*. 'Stall?' I said indignantly. 'What do you mean by it, stall?'

'Stall, meaning avoiding answering, Minister,' interjected Bernard. Like headless chickens in a crisis, these civil servants.

I gritted my teeth. 'I know what stall means, Bernard.' I was trying, not altogether successfully, to keep my temper. 'But what do you mean by sending me out into a typhoon without even giving me an umbrella?'

'An umbrella wouldn't be much use in a typhoon, Minister, because the wind would get underneath and . . .'

The Chairman called upon me at that moment, which was just as well or Bernard might never have lived to tell the tale.

'Have you had sufficient consultation with your officials?' asked the Chairman.

'More than enough,' I replied grimly.

The Chairman nodded to Betty Oldham, who smiled and said: 'Let me read you some of the scandalous facts that Mr Rhodes reveals.'

She then read me the following passage: 'At No. 4 regional supply depot in Herefordshire there are two former aircraft hangars used only for stores, but which are centrally heated to 70° Fahrenheit day and night.' [*Quoted verbatim from Rhodes's book – Ed.*] 'What have you got to say about that?' she asked.

Naturally I had absolutely nothing to say. I pointed out that I couldn't possibly be expected to answer that sort of detailed question without prior notice.

She conceded the point, but claimed that she was asking about a principle. 'What I'm asking is, what conceivable reason could there be for such appalling extravagance?'

The Chairman and the Committee seemed to think I should answer. So I made a stab at it. 'Some materials deteriorate badly at low temperatures. It would depend on what was being stored.'

I'd played right into her hands. 'Copper wire,' she said promptly, and smiled.

'Well . . .' I made another guess at what conceivable reason there could be. 'Er . . . copper can corrode in damp conditions, can't it?'

'It's plastic-coated,' she said, and waited.

'Plastic-coated,' I said. 'Ah well. Yes.' They still seemed to want something of me. 'Well, I'll have it looked into,' I offered. What else could I say?

I'd hoped that would be the end of it. But no. It was only the beginning.

'Mr Rhodes also says that your Department insists on ordering all pens, pencils, paper-clips and so on centrally, and then distributing them against departmental requisitions.'

'That seems very sensible to me,' I replied cautiously, scenting a trap. 'There are big savings on bulk purchases.'

There *was* a trap. 'He demonstrates,' she continued, 'that this procedure is four times more expensive than if local offices went out and bought what they wanted in the High Street.'

I thought of remarking that you can prove anything with figures, but decided against it. Clearly he, and she, wouldn't make this claim without *some* evidence. And my experience of the DAA suggests that Rhodes was probably absolutely right anyway. So I told her that I found this information very interesting and that I'd be happy to change the system if it were shown to be necessary. 'We're not a rigid bureaucracy, you know,' I added.

This remark proved to be a tactical error. 'Oh no?' she enquired acidly. 'Mr Rhodes says that he gave these figures and proposed this change when he was in your Department, and it was turned down on the grounds that people were used to the existing procedure. How's that for a rigid bureaucracy?'

I'd led with my chin there. I really had no defence immediately available to me. Again I offered to have the matter looked into.

'Looked into?' she smiled at me contemptuously.

'Looked into, yes,' I asserted defiantly, but I was losing my nerve.

'You did say in Washington last week that your Department conducted a ruthless war on waste and could teach the world a lesson?' I nodded. She went for the kill. 'How would you reconcile that with spending seventy-five thousand pounds on a roof garden on top of the supplementary benefits office in Kettering?'

I was speechless.

She asked me, with heavy sarcasm, if I proposed to have it looked into. Now I was on the ropes. I started to explain that my responsibility is for policy rather than for detailed administration (which isn't true) and was saved by the bell in the form of Alan Hughes, a more friendly committee member [*i.e. a committee member hoping for office in the government, or some other special favour – Ed.*].

Alan intervened and said: 'Mr Chairman, I think that the Permanent Secretary to the DAA is due to appear before us next week. Would he not be the appropriate person to answer these questions?'

The Chairman agreed, asked that Sir Humphrey be notified in advance. The wretched galley proofs were taken from Mrs Oldham to be shown to him.

October 6th
The headlines weren't good today.

New Allegations of Government Waste

Humphrey and I met to discuss the matter. To my astonishment he attacked me. 'Minister,' he said, 'you have placed me in a very difficult position.'

I was outraged. 'And what about the position you put me in? Here's the Prime Minister asking for economies right, left and centre, and I look as if I'm wasting everything that everyone else has saved.'

Humphrey looked at me as if I were mad. 'Minister, no one else has saved *anything*! You should know that by now.'

I knew that, and he knew that, and he knew I knew that, but the public doesn't know that. 'They all look as if they have,' I reminded him.

'Couldn't you have stalled a bit more effectively?' he complained.

'What do you mean, stalled?' I was deeply indignant.

'Blurred things a bit. You're normally so good at blurring the issue.'

If this was meant to be a compliment it certainly didn't sound like one. But apparently that's how it was intended.

'You have a considerable talent for making things unintelligible, Minister.' My mouth must have dropped open, for he continued, 'I mean it as a compliment, I assure you. Blurring issues is one of the basic ministerial skills.'

'Pray tell me the others,' I replied coldly.

Without hesitation he gave me a list. 'Delaying decisions, dodging questions, juggling figures, bending facts and concealing errors.'

He's quite right, as a matter of fact. But I didn't see what else he could have expected me to do yesterday.

'Couldn't you have made it look as though you were doing something, and then done nothing? Like you usually do?'

I ignored that remark and tried to get at the facts. 'Humphrey,' I began, 'if these revelations are true . . .'

He interrrupted rapidly. 'If. Exactly! If! You could, for instance, have discussed the nature of truth.'

Now it was my turn to explain a thing or two. 'The Select Committee couldn't be less interested in the nature of truth – they're all MPs.'

'You should have said it was a security matter,' said Humphrey, falling back on the usual first line of defence.

Completely idiotic! I asked him how HB pencils could be a security matter.

'It depends what you write with them,' he offered. Pathetic. He can't really think I'd have got away with that.

'And why on earth are we building roof gardens on offices?' I asked.

'We took over the office design from an American company that was going to occupy it. It just happened that nobody noticed the roof garden on the plans.'

I simply stared at him, incredulously.

'A tiny mistake,' he was defiant. 'The sort anyone could make.'

'Tiny?' I could hardly believe my ears. 'Tiny? Seventy-five thousand pounds. Give me an example of a big mistake.'

'Letting people find out about it.'

Then I asked him why we are heating sheds full of wire.

'Do you want the truth?' he asked.

I was taken aback. It's the first time he's ever asked me that. 'If it's not too much trouble,' I replied with magnificent condescension.

'All the staff,' he said, 'use these sheds for growing mushrooms.'

I didn't even know where to begin. So I kept it simple. 'Stop them,' I ordered.

He shook his head sadly, and sighed a heartfelt sigh. 'But they've been doing it since 1945. It's almost the only perk of a very boring job.'

I understand this argument, but it's clearly untenable in public. So next I asked about Rhodes's proposal for saving money on stationery orders. Why hadn't we accepted it?

'Minister,' said Humphrey vehemently, 'that man was a troublemaker. A crank. He had an unhealthy obsession about efficiency and economy.'

'But why didn't we adopt his proposal? It would have saved millions of pounds.'

'It would have meant a lot of work to implement it.'

'So?'

'Taking on a lot more staff.'

This argument was manifest nonsense. I told him so. He seemed unbothered.

'Disprove it,' he challenged me.

'I can't, obviously.'

'Exactly,' he replied smugly.

I stared at him. I had suddenly realised what was going on. 'You're making all this up aren't you?' I said.

He smiled. 'Of course.'

'Why?'

He stood up.

'As an example,' he said in his most superior manner, 'of how to handle a Select Committee.'

[*The following week the same Select Committee met Sir Humphrey. Mrs Oldham questioned him closely on the Rhodes disclosures and proposals. The evidence taken that day is printed below – Ed.*]

Mrs Betty Oldham: This is all very well, Sir Humphrey, but let's get down to details. This heated aircraft hangar for example.

Sir Humphrey Appleby: Indeed, I fully understand the Committee's concern. But it can be very cold in Herefordshire in winter, and even civil servants cannot work in subzero temperatures.

Mrs Betty Oldham: We aren't talking about civil servants. We are talking about coils of wire, with plastic coats to keep them warm.

Sir Humphrey Appleby: Yes, but staff are in and out all the time.

Mrs Betty Oldham: Why?

Sir Humphrey Appleby: Taking deliveries, making withdrawals, checking records, security patrols, fire inspection, stocktaking and auditing, and so forth.

Mrs Betty Oldham: Well, they can wear gloves can't they?

Sir Humphrey Appleby: They could. It's a question of staff welfare policy.

Mrs Betty Oldham: Well, I suggest this policy is costing the taxpayer millions of pounds. (silence) Nothing to say, Sir Humphrey?

Sir Humphrey Appleby: It is not for me to comment on government policy. You must ask the Minister.

Mrs Betty Oldham: But you advise the Minister.

Sir Humphrey Appleby: I think the Chairman is aware that I cannot disclose how I advise my Minister. The Minister is responsible for policy.

Mrs Betty Oldham: All right. So we'll ask the Minister. Now then, what about those stationery requisition savings?

Sir Humphrey Appleby: That would have involved putting very considerable government patronage in the hands of junior staff.

Mrs Betty Oldham: Considerable government patronage? Buying a packet of paper-clips?

Sir Humphrey Appleby: It is government policy to exercise strict control over the number of people allowed to spend its money. I'm sure you'll agree that this is right and proper.

Mrs Betty Oldham: But it's plain common sense to allow people to buy their own paper-clips.

Sir Humphrey Appleby: Government policy has nothing to do with common sense.

Mrs Betty Oldham: Well, don't you think it's time that the policy was changed? (silence) Well, Sir Humphrey?

Sir Humphrey Appleby: It is not for me to comment on government policy. You must ask the Minister.

Mrs Betty Oldham: But the Minister advises us to ask you.

Sir Humphrey Appleby: And I am advising you to ask the Minister.

Mr Alan Hughes: When does this end?

Sir Humphrey Appleby: As soon as you like.

Mrs Betty Oldham: Well, let's come to the roof garden.

Sir Humphrey Appleby: With pleasure. It was part of a wide variety of roof insulation schemes which the government undertook to test, in the interest of fuel economy.

Mrs Betty Oldham: Seventy-five thousand pounds?

Mrs. *Betty Oldham.*

23. This is all very well, Sir Humphrey, but let's get down to details. This heated aircraft hangar for example.——(*Sir Humphrey Appleby.*) Indeed, I fully understand the committee's concern. But it can be very cold in Herefordshire in winter, and even civil servants cannot work in subzero temperatures.

24. We aren't talking about civil servants. We are talking about coils of wire, with plastic coats to keep them warm.——Yes, but staff are in and out all the time.

25. Why?——Taking deliveries, making withdrawals, checking records, security patrols, fire inspection, stocktaking and auditing, and so forth.

26. Well, they can wear gloves can't they?——They could. It's a question of staff welfare policy.

27. Well, I suggest this policy is costing the taxpayer millions of pounds. (silence) Nothing to say, Sir Humphrey?——It is not for me to comment on government policy. You must ask the Minister.

28. But you advise the Minister.——I think the Chairman is aware that I cannot disclose how I advise my Minister. The Minister is responsible for policy.

29. All right. So we'll ask the Minister. Now then, what about those stationery requisition savings?——That would have involved putting very considerable government patronage in the hands of junior staff.

30. Considerable government patronage? Buying a packet of paper-clips?——It is government policy to exercise strict control over the number of people allowed to spend its money. I'm sure you'll agree that this is right and proper.

31. But it's plain common sense to allow people to buy their own paper-clips.——Government policy has nothing to do with common sense.

31. Well, don't you think it's time that the policy was changed? (silence) Well, Sir Humphrey?——It is not for me to comment on government policy. You must ask the Minister.

33. But the Minister advises us to ask you.——And I am advising you to ask the Minister.

Mr. *Alan Hughes.*

34. When does this end?——(Sir *Humphrey Appleby.*) As soon as you like.

Mrs. *Betty Oldham.*

35. Well, let's come to the roof garden.——(Sir *Humphrey Appleby*). With pleasure. It was part of a wide variety of roof insulation schemes which the government undertook to test, in the interest of fuel economy.

36. Seventy-five thousand pounds?——It was thought that the sale of flowers and vegetable produce might offset the cost.

37. And did it?——No.

38. Then why not abandon the garden?——Well, it's there now. And it does insulate the roof. But we aren't building any more.

39. But you've wasted seventy-five thousand pounds.——It was the government's policy to test all the proposals for fuel saving.

40. At this fantastic waste of taxpayers' money? You agree the money was wasted?——It is not for me to comment on government policy. You must ask the Minister.

41. Look, Sir Humphrey. Whatever we ask the Minister, he says is an administrative question for you. And whatever we ask you, you say is a policy question for the Minister. How do you suggest we find out what's going on?——Yes, I do think there is a real dilemma here, in that while it has been government policy to regard policy as the responsibility of Ministers and administration as the responsibility of officials, questions of administrative policy can cause confusion between the administration of policy and the policy of administration, especially when responsibility for the administration of the policy of administration conflicts or overlaps with responsibility for the policy of the administration of policy.

42. That's a load of meaningless drivel, isn't it, Sir Humphrey?——It is not for me to comment on government policy. You must ask the Minister.

The actual report of Sir Humphrey Appleby's evidence to the Select Committee, reproduced by kind permission of HMSO.

[*We have reprinted it in more readable form – Ed.*]

Sir Humphrey Appleby: It was thought that the sale of flowers and vegetable produce might offset the cost.
Mrs Betty Oldham: And did it?
Sir Humphrey Appleby: No.
Mrs Betty Oldham: Then why not abandon the garden?
Sir Humphrey Appleby: Well, it's there now. And it does insulate the roof. But we aren't building any more.
Mrs Betty Oldham: But you've wasted seventy-five thousand pounds.
Sir Humphrey Appleby: It was the government's policy to test all the proposals for fuel saving.
Mrs Betty Oldham: At this fantastic waste of taxpayers' money? You agree the money was wasted?
Sir Humphrey Appleby: It is not for me to comment on government policy. You must ask the Minister.
Mrs Betty Oldham: Look, Sir Humphrey. Whatever we ask the Minister, he says is an administrative question for you. And whatever we ask you, you say is a policy question for the Minister. How do you suggest we find out what's going on?
Sir Humphrey Appleby: Yes, I do think there is a real dilemma here, in that while it has been government policy to regard policy as the responsibility of Ministers and administration as the responsibility of officials, questions of administrative policy can cause confusion between the administration of policy and the policy of administration, especially when responsibility for the administration of the policy of administration conflicts or overlaps with responsibility for the policy of the administration of policy.
Mrs Betty Oldham: That's a load of meaningless drivel, isn't it, Sir Humphrey?
Sir Humphrey Appleby: It is not for me to comment on government policy. You must ask the Minister.

SIR BERNARD WOOLLEY RECALLS:[1]
It was theoretically true, as Sir Humphrey claimed, that Ministers are – and were in the 1980s – responsible for policy. In practice, however, Ministers are responsible for relatively little policy because the useful life of a government is only about two years. The first year is spent learning that commitments made while in Opposition cannot be kept once they are in office: once a government gets in it has to get to grips with the real problems that actually exist, invariably connected with the prevailing economic situation

[1] In conversation with the Editors.

which is always either appalling or catastrophic, and of which the full details of the horror were invariably kept secret from the nation and therefore from the Opposition.

As a new government struggles to sort out these problems it will be dependent on economists and on the Treasury. This is a trifle unfortunate – economists are always in a state of total intellectual disarray and confusion and are too busy arguing with each other to be able to advise politicians who are usually rather ignorant of economics. And the Treasury, on the other hand, has had rather a lot of bad luck with its economic forecasts over the last sixty years or so.

So, after a period of between a year and eighteen months, Ministers come to an understanding of the situation as it actually is. Then there follows about two years of potentially serious government – after which the run-up to the next general election begins. At this point achievement has to be subordinated to the winning of votes – or, rather, winning votes becomes the only measure of achievement. The last two years are rather like swotting for an exam. You don't do anything new, you just try to pass.

Therefore, as he knew only too well, Sir Humphrey's claim that Ministers make policy applies – at most – to two years out of every five. This Select Committee enquiry took place, of course, during the first year that Hacker was in office.

There is one further interesting question raised by this discussion. If the Minister makes policy for two years out of five, who makes policy in the other three years? Obviously, we in the Civil Service used to fill the vacuum. And this created serious problems during the Minister's two years of 'serious government' – which were therefore frequently absorbed in a war between the Minister's policies and the Ministry's policies.

The only time that this eighteen-month vacuum did not occur at the start of a government was when a government was re-elected for a second full term with a working majority. In the early 1980s this had not occurred in Britain for a quarter of a century. This is why it was always absurd to categorise the Civil Service as either Conservative or Labour – we always believed in, and hoped for, regular alternation of governments. This gave us the maximum freedom from control by Ministers who, if they stayed too long in office, were likely to begin to think that they knew how to run the country.

October 13th

Today I read in the papers the reports of Humphrey's appearance before the Select Committee. He's been a big help!

And we've both been called back to make a joint appearance, to sort out the mess that he made.

I called him in and gave him a bollocking.

He said he'd done his best.

I told him: 'You did your best for yourself, perhaps. But you've solved nothing. The day after tomorrow we'll be sitting there, side by side, getting the third degree from the Committee. We must have proper answers – or, at the very least, the *same* answers.'

Humphrey said that we must begin by establishing what our position is.

'Very well,' I agreed. 'What are the facts?'

He got very impatient with me. 'I'm discussing our position, Minister – the facts are neither here nor there.'

Fair enough. So I asked him to outline our position.

He suggested that we choose one of the Civil Service's five standard excuses, to deal with each of their allegations. A different one for each if possible.

I had never before heard of the five standard excuses. Humphrey must be quite anxious about the situation if he's prepared to reveal his techniques to me so openly.

I made notes. I have called each excuse by the name of a famous example of its use.

1 *The Anthony Blunt excuse*
There is a perfectly satisfactory explanation for everything, but security prevents its disclosure

2 *The Comprehensive Schools excuse*
It's only gone wrong because of heavy cuts in staff and budget which have stretched supervisory resources beyond the limit

3 *The Concorde excuse*
It was a worthwhile experiment now abandoned, but not before it provided much valuable data and considerable employment

4 *The Munich Agreement excuse*
It occurred before important facts were known, and cannot happen again
(The important facts in question were that Hitler wanted to conquer Europe. This *was* actually known; but not to the Foreign Office, of course)

5 *The Charge of the Light Brigade excuse*
It was an unfortunate lapse by an individual which has now been dealt with under internal disciplinary procedures

According to Sir Humphrey, these excuses have covered everything so far. Even wars. Small wars, anyway.

I finished making notes, and contemplated the list. It seemed okay, if we could carry it off. But I knew I couldn't manage it without Humphrey.

I smiled at him encouragingly. 'All right,' I said, 'so it's real teamwork from now on, eh, Humphrey?'

'United we stand, divided we fall,' he replied, with a distinctly optimistic air.

I was about to start going through the list to see which excuse we could apply to which allegation, when Bernard reminded me that I had to be at the House in ten minutes for a committee meeting. 'And,' he added nervously, 'Number Ten's been on the phone. Sir Mark Spencer [*the Prime Minister's special political adviser – Ed.*] wonders if you could pop in for a drink sometime tomorrow. I suggested 5.30.'

I pointed out to Sir Humphrey that this was *not* a good sign. Clearly the PM wants me to account for our feeble explanations to the Select Committee.

'Perhaps it *is* just for a drink,' said Sir Humphrey, with more optimism than sense.

'Don't be silly,' I told him. 'You don't get invited to drinks at Number Ten because you're thirsty.' I agreed to meet Humphrey tomorrow, and cook up a story.

'Agree our position, Minister,' he corrected me.

'That's what I said,' I replied, 'cook up a story.'

October 14th

I am very confused this evening.

At 5.30 I went to see Sir Mark Spencer at Number Ten.

Going to Number Ten is a very weird experience. From the outside it just looks like an ordinary terraced Georgian house – big, but not *that* big. But when you step inside the front door and walk along a big wide hall that seems a hundred yards long, you realise that you're actually in a palace.

It's so English, so extremely discreet on the outside. The secret of the house is that it's three or four houses knocked together, and built onto at the back as well. As a result it's pretty hard to find your own way round Number Ten. You go up and down funny little stairs, crossing from one house to another, and in no time you don't even know which floor you're on.

This, according to the drivers' grapevine, is put to creative use by the civil servants, who know the plan of the building inside out and who therefore situate their own offices in the key rooms from which they can monitor and control all comings and goings within the building. Also these are usually the nicest rooms. In fact, there is a persistent rumour that the battle for rooms goes on through every administration, with political staff fighting for the rooms nearest to the PM's office – and fighting also to get the civil servants further away. But it seems that as soon as the government changes, the civil servants move swiftly and smoothly to reoccupy all the lost ground before the new Prime Minister's staff arrive.

I was escorted up to Sir Mark Spencer's office. It was a small, poky, sparse little room, under-furnished, exactly the sort of office in which the permanent civil servants would put a temporary part-time adviser.

[*Sir Mark Spencer was the Managing Director of a well-known and popular multiple chain-store, a byword for efficiency and productivity, who had been brought into Number Ten by the PM to advise personally on economies and increased administrative productivity. So far, it seems, he was still struggling with the problem of getting a decent office. Presumably, if it were not for the PM's personal interest in his work, he would have been found an office in Walthamstow – Ed.*]

I'd only met Sir Mark once before. He is a big fellow, highly intelligent and with a kindly soft-spoken manner. He welcomed me warmly.

'Ah, come in, Jim. Scotch?'

I thanked him.

'How are things going?' he enquired gently, as he brought me my drink.

I told him things were fine. Absolutely fine. I told him that it was a bit of a shock, having Rhodes's book thrown at us out of the blue, but that now the whole situation was under control. 'Humphrey and I will be getting together this evening. We'll be able to explain everything. Nothing for the PM to worry about.'

I hoped that I was being sufficiently reassuring to Sir Mark. As I heard myself speak, however, I rather sounded as though I were reassuring myself.

I paused. But Sir Mark said nothing. He just sat still, looking at me.

I found myself continuing, and making more excuses. 'What beats me is how Malcolm Rhodes got all that information. Most of it happened outside his division. And I wouldn't mind knowing who got those advance proofs to Betty Oldham. The PM must be livid. But it's certainly no fault of mine.'

I paused again. In fact, I had really nothing left to say on the subject. Sir Mark obviously sensed this, because he finally spoke.

'What makes you think the PM is livid?' he asked, in a slightly puzzled tone.

I hadn't expected this question. I thought it was obvious. Why else was I there at Number Ten? I stared at him.

'Let's try and look at this situation logically, shall we?' suggested Sir Mark.

'Of course,' I agreed.

Then he asked me a series of questions. At first I simply couldn't see what he was driving at.

'What has the PM been trying to achieve, in public expenditure?'

'Cuts, obviously.'

Sir Mark nodded. 'And why has there been so little success?'

Again the answer was obvious. 'Because of Civil Service obstruction.'

'And are all the Cabinet committed to this policy of cutting public expenditure?'

I wasn't sure if this was an attack on me. 'I think so, yes. *I* certainly am.'

He stared at me. He seemed unconvinced. Then he said: 'If that is so, why have virtually no Ministers achieved any real cuts?'

'Rome wasn't built in a day, you know.'

'Wrong. It's because the Ministers have gone native.'

'Oh I don't think . . .' I paused again. I had been about to disagree. But what had I just said to Sir Mark? Rome wasn't built in a day. The standard Civil Service answer when pressed for results. But surely *I've* not gone native?

'The Civil Service has house-trained the lot of you,' he said with a little sad smile.

'Well, some of us, perhaps. But I certainly haven't been . . .'

He interrupted me. 'Look, if a Minister were *really* trying to cut expenditure, how would he react to a book exposing massive government waste?'

'Well, he'd, he'd er . . . oh!' I realised I had no immediate answer. 'It would depend on . . . er . . .' I was stuck. So I asked him precisely what he was trying to say.

He didn't answer. That is to say, he answered obliquely. 'Do you know what the Civil Service is saying about you?'

I shook my head nervously.

'That you're a pleasure to work with.' A rush of mixed emotions overwhelmed me. First relief. Then pleasure and pride. Then, suddenly, a dreadful realisation of the awfulness of what he had just revealed!

'That's what Barbara Woodhouse says about her prize-winning spaniels,' he added.

I just sat there, struggling to grasp all the implications. My head was in a whirl.

Sir Mark continued destroying me, in that kindly voice of his. 'I've even heard Sir Humphrey Appleby say of you that you're worth your weight in gold. What does that suggest to you?'

It was only too clear what it suggested. I felt deeply miserable. 'You mean . . . I've failed utterly,' I said.

Sir Mark stood up, picked up my empty glass, and observed that I looked as if I needed another Scotch.

He returned it to me, I sipped it. Then he waited for me to speak again.

'And now,' I mumbled, 'I suppose the PM is not pleased with my performance at the Select Committee because I failed to cover up the failure?'

He sighed heavily and looked at the ceiling. He was becoming impatient. 'On the contrary, the PM is not pleased because you're covering up *too well*.'

This baffled me even more.

He explained. 'You're protecting the Civil Service. You're protecting Humphrey Appleby. The PM and I are doing our level best to expose why cuts in public expenditure are not taking place – and you're helping the Civil Service to defy the Government.'

'Am I?' My brain was reeling. How *could* I be doing that?

'You were wondering where Betty Oldham got the advance proofs of that book. And where Malcolm Rhodes got the inside information.' He smiled at me. And waited. I just stared at him, blankly. 'Can't you guess?' he asked eventually, with pity in his voice.

Suddenly the light dawned. 'You mean . . . the PM?' I whispered.

Sir Mark looked shocked. 'Of course not . . . not directly.'

'You mean,' I whispered again, '*you*?'

He sipped his drink and smiled.

So that was it. Whether wittingly or unwittingly, Malcom Rhodes and Betty Oldham had been put up to this by the PM's special adviser. And therefore, in effect, by the PM.

Therefore . . . therefore what? What do I do at the Select Committee? What does Number Ten want?

'There's only one course open to you,' Sir Mark added enigmatically. 'Absolute loyalty.'

'Ah,' I said, and then realised that my worries were not fully answered. 'But, er, who to?'

'That's your decision,' he said.

I think I know what is expected of me. I *think*.

October 15th

Today we met the Select Committee and I really put the cat among the pigeons.

They started with the plastic-coated copper wire in the heated sheds. Humphrey gave the answer that he and I had agreed he would give when we met earlier today. He said that the error actually occurred before some important facts were known and that he was able to answer the Committee that no such oversight could possibly occur again.

He asked me to agree.

My answer surprised him.

'Yes,' I said. 'Sir Humphrey's reply is absolutely correct. The correct *official* reply.' He glanced at me quickly. 'But I've been thinking very deeply since our last meeting' (which was true!) 'and really there is no doubt that this Committee is on to something.'

Humphrey turned and stared at me in astonishment.

'Of course there's waste,' I continued carefully, 'whatever the excuses that we can always find for individual cases. You have convinced me that our whole attitude is wrong.'

It was clear from the expression on his face that they had not convinced Sir Humphrey.

Nevertheless, I took my courage in both hands, and continued. 'Ministers and their civil servants cover up and defend where we should seek out and destroy.' Sir Humphrey was now absolutely aghast. 'I have spoken to Mr Malcom Rhodes, the author of this invaluable book, and he has agreed to give extensive evidence to an outside independent enquiry which I shall set up.' I could see Sir Humphrey out of the corner of my eye, putting his head in his hands. 'This will examine the whole of government administration, starting with my Department.'

The Chairman looked pleased. 'How does Sir Humphrey react to this?' he asked.

Sir Humphrey lifted his head from his hands and tried to speak. But no words came out.

I quickly answered for him. 'He is in full agreement. We work as a team, don't we Humphrey?' He nodded weakly. 'And I may say he's a pleasure to work with.'

Meanwhile, Betty Oldham had been thrown into a state of confusion. She was still trying to attack me, but there was no longer any reason to do so.

'But Minister,' she complained shrilly, 'this account of what's been going on doesn't square with what you were saying in your Washington speech about a ruthless war on waste.'

I was ready for that. In my most patronising manner I explained my position. 'Well Betty,' I said, 'I'm an old-fashioned sort of chap. I believe in things like loyalty. Whatever you say to them privately, you defend your chaps in public. Eh, Humphrey?'

Humphrey was now eyeing me as if I were a rabid dog.

'In that case,' pressed Mrs Oldham, 'aren't you being rather disloyal to them now?'

'No,' I explained charmingly, 'because in the end a Minister has a higher loyalty – a loyalty to Parliament, a loyalty to the nation. And that loyalty must take precedence, come what may, painful as it may be. My belief is that one is loyal to one's department and one's officials until the evidence is overwhelming. But I must now say in public what I have long been saying in private: that reforms can and will be carried out and I know that in Sir Humphrey I will find my staunchest ally. Isn't that so, Humphrey?'

'Yes Minister,' replied my staunchest ally in a thin choking voice of pure hatred.

After the meeting was over Humphrey, Bernard and I strolled back across Whitehall to the DAA. It was a lovely sunny autumn day with a cool breeze from the river. I was feeling fairly positive about it all, though desperately hoping that I had not misunderstood Sir Mark's intentions. It seemed to me that I had just been as loyal as could be to the PM, even though I'd upset Sir Humphrey more than somewhat.

Humphrey didn't speak all the way back to the Department. He was too angry. Bernard didn't either. He was too frightened.

In fact, nothing was said until we were back in my office. Humphrey had followed me into my room, so clearly he did have something to say to me.

I shut the door and looked at him expectantly.

'That was a big help Minister,' he began bitterly.

'I did my best,' I replied with a modest smile.

He stared at me, trying to understand why I had behaved as I had. He must have thought that I had gone out of my mind.

'You did your best for yourself, perhaps,' he said. 'So this is your idea of teamwork, is it? Most amusing, if I may say so.'

I felt I should explain. So I started to say that I had to do it, that I'd had no choice. He wouldn't listen.

'You had to do *what*? Cravenly admitting everything to that Committee. Don't you realise how utterly calamitous this has been for us?'

'Not for me, I hope,' I replied.

He shook his head, more in sorrow than in anger. 'You hope in vain, Minister. The Department will be up in arms – they will have very little confidence in you in future. And as for Number Ten – well, I shudder to think how the PM may react to a public admission of failure.'

I said nothing. As I sat there, wondering for a moment if I'd made a ghastly mistake, Bernard knocked and came in. He was holding an envelope.

'Excuse me, Minister, sorry to interrupt,' he said nervously, 'but here's a personal letter from the Prime Minister.'

He handed it to me. Sir Humphrey shook his head. I ripped it open. As I read it I was aware of Humphrey's voice.

'I did warn you,' it was saying. 'Bernard, perhaps you should give some thought to drafting a face-saving letter of resignation for the Minister.'

I read the letter. [*We reproduce it overleaf – Ed.*]

10 Downing Street

The Prime Minister 15th October

Dear Jim,

We haven't seen enough of each other lately. Would you be free to lunch at Chequers on Sunday? We shall be just the family. Do please bring Annie and Lucy.

I look forward so much to seeing you and perhaps we could catch up on each other's news.

Then I read it aloud.

Humphrey's face was a picture of confusion. 'I don't think I quite . . .' he said, and then the penny dropped. 'A conspiracy!' he hissed at me. 'That drink with Mark Spencer!'

I just smiled. The gamble had paid off. I reread the letter. It was a triumph. 'We haven't seen enough of each other lately . . . lunch

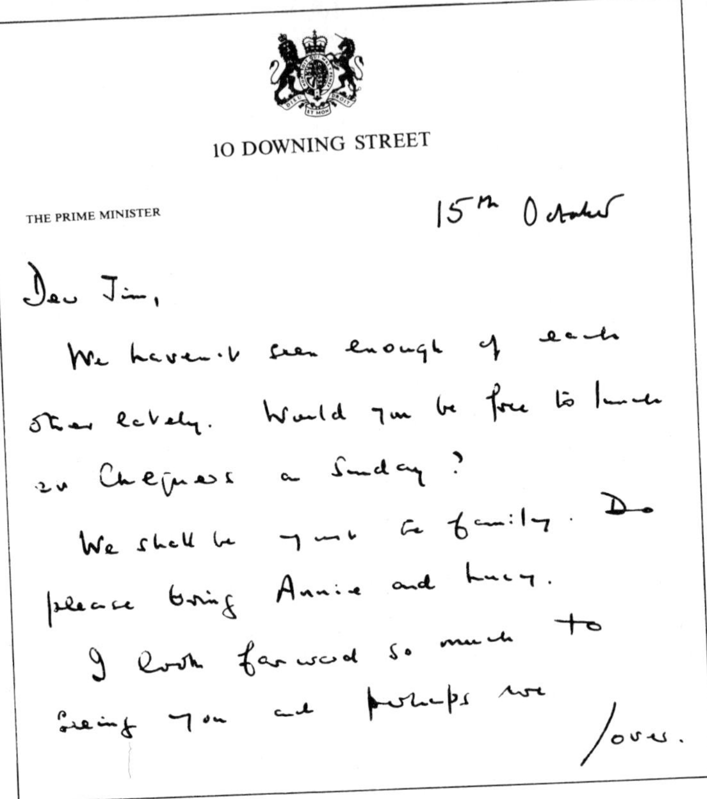

10 DOWNING STREET

THE PRIME MINISTER

15th October

Dear Jim,

We haven't seen enough of each other lately. Would you be free to lunch at Chequers on Sunday?

We shall be just the family. Do please bring Annie and Lucy.

I look forward so much to seeing you and perhaps we

/over.

at Chequers . . . just the family . . .' And it is *handwritten*.

'Do you know what this letter is worth, Humphrey?' I asked with quiet pride.

'I believe the going rate is thirty pieces of silver,' he replied nastily.

I shook my head. 'No Humphrey,' I said with supreme confidence. 'Integrity and loyalty have been rewarded.'

'Loyalty?' he sneered contemptuously. '*Loyalty*?'

I just couldn't resist rubbing his nose in it. 'Yes Humphrey. I supported you just the way you have always supported me. Isn't that so?'

He really didn't know how to answer that. A sort of snorting noise emanated from behind his clenched teeth.

'Did you say something, Humphrey?' I asked politely.

'I think,' said Bernard, 'that he said "Yes Minister."'

15

Equal Opportunities

October 23rd

Today was a fairly quiet Saturday afternoon in the constituency. The end of our first year and I was feeling that I've done pretty well, one way or another: no great cock-ups after my first-ever year in office (or at least, none which we haven't survived somehow) and I have a sense that I am beginning to understand the administrative machine at last.

You may think that a year is rather too long a period in which to achieve an understanding of the one department of which I am the titular head. In political terms, of course, that's true. Nonetheless if, had I become Chairman of ICI after a lifetime as a journalist and polytechnic lecturer and with no previous experience of running a major industry, I had a thorough understanding of how it all worked after only one year, I would be considered a great success.

We politicians blunder into Whitehall like babes in the wood. So few of us have ever run *anything* before, other than a medical practice, a law firm, or a political journal – and suddenly we find ourselves the head of a ministry with between twenty thousand and a hundred thousand employees.

All in all, I think we do pretty well! [*It was in this bullish mood that Hacker had agreed that day to give an interview to Cathy Webb, a fourth-former in one of the comprehensive schools in Hacker's constituency*[1] *– Ed.*]

However, my enthusiastic feelings about my first year in office were, I must admit, a little shaken after I was interviewed at teatime by a precocious schoolgirl for the school magazine.

She began by asking me how I had reached my present eminent position. I summarised my political career so far, culminating, I said, with carefully calculated modesty, 'with the moment when the

[1] Birmingham East.

Prime Minister saw fit, for whatever reason, to invite one to join the Cabinet and, well, here one is.' I didn't want to seem conceited. In my experience the young have a nose for that sort of thing.

She asked me if it isn't a terrific responsibility. I explained to her that if one chooses, as I have chosen, to dedicate one's life to public service, the service of others, then responsibility is one of those things one has to accept.

Cathy was full of admiration, I could see it in her eyes. 'But all that power . . .' she murmured.

'I know, I know,' I replied, attempting the casual air of a man who is used to it. 'Frightening, in a way. But actually, Cathy . . .' (I was careful to use her name, of course, because it showed I did not consider myself above my constituents, even schoolchildren – future voters, after all) '. . . this power actually makes one rather humble!'

Annie hurried in and interrupted me. The phone had been ringing elsewhere in the house.

'Bernard just rang, oh Humble One,' she said. I *wish* she wouldn't send me up like that in front of other people. I mean, I've got a pretty good sense of humour, but there is a limit.

She went on to tell me that Central House[1] wanted me to see some programme on television. On BBC2.

I had already remembered the wretched programme, and made a note *not* to watch.

'Oh Lord,' I said. 'Maureen Watkins MP. One of our backbenchers – not my favourite lady, a rampaging feminist, I don't think I'll bother.'

In the nick of time I noticed Cathy making a note. I had to explain that my remark was 'off the record', a concept that she seemed to have some difficulty with. It reminded me how lucky we are to have those well-trained lobby correspondents to deal with most of the time.

Anyway, she crossed it out. But to my surprise she spoke up in defence of Maureen Watkins.

'I like her,' she said. 'Don't you think that women are still exploited? All of my friends in 4B think that they are exploited at work and at home and that it's still a world designed by men and run by men for the convenience of men.'

I was slightly surprised by this little speech. It didn't sound entirely . . . home-grown, if you know what I mean. Cathy must

[1] Hacker's Party HQ.

have realised, because she had the grace to add: 'You know – like she says.'

I must say, I'm getting a bit fed up with all this feminist crap. Nowadays, if you so much as compliment a woman on her appearance, you're told you're a sexist. This dreadful lesbian lobby is getting everywhere.

So I decided to argue the point with young Cathy. 'Surely it's not like that any longer,' I said with a warm smile. 'Anyway, she doesn't carry any weight in the House, thank goodness.'

'Not in the House, perhaps,' interjected Annie. 'It's full of men.'

I thanked my dear wife for her helpful comment, renewed my smile in Cathy's direction, and asked her if there was anything else she wanted to know.

'Just one last question,' she said. 'As a Cabinet Minister with all this power, what have you actually achieved?'

I was pleased to answer that question. It seemed an easy one. 'Achieved?' I repeated reflectively. 'Well, all sorts of things. Membership of the Privy Council, membership of the party policy committee . . .'

She interrupted. It seemed that she wanted to make the question more specific. What, she wanted to know, had I actually done that makes life better for other people.

Well, of course, I was completely nonplussed. Children ask the oddest questions. Right out of left field, as our American allies would say. Certainly no one had ever asked me such a question before.

'Makes life *better*?' I repeated.

'Yes,' she said.

'For *other people*?' I thought hard, but absolutely nothing sprang to mind. I tried to think as I spoke. 'There must be a number of things. I mean, that's what one's whole job is about, eighteen hours a day, seven days a week . . .'

Cathy interrupted me as I made the mistake of momentarily drawing breath. She has a future with the BBC, that kid! 'Could you just give me one or two examples, though? Otherwise my article might be a bit boring.'

'Examples. Yes, of course I can,' I said, and found that I couldn't.

Her pencil was poised expectantly above her lined exercise book. I realised that some explanation was called for.

'Well,' I began, 'you see, it's difficult to know where to start. So much of government is collective decisions, all of us together, the best minds in the country hammering it out.'

She seemed dissatisfied with my explanation.

'Yes,' she said doubtfully, 'but what is it you'll look back on afterwards and say "I did that"? You know, like a writer can look at his books.'

Persistent little blighter.

I started to explain the facts of political life. 'Yes, well, politics is a complex business, Cathy.' I was careful to use her name again. 'Lots of people have to have their say. Things take time. Rome wasn't built in a day.'

As I looked at her face, I could see an air of disappointment written across it. [*In view of the insight that Hacker's frequently mixed metaphors give us into the clouded state of his mind, we have retained them unless clarity is threatened – Ed.*] I began to feel slightly disappointed with myself. I realised that I could not give a proper answer to her question. I also began to feel more than a little irritated that this wretched child should have produced these feelings of inadequacy in me. Enough was enough. It was time to bring the interview to an end.

I pointed out that time was flying, and that I still had to do my boxes. I hustled her out, emphasising how much I'd enjoyed our little talk, and reminding her that she had agreed to let me approve the article before it was printed.

I returned and sat down heavily in my favourite fireside armchair. I was feeling very brought down.

'Bright kid,' commented Annie.

'That's the last time I ever give an interview to a school magazine,' I responded. 'She asked me some very difficult questions.'

'They weren't difficult,' said Annie firmly. 'Just innocent. She was assuming that there is some moral basis to your activities.'

I was puzzled. 'But there is,' I replied.

Annie laughed. 'Oh Jim, don't be silly.'

I wasn't amused. I gazed gloomily into the carefully arranged embers of the artificial gas log fire.

'What are you sighing for?' Annie asked.

I tried to explain.

'What *have* I achieved?' I asked. 'Cathy was right.'

Annie suggested that, since Cathy and I had agreed I had all that power, I should go and achieve something forthwith. She *will* persist in making these silly suggestions.

'You know I'm only a Cabinet Minister,' I snapped.

Annie smiled. 'It really does make you humble.'

My humility is not in question, and never has been. The point is that I can't change anything in the foreseeable future. Changing things means getting bills through Parliament, and all the time's been taken up for the next two years.

Annie was unimpressed.

'Why don't you reform the Civil Service?' she suggested.

She makes it sound like one simple little task instead of a lifetime of dedicated carnage. Which reforms in particular did she have in mind, I wondered? Anyway, any real reform of the Civil Service is impossible, as I explained to her.

'Suppose I thought up fifty terrific reforms. Who will have to implement them?'

She saw the point at once. 'The Civil Service,' we said in unison, and she nodded sympathetically. But Annie doesn't give up easily.

'All right,' she suggested, 'not fifty reforms. Just one.'

'One?'

'If you achieve *one* important reform of the Civil Service – that would be something.'

Something? It would get into the *Guinness Book of Records*. I asked her what she was proposing.

'Make them put more women in top civil servants' jobs. Women are half the population. Why shouldn't they be half the Permanent Secretaries? How many women are there at the top?'

I tried to think. Certainly not many. I'd hardly come across any.

'Equal opportunities,' I said. I liked the sound it made. It has a good ring to it, that phrase. 'I'll have a go,' I said. 'Why not? There's a principle at stake.'

Annie was delighted. 'You mean you're going to do something out of pure principle?'

I nodded.

'Oh Jim,' she said, with real love and admiration in her voice.

'Principles,' I added, 'are excellent vote-winners.'

Shortly afterwards, Annie developed a headache and went to bed unusually early. I wanted to pursue the conversation with her but she seemed to have lost interest. Odd, that!

October 25th

Today I learned a thing or two about equal opportunities, or the lack of them, in the Civil Service.

Quite coincidentally I had a meeting with Sarah Harrison, who is the only woman Under-Secretary in the DAA.

Sarah really is a splendid person. Very attractive, intelligent, and about thirty-nine or forty years old, which is pretty young for an Under-Sec. She has a brisk and – I suppose – slightly masculine approach to meetings and so forth, but seems to be jolly attractive and feminine in spite of all that.

She has brought me a very difficult letter of complaint from one of the opposition front bench on a constituency matter; something to do with special powers for local authorities for land development in special development areas. I had no idea what it all meant or what I was supposed to do about it.

It turned out that I didn't have to do *anything* about it. She explained that some of the facts were wrong, and other points were covered by statutory requirements so that I didn't have any alternatives anyway.

This is the kind of Civil Service advice that makes a Minister's life easy. No decision needed, not even an apology required. Nothing to do at all, in fact. Great.

I asked her to draft a reply, and she'd already done it. She handed it across my desk for me to sign. It was impeccable. I found myself wondering why they don't make more Under-Secretaries like her – and realised that this was the moment to actually *find out*. So I asked her how many women are there at the top of the Civil Service.

She had an immediate answer to that question. 'None of the Permanent Secretaries. Four out of one hundred and fifty odd Deputy Secretaries.'

I wondered silently if there are any that aren't odd. Presumably not, not by the time they become Deputy Secretaries.

I asked her about her grade – Under-Secretary. As I expected, she knew the precise figure.

'Oh, there's twenty-seven of us.'

That seemed not so bad. 'Out of how many?' I asked.

'Five hundred and seventy-eight.'

I was shocked. Appalled. I wonder why *she* wasn't. At least, she didn't seem to be, she was answering these questions in her usual bright, cheerful, matter-of-fact sort of way.

'Doesn't this appal you?' I asked.

'Not really,' she smiled. 'I think it's comic. But then I think the whole Civil Service is comic. It's run by men, after all.'

As a man who was about to devote himself to the cause of

women's rights, I felt able to rise above that one. I was on her side.

'What can you do about it?' I asked. She looked blank. I rephrased it. 'What can *I* do about it?' I said.

She looked me straight in the eye, with a cool clear gaze. Her eyes were a beautiful deep blue. And she wears an awfully nice perfume.

'Are you serious, Minister?'

I nodded.

'It's easy,' she said. 'Bring top women from the professions and commerce and industry, straight into the top grades. The pay is quite good for women. There's long holidays, index-linked pensions. You'd get a lot of very high-quality applicants.'

'And they could do this job?' I asked.

'Of course.' She seemed surprised at the question.' I mean, with all due respect,[1] if you can make a journalist MP into an instant Minister, why can't you make a senior partner of a top legal firm into an Under-Secretary?' [*Hacker, of course, before he became a Minister, had been a journalist, editing the journal* Reform – *Ed.*] 'Most of the work here only needs about two O-Levels anyway,' she added.

Bernard came in to remind me of my next appointment. He escorted Sarah out. 'Bernard,' I said.

'Yes Minister?' he replied as always. I've been trying to establish a closer personal relationship with him for nearly a year now, why does he persist in such formality?

'I wish you'd call me Jim,' I complained. 'At least when we're alone.'

He nodded earnestly. 'I'll try to remember that, Minister,' he replied. Hopeless!

I waved the papers from my meeting with Sarah. 'Sarah says this complaint is complete nonsense,' I informed him. 'And she's done a reply.'

Bernard was pleased. 'Fine, we can CGSM it.'

'CGSM?' I asked.

'Civil Service code,' he explained. 'It stands for Consignment of Geriatric Shoe Manufacturers.' I waited for the explanation. 'A load of old cobblers,' he added helpfully.[2]

[1] That ominous phrase from a civil servant.

[2] Bernard Wolley was, for once in his life, inaccurate in his pedantry. A cobbler is one who mends footwear, and therefore it is widely held by modern scholars who have researched this part of the Hacker diaries that CGSM stood for a

I took the paper from him.

'I am not a civil servant,' I remarked loftily.' I shall write my own code on it.'

I wrote 'Round Objects' in the margin.

October 27th

Today I had a meeting with Sir Humphrey about equal opportunities. But I had taken care not to let on in advance – in his diary Bernard had written 'Staffing'.

He came in, smiling, confident, benign, patrician, apparently without a care in the world. So I decided to shake him up a bit, then and there.

'Humphrey,' I began, 'I have made a policy decision.'

He froze, half-way down into his chair, in a sort of Groucho Marx position, eyeing me warily with pursed lips.

[*Presumably Hacker intended to say that Sir Humphrey eyed him warily, and that simultaneously he had pursed his lips – Ed.*]

'A policy decision, Minister?' He recovered himself rapidly and pretended to be pleased with this piece of news.

'Yes,' I replied cheerfully. 'I am going to do something about the number of women in the Civil Service.'

'Surely there aren't all that many?' He looked puzzled.

Bernard hastened to explain.

'The Minister thinks we need *more*.'

'Many more,' I added firmly.

Now Sir Humphrey really *was* taken aback. His mind was racing. He just couldn't see what I was driving at. 'But we're actually quite well up to Establishment on typists, cleaners, tea-ladies . . .' He petered out, then sought advice. 'Any ideas, Bernard?'

'Well,' said Bernard helpfully, 'we are a bit short of temporary secretaries.'

Clearly Bernard had not got the point either.

'I'm talking about Permanent Secretaries,' I said.

Sir Humphrey was stunned. He seemed unable to formulate a sentence in reply. So I went on.

'We need some female mandarins.' Sir Humphrey was still mentally pole-axed. He didn't respond at all. Bernard also seemed com-

(*continued from previous page*)
Consignment of Geriatric Shoe Menders. An alternative possibility is that Woolley was merely being facetious, although this possibility has not found favour with the academic community.

pletely baffled. He sought clarification.

'Sort of . . satsumas, Minister?' he enquired desperately.

I'm never quite sure if Bernard has a highly-intelligent deadpan wit, or is faintly moronic. So I merely told him to sit down.

'How many Permanent Secretaries,' I asked Sir Humphrey, 'are there at the moment?'

'Forty-one, I believe.'

A precise answer.

'Forty-one,' I agreed pleasantly. 'And how many are women?'

Suddenly Sir Humphrey's memory seemed to fail him. 'Well, broadly speaking, not having the exact figures to hand, I'm not exactly sure.'

'Well, approximately?' I encouraged him to reply.

'Well,' he said cautiously, '*approximately* none.'

Close but no cigar, as our American allies would say. *Precisely* none was the correct answer. And Sir Humphrey knew that only too well. [*Hacker was right. The Permanent Secretaries form an exclusive little club in all but name, so exclusive that a newly-nominated Permanent Secretary could, in effect, be blackballed. This would be an 'informal' process not fully clear to their political 'Lords and Masters', but nonetheless effective for all that – Ed.*]

I was beginning to enjoy myself. 'And I believe there are one hundred and fifty Deputy Secretaries,' I continued gleefully. 'Do you know how many of them are women?'

Sir Humphrey hedged. Either he genuinely didn't know the answer to this one, or wasn't going to say if he did. 'It's difficult to say,' was the best reply he could manage.

This surprised me. 'Why is it difficult?' I wanted to know.

Bernard tried to be helpful again. 'Well, there's a lot of old women among the men.'

I ignored him. 'Four,' I said to Humphrey. 'Four women Dep. Secs out of one hundred and fifty-three, to be precise.'

Sir Humphrey seemed impressed that there were so many. 'Are there indeed,' he said, slightly wide-eyed.

I had enjoyed my little bit of fun. Now I came bluntly to the point. I had a proposal to make. I've been thinking about it since my first conversation with Sarah.

'I am going to announce,' I announced, 'a quota of twenty-five per cent women Deputy Secretaries and Permanent Secretaries to be achieved within the next four years.'

I think Sir Humphrey was rattled, but it was hard to tell because he's such a smooth operator.

'Minister, I am obviously in total sympathy with your objectives,' he said. This remark naturally increased my suspicions.

'Good,' I said.

'Of course there should be more women at the top. Of *course*. And all of us are deeply concerned by the apparent imbalance.' I noted the skilful use of the word 'apparent'. 'But these things take time.'

I was ready for that one. 'I want to make a start right away,' I replied.

'I agree wholeheartedly,' responded Sir Humphrey enthusiastically. 'And I propose that we make an immediate start by setting up an interdepartmental committee . . .'

This was not what I meant, and he knew it. I told him firmly that I didn't want the usual delaying tactics.

'This needs a sledgehammer,' I declared. 'We must cut through the red tape.'

Bloody Bernard piped up again. 'You can't cut tape with a sledgehammer, it would just . . .' and then he made a sort of squashing gesture. I squashed *him* with a look.

Humphrey seemed upset that I'd accused him of delaying tactics. 'Minister, you do me an injustice,' he complained. 'I was not about to suggest delaying tactics.'

Perhaps I had done him an injustice. I apologised, and waited to see what he *was* about to suggest.

'I was merely going to suggest,' he murmured in a slightly hurt tone, 'that if we are to have a twenty-five per cent quota of women we must have a much larger intake at the recruitment stage. So that eventually we'll have twenty-five per cent in the top jobs.'

'When?' I asked.

I knew the answer before he said it. 'In twenty-five years.'

'No, Humphrey,' I said, still smiling and patient. 'I don't think you've quite got my drift. I'm talking about *now*.'

At last Sir Humphrey got the point. 'Oh,' he said, staggered. 'You mean – *now*!'

'Got it in one, Humphrey,' I replied with my most patronising smile.

'But Minister,' he smiled smoothly, 'it takes time to do things now.' And he smiled patronisingly back at me. It's amazing how quickly he recovers his poise.

I've been hearing that kind of stuff for nearly a year now. It no longer cuts any ice with me. 'Ah yes,' I said, 'the three articles of Civil Service faith: it takes longer to do things quickly, it's more expensive to do things cheaply, and it's more democratic to do things secretly. No Humphrey, I've suggested four years. That's masses of time.'

He shook his head sadly. 'Dear me no, Minister, I don't mean political time, I mean *real* time.' He sat comfortably back in his chair, gazed at the ceiling, and then continued in a leisurely sort of way. 'Civil servants are grown like oak trees, not mustard and cress. They bloom and ripen with the seasons.' I'd never heard such pretentious crap. But he was in full flow. 'They mature like . . .'

'Like you?' I interrupted facetiously.

'I was going to say,' he replied tartly, 'that they mature like an old port.'

'Grimsby, perhaps?'

He smiled a tiny humourless smile. 'I *am* being serious, Minister.'

He certainly was. Apart from being entirely serious about his own importance, he was seriously trying to use all this flimflam to get me to lose track of my new proposal – or, as I think of it, my new policy decision. I decided to go straight for the jugular.

'I foresaw this problem,' I said firmly. 'So I propose that we solve it by bringing in top women from outside the Service to fill vacancies in the top grades.'

Humphrey's face was a picture. He was absolutely aghast. The colour drained out of his face.

'Minister . . . I don't think I quite . . .' His voice petered out as he reached the word 'understood'.

I was enjoying myself hugely.

'Watch my lips move,' I said helpfully, and pointed to my mouth with my forefinger. 'We . . . will . . . bring . . . women . . . in . . . from . . . out- . . . side!' I said it very slowly and carefully, like a deranged speech therapist. He just sat there and stared at me, transfixed, a rabbit with a snake.

Finally he pulled himself together.

'But,' he began, 'the whole strength of our system is that it is incorruptible, pure, unsullied by outside influences.'

I just can't see the sense in that old chestnut and I said so. 'People move from one job to another throughout industry, Humphrey – why should the Civil Service be different?'

'It *is* different. The Civil Service demands subtlety . . .'

'Discretion,' said Bernard.

'Devotion to duty,' said Humphrey.

'Soundness!' said Bernard.

'*Soundness*!' repeated Sir Humphrey emphatically. 'Well said, Bernard. *Soundness*.' Bernard had clearly hit upon one of the key compliments in the Civil Service vocabulary.

[*Bernard Woolley, of course, had an important vested interest in this conversation. If Hacker's policy of bringing women in from outside were implemented, this might well have an adverse effect on the promotion prospects of more junior civil servants such as Woolley. And if women could be brought in to fill top jobs from outside, so could men. What, then, would Bernard Woolley's prospects have been? – Ed.*]

Sir Humphrey went on to explain that civil servants require endless patience and boundless understanding, they need to be able to change horses midstream, constantly, as the politicians change their minds. Perhaps it was my imagination, but it seemed to me that he was putting the word 'minds' in quotes – as if to imply, 'as politicians change what they are pleased to call their minds'.

I asked him if he had all these talents. With a modest shrug he replied: 'Well, it's just that one has been properly . . .'

'Matured,' I interjected. 'Like Grimsby.'

'Trained.' He corrected me with a tight-lipped smile.

'Humphrey,' I said, 'ask yourself honestly if the system is not at fault. *Why* are there so few women Deputy Secretaries?'

'They keep leaving,' he explained, with an air of sweet reason, 'to have babies. And things.'

This struck me as a particularly preposterous explanation, 'Leaving to have babies? At the age of nearly fifty? Surely not!'

But Sir Humphrey appeared to believe it. Desperately he absolved himself of all responsibility or knowledge. 'Really Minister, I don't know. Really I don't. I'm on your side. We do indeed need more women at the top.'

'Good,' I replied decisively, 'because I'm not waiting twenty-five years. We've got a vacancy for a Deputy Secretary here, haven't we?'

He was instantly on his guard. He even thought cautiously for a moment before replying.

'Yes.'

'Very well. We shall appoint a woman. Sarah Harrison.'

Again he was astounded, or aghast, or appalled. Something like that. Definitely not pleased, anyway. But he contented himself with merely repeating her name, in a quiet controlled voice.

'Sarah Harrison?'

'Yes,' I said. 'I think she's very able. Don't you?'

'Very able, for a woman. For a person.' He had corrected himself with scarcely a hesitation.

'And,' I added, 'she has ideas. She's an original thinker.'

'I'm afraid that's true,' agreed Sir Humphrey, 'but she doesn't let it interfere with her work.'

So I asked him what he had against her. He insisted that he had *nothing* against her, that he was totally *pro* her. He confirmed that she is an excellent worker, and he pointed out that he is a great supporter of hers and had in fact advocated her promotion to Under-Secretary only last year at a very early age.

'Would you say she is an outstanding Under-Secretary?' I asked him.

'Yes,' he replied, without equivocation.

'So,' I said, 'on balance it's a good idea, isn't it?'

'On balance? Yes . . . and no.'

I told him that that was not a clear answer. He said it was a balanced answer. Touché. Then he went on to explain that the point is, in his opinion, that she's too young and it's not her turn yet.

I leaped upon that argument. I'd been expecting it. 'That is precisely what's *wrong* with the Civil Service – Buggins' Turn! Whereas the best people should be promoted, as soon as possible.'

'Exactly,' agreed Sir Humphrey, 'as soon as it's their turn.'

'Rubbish. Napoleon ruled Europe in his thirties. Alexander the Great conquered the world in his twenties.'

'They would have made *very* poor Deputy Secretaries,' remarked Sir Humphrey contemptuously.

'At least they didn't wait their turn,' I pointed out.

'And look what happened to them.' Sir Humphrey clearly thought he'd won our little debate. So I decided to make the argument rather more personal.

'Look what's happened to *us*,' I said calmly. 'Instead of this country being run by bright energetic youthful brains it is being run by tired routine-bound fifty-five-year-olds who just want a quiet life.'

Humphrey stared at me coldly. 'Had you anyone specific in mind, Minister?'

I smiled. 'Yes . . . and no, Humphrey.' Game, set and match to yours truly, I felt.

Sir Humphrey decided to move the debate back to the specific problem. He informed me, in his most matter-of-fact fashion, that Sarah Harrison is an excellent civil servant and a bright hope for the future. But he also reiterated that she is our most junior Under-Secretary and that he cannot and will not recommend her for promotion.

There was a clear implication in that final comment that it was ultimately up to him, and that I should mind my own business.

I told him he was a sexist.

I'm surprised he didn't laugh at me. Surprisingly, this trendy insult seemed to cut him to the quick. He was outraged.

'Minister,' he complained bitterly, 'how can you say such a thing? I'm very pro-women. Wonderful people, women. And Sarah Harrison is a dear lady. I'm one of her most ardent admirers. But the fact is that if the cause of women is to be advanced it must be done with tact and care and discretion. She is our only woman contender for a top job. We mustn't push her too fast. Women find top jobs very difficult, you know.'

He *is* a sexist.

'Can you hear yourself?' I asked incredulously.

Unabashed, he continued in the same vein. 'If women were able to be good Permanent Secretaries, there would be more of them, wouldn't there? Stands to reason.'

I've never before heard a reply that so totally begs the question.

'No Humphrey!' I began, wondering where to begin.

But on he went. 'I'm no anti-feminist. I love women. Some of my best friends are women. My wife, indeed.' Methinks Sir Humphrey doth protest too much. And on and on he went. 'Sarah Harrison is not very experienced, Minister, and her two children are still of school age, they might get mumps.'

Another daft argument. Anybody can be temporarily off work through their own ill-health, not just their children's. 'You might get shingles, Humphrey, if it comes to that,' I said.

He missed my point. 'I might indeed, Minister, if you continue in this vein,' he muttered balefully. 'But what if her children caused her to miss work all the time?'

I asked him frankly if this were likely. I asked if she were likely to have reached the rank of Under-Secretary if her children kept having mumps. I pointed out that she was the best person for the job.

He didn't disagree about that. But he gave me an indignant warning: 'Minister, if you go around promoting women just because they're the best person for the job, you could create a lot of resentment throughout the whole Civil Service.'

'But not from the women in it,' I pointed out.

'Ah,' said Sir Humphrey complacently, 'but there are so few of them that it wouldn't matter so much.'

A completely circular argument. Perhaps this is what is meant by moving in Civil Service circles.

[*Later in the week Sir Humphrey Appleby had lunch with Sir Arnold Robinson, the Cabinet Secretary, at the Athenaeum Club. Sir Humphrey, as always, made a note on one of his pieces of memo paper – Ed.*]

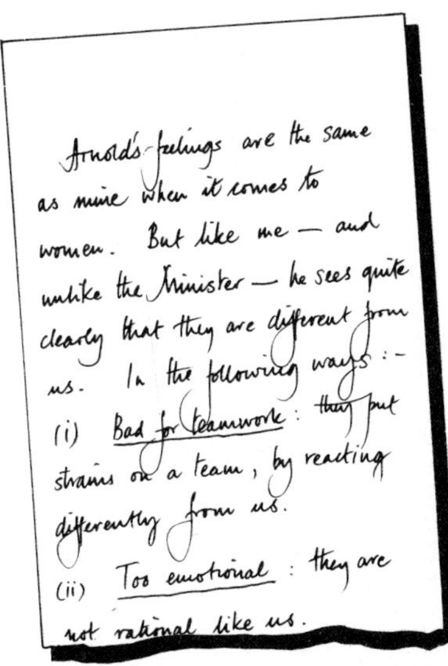

Arnold's feelings are the same as mine when it comes to women. But like me — and unlike the Minister — he sees quite clearly that they are different from us. In the following ways:-

(i) Bad for teamwork: they put strains on a team, by reacting differently from us.

(ii) Too emotional: they are not rational like us.

Arnold's feelings are the same as mine when it comes to women. But like me – and unlike the Minister – he sees quite clearly that they are different from us. In the following ways:–

1. *Bad for teamwork:* they put strains on a team, by reacting differently from us.
2. *Too emotional:* they are not rational like us.
3. *Can't be Reprimanded:* they either get into a frightful bate or start blubbing.
4. *Can be Reprimanded:* some of them can be, but are frightfully hard and butch and not in the least bit attractive.
5. *Prejudices:* they are full of them.
6. *Silly Generalisations:* they make them.
7. *Stereotypes:* they think in them.

I asked Arnold for his advice. Arnold suggested that I lecture the Minister at such length on the matter that he becomes bored and loses interest in the whole idea.

There is a remote chance of success for such a plan. But Hacker does not get bored easily. He even finds *himself* interesting. They all do in fact. All the ones who listen to what they're saying of course. On second thoughts, that is by no means all of them.

But the fact remains that Hacker's boredom threshold is high. He even reads most of the stuff that we put into his red boxes, with apparent interest!

Arnold also suggested that standard second ploy: to tell the Minister that the Unions won't wear it. [*'It' being the importation of women into the Service to fill some top jobs – Ed.*] We agreed that this was a line of action worth pursuing.

We also discussed the feminine angle. His wife [*the Minister's, that is – Ed.*] is in favour of promoting the Harrison female, and may well – from what I know of Mrs Hacker – be behind all this. However, she may not know that Harrison is extremely attractive. I'm sure Mrs H. and Mrs H. have never met. This could well be fruitful.

I pointed out that the Cabinet will be in favour of Hacker's proposal. But we agreed that we could doubtless get the Cabinet to change their minds. They change their minds fairly easily. Just like a lot of women. Thank God they don't blub.

[*Appleby Papers 37/6PJ/457*]

[*It is interesting to compare Sir Humphrey's self-confident account of this luncheon with the notes made by Sir Arnold Robinson on Sir Humphrey's report, which were found among the Civil Service files at Walthamstow – Ed.*]

Told Appleby that I wasn't impressed with his Minister's plan to bring in women from outside, novel though the idea may be.

[*'Wasn't impressed' would be an example of Civil Service understatement. Readers may imagine the depth of feeling behind such a phrase. The use of the Civil Service killer word 'novel' is a further indication of Sir Arnold's hostility – Ed.*]

Suggested that he bore the Minister out of the idea. Appleby claimed that this would not work. Probably correctly.

So I made various other suggestions. For instance, the Trade Union ploy: suggesting to the Minister that the Unions won't wear it. Appleby missed the point completely. He told me that the Unions would like it. He's probably right, but it was completely beside the point!

I also suggested pointing the Minister's wife in the right direction. And suggested that we try to ensure that the Cabinet throws it out. Appleby agreed to try all these plans. But I am disturbed that he had thought of none of them himself.

Must keep a careful eye on H.A. Is early retirement a possibility to be discussed with the PM?

A.R.

Staff Report (Cont.) **CR36**

7. **LONG TERM POTENTIAL**

At present, he/~~she~~ seems

- [x] unlikely to progress further — 1
- or [ ] to have potential to rise about one grade but probably no further — 2
- or [ ] to have potential to rise two or three grades — 3
- or [ ] to have exceptional potential — 4

8. **GENERAL REMARKS**

Please provide any additional relevant information here, drawing attention to any particular strengths or weaknesses.

Told Appleby that I wasn't impressed with his Minister's plan to bring in women from outside, novel though the idea may be.

Suggested that he bore the Minister out of the idea. Appleby claimed that this would not work. Probably correctly.

So I made various other suggestions. For instance, the Trade Union ploy: suggesting to the Minister that the Unions won't wear it. Appleby missed the point completely. He told me that the Unions would like it. He's probably right, but it was completely beside the point!

[*Naturally, Sir Humphrey never saw these notes, because no civil servant is ever shown his report except in wholly exceptional circumstances.*

And equally naturally, Hacker never knew of the conversation between Sir Arnold and Sir Humphrey over luncheon at the Athenaeum.

It was in this climate of secrecy that our democracy used to operate. Civil servants' word for secrecy was 'discretion'. They argued that discretion was the better part of valour – Ed.]

[*Hacker's diary continues – Ed.*]

November 1st

Sir Humphrey walked into my office today, sat down and made the most startling remark that I have yet heard from him.

'Minister,' he said, 'I have come to the conclusion that you were right.'

I've been nothing but right ever since I took on this job, and finally, after nearly a year, it seemed that he was beginning to take me seriously.

However, I was immediately suspicious, and I asked him to amplify his remark. I had not the least idea to which matter he was referring. Of course, asking Humphrey to amplify his remarks is often a big mistake.

'I am fully-seized of your ideas and have taken them on board and I am now positively against discrimination against women and positively in favour of positive discrimination in their favour – discriminating discrimination of course.'

I think it was something like that. I got the gist of it anyway.

Then he went on, to my surprise: 'I understand a view is forming at the very highest level that this should happen.' I think he must have been referring to the PM. Good news.

Then, to my surprise he asked why the matter of equal opportunities for women should not apply to politics as well as the Civil Service. I was momentarily confused. But he explained that there are only twenty-three women MPs out of a total of six hundred and fifty. I agreed that this too is deplorable, but, alas, there is nothing at all that we can do about that.

He remarked that these figures were an indication of discrimination against women by the political parties. Clearly, he argued, the way they select candidates is fundamentally discriminatory.

I found myself arguing in defence of the parties. It was a sort of reflex action. 'Yes and no,' I agreed. 'You know, it's awfully difficult for women to be MPs – long hours, debates late at night, being away from home a lot. Most women have a problem with that and with homes, and husbands.'

'And mumps,' he added helpfully.

I realised that he was sending me up. And simultaneously trying to suggest that I too am a sexist. An absurd idea, of course, and I told him so in no uncertain terms.

I steered the discussion towards specific goals and targets. I asked what we would do to start implementing our plan.

Humphrey said that the first problem would be that the unions won't agree to this quota.

I was surprised to hear this, and immediately suggested that we get them in to talk about it.

This suggestion made him very anxious. 'No, no, no,' he said. 'No. That would stir up a hornet's nest.'

I couldn't see why. Either Humphrey was paranoid about the unions – or it was just a ploy to frighten me. I suspect the latter. [*Hacker was now learning fast – Ed.*]

The reason I suspect a trick is that he offered no explanation as to why we shouldn't talk to the union leaders. Instead he went off on an entirely different tack.

'If I might suggest we be realistic about this . . .' he began.

I interrupted. 'By realistic, do you mean drop the whole scheme?'

'No!' he replied vehemently. 'Certainly not! But perhaps a pause to regroup, a lull in which we reassess the position and discuss alternative strategies, a space of time for mature reflection and deliberation . . .'

I interrupted again. 'Yes, you mean drop the whole scheme.' This time I wasn't asking a question. And I dealt with the matter with what I consider to be exemplary firmness. I told him that I had set my hand to the plough and made my decision. 'We shall have a twenty-five per cent quota of women in the open structure in four years from now. And to start with I shall promote Sarah Harrison to Dep. Sec.'

He was frightfully upset. 'No Minister!' he cried in vain. 'I'm sure that's the wrong decision.'

This was quite a remarkable reaction from the man who had begun the meeting by telling me that I was absolutely right.

I emphasised that I could not be moved on this matter because it is a matter of principle. I added that I shall have a word with my Cabinet colleagues, who are bound to support me as there are a lot of votes in women's rights.

'I thought you said it was a matter of principle, Minister, not of votes.'

He was being too clever by half. I was able to explain, loftily, that I was referring to my Cabinet colleagues. For me it *is* a matter of principle.

A very satisfactory meeting. I don't think he can frustrate me on this one.

November 2nd

Had a strange evening out with Annie. She collected me from the office at 5.30, because we had to go to a party drinks 'do' at Central House.

I had to keep her waiting a while because my last meeting of the day ran late, and I had a lot of letters to sign.

Signing letters, by the way, is an extraordinary business because there are so many of them. Bernard lays them out in three or four long rows, all running the full length of my conference table – which seats twelve a side. Then I whiz along the table, signing the letters as I go. It's quicker to move me than them. As I go Bernard collects the signed letters up behind me, and moves a letter from the second row to replace the signed and collected one in the first row. Then I whiz back along the table, signing the next row.

I don't actually read them all that carefully. It shows the extent of my trust for Bernard. Sometimes I think that I might sign absolutely anything if I were in a big enough hurry.

Bernard had an amusing bit of news for me today.

'You remember that letter you wrote "Round objects" on?' he asked.

'Yes.'

'Well,' he said with a slight smile, 'it's come back from Sir Humphrey's office. He commented on it.'

And he showed me the letter. In the margin Humphrey had written: 'Who is Round and to what does he object?'

Anyway, I digress. While all this signing was going on, Annie was given a sherry by Humphrey in his office. I thought it was jolly nice of him to take the trouble to be sociable when he could have been on the 5.59 for Haslemere. Mind you, I think he likes Annie and anyway perhaps he thinks it's politic to chat up the Minister's wife.

But, as I say, Annie and I had a strange evening. She seemed rather cool and remote. I asked her if anything was wrong, but she wouldn't say what. Perhaps she resented my keeping her waiting so long, because I know she finds Humphrey incredibly boring. Still, that's the penalty you have to pay if you're married to a successful man.

[*A note in Sir Humphrey's diary reveals the true cause of Mrs Hacker's disquiet – Ed.*]

Had a sherry with Mrs Hacker this evening. The Minister was delayed signing letters, which was not entirely coincidental. Naturally I had taken care to ensure that his previous meeting overran somewhat.

I brought the conversation around to the matter of changing and reforming the Civil Service. As expected, she was pretty keen on the whole idea.

Immediately she asked me about the promotion of the Harrison female.

Tuesday 2 NOVEMBER

Had a sherry with Mrs Hacker this evening. The Minister was delayed signing letters, which was not entirely coincidental. Naturally I had taken care to ensure that his previous meeting overran somewhat.

I brought the conversation around to the matter of changing and reforming the Civil Service. As expected, she was pretty keen on the whole idea.

'What about promoting this woman that Jim was talking about?'

I talked about it all with great enthusiasm. I said that the Minister certainly has an eye for talent. I said that Sarah was undoubtedly very talented. And thoroughly delightful. A real charmer.

I continued for many minutes in the same vein. I said how much I admired this new generation of women civil servants compared with the old battle-axes of yesteryear. I said that naturally most of the new generation aren't as beautiful as Sarah, but they all are thoroughly feminine.

Mrs Hacker was becoming visibly less enthusiastic about Sarah Harrison's promotion, minute by minute. She remarked that Hacker had never discussed what Sarah looked like.

I laughed knowingly. I said that perhaps he hadn't noticed, though that would be pretty hard to believe. I laid it on pretty thick – made her sound like a sort of administrative Elizabeth Taylor. I said that no man could fail to notice how attractive she was, *especially* the Minister, as he spends such a considerable amount of time with her. And will spend even more if she's promoted.

My feeling is that the Minister will get no further encouragement from home on this matter.

[*Appleby Papers 36/RJC/471*]

[*Sir Arnold Robinson and Sir Humphrey Appleby were plainly quite confident, as we have already seen, that they could sway a sufficient number of Hacker's Cabinet colleagues to vote against this proposal when it came before them.*

The source of their confidence was the practice, current in the 1970s and 1980s, of holding an informal meeting of Permanent Secretaries on Wednesday mornings. This meeting took place in the office of the Cabinet Secretary, had no agenda and was – almost uniquely among Civil Service meetings – unminuted.

Permanent Secretaries would 'drop in' and raise any question of mutual interest. This enabled them all to be fully-briefed about any matters that were liable to confront their Ministers in Cabinet, which took place every Thursday morning, i.e. the next day. And it gave them time to give their Ministers encouragement or discouragement as they saw fit on particular issues.

Fortunately Sir Humphrey's diary reveals what occurred at the Permanent Secretaries' meeting that fateful Wednesday morning – Ed.]

I informed my colleagues that my Minister is intent on creating a quota of twenty-five per cent women in the open structure, leading to an eventual fifty per cent. Parity, in other words.

Initially, my colleagues' response was that it was an interesting suggestion.

[*'Interesting' was another Civil Service form of abuse, like 'novel' or, worse still, 'imaginative' – Ed.*]

Arnold set the tone for the proper response. His view was that it is right and proper that men and women be treated fairly and equally. In principle we should all agree, he said, that such targets should be set and goals achieved.

Everyone agreed immediately that we should agree in principle to such an excellent idea, that it was right and proper to set such targets and achieve such goals.

Arnold then canvassed several of my colleagues in turn, to see if they could implement this excellent proposal in their departments.

Bill [*Sir William Carter, Permanent Secretary at the Foreign and Commonwealth Office – Ed.*] said that he was in full agreement, naturally. He believes that the Civil Service must institute some positive discrimination in favour of women. But regretfully he felt obliged to point out that it cannot happen in the FCO for obvious reasons. Clearly we cannot post women ambassadors to Iran, or any of the Muslim countries, for instance. Generally speaking most of the Third World countries are not as advanced as we are in connection with women's rights – and as we have to send our diplomats to new postings every three years, and entertain many Islamic VIPs in this country, the proposal would definitely not work for the FCO. Nonetheless he wished to make it clear that he applauded the principle.

Ian [*Sir Ian Simpson, Permanent Secretary of the Home Office – Ed.*] said that he was enthusiastically in favour of the principle. He believes we all could benefit from the feminine touch. Furthermore, women are actually *better* at handling some problems than men. He had no doubt about this. Regretfully, however, an exception would have to be made in the case of the Home Office: women are not the right people to run prisons, or the police. And quite probably, they wouldn't want to do it anyway.

We all agreed that this was probably so.

Peter [*Sir Peter Wainwright, Permanent Secretary of the Department of Defence – Ed.*] said that, alas! the same applies to Defence. Women are hardly the people to control all those admirals and generals. Nor is it a practical possibility to place a woman at the Head of Security.

I observed that M. would have to become F. This provoked a gratifying degree of merriment around the table.

Arnold, speaking for us all, agreed that Defence must clearly be a man's world. Like Industry. And Employment, with all those trade union barons to cope with.

John [*Sir John McKendrick, Permanent Secretary of the Department of Health and Social Security – Ed.*] took an even more positive line. He was happy to inform us that women are already well represented near the top of the DHSS, which has two of the four women Dep. Secs. currently in Whitehall. Neither of them is in line for Permanent Secretary, obviously, as they are Deputy Chief Medical Officers (and in any case they may not be suitable for other reasons). Furthermore, women constitute eighty per cent of the typing grades, so he was delighted to be able to tell us that his Department is not doing too badly by them. He added that, in principle, he was in favour of them going to the very top.

Arnold summed up all the views expressed: the feeling of the meeting was – unquestionably – that in principle we were all thoroughly in favour of equal rights for the ladies. It is just that there are special problems in individual departments.

I raised again the question of the quota and stated that I was against it.

Everyone immediately supported me. There was a feeling that it was not on and a bad idea – in fact a typical politician's idea.

I gave my view: namely, that we must always have the right to promote the best man for the job, regardless of sex.

Furthermore – and I made it clear that I was speaking as an ardent feminist myself – I pointed out that the problem lay in recruiting the right sort of women. Married women with families tend to drop out because, in all honesty, they cannot give their work their full single-minded attention. And unmarried women with no children are not fully-rounded people with a thorough understanding of life.

There was general agreement that family life was essential and that it was hard for spinsters to be fully-rounded individuals.

I summed up my remarks by saying that, in practice, it is rarely possible to find a fully-rounded married woman with a happy home and three children who is prepared to devote virtually her whole life, day and night, to a Government Department. It's Catch-22 – or, rather, Catch-22, sub-paragraph (a). This remark produced more gratifying merriment from my colleagues.

Arnold had allowed considerable time for this discussion, which indicates the importance that he attached to the problem. He concluded the matter by asking everyone present to ensure that all of their respective Ministers oppose the quota idea in Cabinet by seeing that each Minister's attention is drawn to each Department's own special circumstances. But he also asked all present to be sure to recommend the *principle* of equal opportunities at every level.

Through the chair, I made one final point. My Minister sees the promotion of women as one means of achieving greater diversity at the top of the Service. I asked all my colleagues to stress, when briefing their Ministers, that quite frankly one could not find a more diverse collection of people than us.

It was unanimously agreed that we constitute a real cross-section of the nation. [*Appleby Papers – 41/AAG/583*]

[*Hacker's diary continues – Ed.*]

November 4th

Cabinet today. And with a very odd outcome. I put forward my proposal for a quota for women for top Civil Service jobs.

All my Cabinet colleagues agreed *in principle* but then they all went on to say that it wouldn't work in their particular Departments. So in the end they didn't really support me at all.

Curiously enough, I'm no longer getting the support from Annie that I was. Not about the quota, specifically, but about promoting Sarah. I had expected her to be *at least* one hundred per cent behind it. But she goes all distant when I talk about it. In fact, she seems to be dead against it now. Extraordinary.

However, as the quota policy is now in ruins it seems that Sarah's promotion is the only thing left that I can immediately achieve in this area. I have arranged that Humphrey and I speak to her tomorrow. I am determined to push it through.

November 5th

My whole equal opportunities policy is destroyed, and quite frankly I feel pretty bitter about the whole thing in general and women in particular. Or at least one particular woman in particular.

Before I saw Sarah today I told Humphrey that we at least could make one tiny positive step today. Lighting a spark. [*It was Guy Fawkes Day – Ed.*]

'Carrying a torch, even,' he replied. What was that supposed to mean?

Anyway, Sarah came in. I explained the background to her: that we have a vacancy for a Deputy Secretary in the Department and that, in spite of her being the most junior of our Under-Secs but because she is the outstanding person in her grade, we were happy to be able to tell her that Humphrey and I were recommending her for promotion to the rank of Deputy Secretary.

Her reaction was a little surprising.

'Oh,' she said. 'I don't know what to say.' And then she laughed.

I couldn't imagine what she was laughing at.

'You don't have to say anything,' I said.

'A simple thank you should suffice,' said Humphrey.

She was still smiling. Then she dropped the bombshell. 'No – I mean – oh gosh! Look, this is awfully embarrassing – I mean, well, I was going to tell you next week – the fact is I'm resigning from the Civil Service.'

You could have knocked me down with a feather. And Humphrey too, by the look of him.

I said something brilliantly witty and apposite, like 'What?', and Humphrey gasped 'resigning?'

'Yes,' she said. 'So thank you, but no thank you.'

Humphrey asked if there was some problem with her children at home.

Bernard suggested mumps.

I suggested that Bernard shut up.

Sarah said she was joining a merchant bank. As a Director.

She'll earn more than me. Perhaps even more than Humphrey!

I tried to explain to her that this news was a frightful blow. 'You see, Sarah, the reason that I'm telling you of your promotion – or rather, Humphrey and I together – is that I have been fighting a losing battle to improve the promotion prospects of women at the top of the Service. And, well, you were to be my Trojan Horse.'

She then explained the reason for her move. 'Quite honestly, Minister, I want a job where I don't spend endless hours circulating information that isn't relevant about subjects that don't matter to people who aren't interested. I want a job where there is achievement rather than merely activity. I'm tired of pushing paper. I would like to be able to point at something and say "I did that."'

The irony of what she was saying was extraordinary. I understand her feeling only too well.

Sir Humphrey didn't. He looked blank. 'I don't understand,' he said.

She smiled. 'I know. That's why I'm leaving.'

I explained that I *did* understand. But I asked her if she was saying that governing Britain is unimportant.

'No,' she said, 'it's very important. It's just that I haven't met anyone who's doing it.'

She added that she'd had enough of the pointless intrigue. I asked what she had in mind. 'Your using me as a Trojan Horse, for instance. And they probably told you that the unions wouldn't wear it if you promoted me.'

I was staggered. Had there been a leak? I asked her how she knew.

She was delighted. She grinned from ear to ear. 'Oh, I *didn't* know. I just know how things are done here.'

We both stared at Humphrey, who had the grace to look slightly embarrassed.

I made one last effort to persuade her to change her mind. 'Look here, Sarah,' I said sternly, 'you don't seem to appreciate that I've fought quite a battle for you.'

Suddenly her eyes blazed. For the first time I recognised the toughness that had brought her to near the top. And the sense of style and dignity. I realised that I'd said something awfully wrong.

'Oh, have you?' she asked. 'Well, I didn't ask you to fight a battle for me. I'm not pleased at the idea of being part of a twenty-five per cent quota. Women are not inferior beings, and I don't enjoy being patronised. I'm afraid you're as paternalist and chauvinist as the rest of them. I'm going somewhere where I shall be accepted as an equal, on my own merits, as a person.'

I was speechless. Clearly I'd offended her. And I suddenly realised that you can't win.

'May I go now?'

There was, of course, no reason to keep her sitting there. I apologised for offending her, though I couldn't see how I'd done it.

'No,' she said, in a kindly way. 'And thank you – I know you both *mean* well.' And off she went, leaving two very puzzled and deflated chaps.

'Women!' I said.

'Yes Minister,' murmured Humphrey, nodding sadly as if to say 'I told you so!'

[*This was not quite the end of the matter. Recently published papers revealed that Hacker fought on for his twenty-five per cent quota for some considerable time – some weeks, anyway. And, as Sir Harold Wilson once said, a week is a long time in politics.*

Sir Humphrey's ingenuity rose to the occasion. He warned Hacker that the Race Relations Board had heard on the grapevine of his proposed quota for women. He told Hacker that if there was to be any affirmative action within the Civil Service, there must also be a quota of blacks within the Civil Service. Sir Humphrey explained that there was a principle at stake.

Hacker was less than enthusiastic about this new principle. He was certainly not a racist, but he could see clearly that whereas a quota for women was a vote-winner, a quota for blacks was in all probability a vote-loser.

Some days later Hacker raised what he called 'this whole business of minority groups – women, blacks, trades unionists and so forth'.

Sir Humphrey explained to Hacker that women and trades unionists were not minority groups, even though they share the same paranoia which is the hallmark of any minority group.

So finally Hacker proposed what Appleby had always proposed: namely, that they start by creating equal opportunities for both women and blacks. In the recruitment grades.

And they drew up terms of reference for an interdepartmental committee to report on methods of choosing the right individuals to be civil servants, to report four years hence. By which time Hacker would certainly no longer be the Minister – Ed.]

[*In early November Jim Hacker apparently bought a microcomputer. An ex-journalist, he was a competent typist and for the next three months all of his diary was committed to the memory of his computer by means of the word-processing software.*

Unfortunately, in early March of the year following he accidentally erased everything on his floppy disc. Abandoning word-processing for ever, he resumed dictation into the cassette recorder on 10 March – Ed.]

16
The Challenge

March 10th
Wonderful news today. I had a call at home last night to go straight to Number Ten this morning.

When I got there I was told of a big Government administrative reorganisation. Not a reshuffle; I stay Minister of Administrative Affairs at the DAA. But I've been given a new remit: local government. It's quite a challenge.

[*Later that day Hacker was interviewed by Ludovic Kennedy in* The World at One, *a popular radio current affairs programme in the 1970s and 80s.*

We have obtained a transcript of the broadcast discussion, which we reproduce below – Ed.]

BBC Radio

LUDOVIC: And the main news this Thursday p.m. is the government reorganisation which gives an ever-increasing empire to the Minister for Administrative Affairs, the Right Honourable James Hacker MP. It has been said, Mr Hacker, that you are now Mr Town Hall as well as Mr Whitehall?

HACKER: Well, it's awfully flattering of you to put it that way, Ludo ...

LUDOVIC: It wasn't me who put it that way, Mr Hacker, it was the Daily Mirror. I was merely seeking confirmation that you are now this country's chief bureaucrat.

BBC Radio

HACKER: I see. Well, of course, that's nonsense. This government believes in reducing bureaucracy.

LUDOVIC: Figures I have here say that your Department's staff has risen by ten per cent this year.

HACKER: Certainly not.

LUDOVIC: Well, what figure do you have?

HACKER: I believe the latest figure was more like 9.97%.

LUDOVIC: You see, it has been suggested, Mr Hacker, that your department is engaged less in reducing bureaucracy than in increasing it.

HACKER: Yes, but that's only because we've had to take on staff in order to reduce staff.

LUDOVIC: I beg your pardon?

HACKER: It's commonsense. You have to take on more doctors to cure more patients. You have to take on more firemen to extinguish more fires. You have to...

LUDOVIC: (INTERRUPTION) And how do you propose to extinguish local government bureaucracy?

HACKER: Well, it's a challenge, and I'm looking forward to it.

LUDOVIC: Would you agree that there's even more bureaucratic waste there than in Whitehall?

HACKER: Well, yes, that's what makes it a challenge.

LUDOVIC: And how are you going to meet this challenge?

Cont.

BBC Radio

HACKER: Ah, well, it's too early to announce detailed proposals. After all, I've come here direct from Number Ten.

LUDOVIC: You mean Number 9.97?

HACKER: The broad principle is to cut ruthlessly at waste while preserving services intact...

LUDOVIC: That's just what your predecessor said when he was appointed. Do you mean he's failed?

HACKER: Please let me finish. Because we must be absolutely clear about this. And I want to be quite frank with you. The plain fact of the matter is, that, at the end of the day, it is the right - nay, the duty - of the elected government, in the House of Commons, to ensure that government policy, the policies on which we were elected and for which we have a mandate, the policies for which the people voted, are the policies which, finally, when the national cake has been divided up - and, may I remind you, we as a nation don't have unlimited wealth, you know, we can't pay ourselves more than we've earned - are the policies ... er, what was the question again?

LUDOVIC: I was asking if you would agree that your immediate predecessor was a failure?

HACKER: No, on the contrary, quite the reverse, it's just that this job is a really enormous, er...

LUDOVIC: Challenge?

HACKER: Exactly.

[*The following day Sir Humphrey Appleby received a note from Sir Arnold Robinson, Secretary of the Cabinet. We reproduce below the exchange of notes that ensued – Ed.*]

10 DOWNING STREET

From the Cabinet Secretary

March 11th

Dear Humpy,

Heard your chap on the radio yesterday. Sounded as though he wanted to do things about your new Local Government remit. Kept calling it a challenge.

I do want you to be quite clear in your own mind that I wouldn't have given you Local Government if I thought you were going to let Hacker do anything about it.

A.

The reply from Sir Humphrey Appleby:

DEPARTMENT OF
ADMINISTRATIVE AFFAIRS

From the Permanent Under-Secretary of State

Dear Arnold :—

I'm sure he won't be able to.

Nobody else has.

HA

11/iii

A reply from Sir Arnold Robinson:

10 DOWNING STREET

From the Cabinet Secretary

March 12th

Dear Humphy,

That's not the point. We have found in the past that all Local Government reforms rebound on us. Whenever anybody finds a way of saving money or cutting staff in Local Government, you will find it works for Whitehall just as well.

If he needs something to keep him busy get him to look into Civil Defence.

A.

[*On the same date, 12 March, Sir Humphrey made a reference to this exchange of notes in his diary – Ed.*]

Received a couple of notes from A.R. Clearly he's worried that Hacker may overstep the mark. I've made it plain that I know my duty.

Nonetheless, A. made a superb suggestion: that I divert Hacker by getting him to look into Civil Defence. By which he means fall-out shelters.

This is a most amusing notion. Everybody knows that Civil Defence is not a serious issue, merely a desperate one. And it is thus best left to those whose incapacity can be relied upon: local authorities.

It is a hilarious thought that, since the highest duty of government is to protect its citizens, it has been decided to leave it to the Borough Councils.

[*Hacker's diary continues – Ed.*]
March 15th

I met a very interesting new adviser today: Dr Richard Cartwright.

We were having a meeting of assorted officials, of which he was one. I noticed that we hadn't even been properly introduced to each other, which I had presumed was some sort of oversight.

But, as the meeting was breaking up, this shambling figure of an elderly schoolboy placed himself directly in front of me and asked me in a soft Lancashire accent if he could have a brief word with me.

Naturally I agreed. Also, I was intrigued. He looked a bit different from most of my officials – a baggy tweed sports jacket, leather elbows, mousy hair brushed forward towards thick spectacles. He looked like a middle-aged ten-year-old. If I'd tried to guess his profession, I would have guessed prep school science master.

'It's about a proposal, worked out before we were transferred to this Department,' he said in his comforting high-pitched voice.

'And you are . . .?' I asked. I still didn't know who he was.

'I am . . . what?' he asked me.

I thought he was going to tell me what his job is. 'Yes,' I asked, 'you are what?'

He seemed confused. 'What?'

Now I was confused. 'What?'

'I'm Dr Cartwright.'

Bernard chose this moment to intervene. 'But if I may put it another way . . . what *are* you?'

'I'm C of E,' said Dr Cartwright puzzled.

'No,' said Bernard patiently. 'I think the Minister means, what function do you perform in this Department.'

'Don't you *know*?' Dr Cartwright sounded slightly horrified.

'Yes, *I* know,' said Bernard, 'but the Minister wants to know.'

'Ah,' said Dr Cartwright. We'd got there at last. No one would believe that this is how busy people in the corridors of power communicate with each other.

'I'm a professional economist,' he explained. 'Director of Local Administrative Statistics.'

'So you were in charge of the Local Government Directorate until we took it over?'

He smiled at my question. 'Dear me, no.' He shook his head sadly, though apparently without bitterness. 'No, I'm just Under-Secretary rank. Sir Gordon Reid was the Permanent Secretary. I fear that I will rise no higher.'

I asked why not.

He smiled. 'Alas! I am an expert.'

[*It is interesting to note that the cult of the generalist had such a grip on Whitehall that experts accepted their role as second-class citizens with equanimity and without rancour – Ed.*]

'An expert on what?'

'The whole thing,' he said modestly. Then he handed me a file.

I'm sitting here reading the file right now. It's dynamite. It's a scheme for controlling local authority expenditure. He proposes that every council official responsible for a new project would have to list the criteria for failure before he's given the go-ahead.

I didn't grasp the implication of this at first. But I've discussed it with Annie and she tells me it's what's called 'the scientific method'. I've never really come across that, since my early training was in sociology and economics. But 'the scientific method' apparently means that you first establish a method of measuring the success or failure of an experiment. A proposal would have to say: 'The scheme will be a failure if it takes longer than this' or 'costs more than that' or 'employs more staff than these' or 'fails to meet those pre-set performance standards'.

Fantastic. We'll get going on this right away. The only thing is, I can't understand why this hasn't been done before.

March 16th

The first thing I did this morning was get Dr Cartwright on the phone, and ask him.

He didn't know the answer. 'I can't understand it either. I put the idea up several times and it was always welcomed very warmly. But Sir Gordon always seemed to have something more urgent on when we were due to discuss it.'

I told him he'd come to the right place this time and rang off.

Then Bernard popped in. He was looking rather anxious. Obviously he'd been listening-in on his extension and taking notes. [*This was customary, and part of the Private Secretary's official duties – Ed.*]

'That's marvellous, isn't it Bernard?' I asked.

There was a pointed silence.

'You've read the report, have you? Cartwright's report?'

'Yes, Minister.'

'Well, what do you think of it?'

'Oh, it's er, that is, er it's very well presented, Minister.'

The message was clear.

'Humphrey will be fascinated, don't you think?' I said mischievously.

Bernard cleared his throat. 'Well, I've arranged a meeting with him about this for tomorrow. I'm sure he'll give you his views.'

'What are you saying, Bernard? Out with it.'

'Yes, well, as I say,' he waffled for a bit, 'um . . . I think that he'll think that it's er, beautifully . . . typed.'

And then surprisingly he smiled from ear to ear.

March 17th

Today I had the meeting with Sir Humphrey. It was supposed to be about our new responsibilities in the area of local government. But I saw to it that it was about Cartwright's scheme.

It began with the usual confusion between us.

'Local authorities,' I began. 'What are we going to do about them?'

'Well, there are three principal areas for action: budget, accommodation and staffing.'

I congratulated him for putting his finger right on it. 'Well done, Humphrey. That's where all the trouble is.'

He was nonplussed. 'Trouble?'

'Yes,' I said, 'with all those frightful councils. Budget, accommodation and staffing. They all go up and up and up.'

'No, Minister.' He had assumed his patronising tone again. 'I'm afraid you misunderstand. I'm referring to this Department's budget, accommodation and staffing. Obviously they must all be increased now that we have all those extra responsibilities.'

I was even *more* patronising in my response. 'No Humphrey, I'm afraid *you* misunderstand.' I told him that local government is a ghastly mess, and that I was asking what we were going to do to improve it, to make it more efficient and economical.

He didn't answer my question. He hesitated momentarily, and then tried to divert me with flattery. 'Minister, this new remit gives you more influence, more Cabinet seniority – but you do not have to let it give you any more work or worry. That would be foolishness.'

Nowadays I find I'm able to resist his blandishments very easily. Stubbornly I repeated that we have to put a stop to all this ghastly waste and extravagance that's going on.

'Why?' he asked.

I was staggered. 'Why?'

'Yes. Why?'

'Because it's my job, we're the government, we were elected to govern.'

'Minister, surely you don't intend to tamper with the democratic rights of freely-elected local government representatives?'

Humphrey's new-found interest in democracy surprised me slightly. For a moment I couldn't think of an answer to what sounded like a perfectly reasonable point. And then it became clear. There is *no* competition between local government and Westminster – local authorities are given their powers by Westminster. They must act accordingly. Parliament is supreme. We live in a Parliamentary democracy. And there was another aspect to this.

'Local councils aren't democratic at all,' I said. 'Local democracy is a farce. Nobody knows who their local councillor is. Most people don't even vote in local elections. And the ones who *do*, just treat it as a popularity poll on the government in Westminster. Councillors, in practice, are accountable to nobody.'

He looked po-faced. 'They are public-spirited citizens, selflessly sacrificing their spare time.'

'Have you ever met any?' I enquired.

'Occasionally. When there was no alternative,' he replied, with one of his occasional flashes of honesty.

'I've met plenty of them. Half of them are self-important busybodies on an ego trip and the other half are in it for what they can get out of it.'

'Perhaps they ought to be in the House of Commons,' said Humphrey.

I think I must have given him a dirty look, because he added hastily, 'I mean, to see how a proper legislative assembly behaves.'

I decided that we'd done enough beating about the bush. I told

Humphrey that I intended to get a grip on these local councils. And I announced that I had a plan.

He smiled a supercilious smile. '*You* have a plan?'

I told him that I was going to insist that any council official who puts up a project costing over £10,000 must accompany it with failure standards.

'With what?'

'With a statement,' I said, 'that he will have failed if his project does not achieve certain pre-set results or exceeds fixed time or staff or budget limits.'

I had hoped, faintly, that he would think this was my idea. No such luck.

'Minister,' he demanded, 'where did you get the idea for this dangerous nonsense?'

I could see that Dr Cartwright needed my protection. 'From someone in the Department,' I replied evasively.

He exploded. 'Minister, I have warned you before about the dangers of talking to people in the Department. I *implore* you to stay out of the minefield of local government. It is a political graveyard.'

Bernard intervened. Just as nature abhors a vacuum, Bernard abominates a mixed metaphor. 'Actually, Sir Humphrey,' he explained confidentially, 'you can't have a graveyard in a minefield because all the corpses would . . .' and he made a vague explosion gesture. Humphrey gave him a look which reduced him to silence.

I was more immediately interested in why Humphrey, who has been claiming that he got me this local government job, is now saying that it's a minefield and a graveyard. Was this a friendly act?

'Well, what *am* I supposed to do?' I asked.

'Um . . . yes, well . . . quite honestly, Minister, I didn't think you'd *do* anything. I mean, you've never done anything before.'

I brushed aside the insult and the complaints. I told him I wanted specific proposals right away, and immediate plans for the implementation of failure standards by local authorities. I couldn't see why he was getting so worked up about it – and then, the penny dropped: these failure standards could be made to apply to Whitehall as well.

I'd just started to say something along those lines when Humphrey made a chance remark that immediately caught my attention.

'Minister, if you insist in interfering in local government, may I make a positive suggestion that could prove a very real vote-winner?'

I always try to make time to listen to a positive suggestion.

'There is an area of local government that needs urgent attention – Civil Defence.'

I thought at first that this was a completely frivolous suggestion. Everybody regards fall-out shelters as a joke.

He seemed to read my mind. 'At the moment, Minister, you may think they are a joke. But the highest duty of any government is to protect its citizens. And Local Authorities are dragging their feet.'

'Some people,' I said, 'think that building shelters makes nuclear war more likely.'

'If you have the weapons, you must have the shelters.'

'I suppose you're right. But I wonder if we really need the weapons.'

Sir Humphrey was shocked. 'Minister! You're not a unilateralist?'

I told him that I sometimes wonder. He told me that in that case I should resign from the government. I told him that I'm not *that* unilateralist.

'But after all, Humphrey,' I added, 'the Americans will always protect us from the Russians, won't they?'

'The Russians?' he asked. 'Who's talking about the Russians?'

'Well, the independent nuclear deterrent . . .'

He interrupted me. 'It's to protect us against the French.'

I could hardly believe my ears. The French? It sounded incredible. An extraordinary idea. I reminded Humphrey that they are our allies, our partners.

'They are *now*,' he agreed. 'But they've been our enemies for most of the past nine hundred years. If *they* have it, we must!'

It only needed a few seconds' thought to realise the profound truth of what he was saying. Suddenly it didn't seem at all incredible – just common sense, really. If the bomb is to protect us from the *French*, that's a completely different matter, obviously we've got to have it, you can't trust the Frogs, there's no room for discussion about *that*!

Furthermore, there is – unquestionably – increasing public concern about the bomb. And if one can be seen to be doing something about it, it could do one a lot of good politically.

Also I gathered at the Beeb that Ludovic Kennedy is preparing a TV documentary on Civil Defence, and it's bound to be critical of the current situation. So if I were seen to be taking decisive measures . . .

'When do we start?' I asked Humphrey.

He had an immediate suggestion. 'The London Borough of Thames Marsh has spent less on Civil Defence than any authority in the country.'

An excellent starting plan. Thames Marsh is Ben Stanley's borough, that odious troglodite with the wispy moustache. The press hate him.

So I told Bernard to set up the visit, and make sure the press are fully informed. 'Tell them,' I instructed him, 'that I lie awake at night worrying about the defenceless citizens of Thames Marsh.'

'Do you?' asked Bernard.

'I will now!' I said firmly.

March 23rd

I made an official visit to Thames Marsh Town Hall today. There was a very satisfactory turn-out from the press, I noticed, especially photographers.

I met a so-called 'welcoming committee' on the front steps. Loads of flash-guns going off. I was introduced to the Leader of the Council.

'Mr Stanley, I presume,' I said. I'd prepared it of course, but it got a jolly good laugh from the assembled hacks.

The ensuing discussion over cups of tea and sticky buns in the Mayor's Parlour can hardly be described as a meeting of minds. But I made the point I had to make with great effectiveness, and I'm sure it will all be reported. If not, no doubt it will be leaked somehow. [*In other words, Hacker would leak it – Ed.*]

Stanley opened the hostilities by asking me belligerently why I thought I could come swanning down to Thames Marsh from Whitehall, telling them how to run their borough.

In return, I asked him (politely) why he was doing less than any other borough in Britain to protect the people who elected him.

'Simple,' he said, 'we can't find the money.'

I suggested he try looking for it. This produced an outburst of anger, mixed with a good dose of self-righteousness.

'Oh that's *great*,' he snapped, smiling a thin smile, strangely at variance with his malevolent, beady eyes, a crumb or two of the Mayor's Battenburg marzipan cake stuck to his twitching moustache. 'Oh that's great. Stop school meals? Buy no textbooks? Turn the OAPs[1] out into the cold?'

[1] Senior Citizens.

I wasn't impressed by all that cheap electioneering rubbish. It's nothing to do with our Senior Citizens.[1]

'If you want the money,' I said wearily, 'I can tell you exactly where you can find it.'

'You can?' he sneered.

'Yes,' I said. I told Cartwright to tell him, because he had the file.

So Cartwright read him the list that he and I had approved.

DEPARTMENT OF ADMINISTRATIVE AFFAIRS

Directorate of Local Administrative Statistics

PROJECTED ECONOMIES FOR THAMES MARSH

1	Scrap the plans for:	(a)	the new Exhibition Centre
		(b)	the artificial ski slope
		(c)	the jacuzzi pools
2	Close down:	(a)	the feminist drama centre
		(b)	the council's weekly newspaper
		(c)	the monthly magazine
		(d)	the welfare rights research department
		(e)	the Gay Bereavement Centre
3	Halve:	(a)	the members' entertainment allowance
		(b)	the management entertainment allowance
4	Sell:		The Mayor's second Daimler
5	Postpone:		The building of the New Town Hall
6	Cancel:		The twenty councillors' tourism factfinding mission to Jamaica

[1] OAPs.

This list of suggestions would save £21 million on capital account over five years, and £750,000 a year on revenue account.

Stanley read the list. There followed a bemused silence. Finally he came up with an answer.

'That's just stupid,' he said.

I asked why.

'Because,' he explained laboriously, 'it's depriving the disadvantaged of indispensable services.'

'Jacuzzi pools?' I asked innocently.

He knew only too well that he was on a very sticky wicket, so changed his line of defence.

'Look,' he said, completely abandoning the argument that Thames Marsh couldn't find the necessary money, 'I don't care whether we can afford fall-out shelters or not. This is a unilateralist borough. We don't believe in nuclear war in Thames Marsh.'

'Mr Stanley,' I replied carefully. 'I don't believe in nuclear war either. No sane man does. But the provision of fall-out shelters is government policy.'

'It is not Thames Marsh policy,' he snarled. 'Thames Marsh has no quarrel with the USSR.'

'It's not just the USSR we're scared of, it could be the Fr. . . .'

I stopped myself just in time. Had I completed that word I could have caused the biggest international incident of the decade.

'The who?' he asked.

I though fast. 'The fr . . . frigging Chinese' was all I could think of on the spur of the moment. But it served its purpose, and the crisis passed. And I kept talking. I thought I'd better. Not that it was difficult. The idea of each borough in the UK having its own foreign policy was too absurd to contemplate. The TUC has its own foreign policy, each trade union, now each borough, where is it going to end? Soon they'll all want their own Foreign Office – as if we haven't enough problems with the one we've got.

The irony is, in practice it is virtually impossible for *any* institution to have its own foreign policy, even the Government. The Foreign Office sees to that, with the help of Washington, NATO, the EEC and the Commonwealth Secretariat.

So I attempted to show him that he was suffering from delusions of grandeur.

'If the Russians ever invade us,' I suggested sarcastically, 'I suppose they'll stop at the borough boundaries, will they, and say: Hang on, we're not at war with the London Borough of Thames

Marsh. Right wheel Comrades. Annex Chelsea instead'?

The discussion was becoming fairly heated. [*What the press statement would later describe as a 'frank exchange of views' – Ed.*]

But at this moment Bernard intervened and, excusing himself for interrupting us, handed me a little note. It was most revealing. In no time at all I grasped its contents, and its political significance.

I looked at Comrade Ben. 'Oh Mr Stanley,' I said, trying not to smile, 'it seems that *you* would not be called upon to make the supreme sacrifice, in any case.'

'What do you mean?' he asked, knowing perfectly well what I meant.

The note contained the information that there is a fall-out shelter under Thames Marsh Town Hall, with a place reserved in it for, among others, the Leader of the Council. I asked if it was true.

'We didn't build it.' I'd got him on the defensive.

'But you maintain it?'

'It's only a very small one,' he muttered sullenly.

I asked him about his own place in it.

'I was persuaded with deep reluctance that my preservation was a necessity in the interests of the ratepayers of Thames Marsh.'

So I asked him what provision he had made for other essential people: doctors, nurses, ambulance men, firemen, civil rescue squads, emergency radio and television services? 'People who might be almost as important as councillors,' I added sarcastically.

'One of them's a chemist.'

'Oh great,' I said. 'Nothing like an aspirin for a nuclear holocaust.'

[*Later that week Sir Humphrey Appleby lunched with Sir Arnold Robinson, the Cabinet Secretary, at the Athenaeum Club. As usual Sir Humphrey kept a memo of the meeting – Ed.*]

Arnold observed that my Minister had enjoyed quite a little publicity triumph down at Thames Marsh. He seemed pleased, which surprised me.

I'm always worried when this Minister has a triumph of any sort. It invariably leads to trouble because he thinks he has achieved something.

Arnold thinks it's good when Ministers think they have achieved something. He takes the view that it makes life much easier, because they stop fretting for a bit and we don't have to put up with their little temper tantrums.

My worry, on the other hand, is that he will want to introduce his next idea.

Arnold was most interested to learn that we have a Minister with two ideas. He couldn't remember when we last had one of those.

[*Of course, Hacker had not really had any ideas. One was Bernard's and the other was Dr Cartwright's – Ed.*]

Arnold wanted to know about the latest idea, and I was obliged to tell him that it was Cartwright's idiotic scheme to introduce pre-set failure standards for all council projects over £10,000, and to make a named official responsible.

Arnold knew about this scheme, of course, it's been around for years. But he thought (as I did) that Gordon Reid had squashed it. I think Arnold was a bit put out that Cartwright had got it to Hacker, though I don't see how I could have prevented it since Cartwright has now come over to the DAA. After all, he slipped it to the Minister privately, under plain cover. Brown envelope job.

Arnold was adamant that it must be stopped. He's absolutely right. Once you specify in advance what a project is supposed to achieve and whose job it is to see that it does, the entire system collapses. As he says, we would be into the whole squalid world of professional management.

Arnold reminded me (as if I didn't already know) that we already move our officials around ever two or three years, to stop this personal responsibility nonsense. If Cartwright's scheme goes through, we would have to be posting everybody once a fortnight.

Clearly we have to make the Minister understand that his new local authority responsibilities are for enjoying, not for exercising.

I told Arnold that tomorrow Hacker will be living his little triumph all over again, recording a TV interview with Ludovic Kennedy for a documentary on Civil Defence.

Arnold wondered out loud what would happen if we gave Hacker a dossier of the curious ways in which local councillors spend their Civil Defence budgets. I remarked that I couldn't really see how that would help. But Arnold had an idea . . .

Perhaps he should become a Minister!

[*Appleby Papers 39/H1T/188*]

[*It was known that Hacker was delighted by the invitation, expected though it was, to appear on Ludovic Kennedy's television documentary on Civil Defence. He was under the impression that he was being given a chance to discuss a Ministerial success. Before the recording, in fact, it is said that he jocularly asked Kennedy if this represented a change of policy by the BBC.*

We reproduce the transcripts of the interview, which took a course that was, as it turned out, not to Hacker's liking. This, of course, was a result of Sir Arnold Robinson's idea – Ed.]

BRITISH BROADCASTING CORPORATION

LUDOVIC: Minister, you've been claiming recently that you've been having some success in your dealings with local authorities on the matter of Civil Defence.

HACKER: Yes.

LUDOVIC: But hasn't this success been more in the field of publicity than any real achievement?

HACKER: No Ludo. I believe that local authorities are being made to face up to the need because of the increased public interest we are generating.

LUDOVIC: So you agree.

HACKER: What?

LUDOVIC: You are saying that your successes have only been publicity successes.

HACKER: Well, if you want to put it that way: yes. But things are changing.

LUDOVIC: In Thames Marsh?

HACKER: Ah. Thames Marsh. They do, as I have pointed out to the press, have one nuclear fall-out shelter. And one of its places is reserved for Mr Ben Stanley, the leader of the council, who is refusing to build shelters for others! Don't you think this is rather hypocritical?

LUDOVIC: But Minister, is it not reasonable for our elected representatives to be given a chance of survival? Otherwise, who will govern?

BRITISH BROADCASTING CORPORATION

HACKER: In the event of a nuclear holocaust there are more important people than mere politicians - doctors, nurses, firemen, all the people who run the essential services.

LUDOVIC: But don't the Prime Minister and the Home Secretary, for instance, have places reserved in a government fall-out shelter?

HACKER: Ah. Er, um, but ... um, but that's completely different.

LUDOVIC: Why?

HACKER: Well, someone has to er, run the ... you know.

LUDOVIC: But they're not trained in first aid and fire fighting, are they? Surely you're arguing that they should give up their places to doctors and nurses? Have you put it to them?

HACKER: I think we must be careful not to, er, trivialise a very important issue, Ludovic. To give another example, I have just been told of a borough that sent a council delegation to California at the ratepayers' expense to look at fall-out shelters. And when they got back they couldn't do anything about it because they'd spent their whole Civil Defence budget for three years on the trip.

LUDOVIC: Isn't that appalling?

HACKER: Appalling.

[*It is interesting to read Hacker's brief remarks in his diary, written on the evening of the television interview – Ed.*]

March 29th

TV interview went quite well. But I got into a bit of difficulty over Ben Stanley's bunker. I said that politicians weren't as important as doctors and so on.

He asked about the PM's place in a government shelter. I should have seen that one coming.

I got out of it, pretty cleverly on the whole. All the same I'm not sure how happy the PM will be about it.

Fortunately I was able to tell a marvellously funny story about a group of councillors who spent three years' Civil Defence budget on a jaunt to California. So that's all right. On the whole it should do me a bit of good when it goes out next week.

March 30th

A worrying day. I've put my foot in it with the PM in a much bigger way than I'd ever imagined.

That wretched story about the councillors going to California is the root of the trouble. I don't even remember where I got it from – it was in some brief that Bernard passed on to me from the Civil Defence Directorate before the TV programme, I think.

Anyway, Humphrey asked me about it. At first he wouldn't say why. He merely made the observation that he was sure that I knew what I was doing.

He only says that when I've made an appalling cock-up.

Then he revealed that the borough in question contains the PM's constituency. And the PM's election agent was the councillor who led the offending delegation.

At first I thought he was joking. But no.

'Number Ten have been trying to keep it quiet for weeks,' he said. 'Ah well. Truth will out.'

I couldn't see why. Truth *mustn't* out. That's the worst thing that can happen. It'll look like a personal attack, and the PM's very touchy about disloyalty at the moment. I told Humphrey that we must stop the interview going out. I could see no other alternative.

To my astonishment he chose that moment to get to his feet and bring the discussion to a close.

'Unfortunately, Minister, I have no time. I must be going.'

I gasped. 'You can't. This is top priority. I order you.'

'Alas! Minister, it is your orders that are calling me away.'

I couldn't think what he meant. He explained: 'Your scheme for imposing pre-set failure standards on local councils is very complex. You asked for proposals straight away. It is taking every moment of my time. Much as I would like to help . . .'

He paused. Then he seemed to make a proposal. 'On the other hand, if implementing failure standards were not quite so urgent . . .'

'Do you mean,' I asked casually, 'you *could* stop the broadcast?'

He was guarded. 'Minister, we cannot censor the BBC. But . . . I happen to be having lunch tomorrow with the BBC's Director of Policy, perhaps you'd care to join us?'

I couldn't see any point, if we can't censor them. I said so, rather disconsolately.

But Sir Humphrey's reply has given me grounds for hope. 'No Minister, but we can always try to persuade them to withdraw programmes voluntarily once they realise that transmission is not in the public interest.'

'It's not in my interest,' I replied firmly, 'and I represent the public. So it can't be in the public interest.'

Humphrey looked intrigued. 'That's a novel approach,' he said. 'We've not tried that on them before.'

I think that he has more respect for my ideas than he likes to show.

March 31st

A very successful lunch today with Humphrey and Francis Aubrey, the BBC's Director of Policy, a man with a permanently anxious expression on his face. As well he might have.

It started badly though. As soon as I broached the subject he stated his position firmly. 'I'm sorry, Mr Hacker, but the BBC cannot give in to government pressure.' His black bushy eyebrows bristled sternly.

'Well, let's leave that on one side, shall we?' said Sir Humphrey smoothly.

I thought Humphrey was supposed to be on my side.

'No really,' I began, 'I must insist. . .'

But he silenced me, rather rudely I thought. 'Let's leave that on one side,' he repeated. '*Please*, Minister.'

I had no option really. But I later realised that I had underestimated my Permanent Secretary.

He turned to Mr Aubrey and said: 'Frank, can I raise something else? There is considerable disquiet about the BBC's hostility to the Government.'

Aubrey laughed off the idea. 'That's absurd.'

'Well, *is* it?' asked Humphrey. And he leaned across to the empty chair beside him and opened up an enormous briefcase. Not his usual slimline leather job with gold engraved initials, but a big fat bulging leather bag, so heavy that his driver had carried it into the club for us.

I'd been preoccupied and worried, and I'd scarcely noticed it. If I had thought about it I suppose I'd have assumed it contained some documents with such a high security clearance that Humphrey had to take them with him everywhere he went.

In the event, it turned out that it contained a number of files that he intended to show the man from the Beeb.

'We have been documenting instances of bias in BBC current affairs.' He handed over a file with *Bias* written across it in a felt pen in large red letters. Francis Aubrey put down his knife and fork and was about to open it when Humphrey handed over a second file, with the words *Favourable News Stories Not Reported By The BBC*. Then he handed over one file after another, pointing out their contents.

Excessive Publicity For Other Countries' Case Against Britain – 'Especially our Common Market enemies. Er, partners, I mean,' explained Humphrey. *Jokes Against The Prime Minister*. *Unnecessary Publicity for Anti-government Demonstrations*. And finally, one huge file, much fatter than the others, which he heaved across the table, marked, *Ministers' Programme Suggestions Not Accepted*.

Francis Aubrey was clearly shaken by this mass of incriminating allegations and evidence. 'But . . . I'm . . . but I'm sure we've got answers to all these.' He sounded more firm than he looked.

'Of course the BBC's got answers,' I told him. 'It's always got answers. Silly ones, but it's always got them.'

Humphrey was taking a cooler line. 'Of course the BBC has explanations,' he said soothingly. 'But I just thought I ought to warn you that questions are being asked.'

'What sort of questions?' Mr Aubrey was looking even more worried.

'Well,' said Humphrey thoughtfully, 'for example, if Parliament were to be televised, whether it shouldn't be entrusted to ITV.'

'You can't be serious,' he exploded.

'And,' continued Humphrey in the same quiet and thoughtful vein, 'whether the BBC administration has really made the cuts in jobs and premises that we have endured in government. Should a Select Committee be appointed to scrutinise all BBC expenditure?'

Francis Aubrey started to panic. 'That would be an intolerable intrusion.' Resorting to pomposity to hide his thoroughly understandable fears.

I was enjoying myself thoroughly by this time.

'Of course,' said Sir Humphrey agreeably. 'And then there's the extraordinary matter of the boxes at Ascot, Wimbledon, Lord's, Covent Garden, the Proms . . .'

I pricked up my ears. This was news to me.

Francis said, 'Ah yes, but these are a technical requirement. For production and engineering staff, you know.'

At this juncture Humphrey fished about at the bottom of his copious and now nearly empty Gladstone bag, and produced a box of photographs and press cuttings.

'Hmmm,' he said, and smiled and dropped his final bombshell. 'Reports suggest your production and engineering staff are all holding champagne glasses, all accompanied by their wives – or other ladies of equal distinction – and all bearing a remarkable similarity to governors, directors and executives of the corporation and their friends. I'm wondering whether it is my duty to pass the evidence to the Department of Inland Revenue. What's your view?'

And, with that, he handed over the box of photographs.

In silence, an ashen Francis Aubrey looked through them.

As he stopped at a splendid ten by eight portrait Humphrey leaned across, glanced at it, and observed, 'You've come out awfully well, haven't you?'

We fell into silence for some while. F.A. put down the photographs, tried to eat a little more of his Sole Meunière, but clearly it was turning to dust in his mouth. He gave up. I just watched with interest. Humphrey's performance was brilliant, and I had no wish to interrupt it or get in the way.

Humphrey was quietly enjoying his glass of Château Léoville-Barton 1973, a bottle of which he had carefully chosen to go with his roast beef. It tasted okay, though one glass of red is much like another as far as I'm concerned.

Finally Humphrey broke the silence. 'Mind you, I think we may just be able to contain all this criticism of the corporation, provided the files don't get any larger. That's why I am urging my Minister that there is no need to take up the case of the Civil Defence programme formally.'

Francis was looking desperate. He turned the photo of himself face downwards on the pile. 'Look, you do see my position. The BBC cannot give in to government pressure.'

'Of course not,' said Humphrey. This surprised me. I thought that that was precisely what we were trying to achieve. But I had reckoned without the hypocrisy of the Establishment. Or, to put it more kindly, Humphrey was devising some face-saving apparatus for Mr Aubrey.

And that's how it turned out to be. He looked at me.

'We wouldn't want the BBC to give in to government pressure. Would we Minister?'

'No?' I asked, slightly cautiously, recognising a clear cue.

'No, of course we wouldn't,' he went on. 'But the Minister's interview with Ludovic Kennedy did contain some factual errors.'

Francis Aubrey seized on that. He brightened up considerably. 'Factual errors? Ah, that's different. I mean the BBC couldn't give in to government pressure . . ."

'Of course not,' we agreed.

'. . . but we set great store by factual accuracy.'

'Indeed,' said Humphrey, nodding sympathetically. 'And then, some of the information in the interview is likely to be out of date by the time of transmission.'

'Out of date?' he responded eagerly. 'Ah that's serious. As you know, the BBC couldn't give in to government pressure . . .'

'Of course not,' we agreed in unison.

'. . . but we don't want to transmit out-of-date material.'

I saw that I could help Humphrey now.

'And since the recording,' I interjected, 'I've discovered that I inadvertently let slip one or two remarks that might have security implications.'

'Such as?' he asked.

I hadn't expected that question. I thought he'd be too well-bred to ask.

Humphrey came to the rescue. 'He can't tell you what they are. Security.'

Francis Aubrey didn't seem to mind a bit. 'Ah well, we can't be too careful about security, I do agree. If the defence of the realm is at stake, we have to be very responsible. I mean, obviously the BBC can't give in to government pressure . . .'

'Of course not,' we chorused enthusiastically one more time.

'. . . but security, well, you can't be too careful, can you?'

'You can't be too careful,' I echoed.

'You can't be too careful,' murmured Humphrey.

'And in the end, it wasn't a very interesting interview anyway. All been said before. Bit of a yawn, actually.'

F.A. – or Sweet F.A. as I like to think of him now – had brightened up considerably by this time. Colour had returned to his cheeks. His eyes were no longer lustreless and dead. He was now able to expound on the matter of BBC policy and practice with renewed confidence.

'I mean,' he explained, 'if it's boring, and if there are inaccuracies and security worries, the BBC wouldn't *want* to put the interview out. That puts a completely different complexion on it.'

'Completely different,' I said happily.

'Transmission,' he went on, 'would not be in the public interest. But I do want to make one thing absolutely clear.'

'Yes?' enquired Humphrey politely.

'There can be absolutely no question,' Francis Aubrey stated firmly and categorically, 'of the BBC ever giving in to government pressure.'

I think it will be all right now.

April 5th

This afternoon Sir Humphrey popped in to see me. He had just received a message that the BBC had decided to drop my interview with Ludovic Kennedy. Apparently they feel it is the responsible course. Of course they do.

I thanked Humphrey, and offered him a sherry. As I thought about the events of the last few days a new thought occurred to me.

'You know,' I said, 'it seems to me that, somehow, I was trapped into saying those things that would embarrass the PM.'

'Surely not,' said Humphrey.

'Yes,' I said, 'I think I was dropped right in it.'

Humphrey derided this as a ridiculous thought, and asked how I could even think it. I asked him why it was ridiculous to think that Ludo tried to trap me.

'Who?' he asked.

'Ludo. Ludovic Kennedy.'

Humphrey suddenly changed his tune. 'Oh, *Ludovic Kennedy* tried to trap you. I see. Yes. I'm sure he did.'

We both agreed that everyone who works for the media is deceitful, and you can't trust them an inch. But, now I think about it, why was he so surprised that I was talking about Ludo? Who did he *think* I was talking about?

Still, he has got me out of a frightful hole. And it was quite clear what the *quid pro quo* was expected to be. I had to suggest that we lay off the local authorities.

'It must be admitted,' I was forced to concede, 'that local councillors – on the whole – are sensible, responsible people, and they're democratically elected. Central government has to be very careful before it starts telling them how to do their job.'

'And the failure standards?'

'I think they can manage without them, don't you think?'

'Yes Minister.'

And he smiled contentedly.

But I don't intend to let the matter drop for good. I shall return to it, after a decent interval. After all, we had a little unspoken agreement, an unwritten *détente* – but no one can hold you to an unspoken, unwritten deal, can they?

17

The Moral Dimension

May 14th

I am writing this entry, not in my London flat or in my constituency house, but in the first-class compartment of a British Airways flight to the oil sheikhdom of Qumran.

We have been en route to the Persian gulf for about four and a half hours, and we should be landing in about forty-five minutes.

I'm very excited. I've never flown first-class before, and it's quite different. They give you free champagne all the way and a decent meal instead of the usual monosodium glutamate plus colouring.

Also, it's nice being a VIP – special lounge, on the plane last, general red-carpet treatment.

We're going there to ratify the contract for one of the biggest export orders Britain has ever obtained in the Middle East.

But when I say 'we' I don't just mean me and Bernard and Humphrey. In fact, I asked for an assurance in advance that we couldn't be accused of wasting a lot of government money on the trip. Humphrey assured me that we were taking the smallest possible delegation. 'Pared to the bone' was the phrase he used, I distinctly remember. But now I realise that there may have been some ulterior motive in keeping me in the VIP lounge till the last possible minute.

When I actually got onto the plane I was aghast. It is *entirely* full of civil servants. In fact it transpires that the plane had to be specially chartered because there are so many of us going.

I immediately challenged Humphrey about the extravagance of chartering an aircraft. He looked at me as though I were mad, and said that it would be infinitely more expensive for all of us to go on a scheduled flight.

I'm perfectly sure that's true. My argument is with the size of the party. 'Who are all these people?' I asked.

'Our little delegation.'

'But you just said the delegation has been pared to the bone.'

He insisted that it was. I asked him, again, to tell me who they all are. And he told me. There's a small delegation from the FCO because, although it's a DAA mission, the FCO doesn't like any of us to go abroad except under their supervision. I can't really understand that, foreign policy is not at issue on this trip, all we are doing is ratifying a contract that has already been fully negotiated between the Government of Qumran and British Electronic Systems Ltd.

Anyway, apart from the FCO delegation, there is one from the Department of Trade, and one from Industry. Also a small group from Energy, because we're going to an oil sheikhdom. (If you ask me, that's completely irrelevant – I reckon the Department of Energy would still demand the right to send a delegation if we were going to Switzerland – they'd probably argue that chocolate gives you energy!) Then there's a Dep. Sec. leading a team from the Cabinet Office, a group from the COI.[1] And finally, the whole of the DAA mission: my press office, half my private office, liaison with other departments, secretaries, those from the legal department who did the contract, those who supervised the contract . . . the list is endless.

One thing's certain: it's certainly not been pared to the bone. I reminded Humphrey (who is sitting next to me but has nodded off after going at the free champagne like a pig with his snout in the trough) that when we were going to meet the Qumranis in Middlesbrough there were only going to be seven people coming with us.

'Yes Minister,' he had nodded understandingly. 'But Teesside is perhaps not quite so diplomatically significant as Qumran.'

'Teesside returns four MPs,' I remarked.

'Qumran controls Shell and BP.'

Then, suddenly, a most interesting question occurred to me.

'Why are *you* here?' I asked.

'Purely my sense of duty free,' is what I thought he had replied. I interrupted gleefully. 'Duty free?'

He held up his hand, asking to be allowed to finish what he was saying. 'Duty, free from any personal considerations.'

Then, changing the subject suspiciously quickly, he handed me a document headed *Final Communiqué*, and asked me to approve it.

I was still silently fuming about over a hundred Civil Service free-loaders on this trip. The whole lot of them with their trip paid for,

[1] Central Office of Information.

and getting paid for coming. Whereas when I'd asked if Annie could come too I'd been told that a special dispensation would be needed from the King of Qumran before she could attend any public functions with me – and that, in any case, I'd have to pay for her fares, hotel bill, everything.

These bloody civil servants have got it all completely sewn up to their own advantage. This trip is costing me hundreds of pounds because Annie really wanted to come. She's sitting opposite, chatting to Bernard, looking as though she's having a thoroughly good time. That's nice, anyway.

Anyway, I digress. I suddenly realised what was in my hand. Humphrey had written a final communiqué *before* the meeting. I told him he couldn't possibly do that.

'On the contrary, Minister, you can't write the communiqué *after* the meeting. We have had to get agreement from half a dozen other departments, from the EEC Commission, from Washington, from the Qumrani Embassy – you can't do that in a few hours in the middle of the desert.'

So I glanced at it. Then I pointed out that it was useless, hypothetical, sheer guesswork – it may bear no relation to what we actually say.

Sir Humphrey smiled calmly. 'No communiqué ever bears any relation to what you actually say.'

'So why do we have one?'

'It's just a sort of exit visa. Gets you past the press corps.' Oh, I forgot to mention, the back third of this mighty aeroplane is stuffed with drunken hacks from Fleet Street, all on freebies too. Everyone except my wife, for whom I have to pay! 'The journalists need it,' Sir Humphrey was saying, 'to justify their huge expenses for a futile non-event.'

I wasn't sure that I liked my trade mission to Qumran being described as a futile non-event. He obviously saw my face fall, for he added: 'I mean, a great triumph for you. Which is why it's a futile non-event for the press.'

He's right about that. Journalists hate reporting successes. 'Yes, what they really want is for me to get drunk at the official reception.'

'Not much hope of that.'

I asked why not, and then realised I'd asked a rather self-incriminating question. But Humphrey seemed not to notice. Instead, he replied gloomily, 'Qumran is dry.'

'Well, it is in the desert, isn't it?' I said and then I suddenly grasped what he meant. Islamic Law! Why hadn't I realised? Why hadn't I asked? Why hadn't he *told* me?

It seems that we can get a drink or two at our own Embassy. But the official reception and dinner are at the Palace. For five solid hours. *Five hours without a single drinkie.*

I asked Humphrey if we could manage with hip flasks.

He shook his head. 'Too risky. We have to grin and bear it.'

So I sat here and read the communiqué which was full of the usual guff about bonds between our two countries, common interests, frank and useful conversations and all that crap. Humphrey was reading the *FT*.[1] I was wondering what we would do if the talks were *so* far removed from what it says in the communiqué that we couldn't sign it. Suppose there were to be a diplomatic incident at the reception. I'd have to contact London somehow. I'd need some way of directly communicating with the Foreign Secretary, for instance, or even the PM.

And then the idea flashed into my mind.

'Humphrey,' I suggested tentatively, 'can't we set up a security communications room next door to the reception? At the Sheikh's Palace, I mean? With emergency telephones and Telex lines to Downing Street. Then we could fill it with cases of booze that we'll smuggle in from the Embassy. We could liven up our orange juice and nobody would ever know.'

He gazed at me in astonishment. 'Minister!'

I was about to apologise for going too far, when he went on, 'That is a stroke of genius.'

I thanked him modestly, and asked if we could really do it.

Musing on it for a moment, he said that a special communications room would only be justified if there were a major crisis.

I pointed out that five hours without a drink is a major crisis.

We decided that, as the pound is under pressure at the moment, a communications room could be justified.

Humphrey has promised his enthusiastic support for the project.

[*It seems that this diplomatically dangerous prank was put into effect immediately on arrival in Qumran. Certainly, British Embassy files show that instructions for installing a British diplomatic communications room were given on the day the Trade Mission arrived in Qumran. Prince Mohammed gave his immediate permission and a*

[1] *Financial Times*.

Photo by courtesy of FCO, Middle East Desk

telephone hot line to Downing Street was swiftly installed, plus a scrambler, a couple of Telexes and so forth.

This temporary communications centre was situated in a small ante-room near to one of the Palace's main reception areas. The following day the British party arrived at the Palace. James Hacker was accompanied by his wife Annie. The Qumranis had found it difficult to refuse permission as Her Majesty the Queen had previously been received at the Palace and thus the precedent had been set for admitting special women on special occasions.

Shortly after the reception began, at which orange juice was being served, Hacker was presented with a gold and silver rosewater jar, as a token of the esteem in which the Qumrani government held the British – Ed.]

May 17th

Yesterday we went to the teetotal reception at Prince Mohammed's palace, and today I've got the most frightful hangover.

Unfortunately I don't remember the end of the reception awfully clearly, though I do have a hazy memory of Sir Humphrey telling some Arab that I'd suddenly been taken ill and had to be rushed off to bed. Actually that was the truth, if not the whole truth.

It was a very large reception. The British delegation was a bloody sight too big to start with. And then there were an enormous number of Arabs there too.

The evening more or less started with the presentation to me of a splendid gift accompanied by diplomatic speeches about what a pleasure it is to commemorate this day. Subsequently, chatting with one of the Arab guests it transpired that apparently it's a magnificent example of seventeenth-century Islamic Art, or so he said.

I asked what it was for originally. He said it was a rosewater jar. I said I supposed that that meant it was for rosewater, and the conversation was already getting rather bogged down along these lines when Bernard arrived at my elbow with the first of the evening's urgent and imaginative messages. Though I must admit that, at first, I didn't quite follow what he was saying.

'Excuse me, Minister, there is an urgent call for you in our communications room. A Mr Haig.'

I thought he meant General Haig. But no.

'I actually mean Mr Haig, Minister – you know, with the dimples.'

I nodded in a worried sort of way, said 'Ah yes' importantly, excused myself and hurried away to the communications room.

I must say Humphrey had seen to it that someone had set the whole thing up beautifully. Phones, Telex, a couple of our security chaps with walkie-talkies, cipher machines, the works.

And just in case the place was bugged by our hosts I was careful not to ask for a drink but to ask for the message from Mr Haig. Immediately one of our chaps poured some Scotch into my orange juice. It looked browner, but no one could really tell.

SIR BERNARD WOOLLEY RECALLS:[1]

The official reception at the Palace of Qumran was an evening that I shall never forget. Firstly, there was the extraordinary strain of covering up for Hacker's increasing drunkenness. And not only Hacker, in fact: several members of the British delegation were in on the secret and it was notice-

[1] In conversation with the Editors.

able that their glasses of orange juice became more and more golden brown as the evening wore on.

But that evening also saw the start of a most unfortunate chain of events that might have led to an early end of my career.

Mrs Hacker was the only woman present. They'd made her a sort of honorary man for the evening. And while Hacker was off getting one of his refills, she remarked that the rosewater jar would look awfully good on the corner table of her hall in London.

It fell to me to explain to her that it was a gift to the Minister.

At first she didn't understand, and said that it was his hall too. I had to explain that it was a gift to the Minister *qua* Minister, and that she would not be allowed to keep it. I was naturally mindful of the near-scandal caused by the Tony Crosland coffee-pot incident, which had occurred only a few years earlier.

She wanted to know if they were supposed to give it back. Clearly not. I explained that it would have been a frightfully insulting thing to do. So she observed, rather sensibly, that if she couldn't keep it and couldn't give it back, she couldn't see what she *could* do.

I explained that official gifts become the property of the government, and are stored in some basement somewhere in Whitehall.

She couldn't see any sense in that. I couldn't either, except that clearly it is not in the public interest for Ministers to be allowed to receive valuable gifts from anybody. I explained that one might keep a gift valued up to approximately fifty pounds.

She asked me how you found out the value. I said that you get a valuation. And then she flattered me in a way that I found irresistible. She asked me to get a valuation, said that it would be 'wonderful' if it were less than fifty pounds, because it was 'awfully pretty', and then told me that I was absolutely wonderful and she didn't know what they would do without me.

Regrettably, I fell for it, and promised that I would see what I could do.

Meanwhile I was being sent on errands by Hacker. He returned from one of his many trips to the temporary Communications Centre which we'd set up, telling me loudly that there was a message for me from Mr John Walker. From the Scotch Office. Aware that we could easily be overheard, I asked if he meant the Scottish Office.

As I left very much in need of some whisky, Mrs Hacker asked if there was a message for her.

'Of course there is, darling,' the Minister replied hospitably. 'Bernard will collect it for you if you give him your glass.' I shot him a meaningful look and he continued, 'if you give him your glass he'll get you some orange juice too.'

I stayed close to the Minister's side for most of the evening which was just as well because he continually made tactless remarks. At one point he was looking for Sir Humphrey and I led him across to where Sir Humphrey and a man named Ross (from the FCO) were talking to Prince Mohammed.

Unfortunately both Ross and Sir Humphrey looked like Qumranis when approached from behind, as they were both dressed in full Arab robes and

Prince Mohammed and Sir Humphrey Appleby – kindly lent by the Trustees of the Archives of the Anglo-Arabian Friendship League

headdresses. In spite of Prince Mohammed's presence, Hacker was unable to disguise his shock as Sir Humphrey turned. He asked Humphrey why on earth he was dressed up like that.

Sir Humphrey explained that this was a traditional Foreign Office courtesy to our hosts. Ross confirmed that this was spot on, and Prince Mohammed said that indeed he regarded it as a most warm and gracious compliment. Nonetheless Hacker took Sir Humphrey aside and, in a voice that had not been lowered sufficiently, said: 'I can't believe my eyes. What have you come as? Ali Baba?'

I really did find it most awfully funny. Old Humphrey began to explain that when in Rome . . . and so forth. Hacker wasn't having any truck with that.

'This is not Rome, Humphrey,' he said severely. 'You look ridiculous.' This was undeniably true, but Humphrey found it rather wounding to be told. Hacker didn't let it go at that, either. 'If you were in Fiji, would you wear a grass skirt?'

Humphrey replied pompously that the Foreign Office took the view that, as the Arab nations are very sensitive people, we should show them whose side we're on.

Hacker remarked: 'It may come as a surprise to the Foreign Office, but you are supposed to be on *our* side.'

I decided that their conversation should continue in private, so I interrupted them and told Sir Humphrey that the Soviet Embassy was on the line – a Mr Smirnoff. And then I told Hacker, who was looking distinctly thirsty, that there was a message for him from the British Embassy Compound. The school. A delegation of Teachers.

He brightened up immediately, and, hurrying off, made some dreadful pun about going to greet the Teachers at once, before the Bell's goes.

Prince Mohammed sidled up to me, and observed softly that we were all receiving a great many urgent messages. There was no twinkle in his eye, no hint that he had spotted that all the British orange juice was turning steadily browner – and yet, I wondered if he realised what was going on. To this day, of course, I still don't know.

Unwilling to prolong the conversation, I edged away. And I found myself face to face with a smiling Arab who had been close to me earlier in the evening when I was talking to Annie Hacker about the rosewater jar. This next conversation, with its fateful consequences, is the first reason why this whole evening is etched forever on my memory.

Although dressed in traditional Arab style, the smiling Arab spoke perfect English and clearly knew the West only too well.

'Excuse me, *Effendi*,' he began, 'but I could not help overhearing your conversation about valuing the gift. Perhaps I can help.'

I was surprised. And grateful. And I asked if he had any idea how much it was worth.

He smiled. 'Of course. An original seventeenth-century rosewater jar is very valuable.'

'Oh dear,' I said, thinking of Annie Hacker's disappointment.

'You are not pleased?' Naturally, he was a little surprised.

I hastened to explain. 'Yes – and no. I mean if it is too valuable, the Minister is not allowed to keep it. So I was hoping it wasn't.'

He understood immediately, and smiled even more. 'Ah yes. Well, as I was saying, an original seventeenth-century rosewater jar is very valuable but this copy, though excellently done, is not of the same order.'

'Oh good. How much?'

He was a very shrewd fellow. He eyed me for a moment, and then said, 'I should be interested to hear your guess.'

'A little under fifty pounds?' I asked hopefully.

'Brilliant,' he replied without hesitation. 'Quite a connoisseur!'

I asked him if he could sign a valuation certificate. He agreed, but added that our English customs are very strange. 'You are so strict about a little gift. And yet your electronics company pays our Finance Minister a million dollars for his co-operation in securing this contract. Is that not strange?'

Of course, I was utterly horrified. I said that I hoped he didn't mean what I thought he meant.

He smiled from ear to ear. 'Of course. I work for the Finance Ministry. I got my share of the money.'

'For what?'

'For keeping my mouth shut!'

It seemed to me that someone would be asking for that money back from him any time now. But excusing myself as quickly as I decently could, I made my way hurriedly through the crowd, looking for Sir Humphrey. Not easy as he was still dressed up like one of the natives.

I found Sir Humphrey talking to the Minister, of all people. Rather clumsily, I asked if I could have a word with Sir Humphrey in private. Hacker told me that I could speak freely. Momentarily nonplussed, because of the enormity of the information that I was about to reveal to Sir Humphrey, I came up with a foolproof way of removing Hacker from the room for a couple of minutes.

'Minister,' I said, 'you're wanted in the Communications Room. The VAT man.' He looked blank. 'About your '69 returns.' He must have had a great deal too much already for he just stared at me as if I was mad, until I was forced to say, 'Vat 69'.

'Ah. Ah. Yes,' he said, turned gleefully, bumped into a hovering prince, and spilt what was left of his previous drink.

'Bernard,' Sir Humphrey took me by the arm and led me quickly to one side. 'I'm beginning to think that the Minister's had almost as many urgent messages as he can take.'

I was glad he'd led me to a quiet corner. I immediately blurted out that I had just found out the most terrible thing: that the contract was obtained by bribery.

Sir Humphrey, to my intense surprise, was completely unconcerned. Not only that, he *knew*. He told me that all contracts in Qumran were obtained by bribery. 'Everybody knows that. It's perfectly all right as long as nobody knows.'

I was pretty sure that the Minister didn't know. I suggested telling him.

'Certainly not,' Sir Humphrey admonished me.

'But if everybody knows . . .'

'Everybody else,' he said firmly. 'You do not necessarily let Ministers know what everybody else knows.'

At the crucial moment in the discussion two people converged upon us. From our right, His Royal Highness, Prince Feisal. And from our left, the Minister, looking distinctly the worse for wear.

'Ah, Lawrence of Arabia,' cried Hacker as he lurched towards Sir Humphrey. 'There's a message for you in the communications room.'

'Oh?' said Sir Humphrey, 'who is it this time?'

'Napoleon,' announced the Minister, giggled, then fell to the floor.

[*Hacker's diary continues – Ed.*]

May 19th

Back in England, and back at the office. Feel rather jet-lagged. I often wonder if we statesmen really are capable of making the wisest decisions for our countries in the immediate aftermath of foreign travel.

Today there was a most unfortunate story in the *Financial Times*, reporting a story from the French press.

Financial Times Thursday May 19

BES bribery allegation

IT IS ALLEGED in *Le Monde* that the recent British Electronic systems contract with Qumran was won by bribery.

It is said in Paris that this is the latest in a long line of scandals, of which Lockheed and Northrop are two of the most famous examples, revealing a hideous web of corruption woven by Western industrial countries and third world governments that forms a blot on our modern civilisation.

I showed it to Bernard. A lot of use that was!

'Webs don't form blots, Minister,' was his comment.

'What?' I said.

'Spiders don't have ink, you see. Only cuttlefish.' Sometimes I think that Bernard is completely off his head. Spiders don't have cuttlefish. I couldn't see what he meant at all. Sometimes I wonder if he says these idiotic things so that he can avoid answering my questions. [*Another sign of Hacker's growing awareness – Ed.*]

So I asked him, directly, what he thought about publishing a baseless accusation of this kind against British Electronic Systems.

He muttered that it was terrible, and agreed with me that the squalid world of baksheesh and palm-greasing is completely foreign to our nature. 'After all, we *are* British,' I remarked.

He agreed without hesitation that we are British.

But there was something shifty in his manner. So I didn't let it drop. 'And yet,' I said, 'it's not like the *FT* to print this sort of thing unless there's something behind it.'

And I looked at him and waited. Bernard seemed to me to be affecting an air of studious unconcern.

'There isn't anything behind it, is there Bernard?'

He got to his feet, and looked at the newspaper. 'I think the sports news is behind it, Minister.'

Clearly there *is* something behind it, and clearly Bernard has been told to keep his mouth shut. Tomorrow I have a meeting with Humphrey first thing in the morning. And I intend to get to the bottom of this matter.

May 20th

My meeting with Humphrey.

I began by showing him the article in the *FT*. Though I think Bernard must have drawn his attention to it already.

I told him that I wanted to know the truth.

'I don't think you do, Minister.'

'Will you answer a direct question, Humphrey?'

He hesitated momentarily. 'Minister, I strongly advise you not to ask a direct question.'

'Why?'

'It might provoke a direct answer.'

'It never has yet.'

It was clear to me yesterday that Bernard knows something about all this. I don't think he was levelling with me. So today I put him on the spot, in front of Humphrey, so that he couldn't say one thing to his Minister and another to his Permanent Secretary. [*This brilliant move by Hacker struck at the heart of the entire Private Secretary system – Ed.*]

'Bernard, on your word of honour, do you know anything about this?'

He stared at me like a frightened rabbit. His eyes flickered briefly at Sir Humphrey who – like me – was gazing at him in the hope (but without the confidence) that he would say the appropriate thing.

Bernard clearly didn't know how to reply, proof enough that he knew something fishy had been going on.

'Well, I, er, that is, there was, er, someone did . . .'

Humphrey interrupted hastily. 'There was a lot of gossip, that's all. Rumour. Hearsay.'

I ignored Humphrey. 'Come on Bernard.'

'Um . . . well, one of the Qumranis did tell me he had received, er, been paid . . .'

'Hearsay, Minister,' cried Humphrey indignantly.

I indicated Bernard. 'Hearsay?'

'Yes,' Humphrey was emphatic. 'Bernard heard him say it.'

Clearly I was going to get nothing further out of Bernard. But he'd told me all I needed to know.

'Humphrey. Are you telling me that BES got the contract through bribery?'

He looked pained. 'I wish you wouldn't use words like "bribery", Minister.'

I asked if he'd prefer that I use words like slush fund, sweeteners, or brown envelopes. He patronisingly informed me that these are, in his view, extremely crude and unworthy expressions for what is no more than creative negotiation. 'It is the general practice,' he asserted.

I asked him if he realised just what he was saying. After all, I ratified this contract myself, in good faith. 'And in that communiqué I announced to the press a British success in a fair fight.'

'Yes,' he mused, 'I did wonder about that bit.'

'And now,' I fumed, 'you are telling me we got it by bribery?'

'No, Minister,' he replied firmly.

There seemed to be a light at the end of the tunnel. My spirits lifted. 'Ah,' I said, 'we *didn't* get it by bribery.'

'That's not what I said,' he said carefully.

'Well what *did* you say?'

'I said I am not telling you we got it by bribery.'

Pure sophistry if ever I heard any. It seemed there was no light at the end of the tunnel after all. Or if there was, it was turning out to be the proverbial oncoming train. So I asked him how he described the payments that had been made.

'You mean, how does the contract describe them?' he asked, to make it clear that he would never describe them at all, under any circumstances.

To cut a long story short, Bernard gave me a list of informal guidelines for making these payments, a list that is in highly confidential circulation among top multinational companies.

1 Below £100,000

- Retainers
- Personal donations
- Special discounts
- Miscellaneous outgoings

2 £100,000 to £500,000

- Managerial surcharge
- Operating costs
- Ex-gratia payments
- Agents' fees
- Political contributions
- Extra-contractual payments

3 £500,000 +

- Introduction fees
- Commission fees
- Managements' expenses
- Administrative overheads
- Advance against profit sharing

To me the scale of corruption was even more appalling than the fact that it was going on. [*A typical Hacker response. Clearly, corruption was perfectly acceptable to Hacker in smallish amounts. As subsequently became clear in the affair of the rosewater jar – Ed.*]

I asked how the payments were generally made.

'Anything from a numbered account in the Swiss Bank to a fistful of used oncers slipped under the door of the gents.'

He was so casual about it. He couldn't see how shocking it was. He *said* he couldn't, anyway.

I spluttered almost incoherently about bribery and corruption being sin. And a criminal offence.

'Minister.' He gave me a patient smile. 'That is a narrow parochial view. In other parts of the world they see it quite differently.'

'Humphrey! Sin is not a branch of geography!'

But he argued that sin *is* a branch of geography, that in developing countries the size of the 'extra-contractual payment' is the means of showing how serious you are about the deal. When a multinational makes a big 'political contribution' it simply demonstrates that it expects big profits.

[*It is like a publisher's advance to an author. The one who pays the biggest advance is the one who is going for the biggest sales – Ed.*]

'You're telling me,' I asked, 'that winking at corruption is government policy?'

'Oh no Minister! That would be unthinkable. It could never be government policy. Only government practice.'

His double standards leave me quite breathless.

In the middle of this unprecedented discussion [*Not so – Ed.*] the press office rang. They wanted a statement about the Qumran bribery allegation. I had no idea what to say to them. I asked Humphrey for his help.

'I'm sure the press office can draft something convincing and meaningless,' he said obligingly. 'That's what they're paid for, after all.'

I told him he was an appalling cynic. He took that as a compliment, remarking that a cynic is only a term used by an idealist to describe a realist.

I realised from his remark about the press office that he expected me to help with some cover-up if necessary. A shocking suggestion. Or implication, to be precise, since he hadn't exactly suggested it. And then, I also realised I had an alternative.

'I'll tell the truth,' I said abruptly.

'Minister! What are you thinking of!'

'I knew nothing of this. Why should I defend what I never approved?'

Then he trotted out all the usual stuff. That the contract is worth thousands of British jobs, and millions of export dollars, and that we can't throw all that away for some small technical irregularity.

I explained, again, that it is not a small technical irregularity, but corruption!

'No Minister, just a few uncontracted prepayments . . .'

I had heard enough. I was forced to explain to him that government is not just a matter of fixing and manipulating. There is a moral dimension.

'Of course, Minister. A moral dimension. I assure you it is never out of my thoughts.'

'So,' I went on, 'if this question comes up in the House, or if the papers start asking questions, I shall announce an inquiry.'

'Excellent idea,' he agreed. 'I shall be more than happy to conduct it.'

I took a deep breath. 'No Humphrey. Not an internal inquiry. A real inquiry.'

His eyes widened in horror. 'Minister! You can't be serious!'

'A real inquiry!' I repeated emphatically.

'No, no, I beg you!'

'The moral dimension.' It really is time moral issues were made central to our government once again. And I'm the man to do it.

SIR BERNARD WOOLLEY RECALLS:[1]
It was shortly after the day that Hacker threatened a real inquiry into the Qumran deal that I went to Hacker's London flat to collect him *en route* for an official visit to the Vehicle Licensing Centre in Swansea. Some morale-boosting was urgently called for down there, because the installation of the labour-saving computers had caused such delays that thousands more staff had been taken on to sort out the chaos. It looked as though larger computers would now be necessary, at some considerable public expense, partly in order to handle the situation and partly in order to avoid our having to lay off all the extra employees now working there. As job-creation was central to our strategy in the depressed or Special Development Areas [*i.e. Marginal Constituencies – Ed.*] it was important to find something for these chaps to do. Clearly Hacker was not able to make any useful contribution in that area, but Sir Humphrey felt that a goodwill visit from the Minister would keep things friendlier for the time being and would make it look as though something was being done while we all racked our brains and tried to think what!

In any event, to cut a long story short [*too late – Ed.*] I was standing in the Minister's front hall chatting to Mrs Hacker, waiting for the Minister to finish dressing, when I saw the rosewater jar from Qumran, and commented that it looked awfully nice.

Mrs Hacker agreed enthusiastically, and added that a friend of hers had dropped in that day and had been frightfully interested.

[1] In conversation with the Editors.

'Really?'

'Yes.' And then she dropped the bombshell. 'Her name's Jenny Goodwin – from *The Guardian*.'

'*The Guardian*,' I said, quietly stunned.

'Yes. She asked me where it came from.'

'A journalist,' I muttered, aghast.

'Yes. Well . . . *The Guardian,* anyway. She asked what it was worth, and I said about fifty quid.'

'You said about fifty quid.' My bowels had turned to water. I felt hot and cold simultaneously. I could hardly speak. I just tried to keep the conversation going somehow.

'Yes. Fifty quid.' She was looking at me strangely now. 'Funnily enough, she thought it was genuine.'

'She thought it was genuine,' I repeated.

'Yes, Bernard, you sound like an answering machine.'

I apologised.

Mrs Hacker then told me that the journalist, one Jenny Goodwin, had asked if she could ring up the Qumrani Embassy to ask what it was worth.

'To ask what it was worth,' I mumbled, hopelessly.

She looked at me keenly. 'It *is* only a copy, isn't it Bernard?' she asked.

I managed to say that so far as I knew, and so I was led to believe, and so forth, and then the Minister hurried downstairs and my bacon was saved. For the time being. But I knew that the jig was up and that my career was on the line, my neck was on the block, and my next appointment was likely to be at the Jobcentre in the Horseferry Road.

My only hope was that the Minister would come to my defence when the facts came out. After all, I'd always done my best for him. I didn't think I could expect much sympathy or help from Sir Humphrey. But I had no choice but to tell him the whole story as soon as I could.

[*The following morning Bernard Woolley made a special request for an urgent meeting with Sir Humphrey Appleby. Sir Humphrey made a note about it, which we found in the Departmental files at Walthamstow – Ed.*]

BW requested an urgent meeting. He asked for a word with me. I said yes, and waited, but he did not speak. So I told him that I'd said yes.

Again he did not speak. I noticed that he was sweating, but it was a cool day. He seemed to be in a state of considerable mental anguish, such as I had never observed in him before.

I asked the standard questions. I thought perhaps that Woolley had sent the Minister to the wrong dinner, given him the wrong speech, or – worst of all – shown him some papers that we didn't mean him to see.

He shook his head silently, and I divined that the situation was even worse than that. So I told him to sit down, which he did gratefully. I waited.

It slowly emerged that the exquisite rosewater jar, given to the Minister in Qumran, was the root of the problem. Apparently the Minister's wife liked it. Not surprising. BW had explained the rules to her, and she had looked terribly sad. They always do. Then she had asked if it was really worth more than fifty pounds, and said how marvellous it would be if it wasn't. And BW, it seems, had agreed to 'help'.

I understand his motives, but a seventeenth-century vase – well, really!

BW then explained that there was a 'terribly nice Qumrani businessman'. And this fellow had apparently valued it as a copy and not as an original. For £49.95. A most convenient sum.

I asked BW if he had believed this man. He wavered. 'I . . . er . . . he said he was an expert . . . well . . . he spoke Arabic awfully well, so I er . . . accepted his valuation. In good faith. After all, Islam is a jolly good faith.'

Not a convincing explanation, I felt. I told him that he had taken a grave risk, and he was fortunate that no one had asked any questions.

I was intending to let the matter drop, and merely record a reprimand in his report. But at this juncture he informed me that a journalist from *The Guardian* had seen the jar in Hacker's house, that Mrs Hacker had said it was a copy, and that further questions were to be asked.

It is a great tragedy that the press are so horribly suspicious about this sort of thing. But I told BW that we had no option but to inform the Minister.

[*Hacker's diary continues – Ed.*]

May 23rd

Humphrey had made a submission on Friday (sounds like wrestling, doesn't it?). In other words, he submitted a paper to me, suggesting various methods of hushing up this bribery scandal.

Obviously I was not intending to go *out of my way* to reveal it. But equally I couldn't see how I could allow myself to be put in the position of sweeping bribery under the carpet. So if questions were asked, I had every intention of announcing a full independent enquiry chaired by a QC.

I explained this to Humphrey at the start of our meeting this morning. He started going on about the contract being worth £340 million. 'Get thee behind me, Humphrey,' I said, and reminded him of the moral dimension of government. The contract may be worth £340 million, but my job's worth even more to me.

But then Humphrey told me that Bernard had something to tell me. I waited. Bernard was looking very anxious. Finally he coughed and began to speak, rather haltingly.

'Um . . . you know that jar the Qumranis gave you?'

I remembered it well. 'Yes, we've got it in the flat. Most attractive.'

I waited. Clearly he was worried about something.

'I told Mrs Hacker that it was all right to keep it,' he said, 'because I had it valued at under fifty pounds. But I'm not sure . . . the man who valued it was awfully nice . . . I told him Mrs Hacker liked it a lot . . . but he might have been er, being helpful.'

I still couldn't see any problem. So I told him not to worry, and that no one will ever know. In fact, I was rash enough to congratulate him for being jolly enterprising.

Then came the bad news. 'Yes, but you see, Mrs Hacker told me this morning that a *Guardian* journalist came round and started asking questions.'

This was horrifying! I asked to see the valuation. It was written on the back of the menu. [*The Treasury were never awfully happy about valuations written on the backs of menus – Ed.*]

I asked what the jar was really worth. Humphrey had the information at his fingertips. If it's a copy, then the valuation is roughly correct. But if it's an original – £5000.

And I had kept it!

If I'd had a day or two to consider the matter there would have been no problem. It would have been pretty easy to dream up some valid explanation of the situation, one that got both me and Bernard off the hook.

But at that moment Bill Pritchard came bursting in from the press office. And he brought even worse news!

The Guardian had been on the phone to him. They'd been on to the Qumrani Embassy, telling them that my wife had said that this extremely valuable seventeenth-century thing presented to me by the Qumrani Government was a copy. The Qumrani Government was incensed at the suggestion that they insulted Britain by giving me a worthless gift. (Though I can't see the point of giving me a valuable gift if it's got to be stored in the vault forever.) The FCO then phoned Bill and told him it was building up into the biggest diplomatic incident since *Death of a Princess*.

I thought I'd heard enough bad news for one day. But no. He added that Jenny Goodwin of *The Guardian* was in the private office, demanding to see me right away.

I thought Annie had always described Jenny Goodwin as a friend of hers. Some friend! You just can't trust the media! Despicable, muck-raking nosey parkers, always snooping around trying to get at the truth!

Bernard looked beseechingly at me. But it was clear that I had no choice.

'My duty is clear,' I said in my Churchillian voice. 'I have no choice.'

'No choice?' squeaked Bernard, like Piglet confronting the Heffalump.

I made it clear that indeed I had no choice. My wife had not asked him to lie about the value of the gift. He admitted she hadn't. I explained to Bernard that I fully realised that he had done this with the best of possible motives, but that there could be no excuse for falsifying a document.

He protested that he hadn't. But of course he was hair-splitting.

But my trouble is, I never know when to stop. I then launched into a tremendously self-righteous tirade. I told him that I cannot have it thought that I asked him to do this. Then I turned on Humphrey, and told him that I cannot have it thought that I will tolerate bribery and corruption in our business dealings. 'Enough is enough,' I went on, digging my own grave relentlessly. 'If this journalist asks me straight questions about either of these matters I must give straight answers. There is a moral dimension.'

I should have realised, since Humphrey was looking so thoroughly unflappable, that he had an ace up his sleeve. I didn't guess. And he played it.

'I agree with you, Minister. I see now that there is a moral dimension to everything. Will I tell the press about the communications room or will you?'

Blackmail. Shocking, but true! He was clearly saying that if I laid the blame for (a) the bribery and corruption, or (b) the rosewater jar – *neither* of which were my fault – at his door or Bernard's door or *anyone's* door (if it comes to that) then he would drop me right in it.

I think I just gaped at him. Anyway, after a pause he murmured something about the moral dimension. Hypocritical bastard.

I tried to explain that the communications room was not the same thing at all. Completely different, in fact. Drinking is nothing to do with corruption.

But Humphrey would have none of it. 'Minister, we deceived the Qumranis. I am racked with guilt, tormented by the knowledge that we violated their solemn and sacred Islamic laws in their own country. Sooner or later we must own up and admit that it was all your idea.'

'It wasn't,' I said desperately.

'It was,' they chorused.

I would have denied it, but it was their word against mine. And who would ever take the word of a mere politician against that of a Permanent Secretary and a Private Secretary?

Sir Humphrey piled on the pressure. 'Is it fifty lashes or one hundred?' he asked Bernard, who seemed to be brightening up a little.

In what seemed like an interminable pause, I contemplated my options. The more I contemplated my options the more they disappeared, until I didn't seem to have any at all. Finally Bill said that I had to meet the journalist or she would write something terrible anyway.

I nodded weakly. Humphrey and Bernard hovered. I knew that only one possible course was open to me. Attack! Attack is always the best form of defence, especially when dealing with the press.

And after all, dealing with the press is my stock-in-trade. That is what I'm best at.

[*That is what Ministers had to be best at. At that time the Minister's main role was to be the chief public relations man for his Ministry – Ed.*]

I sized her up in no time as she came into the office. Attractive voice, slightly untidy pulled-through-a-hedge-backwards sort of look, trousers, absolutely what you'd expect from *The Guardian* – a typical knee-jerk liberal, Shirley Williams type.

As she came in a rough strategy formed in my mind. I was charming, but cool, and gave her the impression that I was fairly busy and didn't have too much time to spare. If you don't do that, if you let them think that you think they are important, it confirms their suspicions that they are on to something.

So I adopted a brisk tone like the family doctor. 'What seems to be the trouble?' I asked in my best bedside manner.

'Two things,' she said, 'both of them rather worrying to the public.'

How dare she speak for the public, who know nothing about any of it? And never will, if I can help it!

She started with the French allegation of BES corruption in getting the Qumrani contract.

'Absolute nonsense,' I said categorically. If in doubt, always issue an absolute denial. And if you're going to lie, then lie with one hundred per cent conviction.

'But they quoted reports of payments to officials,' she said.

I pretended to lose my rag. I fixed her with a piercing gaze. 'This is absolutely typical. A British company slogs its guts out to win orders and create jobs and earn dollars, and what do they get from the media? A smear campaign.'

'But if they won by bribery . . .'

I talked over her. 'There is no question of bribery – I have had an internal inquiry and all these so-called payments have been identified.'

'What as?' she asked, slightly on the retreat.

Humphrey saw his opportunity to help.

'Commission fees,' he said quickly. 'Administrative overheads.'

He'd given me time to think – 'Operating costs. Managerial surcharge,' I added.

Bernard chimed in too. 'Introduction expenses. Miscellaneous outgoings.'

I thundered on. 'We have looked into every brown envelope,' I found myself saying, but changed it to 'balance sheet' in the nick of time. 'And everything is in order.'

'I see,' she said. She really didn't have a leg to stand on. She had no proof at all. She had to believe me. And I'm sure she knew only too well the risk of incurring the wrath of a Minister of the Crown with false allegations and accusations.

[*We get the impression that Hacker, like many politicians, had the useful ability to believe that black was white merely because he was saying so – Ed.*]

I told her that the allegations she was making were the symptoms of a very sick society for which the media must take their share of the blame. I demanded to know why she wanted to put thousands of British jobs at risk. She had no answer. [*Naturally, as she did not want to put thousands of British jobs at risk – Ed.*] I told her that I would be calling on the Press Council to censure the press for a disgraceful breach of professional ethics in running the story.

'Indeed,' I continued, rather superbly I thought, 'the Council, and the House of Commons itself must surely be concerned about the standards that have applied in this shameful episode, and pressure will be brought to bear to ensure that this type of gutter press reporting is not repeated.'

She looked stunned. She was completely unprepared for my counter-attack, as I thought she would be.

Nervously she collected herself and asked her second question, with a great deal less confidence, I was pleased to see. 'This rose-water jar, apparently presented to you in Qumran?'

'Yes?' I snapped, belligerently.

'Well . . .' she panicked but continued, 'I saw it in your house actually.'

'Yes,' I replied, 'we're keeping it there temporarily.'

'Temporarily?'

'Oh yes,' I was doing my ingenuous routine now. 'It's very valuable, you see.'

'But Mrs Hacker said it was an imitation.'

I laughed. 'Burglars, you silly girl. Burglars! We didn't want gossip going around. Until we've got rid of it.'

Now she was completely confused. 'Got rid of it?'

'Of course. I'm presenting it to our local museum when we get back to the constituency on Saturday. Obviously I can't keep it. Government property, you know.' And then I came out with my master stroke. 'Now – what was your question?'

She had nothing else to say. She said it was nothing, it was all right, everything was fine. I charmingly thanked her for dropping in, and ushered her out.

Humphrey was full of admiration.

'Superb, Minister.'

And Bernard was full of gratitude.

'Thank you, Minister.'

I told them it was nothing. After all, we have to stick by our friends. Loyalty is a much underrated quality. I told them so.

'Yes Minister,' they said, but somehow they didn't look all that grateful.

18

The Bed of Nails

[In politics, August is known as the 'silly season'. This is a time when voters are away on holiday, and trivial issues are pushed in the forefront of the press in order to sell newspapers to holidaymakers. It is also the time when the House of Commons has risen for the summer recess and is thus an excellent time for the government to announce new or controversial measures about which the House of Commons cannot protest until they reconvene in October – by which time most political events that took place in August would be regarded as dead ducks by the media.

It follows that August is also the time when Cabinet Ministers are most off their guard. Members of Parliament are not at hand to question them or harass them, and the Ministers themselves – secure from the unlikely event of an August reshuffle and secure from serious press coverage of their activities – relax more than they should.

Perhaps this is the explanation of the transport policy crisis, which very nearly led to Hacker taking on one of the most unpopular jobs in Whitehall. How he evaded it is a tribute to the shrewd guiding hand of Sir Humphrey, coupled with Hacker's own growing political skills.

Early in the month a meeting took place at Ten Downing Street between Sir Mark Spencer, the Prime Minister's Chief Special Adviser, and Sir Arnold Robinson, the Secretary of the Cabinet. Sir Mark's files contain no reference to this meeting, but as he was not a career civil servant this is not surprising. But Sir Arnold Robinson's diary, recently found in the Civil Service archives Walthamstow, reveal a conspiracy in the making – Ed.]

August 11th.

Lunched with Sir Mark Spencer today. He and the P.M. are keen to bring in an integrated transport policy. I suggested that Hacker could be the best man for the job, as he doesn't know anything at all about the subject. The Secretary of State for Transport, who knows a lot about it, won't touch it with a ten foot barge pole. M.S. and I agreed that this job was indeed a bed of nails, a crown of thorns, a booby trap – which is why I suggested Hacker, of course.

Lunched with Sir Mark Spencer today. He and the PM are keen to bring in an integrated transport policy.

I suggested that Hacker could be the best man for the job, as he doesn't know anything at all about the subject. The Secretary of State for Transport, who knows a lot about it, won't touch it with a ten foot barge pole. M.S. and I agreed that this job was indeed a bed of nails, a crown of thorns, a booby trap – which is why I suggested Hacker, of course.

He is ideally qualified, as I explained to M.S., because the job needs a particular talent – lots of activity, but no actual achievement.

At first M.S. couldn't see how to swing it on Hacker. The answer was obvious: we had to make it seem like a special honour.

The big problem was to get Hacker to take it on before Humphrey Appleby hears of it, because there's no doubt that Old Humpy would instantly smell a rat. '*Timeo Danaos et dona ferentes*'[1] he would be sure to say, though he'd probably have to say it in English for Hacker's benefit as Hacker went to the LSE.[2]

It seemed clear that we had to get a commitment today, especially as my departure for the Florida Conference on 'Government and Participation' is both imminent and urgent, tomorrow at the latest. [*During the 1970s and 1980s it was the custom for senior government officials to send themselves off on futile conferences to agreeable resorts at public expense during the month of August – Ed.*]

Hacker came to meet us at tea-time. I had resolved to flatter him, which almost invariably leads to success with politicians. M.S. and I agreed therefore that we would give the job the title of Transport Supremo, which was a lot more attractive than Transport Muggins.

[1] 'Beware of Greeks bearing gifts' is the usual rough translation.
[2] London School of Economics.

I was also careful not to inform him in advance of the purpose of the meeting, partly because I did not want him to have the opportunity to discuss it with Humpy, and partly because I knew he would be anxious about being summoned to Number Ten. This would surely make him more pliable.

Events turned out precisely as I anticipated. He knew nothing whatever about transport, floundered hopelessly, was flattered to be asked and accepted the job.

It is fortunate that I shall be leaving for the country tonight, before Humpy gets to hear about all this.

[*It is interesting to compare the above recollections with Hacker's account of the same day's events in his diary – Ed.*]

August 11th

An absolutely splendid day today, with a big boost for my morale.

I was summoned to meet Mark Spencer at Number Ten. Naturally I was a bit wary, especially as I knew the PM hadn't been awfully pleased to hear about that business with the rosewater jar, even though no harm came of it all in the end. I thought I might be in for a bit of a wigging, for when I got there I was met by Arnold Robinson, the Cabinet Secretary.

However, the meeting was for quite a different purpose – I've been promoted.

Arnold kicked off by saying they wanted to offer me something that was rather an honour. For a split second I was horrified – I thought they were telling me I was to be kicked upstairs. It was a nasty moment. But, in fact, they want to put me in charge of a new integrated national transport policy.

They asked me for my views on transport. I had none, but I don't think they realised because I carefully invited them to explain themselves further. I'm sure they thought that I was merely playing my cards close to my chest.

'We've been discussing a national integrated transport policy,' they said.

'Well, why not?' I replied casually.

'You're in favour?' enquired Sir Arnold quickly.

I thought the answer required was 'yes' but I wasn't yet sure so I contented myself by looking enigmatic. I'm sure that they were by now convinced that I was sound, because Sir Mark continued: 'Unfortunately, public dissatisfaction with the nationalised transport industries is now at a high enough level to worry the government, as you know.'

Again he waited. 'Can you go on?' I enquired.

He went on. 'We need a policy.' I nodded sagely. 'It's no good just blaming the management when there's an R in the month and blaming the unions the rest of the time.'

Sir Arnold chipped in. 'And unfortunately now they've all got together. They all say that it's all the government's fault – everything that goes wrong is the result of not having a national transport policy.'

This was all news to me. I thought we had a policy. As a matter of fact, I specifically recall that in our discussions prior to the writing of our manifesto we decided that our policy was not to have a policy. I said so.

Sir Mark nodded. 'Be that as it may,' he grunted, 'the PM now wants a *positive* policy.'

I wished Sir Mark had said so earlier. But I can take a hint, and it was not too late. 'Ah, the PM, I see.' I nodded again. 'Well, I couldn't agree more, I've always thought so myself.'

Sir Arnold and Sir Mark looked pleased, but I still couldn't see what it had to do with me. I assumed that it was a Department of Transport matter. Sir Arnold disabused me.

'Obviously the Transport Secretary would love to get his teeth into the job, but he's a bit too close to it all.'

'Can't see the wood for the trees,' said Sir Mark.

'Needs an open mind. Uncluttered,' added Sir Arnold.

'So,' said Sir Mark, 'the PM has decided to appoint a Supremo to develop and implement a national transport policy.'

A *Supremo*. I asked if I were the PM's choice. The knights nodded. I must admit I felt excited and proud and really rather overwhelmed by this extraordinary good piece of news. And there were more compliments to come.

'It was decided,' said Sir Mark, 'that you had the most open mind of all.'

'And the most uncluttered,' added Sir Arnold. They really were grovelling.

I naturally responded cautiously. Firstly because I simply couldn't imagine what the job entailed, and secondly it's always good to play hard to get when you're in demand. So I thanked them for the honour, agreed that it was a pretty vital and responsible job, and asked what it entailed.

'It's to help the consumer,' said Sir Mark. Though when Sir Arnold laboriously pointed out that helping the consumer was always a vote-winner, I reminded him firmly that I was interested purely because I saw it as my duty to help. My sense of public duty.

During the conversation it gradually became clear what they had in mind. All kinds of idiocies have occurred in the past, due to a lack of a natural integrated policy. Roughly summarising now, Sir Mark and Sir Arnold were concerned about:

1 *Motorway planning:* Our motorways were planned without reference to railways, so that now there are great stretches of motorway running alongside already existing railways.

  As a result, some parts of the country are not properly served at all.

2 *The through-ticket problem:* If, for instance, you want to commute from Henley to the City, you have to buy a British Rail ticket to Paddington and then buy an underground ticket to the Bank.

3 *Timetables:* The complete absence of combined bus and railway timetables.

4 *Airport Links:* Very few. For instance, there's a British Rail Western Region line that runs less than a mile north of Heathrow – but no link line.

5 *Connections:* Bus and train services don't connect up, all over London.

Sir A. and Sir M. outlined these problems briefly. They added that there are probably problems outside London too, although understandably they didn't know about them.

The possibilities are obviously great, and it's all very exciting. I suggested having a word with Humphrey before I accepted responsibility, but they made it plain that they wanted *my* opinion and approval. Not his. Rather flattering, really. Also, it shows that they have finally realised that I'm not a straw man – I really run my Department, not like *some* Ministers.

Furthermore it transpired that the PM was due to leave for the airport in thirty minutes on the long trip involving the Ottawa Conference, and the opening of the UN General Assembly in New York, and then on to the meeting in Washington.

Jokingly I asked, 'Who's going to run the country for the next week?' but Sir Arnold didn't seem awfully amused.

Sir Mark asked if he could give the PM the good news that I had taken on the job on the way to the airport.

Graciously, I agreed.

Hacker leaving Downing Street after the meeting (London Press Association)

August 12th

At an early morning meeting with Sir Humphrey, I told him I had good news. 'I've got a new job,' I began.

'Oh dear, the Department will be awfully sorry to lose you,' he responded pleasantly. A bit *too* pleasantly, perhaps.

But I explained that it was merely an extra job, developing and implementing an integrated national transport policy. At the special request of the PM. My Permanent Secretary did not seem pleased. In fact, he seemed to flinch.

'I see,' he replied. 'And what was the *good* news?'

I thought he must have misheard, so I told him again.

'So how,' he enquired drily, '*if* I may be so bold as to enquire, would you define *bad* news?'

I asked him to explain himself.

'Minister,' he said with a heavy sigh, 'are you aware what this job would mean if you accepted it?'

'I have accepted it.'

His mouth dropped open. 'You've *what*?' he gasped.

'I have accepted it.' I went on to explain that it is an honour, and also that we need a transport policy.

'If by "we" you mean Britain, that's perfectly true,' he acknowledged. 'But if by "we" you mean you and me and this Department, we need a transport policy like an aperture in the cranial cavity.'[1]

He went on to describe the job as a bed of nails, a crown of thorns, and a booby trap.

At first I thought he was just being silly or lazy or something. I could see that it would cause him some extra administrative problems, but on the other hand it usually gave Humphrey pleasure to add to his empire – bigger budget, more staff, all that sort of thing.

'No Minister, the point is that *you* are the one who is at risk. My job, as always, is merely to protect the seat of your trousers. The reason that there has never been an integrated transport policy is that such a policy is in everybody's interest *except* the Minister who creates it.'

I couldn't see why.

Humphrey paused for a minute, and gazed at the ceiling contemplatively. 'How can I put it in a manner that is close to your heart?' he asked himself. I waited. So did Bernard. 'Ah, I have it,' he murmured, turning to look at me straight in the eye. 'It is the ultimate vote-loser.'

I was stunned. Vote-*loser*?

Sir Humphrey explained, 'Why do you think the Transport Secretary isn't doing this?'

I was just about to reply that the Transport Secretary is apparently too close to it and can't see the wood for the trees, when Sir Humphrey said: 'He's too close to it, I suppose? Can't see the wood for the trees? Is that what they told you?'

'You tell me another reason then,' I challenged him.

'Why do you think the Transport Secretary suggested the Lord Privy Seal? Why do you think the Lord Privy Seal suggested the Chancellor of the Duchy of Lancaster? Why do you think *he* suggested the Lord President of the Council?'

I had to confess I knew nothing of all this.

Sir Humphrey continued relentlessly. 'And why do you think they invited you to Number Ten behind my back?' I must admit that this explanation never occurred to me. 'Minister, this hideous appointment has been hurtling round Whitehall for the last three weeks like a grenade with the pin taken out.'

He may be right, of course. He's usually pretty well up on all the

[1] A hole in the head.

gossip. But I was not about to concede the point. I felt that Humphrey's attitude was coloured by sour grapes – sour grapes that I had been honoured in this way, and sour grapes that he hadn't been consulted, either by them or by me.

'If I can pull it off,' I said carefully, 'it will be a feather in my cap.'

'If you pull it off,' said Bernard, 'it won't be in your cap any more.' I scowled at him, and he went pink and studied his shoes.

Sir Humphrey wasn't impressed with my argument. He believes that if I do pull it off, no one will feel the benefits for ten years and long before that we will both have moved on. Or up. Or out.

'In the meantime,' he continued, 'formulating policy means making choices. Once you make a choice you please the people you favour but you infuriate everyone else. This is liable to end up as one vote gained, ten lost. If you give a job to the road services, the Rail Board and unions will scream. If you give it to the railways, the road lobby will massacre you. If you cut British Airways' investment plans they'll hold a devastating press conference the same afternoon. And you can't expand, because an overall saving is the Treasury's fundamental requirement.'

I voiced the small hope that, as I am to be the Transport Supremo, my views might carry some weight.

Humphrey could not disguise the sneer on his face. 'Transport Muggins is the Civil Service vernacular, I'm afraid. All the enemies you will make are experts in manipulating the media. PROs, trades unionists, MPs in affected constituencies. There'll be someone on television every night vilifying Hacker's Law, saying that you are a national disaster.'

His attitude angered me. I reminded him that the PM has asked me to perform this task, this necessary duty for my country. I always do my duty. Furthermore, Sir Mark believes that there are votes in it and, if so, I certainly do not intend to look a gift horse in the mouth.

'I put it to you,' replied Sir Humphrey, 'that you are looking a *Trojan* Horse in the mouth.'

I wasn't quite sure what he meant by this. 'Do you mean,' I asked, 'that if we look closely at this gift horse we'll find it's full of Trojans?'

Bernard tried to interrupt, but I silenced him with a look. Sir Humphrey insisted that he be given a chance to prove his point, and offered to arrange a meeting, a preliminary discussion, with Under-Secretaries from the Department of Transport – the Road Division, the Rail Division and the Air Transport Division. 'I think it may illustrate the extent of some of the problems you will encounter.'

'You can arrange it if you like,' I told him. 'But I intend to take this on. If I succeed this could be my Falkland Islands.'

'Yes,' agreed Sir Humphrey, 'and you could be General Galtieri.'

August 15th

When I arrived in my office today I found the most curious memo from Bernard sitting on my desk.

Memorandum
From: The Private Secretary
To: The Minister

Aug 12th

CONFIDENTIAL, FOR THE MINISTER'S EYES ONLY

With reference to your comment at today's meeting with the Permanent Secretary at which you enquired, in connection with looking the Integrated Transport Policy gift horse in the mouth, whether, if the gift horse were a Trojan Horse (as suggested by the Permanent Secretary that so it might prove to be) it would be full of Trojans.

Aug. 12th

CONFIDENTIAL, FOR THE MINISTER'S EYES ONLY

With reference to your comment at today's meeting with the Permanent Secretary at which you enquired, in connection with looking the Integrated Transport Policy gift horse in the mouth, whether, if the gift horse were a Trojan Horse (as suggested by the Permanent Secretary that so it might prove to be) it would be full of Trojans.

May I respectfully draw the Minister's attention to the fact that, if he had looked the Trojan Horse in the mouth, he would have found Greeks inside.

The reason, of course, is that it was the Greeks who gave the Trojan Horse to the Trojans. Therefore, technically it was not a Trojan Horse at all. In fact, it was a Greek Horse. Hence the tag 'Timeo Danaos et dona ferentes', which, as the Minister will recall, is usually and somewhat inaccurately translated as Beware of Greeks Bearing Gifts, or doubtless the Minister would recall had he not attended the LSE.

B.W.

I dictated a reply to Bernard, in which I said that Greek tags are all very interesting in their way, especially to classicists no doubt, but that they were not exactly central to government business.

I added that presumably the modern EEC version of that tag would be Beware of Greeks Bearing An Olive Oil Surplus.

(Rather good that. I must remember to use it next time I have to make an anti-EEC speech.)

To my astonishment, I found yet another memo from Bernard in my red boxes tonight, shortly before writing this entry in my diary. He really is tireless in his pursuit of pointless pedantry.

Memorandum
From: The Private Secretary
To: The Minister

Aug 15th

With reference to your memorandum in reply to my memorandum on the subject of classical tags, your description of the tag Beware of Greeks Bearing Gifts as a Greek tag is, of course, erroneous.

Aug. 15th

With reference to your memorandum in reply to my memorandum on the subject of classical tags, your description of the tag Beware of Greeks Bearing Gifts as a Greek tag is, of course, erroneous.

Just as the Trojan Horse was Greek, the tag which you described as Greek was, in fact, Latin. In fact, this is obvious if you consider that the Greeks would hardly suggest bewaring of themselves – if one can use such a participle: bewaring, that is – and the tag can clearly be seen to be Latin rather than Greek not because ‘timeo’ ends in ‘o’ (because the Greek first person also ends in ‘o’) – actually, if I may digress, there is a Greek word ‘timao’ meaning ‘I honour’ – but because the ‘os’ ending is a nominative singular termination of the second declension in Greek and an accusative plural in Latin.

Incidentally, as a fine point of interest, Danaos is not only the Greek for Greek but also the Latin for Greek.

B.W.

I shall preserve Bernard's memos for posterity. They give a clear indication of how academic brilliance can mislead those who recruit administrative trainees into the Civil Service.

[*A few days later Hacker, Appleby and Bernard Woolley were present at the promised meeting with three Department of Transport Under-Secretaries – Ed.*]

August 17th
We have had a most extraordinary meeting today, the one that Humphrey had promised to arrange with the Under-Secretaries from the Department of Transport.

I can't remember all their names, but each one was from a different division – one from Air, one from Road and one from Rail. It was extraordinarily acrimonious. The one thing that they were all agreed on was that, somehow, my proposals were deeply misguided.

The man from Road Transport, Graham something or other, suggested that it should be government policy to designate road haulage as its own principal means of freight transport. He was promptly interrupted by Richard somebody with a rather irritable thin tired-looking creased face – not surprising when you consider he's been trying to modernise the railways and battle with BR, the NUR and ASLEF for most of his career.

'With the greatest possible respect, Minister, I think that such a policy would be, not to put too fine a point on it, unacceptably short-sighted. It is rail transport that must surely be the favoured carrier under any sane national policy.'

Piers, a smooth fellow from Air, interrupted so fast that he scarcely gave himself time to utter his usual courteous but meaningless preamble. 'If-I-might-crave-your-indulgence-for-a-moment-Minister, I have to say that *both* those proposals are formulae for disaster. Long-term considerations absolutely mandate the expansion of air freight to meet rising demand.'

Graham (Roads) put down his pencil, with a sharp click as it hit my mahogany reproduction conference table. 'Of course,' he snapped, 'if the Minister is prepared for a massive budget increase . . .'

'If the Minister will accept a long and unbelievably bitter rail strike . . .' interrupted Richard (Rail).

And Piers butted in: 'If the public can tolerate a massive rise in public discontent . . .'

I interrupted *them* by holding up my hand. They then confined themselves to staring at each other with intense mutual hostility.

'Hold on, hold on,' I said. 'We're the government, aren't we?'

'Indeed you are, Minister,' Sir Humphrey corrected me.

'So,' I continued, searching for agreement, 'we're all on the same side, aren't we?'

'Indeed we are/quite so/absolutely no question,' replied Richard, Piers and Graham roughly in concert.

'And,' I went on patiently, 'we are trying to find out what's best for Britain.'

Piers put up his hand. I nodded at him. 'Through the chair,' he said, 'I hardly think the end of the national air freight business is best for Britain?'

Our truce had lasted a mere twenty seconds. The war was on again. 'I find it hard to see how Britain is saved by the destruction of the railways,' Richard remarked bitterly.

And Graham, not to be outdone, added with heavy sarcasm that it was not immediately apparent to him how Britain would benefit from a rapid deterioration of the road network.

Again I took a lead. I explained that I was merely trying to examine a few policy options for the government's own freight transport needs. And that therefore I had thought that a preliminary chat with a few friends, advisers, around the table, could lead to some *positive, constructive* suggestions.

I should not have wasted my breath. The positive constructive suggestions were somewhat predictable. Richard promptly suggested a firm commitment to rail transport, Graham a significant investment in motorway construction, and Piers a meaningful expansion of air freight capacity!

So at this point I explained that my overall brief is, among other things, to achieve an overall cut in expenditure.

'In that case,' said Richard grimly, 'there is only one possible course.'

'Indeed there is,' snapped Graham.

'And there can be no doubt what it is,' Piers added in an icy tone.

They all eyed each other, and me. I was stuck. Sir Humphrey came to the rescue.

'Good,' he said with a cheerful smile, 'I always like to end a meeting on a note of agreement. Thank you, gentlemen.'

And they filed out.

The meeting is the sort that would be described in a communiqué as 'frank'. Or even 'frank, bordering on direct', which means that the cleaners have to mop up the blood in the morning.

SIR BERNARD WOOLLEY RECALLS:[1]
The Minister found his meeting with the three Under-Secretaries confusing. This was because of his failure to understand the role of the Civil Service in making policy.

The three Under-Secretaries whom we met that morning were, in effect, counsel briefed by the various transport interests to resist any aspects of government policy that might have been unfavourable to their clients.

This is how the Civil Service in the 1980s actually worked in practice. In fact, all government departments – which in theory collectively represented the government to the outside world – in fact lobbied the government on behalf of their own client pressure group. In other words, each Department of State was actually controlled by the people whom it was supposed to be controlling.

Why – for instance – had we got comprehensive education throughout the UK? Who wanted it? The pupils? The parents? Not particularly.

The actual pressure came from the National Union of Teachers, who were the chief client of the DES.[2] So the DES went comprehensive.

Every Department acted for the powerful sectional interest with whom it had a permanent relationship. The Department of Employment lobbied for the TUC, whereas the Department of Industry lobbied for the employers. It was actually rather a nice balance: Energy lobbied for the oil companies, Defence lobbied for the armed forces, the Home Office for the police, and so on.

In effect, the system was designed to prevent the Cabinet from carrying out its policy. Well, somebody had to.

Thus a national transport policy meant fighting the *whole* of the Civil Service, as well as the other vested interests.

If I may just digress for a moment or two, this system of 'checks and balances', as the Americans would call it, makes nonsense of the oft-repeated criticism that the Civil Service was right wing. Or left wing. Or any other wing. The Department of Defence, whose clients were military, was – as you would expect – right wing. The DHSS, on the other hand, whose clients were the needy, the underprivileged and the social workers, was (predictably) left wing. Industry, looking after the Employers, was right wing – and Employment (looking after the *un*employed, of course) was left wing. The Home Office was right wing, as its clients were the Police, the Prison Service and the Immigration chaps. And Education, as I've already remarked, was left wing.

You may ask: What were we at the DAA? In fact, we were neither right nor left. Our main client was the Civil Service itself, and therefore our real interest was in defending the Civil Service against the Government.

Strict constitutional theory holds that the Civil Service should be committed to carrying out the Government's wishes. And so it was, as long as the Government's wishes were practicable. By which we meant, as long as *we* thought they were practicable. After all, how else can you judge?

[1] In conversation with the Editors.
[2] Department of Education and Science.

[*Hacker's diary continues – Ed.*]

August 19th

Today Humphrey and I discussed Wednesday's meeting.

And it was now clear to me that I had to get out of the commitment that I had made. Quite clearly, Transport Supremo is a title that's not worth having.

I said to Humphrey that we had to find a way to force the PM's hand.

'Do you mean "we" plural – or do Supremos now use the royal pronoun?'

He was gloating. So I put the issue to him fair and square. I explained that I meant both of us, unless he wanted the DAA to be stuck with this problem.

As Humphrey clearly had no idea at all how to force the PM's hand, I told him how it's done. If you have to go for a politician's jugular, go for his constituency.

I told Bernard to get me a map and the local municipal directory of the PM's constituency.

Humphrey was looking puzzled. He couldn't see what I was proposing to do. But I had to put it to him in acceptably euphemistic language. 'Humphrey,' I said, 'I need your advice. Is it possible that implementing a national transport policy could have unfortunate local repercussions? Necessary, of course, in the wider national interest but painful to the borough affected!'

He caught on at once. 'Ah. Yes indeed, Minister,' he replied. 'Inevitable, in fact.' And he brightened up considerably.

'And if the affected borough was represented in the House by a senior member of the government – a very senior member of the government – the *most* senior member of the government . . .?'

Humphrey nodded gravely. 'Embarrassing,' he murmured. 'Deeply embarrasing.' But his eyes were gleaming.

In due course Bernard obtained the street map of the PM's constituency, and a street directory, and he found a relevant section in the business guide too. Once we studied the map, it was all plain sailing!

First we found a park. Humphrey noticed that it was near the railway station, and reminded me that one requirement of a national transport policy is to bring bus stations nearer to railway stations.

So, with deep regret, I made my first recommendation: *Build a bus station on Queen Charlotte's Park.* Someone has to suffer in the national interest, alas!

Second, we found a reference to a big bus repair shop, in the street directory. It seemed to us that it would be more economical to integrate bus and train repairs. There would undoubtedly be a great saving. So our second recommendation was *Close the bus repair shop*.

Then it struck me that the PM's constituency is in commuter country. And we know, of course, that commuter trains run at a loss. They are only really used at rush hours. This means that commuters are, in effect, subsidised.

'Is this fair?' I asked Humphrey. He agreed that this was indeed an injustice to non-commuters. So we made our third recommendation: *Commuters to pay full economic fares.*

Sadly this will double the price of commuter tickets, but you can't make an omelette without breaking eggs.[1]

Humphrey noted that the PM's constituency contained several railway stations – British Rail as well as the Underground. He reminded me that some people take the view that areas with reasonable rail services don't need an evening bus service as well. I regard this as an extremely persuasive view. Accordingly, we made our fourth recommendation. *Stop all bus services after 6.30 p.m.*

We then moved on to consider what to do with all the remaining land after the removal of the bus station into the park.

We had to rack our brains on this matter for a while, but eventually we realised that the whole area seemed very short of parking space for container lorries. Especially at night. So fifth we recommended: *Container lorry park on bus station site.*

Regretfully, on closer study, the map revealed that building a new container lorry park would mean widening the access road. Indeed, it appears that the western half of the swimming baths might have to be filled in. But we could see no alternative: *Widen the access road to the bus station site* was our sixth and last recommendation.

We sat back and considered our list of recommendations. These had nothing whatever to do with the PM personally, of course. They were simply the local consequences of the broad national strategy.

However, I decided to write a paper which would be sent to Number Ten for the PM's personal attention. The PM would undoubtedly wish to be informed of the constituency implications and as a loyal Minister and dutiful colleague I owe this to the PM. Among other things!

[1] Originally said by Frederick the Great, King Frederick II of Prussia.

Humphrey raised one other area of concern. 'It would be awful, Minister, if the press got hold of all this. After all, lots of other boroughs are likely to be affected. There'd be a national outcry.'

I asked if he thought there was any danger of the press getting hold of the story.

'Well,' he said, 'they're very clever at getting hold of things like this. Especially if there's lots of copies.'

A good point. Humphrey's a bloody nuisance most of the time, but I must say that he's a good man to have on your side in a fight.

'Oh dear,' I replied. 'This *is* a problem, because I'll have to copy all my Cabinet colleagues with this note. Their constituencies are bound to be affected as well, of course.'

Humphrey reassured me on this point. He said that we must hope for the best. If it *were* leaked, with all those copies, no one could *ever* discover who leaked it. And as it happened, he was lunching today with Peter Martell of *The Times*.

I found this very reassuring.

I told him not to do anything that I wouldn't do. He told me that I could rely on him.

I'm sure I can.

I wonder how he got on.

[*Sir Humphrey's account of lunch with Peter Martell has been found in his private diary – Ed.*]

19/viii

Lunched with the chap from Printing House Square, and mentioned the recent rumours of the integrated national transport policy.

His first reaction was one of boredom with this hoary old chestnut. Quite a natural reaction, really. But he became

Lunched with the chap from Printing House Square, and mentioned the recent rumours of the integrated national transport policy.

His first reaction was one of boredom with this hoary old chestnut. Quite a natural reaction, really. But he became interested when I hinted of the rumours that the policy may have several unwelcome side-effects.

1 Job loss from integration of the railway terminals.
2 Job loss from joint repair shops.
3 Job loss from streamlining of services.
4 Reduction of bus and train services – causing job loss.

Peter realised that this could be rather a large story, especially in view of the rumours that one of the areas to suffer most will be the PM's own constituency. I can't imagine how these rumours got around.

He asked for hard facts, and I admonished him. He persisted, explaining to me that newspapers are not like the Government – if they make statements they have to be able to prove that they are true.

He pressed me for news of a White Paper or a Green Paper. I gave no help. But I did have to confirm that there is in existence a confidential note from Hacker to the PM with similar notes to all twenty-one of his Cabinet colleagues.

'Oh that's all right then,' he said cheerfully. 'Are *you* going to show it to me or shall I get it from one of your colleagues?'

I reproved him. I explained that it was a confidential document. It would be grossly improper to betray it to anyone, let alone a journalist.

The only way he could possibly obtain a copy of such a document would be if somebody left it lying around by mistake. The chances of that happening are remote, of course.

[*It seems, from Sir Humphrey's account, that he even wrote his private diary in such a way as to prevent it being used as evidence against him. But Peter Martell's subsequent publication of the full details of the confidential note, only one day later, suggests that Sir Humphrey had carelessly left his own copy lying around – Ed.*]

August 22nd

Humphrey did his job well. The full disclosure of my seven-point plan for the Prime Minister's constituency appeared in *The Times* on Saturday. I must say I had a jolly good laugh about it. By 10.30 a.m. I'd received the expected summons for a chat with Sir Mark Spencer at Number Ten. (The PM's still abroad.)

I went this morning, and M.S. came straight to the point.

'I thought I ought to tell you that the PM isn't very pleased.' He waved Saturday's *Times* at me. 'This story.'

I agreed with him heartily. 'Yes, absolutely shocking. I wasn't pleased either.'

'There's obviously been a leak,' he murmured, eyeing me.

'Terrible. Can't trust any of my Cabinet colleagues nowadays.'

This wholehearted agreement threw him momentarily off guard, I think. 'Who are you saying it was?' he asked.

I lowered my voice and explained that I wouldn't want to name names, but as for one or two of my Cabinet colleagues . . . well! I left it at that. Looks speak louder than words sometimes.

He didn't want to leave it there. 'But what are you suggesting?'

I immediately backtracked. I was enjoying myself hugely. 'Well,' I said, 'it may *not* have been one of them, of course. I did send the paper here to Number Ten – could there be a leak *here* somewhere, do you think?'

Sir M. was not amused. 'The PM's office does not leak.'

'Of course not,' I said quickly. 'Perish the thought.'

We all leak of course. That's what the lobby correspondents are there for. However, we all prefer to call it 'flying a kite.'

Sir Mark continued. 'It wasn't only the fact of the leak that was disturbing. It was the implications of the proposals.'

I agreed that the implications were indeed disturbing, which was why I had written a special paper for the PM. National transport policies are bound to have disturbing implications. He disagreed. He insisted that the Transport Policy will not have such implications.

'It will,' I said.

'It won't,' he said. Such is the intellectual cut and thrust to be found at the centre of government.

'Didn't you read what it said?' I asked.

'What it *said* is not what it will *be*,' he replied very firmly. 'I thought perhaps you'd like to see this.' And he handed me a newspaper, one of the London suburban weeklies.

It was the local paper from the PM's constituency.

P.M. Steps In to Stop Transport Re-organisation Proposals

BY NORMAN POTTER

Rumours that services and jobs were threatened in this constituency were scotched today. Apparently the P.M. has given a firm directive to transport supremo designate Jim Hacker.

This was certainly news to me.

'I've had no directive from the PM,' I said.

'You have now.' What a curious way to get a directive from the PM. 'I'm afraid this leak, whoever it comes from, is a verbatim report of a confidential minute dictated by the Prime Minister in Ottawa. So it looks as though the national transport policy will need some rethinking, doesn't it?'

This leak was a skilful counter-move by the PM. I started to explain to Sir Mark that rethinking the policy would be difficult, but he interrupted me unceremoniously.

'I think the PM's view is that Ministers are there to do difficult jobs. Assuming that they wish to remain as Ministers.'

Tough talk. I got the message.

I hastened to assure him that if the policy needed rethinking then I would rethink it until it was well and truly rethought.

Before I left I asked him how the leak had got into the paper. The PM's own local paper. He assured me that he had no idea, but that the PM's office does not leak.

'Shocking, though, isn't it?' he added. 'You can't trust anyone nowadays.'

August 23rd

Another meeting with Humphrey. We appeared to be back to square one.

I was somewhat downcast, as I still appeared to be landed with this ghastly job. To my surprise Humphrey was in good spirits.

'It's all going excellently, Minister,' he explained. 'We shall now produce the other kind of non-proposal.'

I asked him what he had in mind.

'The high-cost high-staff kind of proposal. We now suggest a British National Transport Authority, with a full structure of Regional Boards, Area Councils, local offices, liaison committees – the lot. Eighty thousand staff, and a billion pounds a year budget.'

'The Treasury will have a fit,' I said.

'Precisely. And the whole matter will certainly be handed back to the Department of Transport.'

I was entranced. I asked him to do me a paper with full staff and costing details and a specimen annual budget.

He was way ahead of me. He immediately produced the very document from his folder. 'And there's a one-page summary on the front,' he smiled smugly. Well, he was entitled to be smug!

I told him he was wonderful. He told me it was nothing.

I sat back and glanced through the proposal. It was splendid stuff.

'My goodness,' I reflected, 'if the press were to get hold of *this* . . . eh?'

Humphrey smiled. 'They'll soon be setting up another leak enquiry.'

Bernard was immediately anxious. 'Not really?'

'Bound to.'

'But . . . wouldn't that be embarrassing?'

I was surprised to see that Bernard didn't know the rules of the leak enquiry game. Leak enquiries are never embarrassing because they never actually happen. Leak enquiries are for setting up, not for actually conducting. Members may be appointed, but they hardly ever meet more than once. They certainly never report.

I asked Bernard, 'How many leak enquiries can you recall that named the culprit?'

'In round figures,' added Humphrey.

Bernard thought for a moment. 'Well, if you want it in round figures . . .' He thought again. 'None.'

The right answer. They *can't* report. For two reasons:

1 If the leak came from a civil servant it's not *fair* to publish it. The politicians are supposed to take the rap, that's what they're there for.

2 If the leak came from a politician it's not *safe* to publish it, because he will then promptly disclose all the other leaks he knows of that came from his Cabinet colleagues.

I explained all this to Bernard.

Then Humphrey chimed in. 'There's a third reason. The most important of all. The main reason why it's too dangerous to publish the results of an enquiry is because most leaks come from Number Ten. The ship of state is the only ship that leaks from the top.'

Humphrey was quite right, of course. Since the problem, more often than not, is a leaky PM – as in this case – it's not easy to get the evidence and impossible to publish it if you do.

And by a curious coincidence, a journalist arrived to see me this very morning, shortly after our meeting. Humphrey, most considerately, left a spare copy of our latest high-cost proposal lying around on my desk. I'm awfully absent-minded, I'm always leaving bits of paper lying around, forgetting where I put them – the upshot was that after the journalist had left my office I couldn't find my spare copy anywhere. Extraordinary!

August 25th

It all came to a head today.

Humphrey and I were summoned – together this time – to a meeting at Number Ten. We were ushered into the Cabinet Secretary's office, where Sir Arnold and Sir Mark sat at the far end of a very long room. I think they were trying to intimidate us. But Humphrey and I are made of sterner stuff.

We greeted them cheerfully, and I sat in one of the armchairs in the conversation area. As a Minister of the Crown they were all my servants (nominally, at least) so they could not insist on a desk-bound interview. At my suggestion they joined me in Sir Arnold's armchairs. But he opened the batting. 'Another leak,' he said. 'This is extremely serious.'

'There has indeed been another leak,' I agreed. 'I can't think how it occurred! Our high-cost proposal was all over this morning's papers.'

Humphrey and I agreed earnestly that this new leak was indeed extremely serious.

'It is almost approaching a disciplinary level,' said Sir Arnold.

'I do agree,' I said, 'don't you, Humphrey?'

He nodded emphatically. 'Indeed, if only one could find the culprits it would be a most serious matter for them.'

Sir Mark piped up. He said he could help with that. He thought that if he were to use his influence he could achieve a disclosure from *The Times* of how they got hold of our original transport plans.

I shook Humphrey up a bit by offering to help further.

'Are you sure, Minister?' He sounded a warning note.

'Oh yes,' I said. 'In fact I'm confident that I could find out how the press got hold of the leak about the Prime Minister's opposition to our original plans. Of course, if it transpires that the PM's own office leaks, then that would be even more serious than a leak in a cabinet minister's private office, wouldn't it? The security implications alone . . .'

I let that threat hang in the air, and sat back.

'Ah,' said Sir Mark.

There was a pause while everyone thought and rethought their positions. I felt I had the initiative, so I continued: 'In fact, perhaps we ought to bring in the police or MI5 – after all, the implications of a leak at Number Ten are really very serious indeed.'

Arnold fought back. 'Nevertheless, our first priority must be to investigate the original leak.' He tried to insist.

I contradicted him flatly. 'No. Our first priority must be to track down the leak involving the PM.'

He really couldn't argue with that. And he didn't. He just sat in silence and looked at me. So after a moment, having won the Battle of the Leak Enquiries, I turned to the matter of the Transport Policy.

'At all events,' I said, summing up the situation, 'you will appreciate that the public outcry in response to all these leaks makes it very difficult for me to develop a national transport policy within the DAA.'

Sir Humphrey agreed vigorously. 'The time is unripe. The climate is unpropitious. The atmosphere is unfavourable.'

'And,' I nodded, 'the only two lines of approach are now blocked.'

Again there was a silence. Again Arnold and Mark stared at me. Then they stared at each other. Defeat stared at them both. Finally Sir Arnold resigned himself to the inevitable.

But he tried to put as good a face on it as he could. He raised the oldest idea as if it were the latest inspiration. 'I wonder,' he addressed himself to Sir Mark, 'if it might not be wiser to take the whole matter back to the Department of Transport?'

I seized on the suggestion. 'Now that, Arnold,' I said, flattering him fulsomely, 'is a brilliant idea.'

'I wish I'd thought of that,' said Humphrey wistfully.

So we were all agreed.

But Sir Mark was still worried. 'There remains the question of the leaks,' he remarked.

'Indeed there does,' I agreed. 'And in my view we should treat this as a matter of utmost gravity. So I have a proposal.'

'Indeed?' enquired Sir Arnold.

'Will you recommend to the PM,' I said, in my most judicial voice, 'that we set up an immediate leak enquiry?'

Sir Arnold, Sir Mark and Sir Humphrey responded in grateful unison. 'Yes Minister,' replied the three knights.

19
The Whisky Priest

September 4th
A most significant and upsetting event has just taken place. It is Sunday night. Annie and I are in our London flat, having returned early from the constituency.

I had a mysterious phone call as I walked in through the door. I didn't know who it was from. All the man said was that he was an army officer and that he had something to tell me that he wouldn't divulge on the phone.

We arranged an appointment for late this evening. Annie read the Sunday papers and I read *The Wilderness Years*, one of my favourite books.

The man arrived very late for our appointment. I began to think that something had happened to him. By the time he'd arrived my fantasies were working overtime – perhaps because of *The Wilderness Years*.

'Remember Churchill,' I said to Annie. 'During all his wilderness years he got all his information about our military inadequacy and Hitler's war machine from army officers. So all the time he was in the wilderness he leaked stories to the papers and embarrassed the government. That's what I could do.'

I realised, as I spoke, that I'd chosen inappropriate words to express my feelings. I felt a little ridiculous as Annie said, 'But you're in the government.' Surely she could see what I *meant*!

Anyway, the man finally arrived. He introduced himself as Major Saunders. He was about forty years old, and wore the *de rigueur* slightly shabby baggy blue pinstripe suit. Like all these chaps he looked like an overgrown prep school pupil.

He was not a frightfully good conversationalist to start with. Or perhaps he was just rather overawed to meet a statesman such as myself.

I introduced him to Annie and offered him a drink.

'Thanks,' he said.

'Scotch?'

'Thanks.'

I told him to sit down.

'Thanks.'

I told him there was no need to keep thanking me.

'Thanks,' he said, then corrected himself. 'Sorry.'

Annie told him there was no need to apologise either.

'Sorry,' he said. 'I mean, thanks. I mean . . .'

Clearly my eminence was reducing this chap to a sort of jelly.

Annie offered to go and let us chaps talk in private, but for some reason he seemed anxious for her to stay. Can't think why. Anyway, he asked if she could stay and of course I agreed.

'I have no secrets from Annie,' I explained. 'I tell her everything.'

'Several times, normally,' she added cheerfully.

I do *wish* she wouldn't make jokes like that. People might think that she means them.

I decided to establish whether the slightly cloak-and-dagger air about our meeting was, in fact, necessary. 'Is this matter highly confidential?' I asked.

'Well, fairly,' he replied, rather on edge. Clearly 'fairly' was a bit of traditional British understatement.

'Shall I turn on the radio?' I offered.

He seemed surprised. 'Why – is there something good on?'

I don't know what they teach these army chaps nowadays. I explained that I was suggesting that we play the radio to avoid being bugged. He asked if it was likely that we were being bugged. How does one know the answer to that? But then Annie reminded me that, as I am the Minister in charge of bugging politicians, it wasn't awfully likely.

But Saunders was quite clear that he didn't want our conversation to be on the record, even though I made it clear that I would take notes at the meeting if necessary (which indeed it was). He began by saying that what he was about to tell me he was telling me on a personal basis.

I asked him what he meant, precisely. I do like clarity in language.

'I'm telling you personally,' he repeated. 'Not as Minister of Administrative Affairs.'

I could *sort of* see what he meant. But, on the other hand, I *am* Minister of Administrative Affairs. I sought further clarification.

'Yes, I know you are,' he said. 'But I'm not telling you in that role. I'm telling you as a journalist.'

'Are you a journalist?' I was surprised. 'I thought you were an army officer.'

'No – *you* are a journalist.'

'I'm a Minister.'

'But – what were you before you became a Minister?'

'Your starter for ten, no conferring,' interrupted Annie facetiously. She's always watched too much television and has always had a rather silly infatuation with Bamber Gascoigne merely because he's charming and clever.

In any case, I'd now seen what Saunders was driving at. I put it into simple language, so that we were both clear about what we were both saying.

'You're telling me that what you're telling me – and, incidentally, I don't yet *know* what you're telling me – but, whatever it is that you're telling me, you're telling me as the former Editor of *Reform*. Is that it?'

'Yes,' he replied. 'You were a very fine editor.'

'I wouldn't say that,' I said modestly.

'You've often said that,' said Annie. Another of her bloody jokes. Sometimes she's more hindrance than help.

We still hadn't found a basis for my receipt of his confidential information. So I had to pursue our talks about talks, as it were. 'How,' I wanted to know, 'do I prevent myself from knowing what you are telling me as a former journalist?'

I couldn't see how I could help the Minister knowing if *I* knew.

'I think he means it's a question of hats, dear,' said Annie. Of course it was. Perfectly bloody obvious. I tried to disguise my irritation.

'Fine,' I said, smiling. 'I'm not wearing my Ministerial hat tonight. I understand that. But . . .' and here I think I impressed him with the solemnity of my high office under the Crown, '. . . I must warn you: if I need to tell myself what you tell me, I won't hesitate to do my duty and see that I am properly informed.'

'Fine,' agreed Major Saunders.

It seemed that at last we had some basis on which to open up our conversation. I waited with bated breath.

He took a large gulp of his whisky, put down his glass firmly on the coffee table, and fixed me with a bloodshot stare. 'Who is in charge of selling British weapons to foreigners?'

'Bzzzzz. Hacker, LSE,' said Annie. I silenced her with a filthy look. Then I waited for more from Saunders. After all, he'd requested the meeting because he'd had something to *tell* me, not to ask me.

Saunders realised the ball was still in his court. 'You wrote an article in *Reform* about the sale of British weapons to undesirable foreign buyers.'

I remembered it well. I had called it 'The Dreadful Trade'. In it I argued – as I have always argued – that while it is wholly patriotic to manufacture arms for our defence and even for the defence of our allies, even though some of our allies are scarcely commendable people, we should never sell British weapons to buttress enemies of the realm or Nazi-style dictators. I repeated the gist of my argument to Saunders. He nodded. 'What about terrorists?' he asked.

'Or terrorists,' I added firmly.

He nodded again. I began to have the feeling that I was being led somewhere, as if by a good interrogator or a prosecuting counsel. But I still had no idea of the enormity of the shock that he had in store for me.

'As you know,' he began to explain, 'I recently returned from Rome.' He had told me on the phone that he'd been there as part of a NATO military delegation. 'While I was there I was shown something that they'd captured in a raid on a terrorist HQ. It was a computerised bomb detonator. Very new, very secret and very lethal.'

'Who showed it to you?' I asked.

'I can't possibly tell you. An absolute confidence.'

I was mildly interested in this computerised detonator thing and invited him to continue.

'You set it to calculate the weight of the victim, the speed of his car and so on, to be sure of getting him. And you can reprogramme it remotely by radio after setting it.'

'Gosh,' I said, walking straight into it. 'You don't connect the Italians with that sort of technology, do you?'

'It wasn't made in Italy,' he countered swiftly. 'It was made here.'

It took me a moment or two to grasp the full implications of what he was saying.

'Here?'

'Yes. Under a Ministry of Defence contract.'

I could hardly believe what he was telling me. As a matter of fact, I still find it incredible. And appalling. British weapons being used by Italian Red Terrorists.

I asked him how they got them.

'That's what I want to know,' he answered.

I asked him who else he'd told. He says he's told no one, because he can't. 'If I reported it officially I'd have to disclose the source. But I thought if I told someone near the top of government . . .'

'At the top,' I corrected him firmly.

He paused and nodded. Then he went on to explain that someone at the top of government would be able, in his opinion, to find out how these weapons are being supplied. Because the investigation would have to start here in Britain, and at top level.

I couldn't see how he thought I was to do this, since he had made it clear that he was telling me on a personal basis.

He spelt it out to me. 'You see, now you know personally, even if you don't know officially, you can use your personal knowledge to start official enquiries to get official confirmation of personal suspicions so that what you now know personally but not officially you will then know officially as well as personally.'

After a year in government I can now make sense of, and recall such sentences. Perhaps in another year I'll be speaking like that myself.

'You're not related to Sir Humphrey Appleby, are you?' I enquired semi-humorously. But no. This is not a family talent, this is the language of the governing classes as they try – as always – to have everything both ways.

Saunders heaved a sigh of relief, finished the rest of his Scotch, and remarked that he had just had to tell somebody.

'Absolutely,' I agreed, at my most understanding. 'Well, now I know. Personally.' Two could play this game.

'Marvellous. Going to do something about it, aren't you?'

'Indeed I am,' I agreed emphatically. 'Oh yes. Definitely.'

'And right away?'

'Right away.' I was employing my most decisive manner.

'*What* are you going to do?'

I hadn't actually expected such a direct question. I couldn't see what that had to do with him. He'd done his duty by informing me, it's not for serving army officers to question Ministers of the Crown. Anyway that's the sort of irritating question that you tend to get from backbench MPs and other awkward busybodies who keep wanting to find out what the government's doing.

However, both hc and Annie were sitting waiting for an answer. I had to say something. 'Well, I'm going to think about what you've told me.' They didn't look too impressed. 'Right away!' I added decisively.

'And then?' Persistent bugger.

'And then I'm going to consider various courses of action, without delay.'

He insisted on seeking clarification. Or trying to pin me down. 'You're going to take action without delay?'

'I'm going to *consider* taking action without delay.' I thought I'd better be clear about this.

'Are *you* related to Sir Humphrey Appleby?' enquired Annie.

I rose above it, ignored her, and offered Major Saunders another drink. He declined, stood up preparatory to leaving, and asked for my assurance that he could rely on me to tackle this shocking matter. Naturally I gave him that assurance.

After he left Annie and I discussed him and his extraordinary information. I asked Annie what she made of it.

She didn't reply directly. She just told me that I really was going to do something about it wasn't I?

And I certainly am. If it's true. But I find it hard to believe. Could it happen? It couldn't happen! Could it? I mean, it's not just that it shouldn't but it couldn't. And even if it could, it wouldn't. Would it?

I've just played that last paragraph back. Perhaps I *am* related to Sir Humphrey Appleby.

September 5th

Today I had a serious conversation with Humphrey. Perhaps the most serious conversation that I have ever had or will ever have.

I'm still not quite sure what to make of it.

He came in for his regular Monday morning meeting with me. I hurried through all the usual items on the agenda, and then set the tone for the discussion that I intended to have.

'Humphrey,' I began, 'there is something that I must talk to you about. Something that concerns me deeply. Really profoundly important.'

He enquired whether I was referring to the amendment to the Administrative order on stock control in government establishments, or the procedures for the renewal of local authority leaseholds in Special Development Areas.

This is the level at which he operates. But I was patient. 'No Humphrey,' I explained, 'I'm concerned about a great issue of life and death.'

'Shouldn't that wait till after work?' he asked. You can see what I'm dealing with.

'It is work.'

'Really?' He was surprised. 'Then please go on.'

I asked him how British arms manufacturers sell arms to foreigners. He explained the whole system to me. The manufacturer has to get an export licence from the Department of Trade. Both private companies and government agencies sell arms abroad. They usually sell to foreign governments, but sometimes they sell to arms dealers. Third parties. In other words, perhaps a little man in Manchester buys on behalf of a party in the Channel Islands who has a contract in Luxembourg, and so on.

So I wanted to know if there was any way of controlling who the arms are really going to. Humphrey assured me that there *is* control. The dealer has to provide a document known as an end-user certificate. This certificate must have a signature on it from the ultimate customer who is an approved user acceptable to HMG.[1]

I found myself wondering if this end-user certificate is a real guarantee. I wonder if Humphrey would be surprised if, for instance, an aircraft carrier turned up in the Central African Republic.

[*Sir Humphrey would undoubtedly have been surprised, as would everybody else, as the Central African Republic is one thousand miles inland – Ed.*]

Sir Humphrey stated that it was 'officially impossible' for weapons to turn up in non-approved hands. 'There is stringent security, there are rigorous inspection procedures, and meticulous scrutiny.'

Officially impossible. I know what that phrase means. It means that it's all a façade.

I challenged him with this. He smiled benignly and inclined his head a little. 'I think perhaps this conversation should stop here, Minister, don't you?'

I refused to play the game this time. 'No,' I said. 'But it is as I thought. Last night a confidential source disclosed to me that British arms are being sold to Italian Red Terrorist Groups.'

He nodded gravely. 'I see. May I ask who the confidential source was?'

I was staggered. 'Humphrey! I just said that it's confidential.'

He was unashamed. 'Oh I'm sorry, Minister, I naturally assumed that meant you were going to tell me.'

[1] Her Majesty's Government.

He waited. I waited too. As I sat there, quietly watching him, I observed that he did not seem to be awfully worried about the information that I had just given him. So I questioned him on this. And indeed, he seemed to find it quite unremarkable.

'These things happen all the time, Minister. It's not our problem.'

'Robbery with violence happens all the time. Doesn't that worry you?'

'No Minister. Home Office problem.'

I was almost speechless. He seemed to see himself only as an official, not as a citizen. Of course, that is the hat that he wears when at the office advising me, but there are moral issues involved.

'We are letting terrorists get hold of murderous weapons,' I expostulated.

'We're not.'

I was confused. 'Well, who is?'

'Who knows?' He was at his most bland. 'The Department of Trade? The Ministry of Defence? The Foreign Office?'

I was getting impatient. This was wilful stupidity, no doubt about it. '*We*, Humphrey. The British Government. Innocent lives are being endangered by British weapons in the hands of terrorists.'

'Only Italian lives, not British lives.'

'There may be British tourists in Italy,' I replied, letting the wider issue go temporarily by default. (The wider issue being that no man is an island.)[1]

'British tourists? Foreign Office problem.'

I was wearying of this juvenile buck-passing. 'Look, Humphrey,' I said, 'we have to do something.'

'With respect, Minister . . .' the gloves were coming off now, '. . . we have to do *nothing*.'

It seemed to me that he was somehow suggesting that doing nothing was an active rather than a passive course. So I asked him to elaborate.

He was perfectly willing to do so. 'The sale of arms abroad is one of those areas of government which we do not examine too closely.'

I couldn't accept that. I told him that I have to examine this area, now that I know.

He said that I could say that I didn't know.

[1] 'No man is an Island, entire of itself . . . Any man's death diminishes me, because I am involved in Mankind; And therefore never send to know for whom the bell tolls; it tolls for thee.' – John Donne.

I wanted to be quite clear what he was saying that I should be saying. 'Are you suggesting that I should lie?'

'Not you, no,' came the enigmatic response.

'Who should lie, then?' I asked.

'Sleeping dogs, Minister.'

We were getting no further. Trying to have an argument with Humphrey can be like trying to squash a bowlful of porridge with your fist. I told him that I intended to raise the question and take the matter further as I was not satisfied with such reassurances as Sir Humphrey had been able to give me.

Now he looked upset. Not about bombs or terrorists or innocent lives, but about taking the matter further. 'Please Minister, I beg of you!'

I waited for him to explain further. Perhaps I would now learn something. And I did. But not what I expected.

'Minister, two basic rules of government: Never look into anything you don't have to. And never set up an enquiry unless you know in advance what its findings will be.'

He was still obsessed with rules of government, in the face of a moral issue of these proportions. 'Humphrey, I can't believe it. We're talking about good and evil.'

'Ah. Church of England problem.'

I was not amused. 'No Humphrey, *our* problem. We are discussing right and wrong.'

'You may be, Minister,' he replied smoothly, 'but I'm not. It would be a serious misuse of government time.'

I thought at first that he was joking. But he wasn't! He was serious, absolutely serious.

'Can't you see,' I begged emotionally, 'that selling arms to terrorists is wrong? Can't you *see* that?'

He couldn't. 'Either you sell arms or you don't,' was his cold, rational reply. 'If you sell them, they will inevitably end up with people who have the cash to buy them.'

I could see the strength of that argument. But terrorists had to be prevented, somehow, from getting hold of them.

Humphrey seemed to find this a ridiculous and/or an impractical approach. He smiled patronisingly. 'I suppose we could put a sort of government health warning on all the rifle butts. NOT TO BE SOLD TO TERRORISTS. Do you think that would help?' I was speechless. 'Or better still, WARNING: THIS GUN CAN SERIOUSLY DAMAGE YOUR HEALTH.'

I didn't laugh. I told him that it was rather shocking, in my view, that he could make light of such a matter. I demanded a straight answer. I asked him if he was saying that we should close our eyes to something that's as morally wrong as this business.

He sighed. Then he replied, with slight irritation. 'If you *insist* on making me discuss moral issues, perhaps I should point out that something is either morally wrong or it is not. It can't be slightly morally wrong.'

I told him not to quibble.

He quibbled again. 'Minister, Government isn't about morality.'

'Really? Then what is it about?'

'It's about stability. Keeping things going, preventing anarchy, stopping society falling to bits. Still being here tomorrow.'

'But what *for*?' I asked.

I had stumped him. He didn't understand my question. So I spelt it out for him.

'What is the ultimate purpose of Government, if it isn't for doing good?'

This notion was completely meaningless to him. 'Government isn't about good and evil, it's only about order and chaos.'

I know what he means. I know that all of us in politics have to swallow things we don't believe in sometimes, vote for things that we think are wrong. I'm a realist, not a boy scout. Otherwise I could never have reached Cabinet level. I'm not naïve. I know that nations just act in their own interest. But . . . there has to be a sticking point somewhere. Can it really be in order for Italian terrorists to get British-made bomb detonators?

I don't see how it can be. But, more shocking still, Humphrey just didn't seem to care. I asked him how that was possible.

Again he had a simple answer. 'It's not my job to care. That's what politicians are for. It's my job to carry out government policy.'

'Even if you think it's wrong?'

'Almost all government policy is wrong,' he remarked obligingly, 'but frightfully well carried out.'

This was all too urbane for my liking. I had an irresistible urge to get to the bottom of this great moral issue, once and for all. This 'just obeying orders' mentality can lead to concentration camps. I wanted to nail this argument.

'Humphrey, have you ever known a civil servant resign on a matter of principle?'

Now, *he* was shocked. 'I should think not! What a suggestion!'

How remarkable. This is the only suggestion that I had made in this conversation that had shocked my Permanent Secretary. I sat back in my chair and contemplated him. He waited, presumably curious to see what other crackpot questions I would be asking.

'I realise, for the very first time,' I said slowly, 'that you are committed purely to means, never to ends.'

'As far as I am concerned, Minister, and all my colleagues, there is no difference between means and ends.'

'If you believe that,' I told him, 'you will go to Hell.'

There followed a long silence. I thought he was reflecting on the nature of the evil to which he had committed himself. But no! After a while, realising that I was expecting a reply, he observed with mild interest, 'Minister, I had no idea that you had a theological bent.'

My arguments had clearly left him unaffected. 'You are a moral vacuum, Humphrey,' I informed him.

'If you say so, Minister.' And he smiled courteously and inclined his head, as if to thank me for a gracious compliment.

Bernard had been in the room for the entire meeting so far, though taking very few minutes, I noticed. Unusually for him, he had not said a word. Now he spoke.

'It's time for your lunch appointment, Minister.'

I turned to him. 'You're keeping very quiet, Bernard. What would you do about all this?'

'I'd keep very quiet, Minister.'

The conversation had ground to a halt. I'd thrown every insult at Sir Humphrey that I could think of, and he had taken each one as a compliment. He appears to be completely amoral. Not immoral – he simply doesn't understand moral concepts. His voice broke in on my thoughts. 'So may we now drop this matter of arms sales?'

I told him that we may not. I told him that I would be telling the PM about it, in person. And I told Bernard to make the appointment for me, as it is just the sort of thing the PM wants to know about.

Humphrey intervened. 'I assure you, Minister, it is just the sort of thing the Prime Minister desperately wants not to know about.'

I told him we'd see. And I left for lunch.

SIR BERNARD WOOLLEY RECALLS:[1]

I well remember that I felt fearfully downcast after that fateful meeting. Because I couldn't help wondering if the Minister was right. I voiced this

[1] In conversation with the Editors.

fear to old Humphrey. 'Most unlikely,' he replied. 'What about?'

I explained that I too was worried about ends versus means. I asked Humphrey if I too would end up as a moral vacuum. His reply surprised me. 'I hope so,' he told me. 'If you work hard enough.'

This made me feel more melancholy than before. At that time, you see, I still believed that if it was our job to carry out government policies we ought to believe in them.

Sir Humphrey shook his head and left the room. Later that day I received a memorandum from him. I have it still.

Memorandum
From: The Permanent Secretary
To: B.W.

5/ix

I have been considering your question. Please bear in mind the following points.

I have served eleven governments in the past thirty years. If I had believed in all their policies I would have been:

(i) passionately committed to keeping out of the Common Market

(ii) passionately committed to going into the Common Market.

Memorandum
From: The Permanent Secretary
To: B.W.
I have been considering your question. Please bear in mind the following points.

I have served eleven governments in the past thirty years. If I had believed in all their policies I would have been:

1) passionately committed to keeping out of the Common Market.
2) passionately committed to going into the Common Market.
3) utterly convinced of the rightness of nationalising steel.
4) utterly convinced of the rightness of denationalising steel.
5) utterly convinced of the rightness of renationalising steel.
6) fervently committed to retaining capital punishment.
7) ardently committed to abolishing capital punishment.
8) a Keynesian.
9) a Friedmanite.
10) a grammar school preserver.
11) a grammar school destroyer.
12) a nationalisation maniac.
13) a privatisation freak.
14) a stark, staring, raving schizophrenic.

H.A.

The following day he sent for me, to check that I was fully seized of his ideas and had taken them on board.

Of course, his argument was irrefutable. I freely admitted it. And yet I was *still* downcast. Because, as I explained to Appleby, I felt that I needed to believe in *something*.

He suggested that we should both believe in stopping Hacker from informing the PM.

Of course he was right. Once the PM knew of this business, there would have to be an enquiry. It would be like Watergate, in which, as you know, the investigation of a trivial break-in led to one ghastly revelation after another and finally to the downfall of a President. The Golden Rule is, was, always has been and always will be: Don't Lift Lids Off Cans of Worms.

'Everything is connected to everything else,' Sir Humphrey explained. 'Who said that?'

I ventured a guess that it might have been the Cabinet Secretary.

'Nearly right,' Sir Humphrey encouraged me. 'Actually, it was Lenin.'

He then set me the task – to stop my Minister from talking to the PM.

At first I couldn't see how this could be achieved, and was unwise enough to say. This earned me a sharp rebuke.

'Work it out,' he snapped. 'I thought you were supposed to be a high-flyer – or are you really a low-flyer supported by occasional gusts of wind?'

I could see that this was one of those make-or-break moments in one's career. I went off and had a quiet think, and I asked myself some questions.

1 Could I stop my Minister from seeing the PM? Clearly not.
2 Could Sir Humphrey? No.
3 Could my friends in the Private Office at Number Ten? Or the Cabinet Office? No.

Therefore the approach had to be through the political side. I needed someone close to the PM, someone who was able to frighten Hacker.

Suddenly it was clear. There's only one figure whose job it is to put the frighteners on MPs – the Chief Whip.

I planned my strategy carefully. Hacker had asked me to phone the diary secretary in the PM's private office for him, to make an appointment. I worked out that if Sir Humphrey had a word with the Cabinet Secretary, he (the Cabinet Secretary) could have a word with the PM's diary secretary, then all of them could have a word with the Whip's office.

The Chief Whip would see the point at once. When Hacker arrived to see the PM the Chief Whip would meet him, and say that the PM was rather busy and had asked him to talk to Hacker instead.

I requested a meeting with Appleby, and told him of my plan. He nodded approvingly. So I lifted up his phone.

'What are you doing, Bernard?' he asked.

'I thought you wanted to talk to the Cabinet Secretary, Sir Humphrey,' I replied with mock innocence.

He took the phone from me, and made the call. I sat and listened. When it was done Appleby replaced the receiver, sat back in his chair and eyed me speculatively.

'Tell me, Bernard, do you – as his Private Secretary – feel obliged to tell the Minister of this conversation?'

'What conversation?' I replied.

He offered me a sherry, congratulated me, and told me that I would be a moral vacuum yet.

I believe that it was at this moment that my future was assured. From then on I was earmarked as a future head of the Home Civil Service.

[*Hacker's diary continues – Ed.*]

September 8th

I feel rather guilty and not a little stupid this evening. Also, somewhat concerned for my future. I just hope that Vic Gould [*the Chief Whip – Ed.*] presents me in a favourable light to the PM next time my name is put forward for anything.

I think that Vic owes me a big favour after today. But he's a strange fellow and he may not see it that way.

I wasn't expecting to see him at all. My appointment was with the PM, at the House. When I got to the PM's office I found Vic Gould waiting there.

Vic is a tall imposing figure, with the white hair of an elder statesman, a face like a vulture and a manner that shifts at lightning speed from charm and soft soap to vulgar abuse. A party man to his fingertips.

He was a bit casual, I thought. He said that the PM was rather busy today and had asked him to see me instead.

I felt slightly insulted. I don't report to Vic. He may be responsible for party discipline but he's one of my colleagues, an equal member of this government. Actually, I had no idea that he was so close to the PM. Or maybe he isn't – maybe it's just that he persuaded the PM (who didn't know why I wanted the appointment) that it was a party matter rather than a political one. But what I can't work out is how did *Vic* know what I wanted? And how did the PM arrive at the decision that Vic should see me instead? Sometimes I really do feel a little paranoid.

As it turned out perhaps it's all for the best, *if* Vic can be believed. But can he? Can anybody?

Anyway, when Vic greeted me I refused to tell him what I'd come about. I couldn't see that arms sales to Italian terrorists was a matter for the Chief Whip.

He refused to take no for an answer. 'The PM has asked me to have a preliminary conversation with you, and write a background note. Save time later.'

I couldn't argue with that. So I told Vic that I'd been given this pretty dramatic information. And I told him the whole story of Italian Red Terrorists being supplied with top-secret bomb detonators made in this country. In a government factory!

'And you feel you should tell the PM?'

I was astonished by the question. The PM is in charge of security. I could see no choice.

But Vic disagreed. 'I don't think it's something to burden the PM with. Let's hold it over, shall we?'

I asked if he *actually* meant to do nothing about it. He nodded, and said yes, that was his recommendation.

I refused to accept this, and insisted that the PM had to be told.

'If the PM were to be told,' said Vic carefully, 'there'd have to be an enquiry.'

That was my point. That was what I wanted.

But it was not what Vic wanted. He explained why. 'An enquiry might perhaps reveal that all sorts of undesirable and even hostile governments had been supplied with British-made arms.'

This remark shocked me. Not so much on account of its factual content, but because of the assumption that such matters should not be looked into.

'Are you serious?' I asked.

'I said *perhaps*. Which would – perhaps – be highly embarrassing to some of our Cabinet colleagues. Foreign Secretary, Defence Secretary, Trade Secretary. And to the PM personally.'

I stuck to my guns. 'Doing what's right can be embarrassing. But that's not an argument for not doing it.'

Vic ignored that. 'You know we already sell arms to places like Syria, Chile and Iran?'

I did know. 'That's officially approved,' I explained, meaning that it was therefore beside the point.

'Quite,' agreed Vic. 'And you're happy about what they do with them?'

I hesitated. 'Well, obviously not entirely . . .'

'Either you're in the arms business or you're not,' said Vic with relentless logic.

At that point I became emotional. A big mistake. It's all right to pretend to be emotional, especially in front of the public (or even with the House if it's the right ploy for the moment), but with one's colleagues – especially a cold fish like Vic – it cuts no ice at all.

'If being in the arms business means being among criminals and murderers, then we should get out. It's immoral.'

Vic lost his temper. He glowered at me with a mixture of anger and contempt. 'Oh great. *Great*!'

I felt he really despised me. I could see him wondering how a boy scout like me had ever been allowed into the Cabinet. Or even into *politics*. 'And is it moral to put a hundred thousand British workers out of a job? And what about the exports? Two billion pounds a year down the tube for starters. And what about the votes? Where do you think the government places all these weapons contracts?'

'Marginal constituencies, obviously.'

'Exactly,' he said. QED, he implied.

But I still couldn't quite leave it alone. I tried again. 'Look Vic, all I'm saying is that now I know this is happening I have to tell the PM.'

'Why?'

'Why?' I couldn't understand the question. It seemed self-evident to me.

'Just because you've caught something nasty,' said Vic, 'why do you have to wander about breathing over everyone?'

While I was considering my answer – or to be precise, wondering if I really *had* an answer – he turned the anglepoise lamp on the desk in my direction. He wasn't *exactly* shining it in my eyes, but I did have the distinct feeling that I was being given the third degree.

And his next question did nothing to dilute the impression that I was under interrogation on account of suspect loyalty.

'Are you happy in the Cabinet?'

'Yes, of course I am.

'You want to stay in it?'

My heart sank into my boots. I couldn't speak. My loyalty was now in doubt. Oh my God! I nodded mutely.

'Well then?' He waited for me to say something.

I was sweating. And no longer thinking clearly enough. This was not the meeting that I had expected. I had expected to be on the attack. Instead I found myself fighting a desperate defensive. Suddenly my whole political future seemed to be on the line.

And I still stuck to my guns. I'm not quite sure why. I think I was confused, that's all.

'There is such a thing as duty,' I heard myself say rather pompously. 'There are times when you have to do what your conscience tells you.'

Vic lost his temper again. I could see why. Telling a Chief Whip that you have to follow your conscience really is like waving a red rag at a bull.

And this time it wasn't a quiet irritable loss of temper. It was the Big Shout, for which he is famous throughout the Palace of Westminster. He leapt to his feet. 'Oh for God's sake!' he yelled, obviously at the end of his tether.

His face came close to mine. Almost nose to nose. His angry bulging eyes were so near that they were slightly out of focus. He was utterly contemptuous of me now.

'Must you go around flashing your petty private little individual conscience? Do you think no one else has got one? Haven't you got a conscience about the survival of the government?'

'Of course I have,' I muttered, when the storm seemed to have abated temporarily.

He walked away, satisfied that at least I'd given one correct answer. 'Here's the PM on the verge of signing an international agreement on anti-terrorism . . .'

I interrupted, in self-defence. 'I didn't know about that,' I explained.

'There's a lot you don't know,' snapped Vic contemptuously.

[*It is not surprising that Hacker did not know about a new international anti-terrorist agreement. So far as we have been able to find out, there was none. Vic Gould presumably invented this on the spur of the moment – Ed.*]

He came and sat beside me again. He tried to be patient. Or

rather, he looked as though he was trying to be patient. 'Can't you understand that it's essential to deal with the major policy aspects, rather than pick off a couple of little arms exporters and terrorist groups?'

I hadn't seen it like that. Furthermore, I realised that I'd better see it like that, and quickly, or else Vic would go on shouting at me all day. 'I suppose it is only a couple of little terrorist groups,' I said weakly.

'They can't kill *that* many people, can they?'

'I suppose not,' I agreed, with a little smile to show that I realised that perhaps I'd been a bit naïve.

But Vic had still not finished with the insults. He sneered at me again. 'And you want to blow it all in a fit of moral self-indulgence.'

Clearly moral self-indulgence was the most disgusting thing Vic had ever come across. I felt very small.

He sat back in his chair, sighed, then grinned at me and offered me a cigarette. And dropped the bombshell.

'After all,' he smiled, 'the PM is thinking of you as the next Foreign Secretary.'

I was astounded. Of course it's what I've always wanted, if Martin's ever kicked upstairs. But I didn't know the PM knew.

I declined his offer of a cigarette. He lit up, and relaxed. 'Still, if it's martydom you're after,' he shrugged, 'go ahead and press for an enquiry. Feel free to jeopardise everything we've all fought for and worked for together all these years.'

I hastily explained that that wasn't what I wanted at all, that of course it is appalling if terrorists are getting British bomb detonators, but there's no question that (as Vic had so eloquently explained it) one has a *loyalty*, the common purpose, and things must be put in perspective.

He nodded. 'Of course,' he said, making a concession to my original point of view, 'if you were at the Ministry of Defence or the Board of Trade . . .'

I interrupted. 'Exactly. Absolutely. Ministry of Defence problem. Department of Trade problem. I see that now.' It's just what Humphrey had been trying to say to me, in fact.

We fell silent, both waiting, sure that the problem was now resolved. Finally Vic asked if we could hold it over for the time being, so that we could avoid upsetting and embarrassing the PM.

I agreed that we could. 'In fact,' I admitted, rather ashamed of my naïvety, 'I'm sorry I mentioned it.'

'Good man,' said Vic paternally. I don't *think* he was being ironic, but you can never tell with Vic.

September 10th

Annie had spent the latter part of the week in the constituency, so I wasn't able to get her advice on my meeting with Vic until this weekend.

Not that I really needed advice. By today it was quite clear to me what I had to do. I explained to Annie over a nightcap of Scotch and water.

'On balance I thought the right thing was to let sleeping dogs lie. In the wider interest. As a loyal member of the government. Nothing to be gained by opening a whole can of worms.'

She argued, of course. 'But the Major said they were terrorists.'

I couldn't blame her for taking such a naïve approach. After all, even *I* had made the same mistake till I'd thought it all through properly.

'Yes,' I said. 'But we bombed Dresden. Everyone's a terrorist in a way, aren't they?'

'No,' she said firmly, and gave me a look which defied me to disagree with her.

I had overstated it a bit. 'No, well, but *metaphorically* they are,' I added. 'You ought to meet the Chief Whip, he *certainly* is.'

Annie pursued me. She didn't understand the wider interest, the more sophisticated level on which decisions like this have to be reached. 'But someone in Britain is giving bombs to murderers,' she reiterated.

'Not giving,' I corrected her. 'Selling.'

'That makes it okay, does it?'

I told her to be serious, and to think it through. I explained that an investigation could uncover all sorts of goings-on.

She wasn't impressed with this argument.

'Ah, I see,' she smiled sadly. 'It's all right to investigate if you might catch one criminal, but not if you might catch lots of them.'

'Not if they're your Cabinet colleagues, that's right!' She'd got the point now. But she sighed and shook her head. Clearly, she had not yet taken my new line on board. So I persisted. I really wanted her to understand. And to agree.

'Annie, Government is a very complex business. There are conflicting considerations.'

'Like whether you do the right thing or the wrong thing?'

I was infuriated. I asked her what else she suggested that I could do. She told me to take a moral stand. I told her I'd already tried that. She told me I hadn't tried hard enough. I asked what *else* I could do. She told me to threaten resignation. I told her that they'd accept it.

And once out of office there's no going back. No one ever resigned on a matter of principle, except a few people with a death wish. Most resignations that are *said* to be based on principle are in reality based on hard-nosed political calculations.

'Resignation might be a sop to my conscience and to yours,' I explained, 'but it won't stop the arms supply to the terrorists.'

'It might,' she retorted, 'if you threaten to tell what you know.'

I considered that for a moment. But, in fact, what do I know? I don't know anything. At least, nothing I can prove. I've no hard facts at all. I know that the story is true simply because no one has denied it – but that's not proof. I explained all this to Annie, adding that therefore I was in somewhat of a fix.

She saw the point. Then she handed me a letter. 'I don't think you realise just how big a fix you're in. This arrived today. From Major Saunders.'

12 Randolph Crescent,
Maida Vale,
London, W.9.

Dear Mr. Hacker,

Thank you for seeing me on Monday last. It is such a relief to have told you all about this whole ghastly business of the supply of British weapons to Italian terrorists. I know you will act upon this information, as you promised, and I look forward to seeing some action taken.

Yours sincerely

J.B. Saunders

J.B. Saunders (Major)

This letter is a catastrophe. Major Saunders can prove to the world that he told me about this scandal, and that I did nothing. And it is a photocopy – he definitely has the original.

And it arrived Recorded Delivery. So I can't say I didn't get it.

I'm trapped. Unless Humphrey or Bernard can think of a way out.

September 12th

Bernard thought of a way out, thank God!

At our meeting first thing on Monday morning he suggested the Rhodesia Solution.

Humphrey was thrilled. 'Well done Bernard! You excel yourself. Of course, the Rhodesia Solution. Just the job, Minister.'

I didn't know what they were talking about at first. So Sir Humphrey reminded me of the Rhodesia oil sanctions row. 'What happened was that a member of the government had been told about the way in which British companies were sanction-busting.'

'So what did he do?' I asked anxiously.

'He told the Prime Minister,' said Bernard with a sly grin.

'And what did the Prime Minister do?' I wanted to know.

'Ah,' said Sir Humphrey. 'The Minister in question told the Prime Minister in such a way that the Prime Minister didn't hear him.'

I couldn't think what he and Bernard could possibly mean. Was I supposed to mumble at the PM in the Division Lobby, or something?

They could see my confusion.

'You write a note,' said Humphrey.

'In very faint pencil, or what? Do be practical, Humphrey.'

'It's awfully obvious, Minister. You write a note that is susceptible to misinterpretation.'

I began to see. Light was faintly visible at the end of the tunnel. But what sort of note?

'I don't quite see *how*,' I said. 'It's a bit difficult, isn't it? "Dear Prime Minister, I have found that top-secret British bomb detonators are getting into the hands of Italian terrorists!" How do you misinterpret that?'

'You can't,' said Humphrey, 'so don't write that. You use a more . . . circumspect style.' He chose the word carefully. 'You must avoid any mention of bombs and terrorists and all that sort of thing.'

I saw that, of course, but I didn't quite see how to write such an opaque letter. But it was no trouble to Humphrey. He delivered a draft of the letter to my red box for me tonight. Brilliant.

[*We have managed to find the letter, in the Cabinet Office files from Number Ten, subsequently released under the Thirty-Year Rule – Ed.*]

DEPARTMENT OF ADMINISTRATIVE AFFAIRS

FROM THE MINISTER

Dear Prime Minister, September 12th

My attention has been drawn on a personal basis to information which suggests the possibility of certain irregularities under Section 1 of the Import – Export and Custom powers (Defence) Act, 1939 (c).

Prima facie evidence suggests that there could be a case for further investigation to establish whether or not enquiries should be put in hand.

Nevertheless it should be stressed that available information is limited and the relevant facts could be difficult to establish with any degree of certainty.

Yours sincerely,

James Hacker

James Hacker

[*Hacker's diary continues – Ed.*]
The letter is masterly because not only does it draw attention to the matter in a way which is unlikely to be remarked, but it also suggests that *someone else* should do something about it, and ends with a sentence implying that even if they do, they won't get anywhere. So if at any future date there is an enquiry I'll be in the clear, and yet everyone will be able to understand that a busy PM might not have grasped the implications of such a letter. I signed it at once.

September 13th
I congratulated Humphrey this morning on his letter, and told him it was very unclear. He was delighted.

He had further plans all worked out. We will not send the letter for a little while. We'll arrange for it to arrive at Number Ten on the day that the PM is leaving for an overseas summit. This will mean that there will be further doubt about whether the letter was read by the PM or by the acting PM, neither of whom will remember of course.

This is the finishing touch, and will certainly ensure that the whole thing is written off as a breakdown in communications. So everyone will be in the clear, and everyone can get on with their business.

Including the red terrorists.

And I'm afraid I'm a little drunk tonight, or I wouldn't have just dictated that deeply depressing sentence.

But it's true. And I've been formulating some theories about government. Real practical theories, not the theoretical rubbish they teach in Universities.

In government you must always try to do the right thing. But whatever you do, you must never let anyone catch you trying to do it. Because doing right's wrong, right?

Government is about principle. And the principle is: don't rock the boat. Because if you do rock the boat all the little consciences fall out. And we've all got to hang together. Because if we don't we'll all be hanged separately. And I'm hanged if I'll be hanged.

Why should I be? Politics is about helping others. Even if it means helping terrorists. Well, terrorists are others, aren't they? I mean, they're not *us*, are they?

So you've got to follow your conscience. But you've also got to know where you're going. So you *can't* follow your conscience because it may not be going the same way that you are.

Aye, there's the rub.

I've just played back today's diary entry on my cassette recorder. And I realise that I am a moral vacuum too.

September 14th

Woke up feeling awful. I don't know whether it was from alcoholic or emotional causes. But certainly my head was aching and I felt tired, sick, and depressed.

But Annie was wonderful. Not only did she make me some black coffee, she said all the right things.

I was feeling that I was no different from Humphrey and all that lot in Whitehall. She wouldn't have that at all.

'He's lost his sense of right and wrong,' she said firmly. 'You've still got yours.'

'Have I?' I groaned.

'Yes. It's just that you don't use it much. You're a sort of whisky priest. You do at least know when you've done the wrong thing.'

She's right. I *am* a sort of whisky priest. I may be immoral but I'm not amoral. And a whisky priest – with that certain air of raffishness of Graham Greene, of Trevor Howard, that *je ne sais quoi* – is not such a bad thing to be.

Is it?

20
The Middle-Class Rip-off

September 24th

After my constituency surgery this morning, which I used to do every other Saturday but which I can now manage less often since I became a Minister, I went off to watch Aston Wanderers' home match.

It was a sad experience. The huge stadium was half empty. The players were a little bedraggled and disheartened, there was a general air of damp and decay about the whole outing.

I went with Councillor Brian Wilkinson, Chairman of the local authority's Arts and Leisure Committee and by trade an electrician's mate at the Sewage Farm, and Harry Sutton, the Chairman of the Wanderers, a local balding businessman who's done rather well on what he calls 'import and export'. Both party stalwarts.

Afterwards they invited me into the Boardroom for a noggin. I accepted enthusiastically, feeling the need for a little instant warmth after braving the elements in the Directors' Box for nearly two hours.

I thanked Harry for the drink and the afternoon's entertainment.

'Better enjoy it while the club's still here,' he replied darkly.

I remarked that we'd always survived so far.

'It's different this time,' said Brian Wilkinson.

I realised that the invitation was not purely social. I composed myself and waited. Sure enough, something was afoot. Harry stared at Brian and said, 'You'd better tell him.' Wilkinson threw a handful of peanuts into his mouth, mixed in some Scotch, and told me.

'I'll not mince words. We had an emergency meeting of the Finance Committee last night, Aston Wanderers is going to have to call in the receiver.'

'Bankruptcy?' I was shocked. I mean, I knew that football clubs were generally in trouble, but this really caught me unawares.

Harry nodded. 'The final whistle. We need one and a half million quid, Jim.'

'Peanuts,' said Brian.

'No thank you,' I said, and then realised that he was describing the sum of one and a half million pounds.

'Government wastes that much money every thirty seconds,' Brian added.

As a member of the government, I felt forced to defend our record. 'We do keep stringent control on expenditure.'

It seemed the wrong thing to say. They both nodded, and agreed that our financial control was so stringent that perhaps it was lack of funds for the fare which had prevented my appearance at King Edward's School prize-giving. I explained – thinking fast – that I'd had to answer Questions in the House that afternoon.

'Your secretary said you had some committee meeting.'

Maybe I did. I can't really remember that kind of trivial detail. Another bad move. Harry said, 'You know what people round here are saying? That it's a dead loss having a Cabinet Minister for an MP. Better off with a local lad who's got time for his constituency.'

The usual complaint. It's so unfair! I can't be in six places at once, nobody can. But I didn't get angry. I just laughed it off and said it was an absurd thing to say.

Brian asked why.

'There are great advantages to having your MP in the Cabinet,' I told him.

'Funny we haven't noticed them, have we, Harry?'

Harry Sutton shook his head. 'Such as?'

'Well . . .' And I sighed. They always do this to you in your constituency, they feel they have to cut you down to size, to stop you getting too big for your boots, to remind you that you need them to re-elect you.

'It reflects well on the constituency,' I explained. 'And it's good to have powerful friends. Influence in high places. A friend in need.'

Harry nodded. 'Well, listen 'ere, friend – what we need is one and a half million quid.'

I had never imagined that they thought I could solve their financial problems. *Was* that what they thought, I wondered? So I nodded non-committally and waited.

'So will you use all that influence to help us?' asked Harry.

Clearly I had to explain the facts of life to them. But I had to do it with tact and diplomacy. And without undermining my own position.

'You see,' I began carefully, 'when I said *influence* I meant the more, er, intangible sort. The indefinable, subtle value of an input into broad policy with the constituency's interest in mind.'

Harry was confused. 'You mean no?'

I explained that anything I can do in a general sense to further the cause I would certainly do. If I could. But it's scarcely possible for me to pump one and a half million into my local football club.

Harry turned to Brian. 'He means no.'

Brian Wilkinson helped himself to another handful of peanuts. How does he stay so *thin*? He addressed me through the newest mouthful, a little indistinctly.

'There'd be a lot of votes in it. All the kids coming up to eighteen, too. You'd be the hero of the constituency. Jim Hacker, the man who saved Aston Wanderers. Safe seat for life.'

'Yes,' I agreed. 'That might just strike the press too. And the opposition. And the judge.'

They stared at me, half-disconsolately, half-distrustfully. Where, they were wondering, was all that power that I'd been so rashly talking about a few minutes earlier? Of course the truth is that, at the end of the day, I do indeed have power (of a sort) but not to really *do* anything. Though I can't expect them to understand that.

Harry seemed to think that I hadn't quite grasped the point. 'Jim,' he explained slowly, 'if the club goes to the wall it'll be a disaster. Look at our history.'

We all looked sadly around the room, which was lined with trophies, pennants, photos.

'FA Cup Winners, League Champions, one of the first teams ever into Europe,' he reminded me.

I interrupted his lecture. 'I know all this. But be fair, Harry, it's a local matter. Not ministerial.' I turned to Wilkinson. 'Brian, you're Chairman of the Borough Arts and Leisure Committee. Can't *you* do something?'

Attack is always the best form of defence. Wilkinson was instantly apologising in the same vein as me. 'You're joking. I spent half yesterday trying to raise seven hundred and eleven quid to repoint the chimney of the Corn Exchange Art Gallery.'

'That miserable place?' I asked. 'Why not just let it fall down?'

He said he'd love to. But if it did actually fall down on somebody the Council would be liable. The Borough owns the place. And, ironically, they keep getting offers for the site. There was one from Safefare Supermarkets only last month.

It was as he said this that I had one of my great flashes of inspiration. From out of nowhere 'The Idea' occurred to me. An idea of such brilliance and simplicity that I myself can, even now, be hardly sure that I thought of it all by myself, completely unprompted. But I did! It is ideas of this quality that have taken me to the top of my chosen profession and will take me still higher.

But first I had a question to ask. 'How much did Safefare offer for the site?'

Brian Wilkinson shrugged and wiped his hands on his trousers. 'About two million, I think.'

Then I hit them with it. 'So – if you sold the art gallery you could save the football club.'

They gazed at me, and then at each other, with wild surmise. Both thinking furiously.

'Can I have a look at it?' I asked.

We tore out of Aston Park. The traffic had nearly cleared, the fans dispersed, the police horses had done their Saturday afternoon cavalry charge, and all the hooligans had been trampled on or arrested. We raced through the deserted early evening streets to the Corn Exchange. It was due to shut at 5.30. We got there just after it closed.

We stepped out of Harry's Rolls in front of the art gallery, stood still, and looked up at our target. To tell the truth, I'd never really *looked* at it before. It is a Victorian monster, red-brick, stained glass, battlements and turrets, big and dark and gloomy.

'Hideous, isn't it?' I said to Brian Wilkinson.

'Yeah, well, it's a Grade II listed building, isn't it?' he explained.

That certainly is the problem.

September 25th

Today Brian, Harry and I returned to the art gallery. Fortunately it's open on Sundays too. Annie was pretty fed up this morning. I told her I was going to the art gallery but she didn't believe me. It's not really surprising – I didn't even go into any art galleries when we went to Italy a couple of years ago. My feet get so tired.

The gallery was empty when we got there. So we found the Curator, a pleasant chubby middle-aged lady, and had a little chat with her. She was awfully pleased to see us and of course I didn't tell her the purpose of our call. I just made it look like I was keeping a fatherly eye on the constituency.

I asked her how popular the gallery is. She answered that it is very popular, and smiled at me.

'You mean, a lot of people come here?'

She was careful to be honest. 'Well, I wouldn't say a lot. But it's very popular with those who come.'

A slightly evasive response. I pressed her for details; like, the daily average of visitors through the year.

'Well into double figures,' she said, as if that were rather a lot.

'How well?'

'Um – eleven, on average,' she admitted, but she added emphatically that they were all very appreciative.

We thanked her for her help and pottered off to look at the pictures. My feet started aching instantly.

At Harry's office afterwards we went over the details of the proposition. Eleven people per day at the gallery, fifteen to twenty thousand people every week at Aston Wanderers. There is no doubt in any of our minds that our plan is in the public interest.

And the plan is simplicity itself. Close the art gallery, sell it to Safefare Supermarkets, and use the money for an interest-free loan to Aston Wanderers.

Harry sounded a note of caution. 'There'd have to be a planning inquiry. Change of use. Art gallery to supermarket.'

I could see no problem. There's no question that this scheme will be immensely popular round here. There's bound to be some opposition, of course – there's opposition to *everything* – but art-lovers aren't a very powerful lobby compared to the Supporters' Club. Brian, who is also the Chairman of the Arts Committee, asked me what they could do with the paintings. I suggested that they sell them in the supermarket – if they can!

SIR BERNARD WOOLLEY RECALLS:[1]

Hacker had told me of this plan to save his local football club, but I paid no great attention to it. It seemed to me that it was a constituency matter and not relevant to his Ministerial role.

I was rather surprised to receive a telephone call from Sir Humphrey Appleby about it, asking what – precisely – our political master was up to.

Rather tactlessly I asked him how he found out about it, and was instantly reprimanded. 'Not from you, Bernard, an omission you may perhaps like to explain.'

He asked for a memo. I sent him one, describing the situation and concluding with my opinion that it would be a very popular move that the local people would support. I received a stern reply, which I have always kept. It is an excellent guideline for all policy matters connected with the Arts.

[1] In conversation with the Editors.

Cat. No. 6912

Memorandum
From The Permanent Secretary
To: B.W. September 28th

The Minister's scheme to demolish the Corn Exchange Art Gallery would in your opinion be popular. This is undoubtedly true. It would be distressingly popular. Hideously popular.

I ask you to take a broader view and consider the consequences.

1. <u>The Minister would be re-elected</u>

We, of course, have no Departmental view on this matter. We do not mind whether the Minister is re-elected or not. As far as this Department is concerned, it makes very little difference who the Minister is.

2. <u>Subsidy for the Arts would be threatened</u>

Suppose other football clubs get into difficulty. Or greyhound race tracks. Should dog racing be subsidised if football clubs are subsidised? If not, why not? You say people would want it.

You have sadly misunderstood the purpose of subsidy. Subsidy is for Art. It is for Culture. It is not to be given to what the people want, it is for what the people don't want but ought to have. If they really want something they will pay for it themselves. The Government's duty is to subsidise education, enlightenment and spiritual uplift, not the vulgar pastimes of ordinary people. This is the thin edge of the wedge and an appalling precedent. It must be stopped.

Please arrange a meeting between the Minister and me, asap,[1] nominally to discuss the impending departmental reorganisation.

[1] As soon as possible.

[*Hacker's diary continues – Ed.*]

September 29th

Bernard slipped an extra meeting with Sir Humphrey into my diary, first thing this morning.

My Permanent Secretary wanted to warn me personally that there is a reshuffle in the offing.

Naturally this made me a little nervous, as I wasn't sure if he was dropping an early hint about my being dropped. This was not just paranoia on my part, because I still don't know whether my deal with the Chief Whip on the matter of the bomb detonators has redounded to my credit or debit as far as the PM is concerned.

But Humphrey made it quickly clear that he was actually talking about a departmental reorganisation – what he called 'a real reshuffle'. He was warning me that we may be given extra responsibilities.

God knows if we want them! I certainly feel that I've got quite enough on my plate. But Humphrey was in no doubt that it would be a definite plus.

'We want all responsibilities, so long as they mean extra staff and bigger budgets. It is the breadth of our responsibilities that makes us important – makes *you* important, Minister. If you want to see vast buildings, huge staff and massive budgets, what do you conclude?'

'Bureaucracy,' I said.

Apparently I'd missed the point. 'No, Minister, you conclude that at the summit there must be men of great stature and dignity who hold the world in their hands and tread the earth like princes.'

I could certainly see his point, put like that.

'So that is the reason,' Humphrey continued, 'why every new responsibility must be seized and every old one guarded jealously. Entirely in your interest of course, Minister.'

A real overdose of soft soap. In my interest perhaps, but certainly not *entirely* in my interest. He must think I was born yesterday.

I thanked him for the information and courteously dismissed him. I can really see through him nowadays.

As he was leaving he enquired about the Corn Exchange Art Gallery proposal. I was surprised he'd heard about it as it's not a matter for central government.

To my surprise he heaped abuse upon the scheme. 'It's a most imaginative idea. Very novel.'

I wondered what he'd got against it, and invited him to go on.

'Well . . .' He returned from the door to my desk, 'I just wondered if it might not be a little unwise.'

I asked him why.

'A valuable civic amenity,' he replied.

I pointed out that it is a monstrosity.

He amended his view slightly. 'A valuable civic monstrosity,' he said, and added that it contained a most important collection of British paintings.

He's obviously been misinformed. In fact, as I told him then and there, the collection is utterly unimportant. Third-rate nineteenth-century landscapes and a few modern paintings so awful that the Tate wouldn't even store them in its vaults.

'But an *important* representative collection of unimportant paintings,' insisted Sir Humphrey, 'and a great source of spiritual uplift to the passing citizenry.'

'They never go in,' I told him.

'Ah, but they are comforted to know it's there,' he said.

I couldn't see where this was leading, what it had to do with Humphrey Appleby, or how he could possibly have any views about this collection of paintings at all. He's hardly ever been north of Potters Bar.

I took a stand on a principle. I reminded him that this is a constituency matter, that it concerns the Borough Council and me as constituency MP – not as Minister – and that it was nothing at all to do with him or Whitehall.

He pursed his lips and made no reply. So I asked him *why* he was interested. To my surprise he told me that it was a matter of principle.

This astonished me. Throughout our whole fight on the question of the bomb detonators he had insisted with religious fervour that principles were no concern of his. I reminded him of this.

'Yes Minister.' He conceded the point. 'But principle is what you've always told me that government is all about.'

I was baffled. 'What principle is at stake here?'

'The principle of taking money away from the Arts and putting it into things like football. A football club is a commercial proposition. There is no cause for subsidising it if it runs out of money.'

He seemed to think that he had just made an irrefutable statement of fact.

'Why not?' I asked.

'Why not what?'

'Why is there no cause? There's no difference between subsidising football and subsidising art except that lots more people are interested in football.'

'Subsidy,' he replied, 'is to enable our cultural heritage to be preserved.'

But for whom? For whose benefit? For the educated middle classes. For people like Humphrey, in other words. Subsidy means they can get their opera and their concerts and their Shakespeare more cheaply than if the full cost had to be recouped from ticket sales. He thinks that the rest of the country should subsidise the pleasures of a middle-class few who want to see theatre, opera and ballet.

'Arts subsidy,' I told him simply, 'is a middle-class rip-off. The middle classes, who run the country, award subsidies to their own pleasures.'

He was shocked. Genuinely shocked, I think. 'How can you say such a thing? Subsidy is about education and preserving the pinnacles of our civilisation. Or hadn't you noticed?' he added scathingly.

I ordered him not to patronise me. I reminded him that I also believe in education – indeed, I am a graduate of the London School of Economics.

'I'm glad to learn that even the LSE is not totally opposed to education,' he remarked. I rose above his pathetic Oxbridge joke, and remarked that there is no possible objection to subsidising sport. Sport is subsidised in many ways already. And sport is educational.

Sir Humphrey's sarcasm was in full swing. 'Education is not the whole point,' he said, having said that it *was* the whole point not two minutes earlier. 'After all, we have sex education too – should we subsidise sex perhaps?'

'Could we?' asked Bernard, waking up suddenly like a hopeful Dormouse. Humphrey scowled at him.

I was enjoying the cut and thrust of our intellectual debate, particularly as I seemed to be doing most of the cutting and thrusting.

I proposed to Humphrey that we might, in fact, choose what to subsidise by the extent of public demand. I certainly can't see anything wrong with the idea. It's democratic at least.

Humphrey normally ignores me when I'm being provocative, unless a serious policy decision of mine is at stake. But for some reason it seemed important to him to persuade me to change my mind.

'Minister,' he said, pleading for me to understand his élitist point of view, 'don't you see that this is the thin end of the wedge. What will happen to the Royal Opera House, on this basis? The very summit of our cultural achievement.'

As a matter of fact, I don't think that the Royal Opera House *is* the summit of our achievement. It's a very good case in point – it's all Wagner and Mozart, Verdi and Puccini. German and Italian. It's not *our* culture at all. Why should we subsidise the culture of the Axis Powers?

'The Royal Opera House,' I explained, 'gets about nine and a half million pounds a year of public money. For what? The public can't afford to buy thirty- or forty-quid seats for gala nights – and even if they could, they can't *get* them, there aren't enough. The audience consists almost entirely of big business executives, block-booked by the banks and oil companies and multinationals – and people like you, Humphrey. The Royal Opera House is for the Establishment at play. Why should the workers on the terraces foot the bill for the gentry in the stalls who can well afford to pay the full price for their seats?'

He stared at me as though I'd been brought in by the cat. I waited for a response. Bernard was studying his empty notepad intently.

Finally Sir Humphrey spoke. Very quietly. 'Minister, I am frankly appalled! This is savagery! Barbarism! That a Minister of the Crown should say such things – this is the end of civilisation as we know it. *And* it's a gross distortion of the truth.'

Emotive language from Humphrey! He was indeed upset. I, on the other hand, wasn't a bit upset and was thoroughly enjoying myself.

'A distortion, eh?' I replied cheerfully.

'Yes indeed. Art cannot survive without public subsidy.'

I wound him up some more. 'Did Shakespeare have public subsidy?'

'Yes of course he did.'

'No he didn't, he had patronage. That's quite different. It's a rich man spending his own money, not a committee spending other people's. Why can't the theatre live on its wits? Is it good for art to be dependent on officials and committees? Not necessarily!'

Humphrey made incoherent choking noises. I put up my hand regally, to silence him.

'And, if you persist in arguing in favour of subsidy, what about films? Films are art. Films are educational. Films are – God forbid! –

popular with the public. More than opera, anyway. So why has the Establishment ignored film subsidy?'

He tried to reply, but I refused to yield the floor. I was having much too good a time. 'I'll tell you. Simply because people like you prefer opera.'

Humphrey finally broke. He shouted me down before I'd finished speaking. This has never been known before. 'Minister, films are *commercial*!' He said this with all the contempt of a man who lives in a very high publicly-funded ivory tower.

Then he stood up. Clearly he was not prepared for me to bring the meeting to a close, as is the normal protocol. He had had enough, and was leaving.

'If you will excuse me, Minister, I have to leave early tonight. I simply cannot continue with this appalling discussion.' And he walked swiftly to the door.

I asked him where he was going in such a hurry.

He instantly slowed down and, his eyes moving shiftily from side to side, replied that he was going nowhere in particular.

I didn't like his walking out on me, and I told him that I insisted we talk the matter through. Apart from the immense pleasure of winding him up, I wanted to establish that my constituency affairs were nothing to do with him. Also, I was instinctively suspicious.

'I can't talk about this any further,' he said, flapping a bit and looking at his watch. 'I have to dress . . . I mean . . .'

He faltered and looked at me like a guilty hamster.

What a wonderful coincidence. I smiled lazily. 'Dress?' I asked as casually as I could. 'Where are you going?'

He drew himself up and squared his shoulders.

'Since you insist on knowing – I'm going to the Royal Opera House.'

'Gala performance, is it?'

'Yes it is, since you ask.'

'Lots of Permanent Secretaries going to be there?'

'Some, no doubt.'

I waved him away. 'Off you go, then,' I said graciously. 'I don't want to make you late for your works' outing.'

He stared at me through narrow little eyes, filled with pure hatred. I smiled back at him.

'Well, that's what it is, isn't it? What's on tonight, by the way?'

'*The Flying Dutchman*.'

'Ah. Another of our European partners.'

He turned his head and swept out. I'd never enjoyed a meeting so much in my whole life. Bernard, I think, had never enjoyed one less.

[*At the Opera that evening Sir Humphrey Appleby had a drink in the Crush Bar with Sir Ian Whitworth, Permanent Secretary of the Department of the Environment. We have found an account of the meeting in Appleby's private diary – Ed.*]

Had a chat with Ian W. over a couple of large G and Ts and those delicious little smoked salmon sandwiches in the Crush Bar.

He's having problems with one of his Ministers. Not the Secretary of State, who is easily handled, but one of the junior Ministers: Giles Freeman, the Parly Sec.

Discussed the impending planning inquiry into the sale and redevelopment of the Corn Exchange Art Gallery site. Warned him that it was rather important that we get the right result.

Ian reminded me that his planning inspectors are absolutely independent and there can be no question of undue influence. Quite right too.

On the other hand, if it were a question of his giving certain informal guidelines, putting the inquiry in the right perspective and explaining the background to facilitate an informed appreciation of the issues and implications, he agreed that such a course would be regarded as entirely proper.

Then he asked me what it was, exactly, that I wanted him to fix. I explained that it was a question of a proposed local authority demolition of a Grade II listed building. He misunderstood my intentions at first. He said that he would be only too happy to arrange it, there would be no problems: they'd been knocking down listed buildings all over the place.

I explained that the proposal had to be *rejected*. This amazed him, naturally. And he demanded an explanation. I was forced to reveal that if the sale goes through the proceeds will be used to save the local football club from bankruptcy.

He was visibly shaken. We were unable to continue this conversation as the interval bell went at that moment. Never send to know for whom the bell tolls – it tolls for the Arts Council.

[*Appleby Papers JAL/REL 14041*]

[*The following day Sir Humphrey Appleby received an urgent letter, delivered by hand, from Sir Ian Whitworth, see opposite – Ed.*]

**DEPARTMENT OF
THE ENVIRONMENT**

From the Permanent Secretary

30th September

Dear Humphrey,

I cannot think where that appalling idea came from. If you allow the principle of money being taken from the Arts and given to ordinary people to enjoy themselves, where will it end?

Your Lord and Master may be getting rather het up over the sweaty masses, but I beg you to do your utmost to put an end to this nonsense somehow.

There is no knowing to what this might lead. Today a Midlands art gallery goes to support a local football club – tomorrow the Royal Opera House grant goes to modernise Wembley Stadium.

For my part, I shall certainly keep a special eye on the planning inquiry. As you know, I cannot influence the Inspector, but it should prove helpful if I appoint a chap who is due for promotion.

And I'll see that he's briefed properly, so that the guidelines make it quite clear that the real issue is civilisation versus barbarism.

Yours ever,

Ian.

[*A reply from Sir Humphrey Appleby – Ed.*]

DEPARTMENT OF
ADMINISTRATIVE AFFAIRS

From the Permanent Under-Secretary of State

30/ix

Dear Ian,

As you know, I'm completely in agreement with your view of this shocking affair. Glad to hear that you're taking what steps you can.

Clearly we cannot have Arts money going to support popular sports. It's just subsidising self-indulgence.

See you at Traviata next week, if not before?

Yours

Humphrey

[*Hacker's diary continues – Ed.*]

October 3rd

My usual diary session with Bernard was full of interest this morning. Though I was in a hurry today he insisted on a brief talk with me before we did anything else.

'There is something I should like to suggest to you, Minister, if I may be so bold.'

I told him to be as bold as he liked.

He told me that, in his opinion, I shouldn't get involved with the art gallery/football club affair. I told him he was being rather bold.

'Better for me to be bold than for you to be stumped, Minister.' I like Bernard. He's wasted in Whitehall.

He then informed me that it is axiomatic in Whitehall (though news to me, I must say) that an MP should never get involved in a planning inquiry in his own constituency.

Apparently this is because the local issues are usually finely balanced. Therefore you're bound to offend as many constituents as you please. Either way, you can't win. The same problem as the integrated national transport policy, in fact. And Bernard emphasised that it becomes especially dangerous to become involved if there's a powerful quango lurking in the wings.

This sounded all very sensible in theory, and I was grateful for Bernard's support and care. But in this case I'm not sure that the local arguments *are* finely balanced. I told Bernard that everyone will be on the same side except for a few wet long-haired scruffy art lovers.

Bernard took this on board, and made no direct reply. He simply suggested that we now went through my diary for the morning. I thought he'd conceded my point until we examined the diary closely.

10.15 a.m. The Secretary-General of the Arts Council
(The biggest quango of them all)
10.45 a.m. The Historic Monuments Association
11.00 a.m. The National Trust
11.15 a.m. The Country Landowners' Association
11.30 a.m. The Council for the Protection of Rural England
11.45 a.m. The Country Crafts and Folklore Council

I gazed at Bernard, nonplussed.

'Rural England?' I asked, picking one of the appointments out at random.

'Yes,' said Bernard and made a vague gesture towards the window. 'There's quite a lot of it out there.'

'But why are all these people coming to see me?'

'The Corn Exchange,' he explained patiently. 'It's the Arts and Architecture mafia.'

'So who are the Country Crafts and Folklore Council?'

'The raffia mafia.' He wasn't joking it seems. 'All very influential people. They've all come out of the woodwork. There'll be letters in *The Times*, hostile articles in the Sundays, you'll be accused of vandalism. And you can be sure they'll orchestrate plenty of opposition in your constituency.'

I had a nasty feeling now that he could be right. But I am determined to fight on. This is one I can win.

I admonished Bernard. 'I didn't ask you to put any of these people in my diary, Bernard. What were you thinking of?'

'I was thinking of Sir Humphrey, Minister. He asked me to.'

I told Bernard that I intended to support my excellent scheme, come what may.

The rest of the day was spent in interminable meetings of excruciating boredom listening to all the pressure groups. Tonight I'm feeling absolutely exhausted.

October 4th

Bernard displayed even more ingenuity and tenacity today.

Having taken on board that my art gallery demolition plan is irrevocable, he produced a document for my inspection when I arrived at the office this morning.

He was actually asking me to approve it. He described it as the Local Government Allowances Amendment No. 2 to this year's regulations. 'What is it?' I asked.

He had written me a briefing, summarising the purpose of the document. It's a Statutory Instrument to be laid before the House. 'As Minister responsible for local government we need you to authorise that the revised Paragraph 5 of No. 2 Regulations 1971 shall come into operation on the 18th of March next, revoking Regulation 7 of the Local Government Allowances Amendment Regulations 1954 (b).'

I asked him what he meant, as I took the briefing and gazed at it.

So he showed me the explanatory note, which adds that 'These regulations are to make provision for prescribing the amounts of attendance and financial loss allowances payable to members of local authorities.'

I didn't pay much attention to Bernard's summary, because I was mesmerised by the document itself. I've kept a copy.

> *Explanatory Note:*
> Regulation 3 of the Local Government Allowances Amendment Regulations 1971 ("the 1971 Regulations") substituted a new regulation for Regulation 3 of the 1954 Regulations. Regulation 3 of the Local Government Allowances Amendment Regulation 1972 ("the 1972 Regulations") further amends Regulation 3 of the 1954 Regulations by increasing the maximum rates of attendance and financial loss allowance.
>
> Regulation 7 of 1982 Regulations revoked both Regulations 3 and 5 of the 1971 Regulations, Regulation 5 being a regulation revoking earlier spent regulations with effect from 1st. April next.
>
> These regulations preserve Regulations 3 and 5 of the 1971 Regulations by revoking Regulation 7 of the 1972 Regulations.

[*Hacker's diary continues – Ed.*]

Isn't it remarkable that this immortal prose should be described as an 'explanatory note'?

I finished reading it and looked at Bernard.

'I think that's quite clear, isn't it?' he said.

'Do I have to bother with all this piddling gobbledegook?' I replied.

He was slightly put out. 'Oh, I'm sorry, Minister. I thought that this would be an opportune moment for you to ensure that, as a result of your Ministerial efforts, local councillors would be getting more money for attending council meetings.'

I suddenly realised what he was driving at. I glanced back at Bernard's summary. There it was, in black and white *and* plain English: 'Amounts of attendance and financial loss allowances payable to members of local authorities.' So *that's* what it all means!

He had done excellently. This is indeed an opportune moment to display some open-handed generosity towards members of local authorities.

He asked if he could make one further suggestion. 'Minister, I happen to know that Sir Humphrey and Sir Ian Whitworth have been having discussions on this matter.'

'Ian Whitworth?'

Bernard nodded. 'The Corn Exchange is a listed building. So it's one of his planning inspectors who will be conducting the inquiry. Sir Humphrey and Sir Ian will be laying down some "informal" guidelines for him.'

I was suspicious. Informal guidelines? What did this mean?

Bernard explained carefully. 'Guidelines are perfectly proper. Everyone has guidelines for their work.'

It didn't sound perfectly proper to me. 'I thought planning inspectors were impartial,' I said.

Bernard chuckled. 'Oh *really* Minister! So they are! Railway trains are impartial too. But if you lay down the lines for them, that's the way they go.'

'But that's not *fair*!' I cried, regressing forty years.

'It's politics, Minister.'

'But Humphrey's not supposed to be in politics, he's supposed to be a civil servant. I'm supposed to be the one in politics.'

Then the whole import of what I'd blurted out came home to me. Bernard was nodding wisely. Clearly he was ready and willing to explain what political moves I had to make. I asked him how Humphrey and Ian would be applying pressure to the planning inspector.

'Planning inspectors have their own independent hierarchy. The only way they are vulnerable is to find one who is anxious for promotion.'

'Can a Minister interfere?'

'Ministers are our Lords and Masters.'

So that was the answer. Giles Freeman, the Parly Sec. at the Department of the Environment, is an old friend of mine. I resolved to explain the situation to Giles and get him to intervene. He could, for instance, arrange to give us a planning inspector who doesn't care about promotion because he's nearing retirement. Such a man might even give his verdict in the interests of the community.

All I said to Bernard was: 'Get me Giles Freeman on the phone.'

And to my astonishment he replied: 'His Private Secretary says he could meet you in the lobby after the vote this evening.'

I must say I was really impressed. I asked Bernard if he ever thought of going into politics. He shook his head.

'Why not?'

'Well, Minister, I once looked up politics in the *Thesaurus*.'

'What does it say?'

'"Manipulation, intrigue, wire-pulling, evasion, rabble-rousing, graft . . ." I don't think I have the necessary qualities.'

I told him not to underestimate himself.

[*Three days later Sir Humphrey Appleby received another letter from Sir Ian Whitworth – Ed.*]

DEPARTMENT OF THE ENVIRONMENT

From the Permanent Secretary

7th October

Dear Humphrey,

More bad news. It seems that your Minister has got at Giles Freeman, our ghastly Parly Sec. He has personally insisted on a different planning inspector to the one I chose. One who would be sympathetic to Hacker's scheme.

This is rather worrying, to say the least. There is now every danger that the planning inspector might make up his own mind.

It seems that there is likely to be a great deal of local support for this scheme.

Any ideas?

Ian.

[*We can find no written reply to this cry for help. But the following Monday Sir Humphrey and Sir Ian had lunch with Sir Arnold Robinson, the Cabinet Secretary. This account appears in Sir Humphrey's private diary, and was apparently written in a mood of great triumph – Ed.*]

At lunch with Arnold and Ian today I brought off a great coup.

Ian wanted to discuss our planning problem. I had invited Arnold because I knew that he held the key to it.

Having briefed him on the story so far, I changed the subject to discuss the Departmental reorganisation which is due next week. I suggested that Arnold makes Hacker the Cabinet Minister responsible for the Arts.

Arnold objected to that on the grounds that Hacker is a complete philistine. I was surprised at Arnold, missing the point like that. After all, the Industry Secretary is the idlest man in town, the Education Secretary's illiterate and the Employment Secretary is unemployable.

The point is that Hacker, if he were made Minister responsible for the Arts, could hardly start out in his new job by closing an art gallery.

As for Ian, he was either puzzled or jealous, I'm not sure which. He objected that the reorganisation was not meant to be a Cabinet reshuffle. I explained that I was not suggesting a reshuffle: simply to move Arts and Telecommunications into the purview of the DAA.

There is only one problem or inconsistency in this plan: namely, putting arts and television together. They have nothing to do with each other. They are complete opposites, really.

But Arnold, like Ian, was more concerned with all the power and influence that would be vested in me. He asked me bluntly if we wouldn't be creating a monster department, reminding me that I also have Administrative Affairs and Local Government.

I replied that Art and local government go rather well together – the art of jiggery-pokery. They smiled at my aphorism and, as neither of them could see any other immediate way of calling Hacker to heel, Arnold agreed to implement my plan.

'Bit of an artist yourself, aren't you?' he said, raising his glass in my direction.

[*Appleby Papers NG/NDB/FX GOP*]

October 11th

Good news and bad news today. Good on balance. But there were a few little crises to be resolved.

I was due to have a meeting with my local committee about the Aston Wanderers/Art Gallery situation.

But Humphrey arrived unexpectedly and demanded an urgent word with me. I told him firmly that my mind was made up. Well, it *was* – at that stage!

'Even so, Minister, you might be interested in a new development. The government reshuffle.'

This was the first I'd heard of a reshuffle. A couple of weeks ago he'd said it would be just a reorganisation.

'Not *just* a reorganisation, Minister. A *reorganisation.* And I'm delighted to say it has brought you new honour and importance. In addition to your existing responsibilities, you are also to be the Cabinet Minister responsible for the Arts.'

This was good news indeed. I was surprised that he'd been told before I had been, but it seems he was with the Cabinet Secretary shortly after the decision was taken.

I thanked him for the news, suggested a little drinkie later to celebrate, and then told him that I was about to start a meeting.

'Quite so,' he said. 'I hope you have considered the implications of your new responsibilities on the project you are discussing.'

I couldn't at first see what rescuing a football club had to do with my new responsibilities. And then the penny dropped! How on earth would it look if the first action of the Minister for the Arts was to knock down an art gallery?

I told Bernard to apologise to the Councillors, and to say that I was delayed or something. I needed time to think!

So Humphrey and I discussed the art gallery. I told him that I'd been giving it some thought, that it was quite a decent little gallery, an interesting building, Grade II listed, and that clearly it was now my role to fight for it.

He nodded sympathetically, and agreed that I was in a bit of a fix. Bernard ushered in the Councillors – Brian Wilkinson leading the delegation, plus a couple of others – Cllrs Noble and Greensmith.

I had no idea, quite honestly, what I was going to say to them. I ordered Humphrey to stay with me, to help.

'This is my Permanent Secretary,' I said.

Brian Wilkinson indicated Bernard. 'You mean he's only a temp?' Bernard didn't look at all pleased. I couldn't tell if Brian was sending him up or not.

I was about to start the meeting with a few cautious opening remarks when Brian plunged in. He told me, with great enthusiasm, that it was all going great. All the political parties are with the plan. The County Council too. It was now unstoppable. All he needed was my Department's approval for using the proceeds from the sale of the art gallery as a loan to the club.

I hesitated. 'Yes,' I said. 'Well – um . . . there is a snag.'

Wilkinson was surprised. 'You said there weren't any.'

'Well, there is.' I couldn't elaborate on this terse comment because I just couldn't think of anything else to say.

'What is it?' he asked.

My mind was blank. I was absolutely stuck. I said things like 'apparently . . . it seems . . . it has emerged,' and then I passed the buck, 'I think Sir Humphrey can explain it better,' I said desperately.

All eyes turned to Sir Humphrey.

'Um . . . well. It just can't be done, you see,' he said. It looked for a dreadful moment that he was going to leave it at that – but then, thank God, inspiration struck. 'It's because the art gallery is a trust. Terms of the original bequest. Or something,' he finished lamely.

I picked up the ball and carried on running with it, blindly. 'That's it,' I agreed emphatically, 'a trust. We'll just have to find something else to knock down. A school. A church. A hospital. Bound to be something,' I added optimistically.

Councillor Brian Wilkinson's jaw had dropped. 'Are we supposed to tell people that you've gone back on your word? It was your idea to start with.'

'It's the law,' I whined, 'not me.'

'Well, why didn't you find this out till now?'

I had no answer. I didn't know what to say. I broke out in a cold sweat. I could see that this could cost me my seat at the next election. And then dear Bernard came to the rescue.

He was surreptitiously pointing at a file on my desk. I glanced at it – and realised that it was the gobbledegook amending Regulation 7 of the Amendment of Regulations Act regulating the Regulation of the Amendments Act, 1066 and all that.

But what was it all about? Cash for Councillors? *Of course*!

My confidence surged back. I smiled at Brian Wilkinson and said, 'Let me be absolutely frank with you. The truth of the matter is, I *might* be able to get our scheme through. But it would take a lot of time.'

Wilkinson interrupted me impatiently. 'Okay, take the time. We've spent enough.'

'Yes,' I replied smoothly, 'but then something else would have to go by the board. And the other thing that's taking my time at the moment is forcing through this increase in Councillors' expenses and allowances. I can't put my personal weight behind both schemes.'

I waited. There was silence. So I continued. 'I mean, I suppose I could forget the increased allowances for Councillors and concentrate on the legal obstacles of the art gallery sale.'

There was another silence. This time I waited till one of the others broke it.

Finally Wilkinson spoke. 'Tricky things – legal obstacles,' he remarked. I saw at once that he understood my problem.

So did Humphrey. 'This is a particularly tricky one,' he added eagerly.

'And at the end of the day you might still fail?' asked Wilkinson.

'Every possibility,' I replied sadly.

Wilkinson glanced quickly at his fellow Councillors. None of them were in disagreement. I had hit them where they lived – in the wallet.

'Well, if that's the way it is, okay,' Wilkinson was agreeing to leave the art gallery standing. But he was still looking for other ways to implement our scheme because he added cheerfully, 'There's a chance we may want to close Edge Hill Road Primary School at the end of the year. That site could fetch a couple of million, give or take.'

The meeting was over. The crisis was over. We all told each other there were no ill-feelings, and Brian and his colleagues agreed that they would make it clear locally that we couldn't overcome the legal objections.

As he left, Brian Wilkinson told me to carry on the good work.

Humphrey was full of praise. 'A work of art, Minister. Now, Minister, you have to see the PM at Number Ten to be officially informed of your new responsibilities. And if you'll excuse me, I have to go and dress.'

'Another works' outing?'

'Indeed,' he said, without any air of apology.

I realised that, as Minister responsible for the Arts, the Royal Opera House now came within my purview. And I've hardly ever been.

'Um . . . can I come too?' I asked tentatively.

'Yes Minister,' he replied with great warmth.

And we had a jolly good evening – good music, great singing, smart people and some delicious little smoked salmon sandwiches in the Crush Bar.

Maybe I was wrong. The middle classes are entitled to a few perks, aren't they?

21
The Skeleton in the Cupboard

November 16th
An interesting situation emerged today from another meeting to which my old friend Dr Cartwright came.

It was a fairly dull routine meeting to start with, all about local government administration. As Humphrey predicted, our Department was increasing in size, staffing and budget. He is plainly in his element. So far, however, it hasn't involved much in the way of policy decisions, which is where I come in.

We'd reached item seven on the agenda, and so far it had been pretty uneventful. The only interest had been in Bernard's pedantic linguistic quibbles, about which he is becoming obsessional.

'Item seven,' I asked, 'what's it about?'

'If I may just recapitulate,' began Sir Humphrey.

Bernard made a little sign and caught my eye.

'Yes Bernard?'

'Um – one can't actually recapitulate an item if one hasn't started it yet,' he volunteered.

Sir Humphrey, who doesn't like to be corrected by *anyone,* let alone a mere Private Secretary, thanked him coldly and proceeded to complete his sentence, thus demonstrating to Bernard that the correction was both impertinent and unnecessary.

'Thank you, Bernard, where would we be without you? Minister, may I just, recapitulating *on our last meeting* and on our submissions which you have doubtless received in your boxes . . .'

I was thoroughly amused, and not paying full attention. 'Doubtless,' I interrupted cheerfully, and then realised that I didn't know what he was talking about. After all, they give me mountains of paper to read virtually every day, I can't remember everything.

'Which minutes?' I asked.

'On the proposal to take disciplinary action against the South-West Derbyshire County Council.'

I still had no idea what the proposal was. But I didn't like to admit it, it's always better to make them think that one is completely on top of the job. So I casually asked Bernard to remind me.

The problem was that the council in question had failed to complete their statutory returns and supply us with the statistical information that the DAA requires.

I asked what we were going to do about it. Apparently a policy decision was required from me. Sir Humphrey offered me assorted alternatives. 'A rebuke from the Minister, a press statement about their incompetence, withholding various grants and allowances, or, ultimately, as you are no doubt fully aware . . .'

'Yes, yes,' I interrupted helpfully.

'Good,' he said, and fell silent.

Again I was in a bit of a hole. I had no idea what he'd been about to say. But clearly he was waiting for my comments.

'I'm fully aware of . . . what?' I prompted him.

'What?'

'What am I fully aware of?'

'I can't think of anything.' Then he realised what he'd said because he added hastily, 'I mean, I can't think what you are . . .'

'You were saying,' I explained, feeling somewhat embarrassed by now. (After all, seven assorted officials of various ages and ranks were silently watching my display of confusion and ineptitude.) 'You were saying: "ultimately, as I'm fully aware" . . .'

'Ah yes, Minister.' Now he was on the ball again. 'Ultimately, taking the local authority to court.'

I asked if a failure to complete returns is all that serious.

Eight officials looked shocked! I was told categorically that it is not merely serious, but catastrophic!

I wanted to know why. Sir Humphrey was quick to explain.

'If local authorities don't send us the statistics we ask for, then government figures will be nonsense. They'll be incomplete.'

I pointed out that government figures are a nonsense anyway. No one denied it, but Bernard suggested that Sir Humphrey wanted to ensure that they are a complete nonsense.

He was rewarded with another withering look from his boss.

I was worried about making an example of South-West Derbyshire, which I happened to know is controlled by my party. Humphrey realised that this was on my mind, and raised the matter with me. I responded by suggesting that we pick on an opposition council instead.

This went down badly. I can't see why. What does he expect? Anyway, the suggestion was met with pursed lips from Sir Humphrey, and everyone else looked down at their blotters.

So I asked if South-West Derbyshire are really all that bad. And suddenly everyone had plenty to say.

One Under-Sec. told me that they won't return their blue forms (whatever they are, something to do with finance I think). An Assistant-Sec. told me that they replied to the DAA's Ethnic Personnel Breakdown Request in longhand, on the back of a departmental circular. And a delightfully attractive lady Assistant-Sec. was appalled because she still hadn't received their Social Worker Revised Case-load Analysis for the last two quarters. Or their Distributed Data Processing Appropriation Tables. 'They're unbelievable,' she said. 'Really evil.'

This was a definition of evil? Someone who doesn't return his blue form? 'Yes,' I said with heavy irony, 'I don't see how life still goes on in South Derbyshire.'

Sir Humphrey took my remark at face value. 'Exactly, Minister. They really are in a class of their own for incompetence.'

Still worried about my party problems, I enquired if they had no redeeming features. And my old friend Dr Cartwright piped up cheerfully. 'Well, it is interesting that . . .'

Sir Humphrey cut right across him. 'So if that's all right, Minister, we can take appropriate coercive action?'

Dr Cartwright had another try. 'Except that the Minister might . . .'

Again Sir Humphrey interrupted him. 'So can we take it you approve?' It was all beginning to look distinctly fishy.

I decided not to give an immediate answer. 'It's a difficult one. They're friends of ours.'

'They're no friends of good administration.'

I refused to be pressured. 'Give me twenty-four hours. I'll have to square the party organisation. Get the Chairman invited to a drinkies do at Number Ten or something. Soften the blow.'

And I insisted that we press on to the next item.

As the meeting broke up I noticed Dr Cartwright hovering, as if he wanted a private word with me. But Sir Humphrey took him by the arm and gently guided him away. 'I need your advice, Dick, if you could spare me a moment.' And they were gone.

Having thought about this overnight, I think I'll question Bernard more closely tomorrow.

November 17th

A fascinating day.

I raised the matter with Bernard as soon as I got to the office. I told him that my instincts told me that there is a good reason not to discipline South-West Derbyshire.

'Furthermore, Dr Cartwright seemed to be trying to tell me something. I think I'll drop in on him.'

'Oh, I wouldn't do that, Minister,' he said rather too hastily.

'Why not?'

He hesitated. 'Well, it is, er, understood that if Ministers need to know anything it will be brought to their attention. If they go out looking for information, they might, er they might . . .'

'Find it?'

'Yes.' He looked sheepish.

I remarked that it may be 'understood', but it's not understood by me.

Bernard obviously felt he had better explain further. 'Sir Humphrey does not take kindly to the idea of Ministers just dropping in on people. "Going walkabout", he calls it.'

I couldn't see anything wrong with that. I reminded him that the Queen does it.

He disagreed. 'I don't think she drops in on Under-Secretaries. Not in Sir Humphrey's department.'

I took a firm line. I asked Bernard for Dr Cartwright's room number.

He virtually stood to attention. 'I must formally advise you against this, Minister,' he said.

'Advice noted,' I said. 'What's his room number?'

'Room 4017. Down one flight, second corridor on the left.'

I told him that if I wasn't back within forty-eight hours he could send a search party.

SIR BERNARD WOOLLEY RECALLS:[1]

I well recall the day that Hacker went walkabout. This was the kind of situation that highlighted the dilemma of a Minister's Private Secretary. On the one hand I was expected to be loyal to the Minister, and any sign of disloyalty to him would mean that I had blotted my copybook. On the other hand, Sir Humphrey was my Permanent Secretary, my career was to be in the Civil Service for the next thirty years, and I owed a loyalty there also.

This is why high-flyers are usually given a spell as Private Secretary. If

[1] In conversation with the Editors.

one can walk the tightrope with skill and manage to judge what is proper when there is a conflict, then one may go straight to the top, as I did.

[*'Walking the tightrope' is Sir Bernard's phrase for betraying confidences from each side to the other while remaining undetected – Ed.*]

After the Minister left his office I telephoned Graham Jones, Sir Humphrey Appleby's Private Secretary. I let him know that the Minister had gone walkabout. I had no choice but to do this, as I had received specific instructions from Sir Humphrey that this should be discouraged [*i.e. prevented. – Ed.*].

I actually counted out ten seconds on my watch, from the moment I replaced the receiver, so well did I know the distance from his office to the Minister's, and Sir Humphrey entered the office on the count of 'ten'.

He asked me what had happened. Carefully playing it down, I told him that the Minister had left his own office. Nothing more.

Sir Humphrey seemed most upset that Hacker was, to use his words, 'loose in the building'. He asked me why I had not stopped him.

As it was my duty to defend my Minister, even against the boss of my own department, I informed Sir Humphrey that (a) I had advised against it, but (b) he was the Minister, and there was no statutory prohibition on Ministers talking to their staff.

He asked me to whom the Minister was talking. I evaded the question, as was my duty – clearly the Minister did not want Sir Humphrey to know. 'Perhaps he was just restless' is what I think I said.

I recall Sir Humphrey's irritable reply: 'If he's restless he can feed the ducks in St James's Park.'

Again he asked who the Minister was talking to, and again I evaded – under more pressure by this time – by seeking confirmation that the Minister could talk to anyone he liked.

Sir Humphrey's reply made it clear to me that he attached the greatest departmental importance to the issue. 'I am in the middle of writing your annual report,' he told me. 'It is not a responsibility that either of us would wish me to discharge while I am in a bad temper.' Then he asked me *again* to whom the Minister was talking.

I realised that I had gone as far as I safely could in defending the Minister's interests. And yet as his Private Secretary, I had to be seen to be standing up for him.

So I resorted to a well-tried formula. I asked for Sir Humphrey's help. Then I said: 'I can quite see that you should be told if the Minister calls on an outsider. But I can't see that it is necessary to inform you if he just wanted, to take a purely hypothetical example, to check a point with, say, Dr Cartwright. . . .'

He interrupted me, thanked me, and left the room. I called '4017' after him – well, why not?

I had passed the test with flying colours. I had managed to see that Sir Humphrey knew what he wanted, without actually telling him myself.

The hypothetical example was, and is, an excellent way of dealing with such problems.

[*Hacker's diary continues – Ed.*]
When I got to Cartwright's office I certainly learned a thing or two. Cartwright was delighted to see me, and told me quite openly that I had been misled at yesterday's meeting. I was intrigued.

'But all those things they told me about South-West Derbyshire – aren't they true?'

'They may be, for all I know.'

I asked him precisely what he was saying. To my surprise I got a completely straight answer. I can see why he's going to rise no higher.

'I'm saying that, nevertheless, South-West Derbyshire is the most efficient local authority in the UK.' And he blinked at me pleasantly from behind his half-moon reading glasses.

I was surprised, to say the least. 'The most efficient? But I'm supposed to be ticking them off for being the *least* efficient.'

Then he showed the figures.

This in itself was a surprise, as I'd been told that they didn't send us the figures. This was true – but no one had told me that they kept their own records perfectly well, which were available for us to see.

And the figures are impressive. They have the lowest truancy record in the Midlands, the lowest administrative costs per council house, the lowest ratio in Britain of council workers to rate income, and a clean bill of public health with the lowest number of environmental health officers.[1]

And that's not all. It seems that virtually all the children can read and write, despite their teachers' efforts to give them a progressive education. 'And,' Cartwright finished up, 'they have the smallest establishment of social workers in the UK.'

From the way he reported this fact I gathered he thought that this was a good thing. I enquired further.

'Oh yes. Very good. Sign of efficiency. Parkinson's Law of Social Work, you see. It's well known that social problems increase to occupy the total number of social workers available to deal with them.'

It was at this critical juncture that Sir Humphrey burst into Cartwright's office. I believe that his arrival in Cartwright's office at that moment was no coincidence.

We had a pretty stilted conversation.

'Oh, Minister! Good Heavens!'

[1] Rat-catchers.

'Oh. Hello Humphrey!'

'Hello Minister.'

'What a coincidence.'

'Yes. Indeed. What a surprise.'

'Yes.'

'Yes.'

For some reason he was making me feel guilty, and I found myself trying to explain my presence there.

'I was just, er, passing.'

'Passing?'

'Yes. Passing.'

'Passing. I see.' He considered my explanation for a moment. 'Where were you going?'

I was trapped. I had no idea what else was on Cartwright's floor. I decided to be vague.

'Oh,' I said airily, 'I was just going . . . past.' I said it as if 'past were a specific place to go. 'Past the door,' I added. I was aware that I sounded fearfully unconvincing but I blundered on. 'Cartwright's – Richard's door. Dick's door. So I thought "hello"!'

'And then did you think anything further?' He is relentless.

'Yes. I thought, why should I just pass the door? I might as well . . . open it.'

'Good thinking, Minister. That's what doors are for.'

'Quite.' I summoned up my courage and finally got to the point. 'And I'd remembered one or two points I wanted to clear up.'

'Good. What points?'

I couldn't see why I should tell him. Or why I shouldn't be in Cartwright's office. Or why he was successfully making me feel guilty? Or why he should consider that he had the right to approve everything that the DAA staff say to me. He behaves as though they are his staff, not mine. [*They were – Ed.*]

But I also couldn't see how not to answer him.

'Oh, just some odd points,' I replied finally, making a suitably vague gesture.

He waited. Silence. Then he repeated it. 'Just some odd points.'

'Yes,' I said.

'How odd?' he asked.

'Well it's not all *that* odd,' I said, argumentatively, wilfully misunderstanding him. 'We had a meeting yesterday, didn't we?'

Sir Humphrey was now tired of the fencing.

'Minister, may I have a word with you?'

'Certainly,' I said, 'as soon as Richard and I have . . .'

He interrupted. 'I mean now.'

Now it was my turn to embarrass him a little. 'Okay. Go ahead.' I knew he wouldn't want to talk in front of one of his juniors.

'Upstairs, Minister, in your office if you please.'

'But I'm sure Richard doesn't mind.'

'Upstairs, Minister. I'm sure Dr Cartwright can spare you for a few moments.'

Cartwright missed the heavy sarcasm completely. 'Oh yes,' he said with an obliging smile.

Sir Humphrey opened the door. Having been made to feel like a naughty schoolboy, I marched out of Cartwright's office.

I wonder how he knew I was in that office. I know Bernard wouldn't have told him, so somebody must have seen me and reported it. I might as well be in the Soviet Union. Somehow I've got to get my freedom – but that involves winning the psychological war against Humphrey. And somehow, he always manages to make me feel guilty and unsure of myself.

If only I could find a chink in his armour. If I ever do, he's *had* it!

Anyway, that tense little sparring match in Cartwright's office wasn't the end of the matter. A few minutes later, back in my office after an icy silent journey up in the lift and along the endless corridors, the row came to a head.

He told me that I cannot just go around talking to people in the Department, and expressed the sincere hope that such a thing would not occur again.

I could scarcely believe my ears. I ordered him to explain himself.

'Minister, how can I advise you properly if I don't know who's saying what to whom? I must know what's going on. You simply cannot have completely private meetings. And what if you're told things that aren't true?'

'If they're not true you can put me right.'

'But they may be true.'

'In *that* case . . .' I began triumphantly. He interrupted me, correcting himself hastily.

'That is, not *entirely* false. But misleading. Open to misinterpretation.'

I faced him with a straight question. 'The fact is, you're just trying to keep things from me, aren't you, Humphrey?'

He was indignant. 'Absolutely not, Minister. Records must be kept. You won't be here forever, nor will we. In years to come it may be vital to know what you were told. If Cartwright were moved tomorrow, how could we check on your information?'

On the face of it, that was a specious argument. 'Cartwright *isn't* being moved tomorrow,' I said.

'Oh, isn't he?' came the insolent response.

Bernard interrupted us. Alex Andrews of *The Mail* wanted to do an interview with me for tomorrow. I agreed of course. I told Bernard to stay with us and minute our conversation. Humphrey had given me *his* views on my private meeting with Cartwright. Now he was going to hear *mine*.

I began by repeating what Cartwright had told me: namely, that in his opinion – and the opinion of everyone who knows anything about local government – the South-West Derbyshire County Council is the most efficient in the country.

'Inefficient, I think he means, Minister.'

'Efficient, Humphrey. Effective. Economical. They're just not particularly interested in sending pieces of blue paper to Whitehall.'

Humphrey then explained something that I hadn't quite grasped yet. Apparently they *have* to return those sodding blue forms, it's a statutory requirement.

And we know why. We know who decreed that it should be so.

Even so, statutory requirements can be overlooked occasionally. Discretion can be exercised. So I asked Humphrey what happens if they don't send in their blue forms. South-West Derbyshire carries on, rather well apparently.

'But,' said Humphrey, not seeing at all what I was getting at, 'if they don't send us the information and plans and requests for permission, well, what are we here for?'

An excellent question, as I told him immediately. I asked it at once. 'What *are* we here for?'

'To collate the information, inspect the plans, and grant or withhold permission.'

'And if we didn't?' I asked.

He gazed at me studiously. I might have been talking Ancient Chinese, for all the sense I was making to him.

'I'm sorry, Minister, I don't understand.'

I persevered. 'If we didn't. If we weren't here and we didn't do it – then what?'

'I'm sorry, Minister, you've lost me.'

Yet again, Humphrey demonstrates that his trouble is that he is concerned with means and not ends.

[*Many civil servants of the time deflected criticisms about ends and means by stating flippantly that the only ends in administration are loose ends. If administration is viewed in a vacuum this is, of course, true. Administration can have no end in itself, and is eternal. For ever and ever, amen – Ed.*]

[*Hacker's diary continues – Ed.*]

The upshot of the whole argument was that I refused to discipline the most efficient local authority in Britain, on the grounds that I would look like an idiot if I did.

Sir Humphrey told me that was my job. I *think* he meant to discipline South-West Derbyshire, rather than to look like an idiot, but I'm not certain. He said that I had no alternative to consider, no discretion to exercise, and that the Treasury and the Cabinet Office insist.

[*By Cabinet Office Sir Humphrey clearly meant the Cabinet Secretary rather than the PM. But he could never have said so – the fiction had to be preserved that Britain was governed by Ministers who told civil servants what to do, not vice versa – Ed.*]

I still refused to co-operate.

'Minister. You don't seem to understand. It's not up to you or me. It's the law.'

And there we left it. I felt a bit like a dog refusing to go for a walk – sitting down and digging in my paws while being dragged along the pavement on my bottom.

But there must be some way out. The more I think of it, the less willing I am to discipline that council until there is *really* no alternative.

And the more I think of it, the more I conclude that Bernard must have told Humphrey that I'd gone to talk to Cartwright.

November 18th

I had no free time to talk to Bernard on his own yesterday.

But first thing this morning, while I was doing my letters, I had a serious word with Bernard. I asked him how Humphrey had found out yesterday that I was with Cartwright.

'God moves in a mysterious way,' he said earnestly.

'Let me make one thing quite clear,' I said, 'Sir Humphrey is not God. Okay?'

Bernard nodded. 'Will you tell him, or shall I?' he replied.

Very droll. But again I asked him how Humphrey knew where to find me.

I am fortunate that my dictaphone had been left running. I noticed it some minutes later. As a result I am able to record his reply for posterity in this diary.

'Confidentially, Minister, everything you tell me is in complete confidence. So, equally, and I'm sure you appreciate this, and by appreciate I don't actually mean appreciate, I mean understand, that everything that Sir Humphrey tells me is in complete confidence. As indeed everything I tell you is in complete confidence. And for that matter, everything I tell Sir Humphrey is in complete confidence.'

'So?' I said.

'So, in complete confidence, I am confident you will understand that for me to keep Sir Humphrey's confidence and your confidence means that my conversations must be completely confidential. As confidential as conversations between you and me are confidential, and I'll just get Alex Andrews as he's been waiting to see you, Minister.'

There it is. Word for word. What was I supposed to make of that? Nothing, of course.

My meeting with Alex Andrews of *The Mail* was today. I'd been very keen to fit him in at the earliest opportunity. I'd been hoping for a Profile, or something of that sort, but no such luck. Still, I've done him a good turn today, it's no skin off my nose, and perhaps he'll do the same for me one day.

He asked for my help in a fascinating story that he had just come across. 'Did you know that your government is about to give away forty million pounds' worth of buildings, harbour installations, a landing-strip, to a private developer? For nothing?'

I thought he was having me on. 'Forty million pounds?'

'Scout's Honour.'

'Why ask me?' I said. Suddenly I had a dreadful moment of panic. 'I didn't do it, did I?'

[*You may think that Hacker should have known if he had done it. But a great many things are done in a Minister's name, of which he may have little or no awareness – Ed.*]

Alex smiled, and told me to relax. Thank God!

Then he told me the story. It goes back a long way. Almost thirty years ago the Ministry of Defence took a lease on a Scottish island. They put up barracks, married quarters, an HQ block, and the harbour and airstrip. Now the lease has expired and they all become the property of the original landowner. And he is turning it into an instant holiday camp. Chalets, yachting marina, staff quarters – it's all there. He is going to make a fortune.

I listened, open-mouthed. 'But he can't do that!' I began. 'The law says that . . .'

Andrews interrupted me. 'You're talking about English law. This contract was under Scottish law and some idiot didn't realise the difference.'

I was relieved that at least I am in the clear. Even *The Mail* can't blame me for a cock-up in the early fifties. Though I'm sure they would if they could. And I couldn't at first see what he wanted from me. He already had the story. Thirty years late, as quick with the news as ever – still, not bad for Fleet Street!

They are running the story tomorrow. But apparently they don't want to leave it at that. The Editor wants Alex to follow up with an investigative feature. He wants him to go through the files, and find out exactly how it happened.

I couldn't see the point, not now.

'Well,' he explained, 'there may be lessons for today. And we might find who was responsible.'

I asked why it would matter? It would, in any case, have been handled by quite a junior official.

He nodded. 'Okay, but that was thirty years ago. He could be in a very senior position now, even a Permanent Secretary, running a great department, responsible for spending billions of pounds of public money.'

A very unlikely eventuality, in my opinion. These hacks will do anything to try and find a story where there isn't one.

He agreed it was pretty unlikely. But he asked to see the papers.

Naturally I had to be a bit cautious about that. I can't just hand files over, as he well knows. But I advised him that, as it was a thirty-year lease that was in question, he would be able to get the papers from the Public Record Office under the Thirty-Year Rule.

He was unimpressed. 'I thought you'd say that. I've asked for them already. But I want a guarantee that I *will* get them. All of them.'

I hate being asked to guarantee anything. I don't really think it's fair. And anyway, was I in a position to? 'Well,' I said, carefully feeling my way, 'Defence papers are sometimes . . .'

He interrupted me. 'Don't come that one. It's not top security.

Look, you made a manifesto commitment about telling voters the facts. This is a test case. Will you guarantee that no papers are removed before the files are opened?'

I could see no reason not to give him that guarantee. 'Fine,' I said, throwing caution to the winds. 'No problem.'

'Is that a promise?' Journalists are suspicious bastards.

'Sure,' I said with a big reassuring smile.

'A real promise? Not a manifesto promise?'

Some of these young Fleet Street fellows can be really rather insulting.

'Your trouble, Alex,' I said, 'is that you can't take yes for an answer.'

'Because otherwise,' he continued as if I hadn't even spoken, 'we do the feature on Ministers ratting on manifestos.'

Clearly I shall now have to stand by that promise. It's fortunate that I have every intention of doing so.

[*The following day* The Mail *ran the story, exactly as predicted in Hacker's diary (see opposite). That night Sir Humphrey's diary contains the following entry – Ed.*]

Horrible shock.

A story in today's *Mail* about the Glenloch Island base.

I read it on the 8.32 from Haslemere to Waterloo. Was seized instantly by what Dr Hindley calls a panic attack. A sort of tight feeling in the chest, I felt I couldn't breathe, and I had to get up and walk up and down the compartment which struck one or two of the regulars on the 8.32 as a bit strange. Or perhaps I just *think* that because of the panic attack.

Fortunately Valium did the trick as the day wore on, and I'll take a few Mogadon[1] tonight.

I tell myself that no one will ever connect that incident with me, and that it's all ancient history anyway, and that that's the last that anyone will want to know about it.

I tell myself that – but somehow it's not helping!

Why has this come up now, so many years later, when I thought it was all forgotten?

If only there was someone I could talk to about this.

Oh my God . . .

[*Hacker's diary continues – Ed.*]

November 21st

They ran that story in *The Mail* today. Quite amusing.

[1] Brand of sleeping pills in common use in the 1980s.

Tax payers lose £40 million!

Developer's Multi-Million Pound Bonanza From Government Error

By ALEX ANDREWS

An elementary mistake by a junior government official thirty years ago has cost British tax payers at least forty million pounds. The lucky beneficiary is a German property developer.

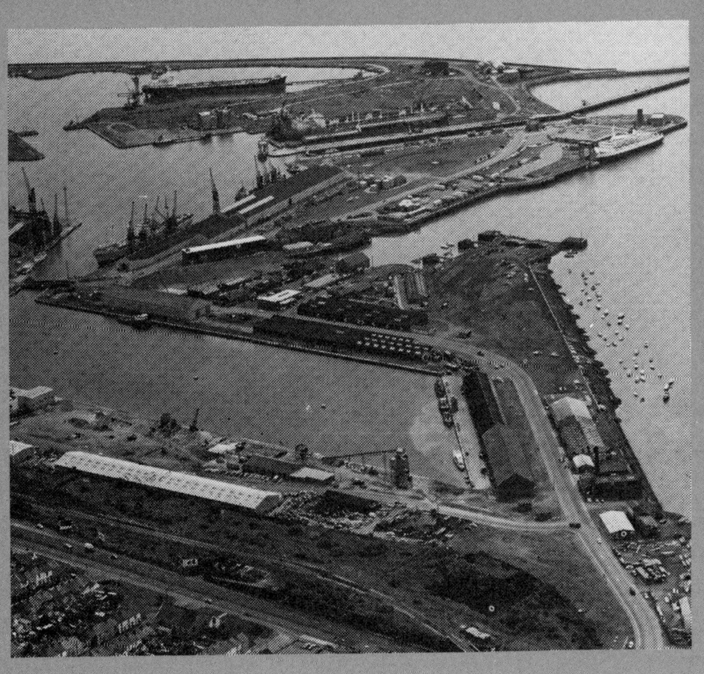

November 22nd

Today was the happiest day of my ministerial life.

All my prayers were answered.

As Humphrey and I were finishing up our weekly departmental meeting I asked him if he'd seen the story in yesterday's *Mail*.

'I'm not sure,' he said.

I reminded him. I knew he must have seen it, someone must have drawn his attention to it. 'You know,' I added, 'about that frightful cock-up thirty years ago over the terms of that Scottish island base.'

Now, as I think back, he seemed to flinch a little as I said 'that frightful cock-up'. Though I must say, I wasn't really aware of it at the time.

Anyway, he did remember the article, and he said that he believed that he *had* glanced at it, yes.

'I must say,' I said, chuckling, 'I think it's pretty funny – forty million quid down the tube. Someone really boobed there, didn't they?'

He nodded and smiled, a little wanly.

'Still, it couldn't happen in your Department could it?'

'No,' he said with absolute firmness. 'Oh no. Absolutely.'

I said that I'd been wondering who it was.

'That, Minister, is something that we shall never know.'

I pointed out that it must be on the files. Everything is always put in writing, as he so constantly reminds me.

Humphrey agreed that it would be on the record somewhere, but it would take ages to find out and it's obviously not worth anyone's time.

'Actually, you're wrong there,' I said. '*The Mail* are doing a big feature on it when the papers are released under the Thirty-Year Rule. I've promised them a free run of all the files.'

Humphrey literally rocked backwards on his feet.

'Minister!'

I was slightly shaken by his anger. Or was it anger? I couldn't tell.

'It's all right, isn't it?' I asked anxiously.

Yes, it *was* anger! 'All right? *All right*? No, it is certainly not all right.'

I asked why not. He told me it was 'impossible and unthinkable'. That didn't sound like much of an explanation to me, and I said as much.

'It . . . it's . . . top security, Minister.'

'A few barracks?'

'But there were secret naval installations, anti-submarine systems, low-level-radar towers.'

I pointed out that he couldn't possibly know what had been there. He agreed at once, but added – rather lamely, I thought – that that's the sort of thing those island bases always had.

'They'll have been dismantled,' I said. His objection was clearly quite irrelevant.

'But the papers will have references.'

'It's ancient history.'

'Anyway,' he said with evident relief, 'we'd have to consult. Get clearances.'

A few months ago I would have accepted that sort of remark from Humphrey. Now, I'm just a little older and wiser.

'Who from?' I asked.

He looked wildly about, and spoke completely incoherently. 'Security implications . . . MI5, MI6 . . . the national interest . . . foreign powers . . . consult our allies . . . top brass . . . CIA . . . NATO, SEATO, Moscow!'

'Humphrey,' I asked carefully, 'are you all right?'

'*Not* Moscow, no, I don't mean Moscow,' he corrected himself hastily. I got the impression that he was just saying the first words that came into his head, and that the word Moscow had been uttered simply because it rhymed.

He could see I wasn't convinced, and added: 'There could be information that would damage people still alive.'

This seemed to matter to him greatly. But it cut no ice with me.

'Whoever drafted that contract,' I insisted, '*ought* to be damaged if he's still alive.'

'Oh, quite, absolutely, no question of protecting officials. Of course not. But responsible Ministers . . .'

I interrupted him. I wasn't the least concerned about some Minister who'd been responsible thirty years ago. It couldn't matter less. Anyway, the other lot were in office then, so it's fairly amusing.

I simply couldn't figure out the reason for his intense opposition to releasing these papers. I asked him why he was *so* concerned.

He sat back in his chair and crossed his legs casually. 'I'm not. Not at all. I mean, not personally. But it's the principle, the precedent . . . the . . . the . . .' he was lost for words '. . . the policy.'

Trapped. I'd got him. 'Policy's up to me, Humphrey, remember?' I said with a smile. And before he could continue the argument I added, 'And I've promised, so it's done now, okay?'

He just sat there, sagging slightly, looking at me. Evidently he was trying to decide whether or not to say something. Finally he gave up. He stood wearily and, without looking at me, walked silently out of the room and shut the door behind him.

He seemed tired, listless, and quite without his usual energy.

Bernard had been present throughout the meeting. He waited, patiently, as usual, to be either used or dismissed.

I gazed at the door which Humphrey had closed quietly behind him.

'What's the matter with Humphrey?' I asked. There was no reply from Bernard. 'Have I done something wrong?' Again there was no reply. 'There *aren't* any security aspects, are there?' This time I waited a while, but answer came there none. 'So what is the problem?' I turned to look at Bernard, who appeared to be staring vacantly into space like a contented heifer chewing the cud.

'Am I talking to myself?'

He turned his gaze in my direction.

'No Minister, I am listening.'

'Then why don't you reply?'

'I'm sorry,' he said. 'I thought your questions were purely rhetorical. I can see no reason for Sir Humphrey to be so anxious.'

And then the penny dropped.

Suddenly I saw it.

I didn't know how I could have been so blind. So dumb. And yet, the answer – obvious though it was – seemed scarcely credible.

'Unless . . .' I began, and then looked at Bernard. 'Are you thinking what I'm thinking?'

He looked puzzled. 'I don't think so, Minister,' he replied cautiously, and then added with a flash of cheerful honesty, 'I'm not thinking anything really.'

'I *think*,' I said, uncertain how to broach it, 'that I smell a rat.'

'Oh. Shall I fetch an Environmental Health Officer?'

I didn't like actually to put my suspicions into words. Not yet. I thought I'd go carefully. So I asked Bernard how long Sir Humphrey had been here at the Department of Administrative Affairs.

'Oh, all his career, hasn't he? Ever since it was founded.'

'When was that?' I asked.

'1964. Same time that they started the Department of Economic Affairs . . .' he stopped dead, and stared at me, wide-eyed. 'Oh,' he said. 'Now I think I'm thinking what you're thinking.'

'Well?' I asked.

He wanted to be cautious too. 'You're thinking: where was he before 1964?'

I nodded slowly.

'It'll be in *Who's Who.*' He stood, then hurried to the glass-fronted mahogany bookcase near the marble fireplace. He fished out *Who's Who*, talking as he leafed through the pages. 'He must have been in some other Department, and been trawled when the DAA started. [*'Trawled', i.e. caught in a net, is the standard Civil Service word for 'head-hunting' through other departments – Ed.*]

He ran his forefinger down a page, and said in one sentence: 'Ah here we are oh my God!'

I waited.

Bernard turned to me. 'From 1950 to 1956 he was an Assistant Principal at the Scottish Office. Not only that. He was on secondment from the War Office. His job was Regional Contracts Officer. Thirty years ago.'

There could be no doubt who the culprit was. The official who had chucked away that forty million pounds of the taxpayers' money was the current Permanent Under-Secretary of the Department of Administrative Affairs, Sir Humphrey Appleby, KCB, MVO, MA (Oxon).

Bernard said, 'This is awful,' but his eyes were twinkling.

'Terrible,' I agreed, and found myself equally unable to prevent a smile creeping across my face. 'And the papers are all due for release in a few weeks' time.'

I suddenly felt awfully happy. And I told Bernard to get Humphrey back into my office at once.

He picked up the phone and dialled. 'Hello Graham, it's Bernard. The Minister wondered if Sir Humphrey could spare some time for a meeting some time in the next couple of days.'

'At once,' I said.

'In fact, some time during the course of today is really what the Minister has in mind.'

'At once,' I repeated.

'Or to be precise, any time within the next sixty seconds really.'

He listened for a moment, then replaced the receiver. 'He's coming round now.'

'Why?' I was feeling malicious. 'Did he faint?'

We looked at each other in silence. And we both tried very hard not to laugh.

Bernard's mouth was twitching from the strain.

'This is very serious, Bernard.'

'Yes Minister,' he squeaked.

I was, by now, crying from the effort not to laugh. I covered my eyes and my face with my handkerchief.

'No laughing matter,' I said, in a strangled muffled gasp, and the tears rolled down my cheeks.

'Absolutely not,' he wheezed.

We recovered as best we could, shaking silently, but didn't dare look at each other for a little while. I sat back in my chair and gazed reflectively at the ceiling.

'The point is,' I said, 'how do I best handle this?'

'Well, in my opinion . . .'

'The question was purely rhetorical, Bernard.'

Then the door opened, and a desperately worried little face peeped around it.

It was Sir Humphrey Appleby. But not the Humphrey Appleby I knew. This was not a God bestriding the Department of Administrative Affairs like a colossus, this was a guilty ferret with shifty beady eyes.

'You wanted a word, Minister?' he said, still half-hidden behind the door.

I greeted him jovially. I invited him in, asked him to sit down and – rather regretfully – dismissed Bernard. Bernard made a hurried and undignified exit, his handkerchief to his mouth, and curious choking noises emanating from it.

Humphrey sat in front of me. I told him that I'd been thinking about this Scottish island scandal, which I found very worrying.

He made some dismissive remark, but I persisted. 'You see, it probably hasn't occurred to you but that official could still be in the Civil Service.'

'Most unlikely,' said Sir Humphrey, presumably in the hope that this would discourage me from trying to find out.

'Why? He could have been in his mid-twenties then. He'd be in his mid-fifties now,' I was enjoying myself thoroughly. 'Might even be a Permanent Secretary.'

He didn't know how to reply to that. 'I, er, I hardly think so,' he said, damning himself further.

I agreed, and said that I sincerely hoped that anyone who made a howler like that could *never* go on to be a Permanent Secretary. He nodded, but the expression on his face looked as though his teeth were being pulled out without an anaesthetic.

'But it was so long ago,' he said. 'We can't find out that sort of thing now.'

And then I went for the jugular. This was the moment I'd been waiting for. Little did I dream, after he had humiliated me in front of Richard Cartwright, that I would be able to return the compliment so soon.

And with the special pleasure of using his own arguments on him.

'Of course we can find out,' I said. 'You were telling me that everything is minuted and full records are always kept in the Civil Service. And you were quite right. Well, legal documents concerning a current lease could not possibly have been thrown away.'

He stood. Panic was overcoming him. He made an emotional plea, the first time I can remember him doing such a thing. 'Minister, aren't we making too much of this? Possibly blighting a brilliant career because of a tiny slip thirty years ago. It's not such a lot of money wasted.'

I was incredulous. 'Forty million?'

'Well,' he argued passionately, 'that's not such a lot compared with Blue Streak, the TSR2, Trident, Concorde, high-rise council flats, British Steel, British Rail, British Leyland, Upper Clyde Ship Builders, the atomic power station programme, comprehensive schools, or the University of Essex.'

[*In those terms, his argument was of course perfectly reasonable – Ed.*]

'I take your point,' I replied calmly. 'But it's still over a hundred times more than the official in question can have earned in his entire career.'

And then I had this wonderful idea. And I added: 'I want you to look into it and find out who it was, okay?'

Checkmate. He realised that there was no way out. Heavily, he sat down again, paused, and then told me that there was something that he thought I ought to know.

Surreptitiously I reached into my desk drawer and turned on my little pocket dictaphone. I wanted his confession to be minuted. Why not? All conversations have to be minuted. Records must be kept, mustn't they?

This is what he said. 'The identity of this official whose alleged responsibility for this hypothetical oversight has been the subject of recent speculation is not shrouded in quite such impenetrable obscurity as certain previous disclosures may have led you to assume, and, in fact, not to put too fine a point on it, the individual in question was, it may surprise you to learn, the one to whom your present interlocutor is in the habit of identifying by means of the perpendicular pronoun.'

'I beg your pardon?' I said.

There was an anguished pause.

'It was I,' he said.

I assumed a facial expression of deep shock. 'Humphrey! No!'

He looked as though he was about to burst into tears. His fists clenched, knuckles whitened. Then he burst out. 'I was under pressure! We were overworked! There was a panic! Parliamentary questions tabled.' He looked up at me for support. 'Obviously I'm not a trained lawyer, or I wouldn't have been in charge of the legal unit.'

[*True enough. This was the era of the generalist, in which it would have seemed sensible and proper to put a classicist in charge of a legal unit or a historian in charge of statistics – Ed.*] 'Anyway – it just happened. But it was thirty years ago, Minister. Everyone makes mistakes.'

I was not cruel enough to make him suffer any longer. 'Very well Humphrey,' I said in my most papal voice. 'I forgive you.'

He was almost embarrassingly grateful and thanked me profusely.

I expressed surprise that he hadn't told me. 'We don't have any secrets from each other, do we?' I asked him.

He didn't seem to realise that I had my tongue in my cheek. Nor did he give me an honest answer.

'That's for you to say, Minister.'

'Not entirely,' I replied.

Nonetheless, he was clearly in a state of humble gratitude and genuinely ready to creep. And now that he was so thoroughly softened up, I decided that this was the moment to offer my *quid pro quo*.

'So what do I do about this?' I asked. 'I've promised to let *The Mail* see all the papers. If I go back on my word I'll be roasted.' I looked him straight in the eye. 'On the other hand, I might be able to do something if I didn't have this other problem on my plate.'

He knew only too well what I was saying. He's done this to me often enough.

So, immediately alert, he asked me what the other problem was.

'Being roasted by the press for disciplining the most efficient council in Britain.'

He saw the point at once, and adjusted his position with commendable speed.

After only a momentary hesitation he told me that he'd been thinking about South-West Derbyshire, that obviously we can't change the law as such, but that it might be possible to show a little leniency.

We agreed that a private word to the Chief Executive would suffice for the moment, giving them a chance to mend their ways.

I agreed that this would be the right way to handle the council. But it still left one outstanding problem: how would I explain the missing papers to *The Mail*?

We left it there. Humphrey assured me that he would give the question his most urgent and immediate attention.

I'm sure he will. I look forward to seeing what he comes up with tomorrow.

November 23rd

When I arrived at the office this morning Bernard informed me that Sir Humphrey wished to see me right away.

He hurried in clutching a thin file, and looking distinctly more cheerful.

I asked him what the answer was to be.

'Minister,' he said, 'I've been on to the Lord Chancellor's Office, and this is what we normally say in circumstances like this.'

He handed me the file. Inside was a sheet of paper which read as follows:

'This file contains the complete set of available papers except for:

(a) a small number of secret documents
(b) a few documents which are part of still active files
(c) some correspondence lost in the floods of 1967
(d) some records which went astray in the move to London
(e) other records which went astray when the War Office was incorporated into the Ministry of Defence
(f) the normal withdrawal of papers whose publication could give grounds for an action for libel or breach of confidence or cause embarrassment to friendly governments.'

[*1967 was, in one sense, a very bad winter. From the Civil Service point of view it was a very good one. All sorts of embarrassing records were lost – Ed.*]

I read this excellent list. Then I looked in the file. There were no papers there at all! Completely empty.

'Is *this* how many are left? None?'

'Yes Minister.'

DEPARTMENT OF ADMINISTRATIVE AFFAIRS

This file contains the complete set of available papers except for:

(a) a small number of secret documents

(b) a few documents which are part of still active files

(c) some correspondence lost in the floods of 1967

(d) some records which went astray in the move to London

(e) other records which went astray when the War Office was incorporated into the Ministry of Defence

(f) the normal withdrawal of papers whose publication could give grounds for an action for libel or breach of confidence or cause embarrassment to friendly governments.

Approved J.H.